Legal Conceptions of National Security Relevant to Counter-Terrorism and Human Rights Law and Policy

Legal Conceptions of National Security Relevant to Counter-Terrorism and Human Rights Law and Policy

Ogechi Joy Anwukah, PhD

Published by:

Vandeplas Publishing, LLC — November 2022

801 International Parkway, 5th Floor
Lake Mary, FL. 32746
USA

www.vandeplaspublishing.com

ISBN: 978-1-60042-526-4

LEGAL CONCEPTIONS OF NATIONAL SECURITY RELEVANT TO COUNTER-TERRORISM AND HUMAN RIGHTS LAW AND POLICY

Ogechi Joy Anwukah, PhD

Table of Contents

Abstract

The event of 9/11 ushered in some critical national security questions. One of such question is on how to effectively counter terrorism without the flagrant violation of human rights. No doubt, issues bothering on 'terrorism' and 'counterterrorism' are national security issues. Hence, this book examines the attitude of the European Court of Human Right towards the issues of national security and human rights in the fight against terrorism. This is carried out by evaluating the laws of the ECHR. Accordingly, this book sets out to critically review and ultimately revise existing legal/judicial conceptions of "national security". Hence, the overall purpose of this book is to carry out an exhaustive search for the formulation of a comprehensive definition of national security against the background of counterterrorism. To further illustrate the practicality of such a definition in the "fight against terrorism", a theory will be propounded in this book. Through the ECHR case law, this book will expose the impunity with which sovereign states violate the principles of the rule of law while countering terrorism. In addition, this book argues the issue of the absolute nature of Article 3 of the ECHR with special reference to deportation in the fight against terrorism. It highlights the challenges sovereign states face when deporting persons whom they consider threats to others and to the nation. This book contends with the trade-off of rights of a single individual (article 3 ECHR right of a terrorist/terrorist suspect whose activities has the potential to threaten national security) as opposed to the right to life of many innocent civilians. This book makes a case for the adoption of a comprehensive definition of national security, which could serve as a model for policy makers to adopt in the formulation and implementation of counterterrorism measures.

Acronyms

RIS	Romanian Intelligence Service
UNSC	United Nations Security Council
UN	United Nations
OAU	Organisation for Arica Unity
AU	African Union
EU	European Union
RAN	EU Radicalization Awareness Network
SCO	Shanghai Co-operation Organisation
ECHR	European Convention on Human Rights
CIA	Central Intelligence Agency
HVD	High Value Detainees
RDI	Rendition Detention Interrogation Programme
NATO	The North Atlantic Treaty Organisation
SC	Security Council
EITs	Enhanced Interrogation Techniques
UNCAT	United Nations Convention Against Torture
PKK	Workers Party of Kurdistan
ASEAN	Association of Southeast Asian Nations
WMD	Weapons of Mass Destruction
FBI	Federal Bureau of Investigations

UBOP	Department of Fight Against Organised Crime
RUC	Royal Ulster Constabulary
GNP	Gross National Product
IAEA	International Atomic Energy Agency
FARC	Revolutionary Armed Forces of Colombia
RATS	Regional Anti-Terrorist Structure
ICCPR	International Covenant on Civil and Political Rights
UDHR	Universal Declaration on Human Rights
AMIB	African Union Mission in Burundi
IRA	Irish Republican Army
ICJ	International Court of Justice
DPP	Director of Public Prosecutions
GCC	Gulf Cooperation Council
GIA	Islamic Terrorist Group
ATCSA	Anti-terrorism, Crime and Security Act
ECAP	European Capabilities Action Plan
DCPS	Department for Control and Professional Standards
SIAC	Special Immigration Appeals Commission
ASIO	Australian Security Intelligence Organisation Legislation Amendment (Terrorism) Act
CPT	European Committee for The Prevention of Torture and Inhuman or Degrading Treatment or Punishment
USA Patriot Act	Uniting and Strengthening America by Providing Appropriate Tools Required to Intercept and Obstruct Terrorism Act

Acknowledgements

I wish to express my profound gratitude to Professor Christian N. Okeke, Professor Steven Greer, Professor Michael Salter, Dr Chukwuemeka Ibeachu and my family for their contiuned support all thorugh this work. My deepest gratitude goes to Almighty God.

Chapter 1
Introduction

1.1 Introductory Remarks

Since the issue of terrorism is not a new phenomenon, why then is 'national security' an issue today? Is it the case that this is a rhetoric designed to enhance the perception of the need for a "tough" response to designated "security threats" and thereby play into a populist/tabloid agenda; for example, the one appealed to successfully by Donald Trump?

> 'The attacks of September 11th propelled terrorism from obscurity to prominence in the wider field of international relations and foreign and security policy. It now took center stage in the grand strategy debate. Scholars who had previously ignored terrorism now acknowledged it was a major security concern..."[1]

The prevention and punishment of ideologically motivated violence without the excessive infringement of political freedoms and human rights poses a great challenge for a democratic society. The terrorist attack of 9/11 intensified such challenge. Ideally, the principles of political freedom, due process and protection of privacy, which constitute an integral part of a free and democratic society,[2] ought not to be infringed upon when responding to terrorism. Ironically, it can be argued that nation states have subverted many rights and freedoms that make the defence of a nation worthwhile in the name of enhancing national security.[3]

---

1 B. Nacos, *Terrorism and Counterterrorism* (5th edn, Taylor and Francis Group, Abingdon 2016), Chapter 10

2 D. Cole, et al., *Terrorism and The Constitution: Sacrificing Civil Liberties in The Name of National Security* (3rd edn, The New Press Company Inc, New York 2006), 1

3 ibid

This book sets out to critically review and ultimately revise existing legal/judicial conceptions of "national security" within the law of European Convention on Human Rights (ECHR). These have emerged in relation to current terrorism threats, considering appropriately defined and applied human rights imperatives. Hence, the overall aim of this book is to carry out an exhaustive search for the formulation of a comprehensive definition of national security against the background of counterterrorism. This could serve as a model for the resolution of the acute conflict between the principles of the rule of law, national security and human rights. To further demonstrate the practicality of such a definition in the "fight against terrorism", a theory will be propounded in this book. Such theory will examine the 'legality', 'rationality' and 'objectivity' of the formulation and implementation of some of the counterterrorism measures adopted by sovereign states in the "fight against terrorism". Thus, it will expose the acute and conscious violations of human rights in the "fight against terrorism". The element of originality lies both in the results of such an exhaustive search for a comprehensive model of the meaning, scope, implications and limits of judicial conceptions of "national security," the theory propounded and the possible resolution, in part at least, of the acute conflict in the "fight against terrorism between the rule of law, national security and human rights protection.

This introductory chapter provides literature in the field as well as the relevance of this research. Subsequently, it gravitates into the research questions and the research methodology adopted to fully facilitate the exposition of the research questions. Essentially, it is contended that the adoption of the black-letter approach, scientific methodological approach of "immanent critique," and socio-legal studies of "law in action" will strengthen the theoretical and analytical dimensions of the issues under consideration. This chapter also provides a descriptive outline of the structure of this book.

1.2 CONTEXTUAL BACKGROUND

The consistent paradigm after the 9/11 attack is the emergence of a 'new terrorism'[4] and the urgency for a proportionate 'new' terrorism response. Hence, from a US policy standpoint, the 9/11 attack has been considered the most destructive

4 M. Mohammed Nia, 'From Old to New Terrorism: The Changing Nature of International Security' (2010) vol 1 (18) Globality Studies Journal 1

attack in its history (although, in magnitude it is small when compared to the death toll stemming from the systematic genocide of Native Americans in the 18th and 19th centuries).[5] Therefore, the weight of the subsequent anti-terrorist policy will be radically different from what is already on ground in some countries, like the USA and the UK. The intent is to obviate future attacks, thereby fortifying a sense of optimising national security. Former UK Prime Minister, Gordon Brown, asserted that: 'the new terrorist threats...multidimensional in its operation...has changed the rules of the game and so changed how we need to protect ourselves against it'.[6] This is a version of the extraordinary response to extraordinary threats' position.

The threat posed by terrorism is global, borderless and dispersed in its networking system.[7] Such a threat transcends nations. It is not always confined within a geographical boundary, because of its aims[8] and the use of information technology. For instance, vulnerable individuals might become radicalised through the internet. People who are scattered all over the world participate in various online chat rooms, websites and forums that make up the online community. If extremist information or terrorist incitements are available on the internet, the extent to which such message/s could spread around the globe is uncertain. Such threat/s might emanate from organised terrorist groups, sympathetic groups, or individuals all over the globe. They can interact with each other through the internet, express their support for terrorist ideologies, manipulate public opinion, coordinate attacks and garner the resources they require to act independently.[9] Information technology is a powerful tool for the predations of terrorists.

5 P. Bartrop, et al., *Modern Genocide: The Definitive Resource and Document Collection* (ABC-CLIO LLC, California 2015), 1973

6 A. Field, 'New Terrorism: Revolution or Evolution?' (2009) vol 7(2) Political Studies Review, 195-207

7 J. Robb, *Brave New War: The Next Stage of Terrorism and The End of Globalisation* (John Wiley & Sons Inc, New Jersey 2007), 3; M. Miklaucic, et al., *Convergence: Illicit Networks and National Security in The Age of Globalization* (National Defense University Press, Washington D.C 2013)

8 S. Greer, 'Human Rights and The Struggle Against Terrorism in The United Kingdom' (2008) vol 2 European Human Rights Law Review 163-172

9 D. Benjamin, *The Next Attack: The Failure of The War on Terror and A Strategy for Getting It Right* (Henry Holt and Company LLC, New York)

The challenge posed by such designated threats emanates from its peculiar nature. For example, its agents are mostly independent and self-starting, and often reside and operate in the country they target.[10] The maturation of international terrorism embodies a broad spectrum of activity that goes beyond carrying out the actual attack. For example, it encompasses education and research, recruitment, radicalisation, creation of terrorist cells, training, planning, financing, communications, coordination and the acquisition of necessary materials.[11] There are many known and unknown terrorist groups such as the Islamic State of Iraq and the Levant (ISIL), Boko Haram. Al-Qaeda is also a recognised terrorist organisation; some individuals and small groups are inspired and enthused by Al-Qaeda but have no immediate operational ties to it.[12] Some terrorist groups parade themselves as Al-Qaeda, yet, no history of violence can be traced to them. All such factors constitute an acute challenge for nations in the fight against terrorism.[13] It therefore remains uncertain when the fight against terrorism will end, since it is also perpetrated by some unknown groups and splinter factions of known groups. Perhaps, it might be safe to say that the fight against terrorism is complicated.

It is accepted that the 9/11 attack had a catastrophic effect, not only on the United States, but on the world at large. However, there have been far greater tragic losses of life in other parts of the world every few months since then, which have not been characterised in the same intense and dramatic manner. Perhaps, countries could save more lives than are taken by terrorism, through stricter drink driving laws and laws relating to young men driving too early, or diet and air pollution issues. However, anti-terrorism efforts could be sustainable and lasting if the applicable measures respect human rights, foster social justice, enhance democracy, and uphold the rule of law.[14] Essentially, where governments must derogate from human rights to enhance national security, then

---

10 B. Hoffman, 'Rethinking Terrorism and Counterterrorism Since 9/11' (2002) vol 25(5) Studies in Conflict and Terrorism 303-316

11 M. Alarid, Recruitment and Radicalisation: The Role of Social Media and New Technology (2016) Centre for Complex Operations 313-330

12 D. Benjamin, op cit

13 D. Prieto, 'War About Terror: Civil Liberties and National Security After 9/11' (2009) Council on Foreign Relations 7

14 E. Flynn, 'Counterterrorism and Human Rights: The View from The United Nations' (2005) vol 1 European Human Rights Law Review 29-49

the conditions stipulated in Article 15 for example, of the European Convention on Human Rights (ECHR) ought to be complied with. Also, it is pertinent that counterterrorism measures adopted by nations are such that can maintain foreign relationships, since terrorism is also a global affair. For instance, there was an immediate need for the Libyan government to safeguard United States' diplomats and property during the 2012 attack on the United States' Embassy in Libya. Thus, if foreign relations amongst nations are not maintained, it might be difficult for them to respond accordingly when the need arises.

1.3 CRITICAL LITERATURE REVIEW ON THE IDEA OF NATIONAL SECURITY

Existing published research has shown that there is still no clearly expounded or definitive judicial definition of "national security."[15] In effect, the issue of defining national security has been a topic in many academic, political books and journal articles. There has been a considerable amount of written work on the definition of national security. Predominantly, such works are written by political scientists, military personnel, and academic scholars. Such texts have reflected different understandings of national security leading to divergent definitions of the same by different schools of thought. For instance, the some Liberals define national security in terms of individual liberty and moral autonomy.[16] Liberalism promotes democracy. Liberals such as Immanuel Kant see democratic governments as legitimate custodians of the interests of the people.[17] There is the realist school who define national security in terms of power".[18] They focus on state security. Realists define national security in terms of power and survival.[19] In other words, to maintain sovereignty.[20] Whereas the liberal

15 M. Filippo, 'Terrorist Crimes and International Co-operation: Critical Remarks on The Definition and Inclusion of Terrorism in The Category of International Crimes' (2008) vol 19(3) The European Journal of International Law 533-570

16 S. Jack, 'One World, Rival Theories' (2004) vol 1(145) Foreign Policy 56

17 A. Jordan, et al., American *National Security* (6th edn The John Hopkins University Press, Baltimore 2011), Ch 1

18 C. Rudolph, *National Security and Immigration: Policy Development in The United States and Western Europe Since 1945* (Stanford University Press, California 2006), 23

19 A. Jordan, op cit

20 ibid

communitarian school concentrates on both individual rights and the advancement of the common good, and that neither should be a priori trump the other.[21] The liberal communitarian school sees national security in terms of creating a balance between individual rights and social responsibilities, which emanates from the need to serve the common good.[22] They hold that nations should pay attention to two principal values: the dignity of individuals which is the foundation of individual rights and the importance of the common good. They contend for balance between the core values in the society as opposed to tilting towards a particular core value.[23]

Alternatively, national security has been traditionally defined by many scholars as military security.[24] A Harvard Professor, Charles Maier defined national security in terms of national power.[25] Conversely, Captain Bernard Thillaye, in his thesis, succinctly defined national security as the matter of guarding national values and interests from internal and external dangers.[26] Scholars such as Jaswant Sing, [27]Cynthia Watson,[28] Walter Lippmann,[29] have defined national security in terms of defence and foreign policy. Arnold Wolfers defines it in relation to the protection of values previously acquired by a state.[30] This definition, though simple, suggests a scope of national security beyond military dimension. Similarly, Feyzioglu has argued that national security cannot focus exclusively on military security. He argues that issues such as health, trade, education,

21 A. Etzioni, 'A Liberal Communitarian Approach to Security Limitations on The Freedom of The Press' (2014) vol 22(4) William &Mary Bill of Rights Journal 1146

22 ibid

23 A. Etzioni, et al., *Privacy in A Cyber Age: Policy and Practice* (1st edn, Palgrave Macmillan, New York 2015), xi

24 J. Morkuniene, *Social Philosophy: Paradigm of Contemporary Thinking* (1stedn, The Council for Research in Values and Philosophy, Washington D.C 2004), 187

25 IBP Inc, *Global National Security and Intelligence Agencies Handbook* (1st vol International Business Publications, Washington D.C), 10

26 B. Thillaye, *Politico-Strategic Forecasting* (MA thesis, Royal Military College of Canada 1972), 79

27 J. Singh, *National Security: An Outline of Our Concerns* (Lancer Publishers and Distributors, India 1996), 19

28 C. Watson, *US National Security: A Reference Handbook* (ABC-CLIO Inc, Santa Barbara 2002), 2

29 P. Paleri, *National Security: Imperatives and Challenges* (Tata McGraw-Hill Publishing Company Limited, New Delhi 2008), 45

30 L. Neack, *Elusive Security: States First, People Last* (Rowman & Littlefield Publishers Inc, Maryland 2007), 16

industry, agriculture, transportation and public are issues of national security policies.[31]

On the other hand, there are others who contend that 'individuals' as opposed to the 'state' ought to be the focal point in defining national security. It has been reported that in the last 100 years, many people have been killed by their own governments rather than by foreign armies.[32] This research notes that violent conflicts within states now make up more than 95% of armed conflicts.[33] Hence, Paleri defines national security in terms of 'human security'. He concludes that the well-being of 'people' is central to the definition of national security[34]. According to him, national security is the apparent physiological, mental and emotional well-being of the people of a nation defined accordingly as a measurable state.[35] By way of extension, others, such as George Kennan, defined national security as the continued ability of a country to pursue its internal life without serious interference.[36] Arguably, he sees national security as internal security. In essence, some scholars have defined national security as the ability to survive and develop.[37] According to R.McNamara, security means development.[38] Along such lines, the UN Environment Programme (UNEP) defined national security as the requirement to maintain the survival of the nation state through the use of economic, military and political power and the exercise of diplomacy."[39]

31 U. Cizre, *Democratic Oversight and Reform of The Security Sector in Turkey* (Deutsche Nationalbibliothek, Germany 2005), 28

32 P. Paleri, op cit

33 ibid

34 P. Paleri, *National Security: Imperatives and Challenges* (Tata McGraw-Hill Publishing Company Limited, New Delhi 2008), 57-58

35 ibid

36 S. Ronis, *Economic Security Neglected Dimension of National Security* (National Defense University Press, Washington DC 2011), 5

37 ibid

38 J. Morkuniene, *Social Philosophy: Paradigm of Contemporary Thinking* (1[st]edn, The Council for Research in Values and Philosophy, Washington D.C 2004), 188

39 A. Amiri, *Freedom of Information and National Security: A study Of Judicial Review Under US Law* (Herbert UtzVerlag GmbH, EU 2014), 20

In redefining national security, a group of scholars' advocate a broader security agenda, where other issues will receive attention as national security priorities.[40] Hence, they feel that transnational threats, environmental factors and terrorism have been ignored. Amongst many others, Lester Brown, Jessica Tuchman Mathews, Michael Renner and others have suggested the redefinition of national security to include resource and environmental threats.[41] Similarly, Richard Ullman and others proposed redefining national security to incorporate other threats stretching from earthquakes to environmental degradation.[42] Disputably, scholars like Daniel Deudney, in defining national security, posit that it would be misleading to link environmental problems or solutions to national security threats. He argues that environmental degradation is not likely to cause interstate wars.[43] However, people like Franklin. P. Huddle has defined national security as global security.[44] He contends for cooperative efforts by sovereign states in solving problems of security. He forcefully maintains that individual and national security is meaningless without global security.

From the foregoing, it might be safe to say that the word 'national security' lacks conceptualisation. Very few definitions of national security are conceptual, such as those of Jaswant Sing and Captain Bernard Thillaye.[45] Some scholars see national security as 'the ability of a nation',[46] a condition,[47] a requirement.[48] Other scholars define it in terms of its aims or focus on some aspects of national security or threats to national security. Again, national security has been defined narrowly in the sense that most scholars have defined it separately and in bits. They have defined it as focusing on a particular element or aspect of national security. For instance, some academics have defined national security

---

40 ibid

41 ibid

42 R. Ullman, 'Redefining Security' (1983) vol 8(1) International Security 129-153

43 D. Deudney, 'The Case Against Linking Environmental Degradation and National Security' (1990) vol 19(3) Journal of International Studies 162-177

44 K. Conca, et al., *Green Planet Blues: Critical Perspective on Global Environmental Politics* (5th edn, Westview Press, Colorado 2015), 51

45 B. Thillaye, op cit

46 C. Watson, op cit

47 P. Paleri, op cit

48 A. Amiri, op cit

as a circumstance borne out of a military or defence advantage over any foreign nation or group of nations, or a friendly foreign relations position, or a defence position capable of successfully protesting hostile or destructive action.[49] Thus, defence considerations are at the core of prevailing conceptions of national security.[50]

The definition of national security in this book is both 'conceptual' and 'prescriptive' in nature. It is conceptual in the sense that it succinctly states the 'meaning' of national security. It states what 'national security' is. Essentially, in simple terms it gives an understanding of national security. Hence, the definition that will be formulated in this book will state conditions such as 'fundamental principles' that will improve on the existing definitions of national security in the current scholarship. It is prescriptive in the sense that it provides a framework for the formulation and implementation of national security policies. Basically, understanding the concept of national security is radically different from prescribing the means through which security can be achieved. In effect, an understanding of the concept will assist in the formulation of strategies for the realisation of such concept. The definition of national security formulated in this book answers the questions of "what" "when", "why" and "how" of national security. The definition formulated in this book, proffers answers to critical national security policy questions: First, what is the meaning of national security? Second, when should national security measures be put in place? Third, why should there be national security? Ultimately, how can national security be achieved? To this point, this book defines national security expansively.

Several works have examined and identified weaknesses in the definitions of national security such as Rajpal Budania's work.[51] As a result, some scholars have expanded their definitions of national security to include other aspects (such as those mentioned above).[52] Nevertheless, where some works have

49 H. Keller, et al., 'State Security v Freedom of Expression: Legitimate Fight against Terrorism or Suppression of Political Opposition?' (2010) vol 10(1) Human Rights Law Review 151-168

50 A. Dupont, et al., 'Australia's National Security Priorities: Addressing Strategic Risk in A Globalised World' (2012) vol 66(1) Australian Journal Of International Affairs 34-51

51 R. Budania, India's National Security Dilemma: The Pakistan Factor and India's Policy Response (Indus Publishing Company, New Delhi 2001), 14

52 U. Cizre, op cit

defined national security expansively, there is a gap in the conceptualisation and adoption of a methodology. This is a loophole that is closed in this book.

1.4 ORIGINALITY AND RELEVANCE OF THIS RESEARCH

The originality of this book is predicated upon the adoption of the black letter standard in the evaluation, assessment, formulation of a comprehensive definition of national security and the formulation of the theory of 'preservative legitimacy 'in this book. The black letter standard has its focus on statutes and case laws.[53] As seen above, some works have explored the definition of national security, however, such assessments have not established that their definition answered the four critical national security questions mentioned above based on the black-letter approach. Again, there is hardly any expansive definition of national security in the sense of crafting some of the basic elements of national security into a comprehensive whole using such approach. Such a gap in the existing academic scholarship does not imply that such definitions are irrelevant; but rather, as will be demonstrated, the adoption of the black letter standard in this book allows for a different assessment and more meaningful results. Its adoption in the examination of the concept of national security, especially in a post-9/11 world, creates room for a better understanding of the position of law when evaluating cases of human rights violation in the fight against terrorism.

It also helps to reveal the challenges of securing a nation in an ongoing terrorist environment. For instance, the black letter approach will expose the dichotomy between law (domestic and international) and some of the measures adopted by sovereign states as counterterrorism measures. Therefore, it will show some of the constraints placed on sovereign states by law in their exercise of authority in certain national security issues (such as in deportation cases). As a result, it makes room for more distinct and constructive reform suggestions. Importantly, it will ensure a coherent progression of this work from the identification of some basic elements of national security through the evaluation of some cases, assessment of the implications of such elements on national security, the possibility of striking a viable balance between the competing interests in the war against terror, proposed definition of national security, and recommendations.

53 C. Morris, et al., *Getting a PHD in Law* (Hart Publishing Limited, United Kingdom 2011), Ch 3

Such an approach will ensure a focused discourse, progress and determination of research questions.

The high level of security concerns post-9/11 has made a comprehensive definition of national security based on the black-letter approach a necessity. The adoption of such an approach, is not only necessary for bridging the gap in the existing academic scholarship but is also needed in the assessment of the counterterrorism measures adopted by sovereign states for the enhancement of national security. Hence, the book will expose some human rights' violations practiced by sovereign states in countering terrorism. The analysis of different provisions of law will show the challenges of compliance by sovereign states and at the same time some conflicts between law and practice of national security.

The issue of national security is a recurring theme in matters of terrorism and counterterrorism. As a result, there is a need for other approaches and perspectives on the definition of national security. Arguably, the system of the black-letter approach proffers one such perspective. The adoption of such an approach implies that presumptions will be eliminated in the examination of certain crucial elements in the discourse as references will be made to laws, case laws, and conventions.

1.5 RESEARCH QUESTIONS

The following questions will be asked to achieve the set aims of this work: First, how do the social and political scientists define the concept of national security? Secondly, how has the ECHR courts defined national security? Does national security have a generally accepted definition within the existing academic scholarship, or can one be formulated? Third, do the different aspects of 'national security' identified in this book have some practical impacts on national security, and if so, what are they, where, and under what conditions Fourth, must the protection of human rights always 'trump' the protection of national security or vice-versa? Fifth, what is the possibility of establishing a viable balance between the competing interests of national security, rule of law and human rights? These are no givens, but conceptions and interpretive constructs that need to be understood in their meanings and complexities and relativities in the fight against terror, based on the reformed definition of the idea of national security formulated in this book. What are the concrete and specific policy recommendations and law reform suggestions?

1.6 RESEARCH METHODS

My research methods will be exclusively textual, and library based. Three different approaches will be applied for different phases of the book. The "black-letter" (or positivist-normative) approach to the conduct of legal research will be used essentially to address the questions in this book that are relevant to the interpretation and application of legal doctrines concerning conceptions of national security (Chapter 3). Such research questions are descriptive-expository in the sense that they ask 'what'-type questions, and therefore require the black-letter approach based on legal positivism to answer them in strictly normative-doctrinal terms. For instance, such expository methodology is used in reviewing national security case laws to generate and express an ideally well-grounded definition and analysis of key legal sub-categories with respect to the doctrinal phase.

By contrast, for the entire work, I apply the social scientific methodological approach of "immanent critique," often deployed within policy oriented legal studies. This will be deployed in the evaluation and assessment of the critical issues under consideration.[54] For instance, in the bid to critically review and ultimately revise existing legal/judicial conceptions of "national security" within the law of European Convention on Human Rights (ECHR) the immanent critique will be applied. Such methodology allows for the assessment of internal standards. Hence, the assessment of legal/judicial conceptions of national security in this book will be judged by the standard of the ECHR law itself and not by any external standard. Also, in attempting to strike a viable balance between the conflicting interests in the fight against terrorism, this book will examine the practice of sovereign states in the formulation and implementation of their counterterrorism measures adopting the immanent critique methodology. It will do this by assessing the ECHR case laws on issues relevant to national security and counterterrorism and then evaluate the practice to ascertain the consistency and compliance of nation states with the law of the ECHR as opposed to other

54 M. Neufeld, *The Restructuring of International Relations Theory* (Cambridge University Press, Cambridge 1995), 5

laws in their formulation and implementation of counterterrorism policies and measures. Evaluation of the practice is realized through necessary references to state reports, counterterrorism polices/measures, reports/statements from non-governmental organisations (NGOs), rapporteur reports.

A further assessment on the consistency between theory and practice of the laws of the ECHR takes into consideration the practicality of normative standards as well as the challenges of implementation. The immanent critique methodology will be adopted in the examination of identified discrepancies and tensions between theory and practice with the intention to resolve these through proposed policies and reforms. In conjunction with the immanent critique, the expressly policy-oriented methodology of socio-legal studies of "law in action" will also be applied in synthesising the social and public policy implications of my topic. It will be applied to uncover the political element of the law, illustrate whether laws have achieved their intended purpose, and helping in law reform proposals by connecting law and policy goals. It will be used to reveal the practicality of the law by exposing its effect on people. For instance, it will be applied in the analysis of some counterterrorism measures and their effects on the members of society.[55] In short, the methodology will integrate doctrinal analysis (normativism), immanent critique of discrepancies and contradictions between the promise and performance of legally relevant doctrines, and the type of policy analysis common to socio-legal studies of law in action.

1.7 RESEARCH OUTLINE

This book is structured in seven chapters. The second chapter will briefly assess the historical background and the non-judicial account of national security. The intention is to examine the different accounts of national security by different schools of thoughts and scholars within the field of international relations. It finds that national security has been narrowly perceived within the existing academic scholarship and that certain contingencies such as wars also play a role in determining some conceptions/ideas of "national security". The third chapter evaluates the concept of national security in the law of the European Convention on Human Rights, where ECHR cases will be analysed. The aim is

55 C. Morris, et al., *Getting A PHD In Law* (Hart Publishing Ltd, Oxford 2011), Ch 3

to identify and elucidate the perceived meaning, scope and purpose of prevailing judicial and legislative interpretations of national security within the ECHR. It discovers possible interpretations of "national security" contained within existing case laws, and, as prompted by reference to violations of human rights and controversial anti-terror laws. Essentially, this entails a literature review to identify key issues and locate my own research questions within the context of an already rich and growing field of academic analysis of law and security issues. Hence, it establishes some basic elements of national security based on the cases analysed. The fourth chapter discusses and critically analyses the practical implications of such elements on the real practice of national security. It evaluates applicable case laws to establish a critical analysis of some of the pragmatic effects of such identified aspects of national security on the activity of national security. The aim here is to come up with enhanced policy decisions and proposals. It proposes conceivable means of promoting national security seen as a way of meeting a crucial human need for security. The fifth chapter reviews and critically discusses a range of judicial cases (both domestic and those of the ECHR) applicable to sovereign states concerning the interpretation and application of "national security issues". The aim is to answer the question whether–and if so on what interpretive basis–such judicial applications of the category of national security have succeeded in striking a "viable balance" between national security imperatives, and those countervailing human rights protections that are deemed "necessary in a democratic society". The sixth chapter provides and sets out this book's comprehensive definition of "national security" that can be shown to be contextually appropriate for anti-terrorism measures. The aim is to expressly develop a comprehensive "national security" definition and credible theory of such a category, whose nature more adequately encompasses existing, largely implicit, judicial and legislative interpretations of its meaning, scope and purpose other than those contained within the existing legal and constitutional scholarship. The goal is to expressly supplement the existing academic literature in ways that will be resolving difficulties within it. The seventh chapter ultimately concludes this book by drafting concrete and specific policy recommendations and law reform suggestions based on the results of previous chapters. This book will suggest an alternative account of the meaning, scope and rationale for "national security" in relation to its implications for reforming the following areas: anti-terrorism legislation, immigration (especially deportation cases), and 'people's security'. It will unravel the implications of the theory and definition of national security formulated in this book (policy, social and academic implications), as well as areas of further research.

This book is not limited to the identification of particular threats to national security. Rather, in analysing the facets of national security it will ascertain and elucidate areas of 'national insecurity'. Hence, it sets out to view national security expansively. This book will articulate and define national security respectively based on the different aspects of national security identified and analysed with the intention of crafting such segmental definitions into a comprehensive whole. I have not come across any book or an article, where each of the different facets of national security have been identified through the ECHR case laws, analysed and specific definitions of national security proffered based upon the various facets identified, and an expansive definition of national security formulated based on such segmental definitions given. At the same time as pointed out above, such a definition answers the four cardinal questions of national security.

Chapter 2
The Non-Judicial Concept Of National Security

2.1 INTRODUCTION

The period immediately following the Second World War demonstrated a great increase of interest in national and international security. The concept developed in the United States of America after the Second World War.[56] The use of the concept of 'security' first became prevalent at that time both theoretically and practically. It was also at this time that the exact meaning of the concept was deliberated upon. Political scientists started discussing what the concept of 'security' meant during the beginning of the cold war era. As a result, Walter Lippmann came up with an initial and significant definition of national security.[57] Thus, according to Walter Lippmann, "A nation is secure to the extent to which it is not in danger of having to sacrifice core values if it wishes to avoid war and is able, if challenged, to maintain them by victory in such a war."[58] The impact of this definition facilitated the specification of 'what is' and 'is not' to be considered 'security'. The concentration of Walter Lippmann's definition of national security is on the security of the core values of a single state from military threats. The definition also impacted the earlier realist tradition.[59]

Another, theoretical influence on the study of 'security' was made by Arnold Wolfers,[60] who acknowledged that the concept of 'security' is an ambiguous concept with diversified meanings. As a starting point, he recognized Walter

---

56 I. Inc, *Global national security and intelligence agency handbook: Strategic information and contacts* (vol 1 International Business Publications United States of America, Washington 2015), 9

57 J. Wiener, et al, *International relations* (EOLSS Publishers Co Ltd United Kingdom, Oxford 2009), 200

58 L. Meng, et al., op cit

59 ibid

60 P. Bilgin, et al., *Global security and international political economy* (vol 111 EOLSS Publication Co Ltd United Kingdom, Oxford 2010), 93

Lippmann's definition of national security and pointed out that the definition must be qualified in some respect if it must serve as an analytical tool and not only imply the common usage of the concept. Hence, Arnold Wolfers proposes the distinction between objective and subjective security. Objective security connotes the real state of security for a nation state, while the subjective usage covers how a state sees its own security situation.[61] National security as a term has long been used by politicians as a rhetorical phrase and by military leaders to describe a policy objective.[62] However, recently social scientists have adopted the concept of national security to suggest both an analytical concept and a field of study. When social scientists refer to the concept, they generally mean the ability of a nation to protect its internal values from external threats. The field of study attempts to analyse the way nation states plan, make and evaluate the decisions and policies orchestrated to increase this ability.[63]

This chapter will assess the non-judicial account of national security. It will look at how social and political scientists in the field of international relations perceive the concept of national security. Thus, it will explore a brief historical background as well as the various definitions and perceptions of the concept. Essentially, the purport of this chapter emanates from the need to have an insight into the origin and the non-judicial conceptions of national security within the existing academic scholarship. Basically, this chapter will investigate the various accounts of national security by different schools of thoughts and scholars. Notably, the evaluation of the non-judicial concept of national security in this chapter is not all inclusive. However, it elucidates some ideas of national security by different schools of thoughts and definitions of some academic scholars outside the purview of the law. It will conclude by stating the findings from the analysis herein. This chapter will be divided into subsections. Particularly, this chapter will tackle the question: How do the social and political scientists explain or define the concept of national security?

61 ibid

62 M. Neocleous, *Critique of security* (Edinburgh University Press Ltd United Kingdom, Edinburgh 2008), 77

63 International encyclopedia of the social sciences, 'National security' (2008) *https://www.encyclopedia.com/social-sciences/applied-and-social-sciences-magazines/national-security-0 accessed 15* November 2018

An evaluation of the concept of national security is inherently challenging. Although the concept is not a new phenomenon, it is broad and elastic. The concept of national security is open to numerous interpretations and is usually debatable. The origin of security can be examined through behavioral, historical, political and methodological approaches.[64] The early conceptions of national security was narrowly concerned with military matters. Nevertheless, academic works of the 1950s and 1960s considerably widened the scope of the field exclusively beyond military affairs.[65] The concept of national security is evolutionary in its original form with respect to a human system and, therefore essential to a nation state. It embraces the well-being of the people of the nation and not only their physical security. It consists of both military and non-military elements. Given that the concept of national security is evolutionary and related to human aspirations of survival, the period in the study of national security will be theoretically the period of the entire human existence in organized groups.[66] It has been presumed that the concept of national security is not a function of time. But it is connected to it.[67]

2.2 A HISTORICAL ACCOUNT OF THE CONCEPT OF NATIONAL SECURITY

The origin of the concept of national security as a philosophy of sustaining a stable nation state could be trailed to the peace of Westphalia in 1648; where the concept of a sovereign state governed by a sovereign, became the foundation of a new international order of nation states. Nevertheless, as an academic concept, national security is a phenomenon which was initially introduced to the United States sequel to the Second World War. This concept to a great extent has taken over other concepts that describe the challenge of nation states to overcome external and internal threats.

64 P. Paleri, op cit, 11

65 ibid

66 P. Paleri, *National security: Imperatives and challenges* (Tata McGraw-Hill Publishing Company Limited India, New Delhi 2008), 10

67 ibid

The concept of national security became an official guiding principle of foreign policy in the United States when the National Security Act 1947 was signed by United States President Harry. S. Truman.[68] Alongside its 1949 amendment, this Act created important facets for American national security. For instance, the precursor to the Department of Defence, established the National Security Council and the Central Intelligence Agency.[69] Notably, the concept of national security was not defined in the Act. As a result, issues threatened by other state interests such as domestic concerns were discussed and decided as issues of national security. At this time, it was known that national security extends beyond military security, but this realisation was understated from the onset.[70] The US National Security Act of 1947 was introduced to advise the President on the integration of domestic, military and foreign policies relating to national security.[71] The institute for Defence Studies and Analyses in India realised in 1965 that "national security is a wider concept than defence".[72] National security extends to non-military issues such as protection of human rights. A British scholar Barry Buzan described 'national security' as a politically powerful concept.[73] Arnold Wolfers wrote, that national security is an ambiguous symbol.[74] Thus, the concept of national security is historically cited at various levels but not universally defined.[75] The next section will explore the definitions and ideas of national security outside the ambit of the law.

68 ibid

69 ibid

70 ibid

71 R. McMahon, et al, *Guide to U.S. Foreign policy: A diplomatic history* (vol 1 SAGE Publications Inc. United States, Los Angeles 2012), 244

72 I. Inc, op cit

73 J. Romm, *Defining national security: the non-military aspect* (Council on Foreign Relations Press USA, New York 1993), 4

74 M. Leffler, "National Security" (1990) vol 77 (1) The Journal of America History 144

75 F.Costigliola, et al, *Explaining the history of American Foreign relations* (3rd edn Cambridge University Press United States, New York 2016), 26

2.3 THE NON-JUDICIAL IDEAS/DEFINITIONS OF NATIONAL SECURITY

National security is increasingly becoming a desired and prized goal both domestically and internationally. However, great ambiguity surrounds the concept.[76] Even at this developing stage, the field of national security is distinguished by many works of scholars from different disciplines. Concepts from various disciplines such as social science, economics, psychology, political science, sociology and anthropology have been applied to national security issues.[77] The concept of national security has been evaluated by many schools of thought. For instance, the realist school.

2.3.1 THE REALIST SCHOOL OF THOUGHT

Since the commencement of the discipline, realism has been the leading theory of international relations. Statism is the focal point of realism.[78] Hence, for the realist school, the decisive factor of national security is to secure the state. The state is its main actor and sovereignty is its distinctive characteristics. Barry Buzan a professor of International Relations concurs that the state is key to the concept of security and contends that national security acting as a compass for the state's foreign policy is committed to safeguarding the four component elements of a state: its physical base (population and territory), the idea of the state (its nationality and organizing ideologies), its institutions (the machinery of government) and finally its sovereignty.[79] Realists posits that, it is the element of sovereignty that provides both security and order to the political community within the territorial boundaries of a state.[80] Hence, national security in this framework is the requirement to maintain the survival of the nation state.[81] Accordingly Simonie F. defined national security as, "that part of government

76 O. Nnoli, *National security in Africa: A radical new perspective* (Pan African Centre for Research on Peace and Conflict Resolution (PACREP) Nigeria, Enugu 2006), 139

77 International encyclopedia of the social sciences, op cit

78 J. Baylis, et al., *The globalization of world politics: An introduction to international relations* (5th edn Oxford University Press United States, New York 2011), 96

79 S. Smith, et al., *Foreign Policy: Theories. Actors. Cases* (1st edn, Oxford University Press USA, New York 2008), 160

80 ibid

81 J. Akpeninor, op cit, 11

policy having as its objective the creation of national and international political conditions favourable to the protection or extension of vital national values against existing and potential adversaries."[82] John Mroz defined security as, "the relative freedom from harmful threat."[83]

Realists view international politics as a dangerous, and conflict prone domain, where security cannot be guaranteed. This school has its emphasis on the central concept of 'power'.[84] It sees the world as a dangerous place and asserts that states must ensure their survival by procuring and efficiently applying power.[85] In the anarchic international environment, states are fearful of each other as a result of mutual misunderstandings; security becomes high priority. States strive to gain security, earn military superiority and improve their individual security status by increasing military expenditure to pursue balance of power. This situation makes the 'security dilemma' inevitable.[86] In the international relations theory, anarchy is defined as the lack of a single authority having sovereign power over the states in the international system.[87] Hence, realists affirm that states must seek self-help strategies in order to survive.[88] Thus, Thomas Hobbes in his Leviathan, contends that the concept of national security covers a social contract in which each person's original power is yielded to a sovereign who regulates conduct.[89] Giacomo Luciani defined national security as, "the ability to withstand aggression from abroad."[90]

---

82 C. Hughes, et al., op cit

83 J. Mroz, *Beyond security: Private perceptions among Arabs and Israelis* (International Peace Academy, New York 1980), 105

84 M. Meese, et al., *American national security* (7th edn, John Hopkins University Press USA, Maryland 2018), chapter 1

85 M. Meese, et al., op cit

86 A. Liff, et al., "Racing toward tragedy? China's rise, military competition in the Asia Pacific and the security dilemma" (2014) vol 39 (2) International Security pp 52-91

87 R. Fawn, *Globalising the regional, Regionalising the global* (Cambridge University Press United Kingdom, Cambridge 2009), 37

88 W. Carlsnaes, et al., *Handbook of International Relations* (1st edn Sage Publication Ltd United Kingdom, London 2002), 372

89 J. Akpeninor, *Modern concepts of security* (AuthorHouse Publishers USA, Indiana 2012), 1

90 G. Luciani, 'The economic content of security' (1989) vol 8(2) Journal of Public Policy 151

According to the realists, acknowledging the importance of power and integrating all policies towards achieving a realistic balance of power is the only way to achieve peace. Thus, the earlier proponents of the realist school- from Thucydides to Hobbes and Clausewitz- almost all considered war as a legitimate means of securing national security.[91] The realist and the neo-realist believe that the state acts as a function of its selfish interest. For instance, the search for greater security by increasing its military power even at the detriment of others.[92] Thus, Penelope Hartland-Thunberg defined national security as, "the ability of a nation to pursue successfully its national interests, as it sees them, any place in the world."[93] The realist and neo-realist accept that globalization pose new concerns for national security. Nevertheless, they deny that states are no longer the only focal point in national security issues.[94]

2.3.2 THE LIBERAL SCHOOL OF THOUGHT

Liberalism is a second major international relations tradition that has its base in the political literature of Immanuel Kant and other enlightenment thinkers.[95] While the main ideology of the realist school is state security, the main ideology of the liberal school, as pointed out in the first chapter of this book, is individual liberty and moral autonomy.[96] The liberal school views the realist school as inadequate because of the absence of moral vision. It opines that the status of the state as the main actor in international politics is dependent on whether the state can be seen as the legitimate guarantors of the rights and aspirations of its population. Whereas realists may assume that a state is unitary and may not analyse domestic institutions, liberals see societal actors as having fundamental

91 N. Gandhi, *National security: Emerging dimensions and threats* (Pentagon Security International India, New Delhi 2010), 17

92 R. Budania, *India's national security dilemma: The Pakistan factor and India's policy Response* (Indus Publishing Company India, New Delhi 2001), 35

93 P. Thunberg, 'National economic security: Interdependence and vulnerability' in Frans A.M. Alting von Geuseu and Jacques Pelkman (Tilburg: John. F. Kennedy Institute 1982), 50

94 I. Bellany, "Towards a theory of national security" (1981) vol 29 (1) Political Studies pp 102

95 M. Meese, et al., op cit

96 J. Haynes, et al, *The world politics: International relations and globalization in the 21st century* (Routledge Publishers USA, New York 2013), 135

importance. Thus, states are not unitary actors.[97] According to the liberal school, democratic institutions, as well as liberal democratic values within a population, will have a crucial effect on foreign policy behavior.[98] Like Realism, liberalism has its pros and cons. Historically, liberal democracies have rarely fought each other, even though the process of democratization can jeopardise international peace and security. Essentially, as opposed to realism, liberal thinking recognizes state cooperation over mutual interests, interdependence through the establishment of regimes and institutions, and the spread of democracy.[99]

2.3.3 THE IDEALIST SCHOOL OF THOUGHT

In contrast to the realist school of thought, the idealist school considers security from the perspective of 'peace'. They posit that international life is found based on the search for peace as opposed to power. This school is of the view that peace and security cannot be enhanced by the search for a balance of power but through the satisfaction of the needs of all nations and the democratization of international life. The idealists pursued the aim of generating an international society or a social pact among states which would eliminate all forms of violence. The basis of idealism is peace and non-violence.[100] For instance, Laurence Martin defined security as, "the assurance of future well-being."[101] The idealist perspective of the concept of security is not devoid of weaknesses. For instance, the idealist school has not clearly defined the word "peace". They see the crafting of the definition of the word 'peace', as a difficult task. The definition of keywords makes for better understanding and elimination of unnecessary broad and unwanted interpretations.[102]

97 D. Peters, *Constrained balancing: The EU's security policy* (Palgrave Macmillan United States, New York 2010), 213

98 M. Meese, et al., op cit

99 P. Morgan, *Security in international politics: Traditional approaches [in] contemporary security studies* (Oxford University Press United States, New York 2007), 13-34

100 R. Budania, op cit

101 L. Martin, 'Can there be national security in an insecure age?' (1983) vol 60(3) Encounter 12

102 L. Singh, *National security problem in India: A case study of the insurgency problem in Nagaland and Manipur* (A.P.H Publishing Corporation India, New Delhi 2000),15

2.3.4 THE LIBERAL COMMUNITARIAN SCHOOL OF THOUGHT

The liberal communitarian school ascertains that a nation is confronted with two legitimate normative and legal claims-protecting national security and human rights. They argue that neither can be maximized nor totally reconciled as there is an unavoidable tension between these two claims. Thus, according to Michael H.H. Louw, national security includes, "traditional defence policy and also the non-military actions of a state to ensure its total capacity to survive as a political entity in order to exert influence and to carry out its internal and international objectives."[103] Impliedly, the idealists assert that the nation should be committed to individual rights and the advancement of the common good and neither should be prioritised over the other. This school is dedicated to achieving a balance between individual rights and social responsibilities which emanates from the need to serve the common good.[104] Essentially, Fischer and Green writes, "Security implies a stable, relatively predictable environment in which an individual or group may pursue its ends without disruption or harm or without fear of such disturbance or injury".[105]

Practically speaking, according to the idealist school, a society can lose the viable balance either by committing immensely to national security or to human rights. Considering the unavoidable change of events, even societies who have attempted to strike a viable balance will generally need to amend it subsequent to changes in historical situations (such as the 9/11) and technological developments (such as innovations of smart small cell phones).[106] Hence, the turf is not strictly on national security or human rights but it is on where the boundary lies between these two legitimate interest. The liberal communitarian ideology is reflected in the American constitution. Thus, the Fourth Amendment bans only unreasonable search, and therefore, allegedly recognizes a full category of reasonable searches. Generally, they are reasonable because they serve the common good (public interest: national security).[107]

---

103 C. Hughes, et al., *Security studies: A reader* (1st edn, Routledge publisher USA, New York 2011)

104 A. Etzioni, op cit

105 J. Akpeninor, op cit, 3

106 A. Etzioni, 'The standing of the public interest' (2014) vol (20) Barry Law Review 193

107 A. Etzioni, 'A liberal communitarian conception of privacy' (2012) vol 29 (3) Journal of Computer And Information Law 421

2.4 ANALYSIS

The perception of the concept of national security differ from different schools of thought and from different scholars. Elements such as, the nature of states, historical events (such as wars), the abilities of states to handle threats play a crucial role in the evaluation of national security conceptions or the idea of national security. The way national security is perceived is important because that will determine the level of interest and the amount of resources that will be allocated to it.[108] Bernard Brodie observed that, not everyone view security as a matter of degree. He demonstrated this view with a statement by General Jacob L. Devers: "National security is a condition which cannot be qualified. We shall either be secure, or we shall be insecure. We cannot have partial security. If we are only half secure, we are not secure at all".[109] Considering the modern-day model of terrorism, it might be safe to say that the concept of national security is still evolving as pointed out above. There are tendencies for unexpected elements to come up in the future. Hence, it might not be possible to ascertain every factor that might affect the national security of a nation. It is a subject that is very debatable. Hence, the shortcoming could be numerous.

Security is an indispensable element in nation states. Some scholars posit that a major way to ensure national security is through the use of force. However, the evolving nature of the concept of national security has shown the need for new thinking on security and defense. Hence, some scholars contend that national security extends beyond the threat or the use of force against the nation and thus, defense is no longer the major element to security.[110] Scholars such as Richard Ullman measure security in terms of the threats it faces and its vulnerability to them because the security of a nation increases as the vulnerability decreases and vice versa.[111]

Essentially, maximum security cannot be achieved by only military power. At the same time, the state cannot also be the only referent point in the determination

108 J. Cohen, *How many people can the earth support* (W.W. Norton & Company, Inc United Kingdom, New York 1995), 271

109 D. Baldwin, "The Concept of Security" (1997) vol 23 Review of International Studies 14

110 N. Gandhi, op cit, 21

111 D. Roy, *The new security agenda in the Asia-Pacific region* (Macmillan Press Ltd United Kingdom, London 1997), 32

of national security issues. Along these lines, the state has shown that it cannot always be a guarantee for both national and international security.[112] This could be illustrated by human rights violations by nation states in the fight against terrorism as will be seen in subsequent chapters of this book. Notably, traditional security thinking cannot effectively cope with the current paradigm shift in national security phenomenon. External military threats cannot possibly be the only threats to national security. Some non-military threats such as transnational organized crimes, terrorism, immigration, drug trafficking can pose serious threats to national security. Transnational organised crime is a wide-ranging security issue involving social, economic, political and cultural aspects. For instance, terrorism could be devastating not only on nation states but on lives and property too.

However, attention should be paid to the causes of insecurity and proffering ways of eliminating or reducing threats to security. The concept of national security could be described as vague. This has played a difficult role in crafting an all-encompassing definition of national security. As a result, Barry Buzan has aptly stated that, both Realist and Idealist have greatly weakened their analysis of security by the former equating security with the idea of power and latter subsuming it under peace. He suggests: "An expanded and clarified concept of national security can fill the ground between power position of the Realist and the peace position of the Idealists."[113]

More so, the critics of traditional definitions of security contend that invasion, war, and violent coercion are not the only potential threats to national security or necessarily the most troubling threats to national security.[114] Hence, the concept of national security has gained attention beyond military fixation. An extensive range of non-military threats persists. For instance, issues of mass migration, transnational organized crime.[115] Even though the realist school has its short fall, its approach to national security has not entirely lost its importance in international politics. The appearance of more unconventional threats

112 N. Al-Rodhan, *Neo statecraft and meta-geopolitics: Reconciliation of power, interests and justice in the 21st Century* (LIT VERLAG GmbH & Co. KG. Wien Germany, Zurich 2009), 132

113 R. Budania, op cit

114 A. Cottey, *Security in 21st century Europe* (2nd edn Palgrave Macmillan United Kingdom, London 2013), 7

115 ibid

to national security has not nullified the traditional threats to security. Though national security experts presently recognise the essence of economic dimensions of power and admit that traditional instruments such as armies and navies cannot be deployed against economic challenges, the nation state is still at the center-stage involved in a continuous footing for advantage against other states.[116] Against the background of a surge in the proliferation of dangerous weapons and the magnitude of ethno-religious conflicts, the importance of the state is likely to remain intact despite changes in its role.[117]

Importantly, one major impediment to the efforts made in countering terrorism is the failure of both judiciary and international law to formulate a comprehensive definition of "national security". It might be safe to say that the world has become unpredictable and complex as a result of unprecedented strategies for terrorism. Hence, it becomes essential to craft in a 'comprehensive' sense the definition of national security. Nevertheless, Stephen Walt, an international affairs professor, pointed out that too much broadening of the concept of national security has the danger of rendering the concept meaningless.[118] At the same time Barry Buzan argued that "An undefined notion of national security offers scope for power maximising strategies to political and military elites, because of the considerable leverage over domestic affairs which can be obtained by invoking it".[119] Ultimately, the essence of a comprehensive definition of national security which could serve as a normative standard cannot be overemphasized.

2.5 SUMMARY

The concept of national security has been widened with an increasing recognition that threats to national and international security has expanded beyond military threats. Security does not merely connote the capacity to protect from war. However, it also implies the ability to protect from other potential risks to survival and well-being. In addition, there is presently a greater concern to address the underlying sources of threat rather than just the defensive mechanisms to

116 N. Gandhi, op cit, 21

117 ibid

118 S. Walt, 'The renaissance of security studies' (1991) vol 35(2) International Quarterly Studies 213

119 Ibid, 4

avert the threats themselves. Also, there is more consciousness regarding the role of nation states in generating threats than external sources of threats.[120] Arguably, a span of non-military approaches can be used to guard against military and non-military threats to national security. The growing interrelationship among states strengthens the argument that, security cannot be realised at the cost of security for others. Furthermore, security requires cooperation and coordination among individuals, groups and nation states.[121]

It is important to note that, there is no last straw in the pursuit for national security. Hence, it becomes imperative for nation states to be vigilant towards the dynamics of both the global as well as the national environment to adjust to the realities of the time. Remarkably, national security is a relative concept. Ultimately, the security interest/s of nation states vary. It therefore becomes incumbent on nation states to evaluate the acceptable level of insecurity within their nation state. Accordingly, an unbiased evaluation of threat/s to national security, an accurate threat assessment and well-articulated national security strategies are indispensable requirements for safe guarding and promoting the national security of any nation state.

2.6 CONCLUSION

This chapter set out to evaluate the non-judicial conceptions of national security. It did this by examining the different accounts of national security by social and political scientists in the field of international relations. This chapter examined their definitions, perceptions and idea of national security at various times. The intention of this evaluation is for the development of the conception of national security outside the purview of the law in this work. Therefore, it finds that the concept of national security has been narrowly defined by different scholars within the existing academic scholarship. It finds that the concept of national security has shifted from the traditional perception, where national security is basically defined as military security. Hence, it has extended to non-military threats. It finds that the concept of national security could be subjective in the sense that, the political atmosphere/events at a specific time could

120 R. Budania., op cit, 41

121 ibid

be instrumental to the formulation of a national security ideology/definition/ policy.

The mechanisms for the maintenance of international peace and stability differ among the various schools of thought. For instance, realists would probably discharge any suggestions that, permanent peace among states is possible. However, they would hold that periods of relative peace and stability can be realised if states carefully look to their interest (power) and pay enough attention to maintaining a balance of power in the international system.[122] On the other hand, liberals would identify mechanisms for the reinforcement of peaceful relations among states. For example, common democratic values, close economic ties, free trade and international institutions.[123] Conclusively, to enhance national security in a world typified by threats without borders, new ways of conceptualizing national security beyond the international relations standard is crucial. The age-long perspectives of international relations such as that of the realist and the liberals are narrowly focused. However, these perspectives provide useful insights on the idea of national security. Hence, the comprehensive definition of national security that will be formulated in this book will gravitate towards the liberal communitarian school of thought.

By examining the non-judicial conceptions of national security, the platform is now set for the subsequent chapter to evaluate the 'judicial' conceptions of national security. This might help to provide a wider understanding of the concept of 'national security' as it will constitute a shift from the social and political background of the concept into the legal conceptions. The analysis will be based mostly on the ECHR caselaw, where an assessment of how the courts defined/ interpreted national security will be made, and if national security has a generally acceptable judicial definition.

122 A. Cottey, op cit, 15

123 ibid

CHAPTER 3
THE CONCEPT OF NATIONAL SECURITY IN THE LAW OF EUROPEAN CONVENTION OF HUMAN RIGHTS

3.1 INTRODUCTION

The issue of international terrorism and national security as it relates to human rights is of great concern.[124] Promulgations made in restriction of individual liberty to enhance state security, especially after the 9/11 terrorist attack, have accentuated such concern.[125] Hence, domestic states are faced with the challenge of effectively dealing with threats to state security and public safety without conceding unjustifiably such features that characterise them as democratic.[126] This chapter will perceive national security as a legal idea. In other words, it will look at national security from the legal perspective. This chapter will be divided into subsections where mostly ECHR laws will be analyzed for the assessment of judicial concept of national security. This chapter will address the following questions. How the ECHR courts defined National Security? Does National Security have a generally acceptable judicial definition, or can one be formulated?

The term 'national security' is elastic; its meaning and implication have expanded, contracted and shifted over time.[127] In Silencing Science, Relyea's discussion on 'National Security' depicts that the concept of national security can

124 I. Cram, 'Beyond Lockean Majoritarianism? Emergency, Institutional Failure and the UK Constitution' (2010) vol 10 (3) Human Rights Law Review 461

125 B. Trujilo, et al., 'Immigration reform, national security after September 11 and the future of North American integration' (2007) 91 Minnesota Law Review 1374

126 I. Cram, op. cit.

127 A. Amos, et al., *American National Security* (6th edn, The John Hopkins University Press, Maryland 2009), 3

be applied in different ways.[128] Thus, it legally justifies deportation, immigration, deprivation of citizenship, anti-terrorism, control orders, military technology and intelligence sharing. National Security has not been defined expressly by judges; rather, an inference could be drawn from the context in which a judge perceives as threatening national security in a particular case. Hence, to see how the ECHR courts, perceive national security, this chapter will analyse some human rights cases.

3.2 NATIONAL SECURITY VERSUS HUMAN RIGHTS PROTECTION (LEGAL CONCEPTIONS OF NATIONAL SECURITY)

The protection of human rights constitutes a major challenge in the bid to effectively address national security issues. It might appear that the protection of human rights is antithetical to national security, but the truth of the matter is that human rights protection, such as the protection of freedom of expression, is an integral part of national security. Most of such rights have exceptions or can be derogated from on grounds of national security. For instance, Article 10 of the European Convention on Human Rights (ECHR) provides for freedom of expression, which states:

> 1. "Everyone has the right to freedom of expression. This right shall include freedom to hold opinions and to receive and impart information and ideas without interference by public authority and regardless of frontiers. This Article shall not prevent States from requiring the licensing of broadcasting, television or cinema enterprises.
>
> 2. The exercise of these freedoms, since it carries with it duties and responsibilities, may be subject to such formalities, conditions, restrictions or penalties as are prescribed by law and are necessary in a democratic society, in the interests of national security, territorial integrity or public safety, for the prevention of disorder or crime, for the protection of health or morals, for the protection of the reputation or rights of others,

128 G. Moran, *Silencing scientists and scholars in other fields: Power, paradigm controls, peer review and scholarly communication* (Ablex Publishing Corporation, England 1998), 7

> for preventing the disclosure of information received in confidence, or for maintaining the authority and impartiality of the judiciary."[129]

It follows that one of the elements of freedom of opinion and expression is freedom of information. In the broadest sense, freedom of expression includes all kinds of expressions and messages ranging from political, religious, philosophical, cultural, and commercial to economic.[130] Freedom of expression is an integral aspect of human rights, especially in a democratic society. However, such freedom is not absolute; its exercise must be congenial to paragraph (2) of Article 10 of the ECHR. The limitations placed on freedom of expression must be prescribed by law and must be expedient in a democratic society.[131]

The acute conflict between the fight against terrorism, national security and human rights protection was demonstrated in the case of ***Gerger v Turkey***[132] the applicant was accused of disseminating propaganda against the Turkish nation at a memorial ceremony of those who were convicted for seeking to obliterate the Turkish constitutional order.[133] Subsequently, the applicant was convicted in a National Security Court for promulgating propaganda against the Turkish nation and the territorial integrity of the state.[134] The National Security Court lent credence to extracts from the applicant's message, which was read out at the memorial ceremony. For instance, he wrote:

> "The Turkish Republic is based on negation of the rights of workers and Kurds...any hint of human action, any aspiration for freedom, any claim to assert the rights of the workers and the Kurds has always met with a reaction on the part of the rulers that has been ruthless in its denial and destruction...the rulers have always distinguished themselves through a

129 European Convention on Human Rights 1950

130 G. Cohen-Jonathan, 'Television without frontiers and Human Rights in Europe' (1992) International Business Law Journal 613

131 M. Macovei, *Freedom of Expression: A guide to the implementation of article 10 of the European Convention on Human Rights* (2nd edn, Human Rights Handbooks, Germany 2004), 9

132 Gerger v Turkey (1999) ECHR 24919/94 Grand Chamber

133 ibid., para 11

134 ibid., para13

> cruel militarism that is the product of... the fundamental nature of the Republic and its subservience to imperialism."135

The applicant appealed, alleging that his conviction amounted to an interference with the exercise of his right to freedom of expression as provided under Article 10 of the ECHR. The Government maintained that since the ceremony in which the applicant's message was read out was in memory of those who took part in acts of terrorism, the passages of his message were intended to:

> "...incite citizens of Kurdish origin to engage in armed combat against the Turkish State, supported separatist violence and glorified the Kurdish independence movement. The message was a criticism of the Turkish authorities but also an encouragement for Kurdish terrorism and the activities of the PKK."[136]

The Appeal Court pointed out that the contextual setting where an opinion or message is given should be considered more, rather than the incendiary nature of the words of a message in a democratic society. It asserted that some essential feature calls for consideration prior to the declaration of a message as a threat to national security. For instance, whether the intention of the language used in the message is to breed violence. However, even if the intention of the language used in a message is to stimulate violence, the consequence of such language should be given more consideration since an 'intention' may result in a mere 'mental exercise'. On the other hand, where it is ascertained that the intention of the language used in a message was to whip up violence, preventive measures need to be put in place on grounds of national security to forestall the manifestation of the violence. The question is how can the intention be established? The easiest way to ascertain intent is through action.

The Appeal Court also held that the following elements needed to be examined in determining whether the appellant's message could be recognised as a threat to national security.

---

135 ibid., para.10

136 ibid., para. 44

> "Was the language intended to inflame or incite violence? Was there a real and genuine risk that it might do so? Did the author of the offending text occupy a position of influence in society of a sort likely to amplify the impact of his words? Was the publication given a degree of prominence either in an important newspaper or through another medium which was likely to enhance the influence of the impugned speech? Were the words far away from the centre of violence or on its doorstep?"[137]

Hence the Appeal Court jointly concurred with the Lower Court's judgment, which revealed that Article 10 of the ECHR (freedom of expression) may protect 'fighting' words. The Court considered the small group of people who attended the commemorative ceremony as being incapable of disrupting national security, public order and territorial integrity. Hence, the Court lent more credence to the contextual setting rather than the words in the message. For instance, the applicant spoke of his "*solidarity with the revolutionary cause*".[138]

He described the Turkish republic as one:

> "Based on negation of the fundamental rights of workers and Kurds, the rulers, whose aim had been to eradicate social and political activity in the country and to weigh society down with the yoke of non-pluralism and dependence to 'break any resistance and stifle any revolt by the masses';" the spirit of resistance and revolt of those heroic years, a nightmare for the rulers, has been with the country for more than twenty years."[139]

Justice Bonello concurred with the judgment of the majority, but declined the endorsement of the primary test applied by the Court in determining whether the interference by the domestic authorities with the applicant's freedom of expression was justifiable in a democratic society. He adopted a narrow criterion, stating:

---

137 ibid

138 ibid., para 10

139 ibid; D. Jacobs, World Book Focus on Terrorism (World Book Inc. Chicago 2003); 147

> "I believe that punishment by the national authorities of those encouraging violence would be justifiable in a democratic society only if the incitement were such as to create a 'clear' and 'present' danger."[140]

The above assertion depicts that the justification for restricting a person's freedom of expression should be such that instantaneous violence ought to have been the aftermath of the expression. According to Justice Bonello, the passages in the appellant's message had no chance of imminently threatening the national order regardless of how violent the words were. He stated:

> "The guarantee of freedom of expression does not permit a state to forbid or proscribe advocacy of the use of force except when such advocacy is directed to inciting or producing imminent lawlessness and is likely to incite or produce such action. It is a question of proximity and degree."[141]

He further pointed out that if the expression in question is not capable of igniting a grievous action, let alone a clear and present one, it falls short of the yardstick for measuring expressions capable of instigating violence.

Justice Bonello stated:

> "No danger flowing from speech can be deemed clear and present, unless the incidence of the evil apprehended is so imminent that it may befall before there is opportunity for full discussion. If there be time to expose, through discussion, the falsehood and the fallacies, to avert the evil by the process of education, the remedy to be applied is more speech, not enforced silence."[142]

It could be argued that the Court adopted a narrow approach towards the concept of national security by holding that there was a violation of Article 10 of the ECHR. Even though the applicant used such words as 'resistance', 'struggle'

140 ibid; Council of Europe, *"Apologie Du Terrorisme" and "Incitement to Terrorism"* (Council of Europe Publishing, Strasbourg 2006), 47

141 ibid; T. Christiano, *The Constitution of Equality: Democratic Authority and its Limits* (Oxford University Press, Oxford 2008), 135

142 ibid; A. Moucheboeuf, *Minority Rights Jurisprudence Digest* (Council of Europe Publishing, Strasbourg Cedex 2006), 229

and 'liberation' in his message, the Court refused to acknowledge its tendency to provoke violence, armed resistance or an uprising even though the PKK had been escalating its operations in south-east Turkey.[143]

Analytically, in determining whether a message constitutes a threat to national security, the author of the message need not be influential in society, although the societal position of the author of a message might be a boost to violence. Nevertheless, a message by an ordinary member of a group whose interest is contrary to national security is sufficient to inflame violence. The fact that such a message is not published in an important newspaper or any other important medium is immaterial.

Thus, it is recognised law (Prevention of Terrorism Act: Law No. 3713) that written and spoken propaganda cannot be made in assemblies or meetings, which can destabilise the constitutional order. If the message is made far away from the centre of the violence it might constitute a potential threat to national security, but where the message is on the doorstep it might cause an imminent threat to national security. In the present case, the fact that the message was read out to a group of people who attended a memorial ceremony does not erode the possibility of the message being capable of inciting the group to violence. A message may have an instant or a remote effect.

By contrast, Justice Gölcüklü disassociated himself from the opinion of the majority and adopted a broad approach towards the meaning of national security. He contemplated the effect of the applicant's comments not just on the small group that attended the ceremony, but also on its effect on the public at large. Hence, he said, "Those statements obviously incite and condone violence and amount to a public invitation to hatred and action".[144] He construed the content of the applicant's message strictly by envisaging its potential of destabilising national security considering the activities of the PKK in Turkey. For example, the applicant said "...the Turkish Republic was based on negation of the fundamental

143 ibid., paras 49, 50; J. Weiner, *Referral of Iranian President Ahmadinejad on the Charge of Incitement to Commit Genocide* (The Jerusalem Centre for Public Affairs, Jerusalem 2007), 9

144 ibid; Vivienne O'Connor, et al., *Model Codes for Post-Conflict Criminal Justice Volume 1* (United States Institute of Peace Press, Washington D.C), 350

rights of workers and Kurds"[145], though the latter had no connection with the memorial ceremony that had been organised. Justice Gölcüklü argued that the present case is homogenous with the case of ***Zana v Turkey*** where Zana's statements obviously incited and condoned violence and amounted to a public invitation to hatred and action. Perhaps the opinions of most of the judges who determined Gerger's case would have been different post 9/11, considering the paradigm shift in modern tactics of terrorism. Essentially, freedom of expression is one of the rights that have suffered a flagrant violation by sovereign states in the "fight against terrorism" due to the fear of radicalisation. Hence, this book will further expose acute and conscious violations of some ECHR rights in an attempt to enhance national security post 9/11.

3.2.1 SUMMARY

In summary, national security does not connote a fight against human rights. National security and human rights protection are pertinent to ensure that society is "free" and "safe". They are interrelated. Prioritising one above the other creates a false dichotomy. The 9/11 attack was an eye opener to the advancement in terrorist schemes and strategies. Often, nations promulgate laws that restrict human rights in times of crisis. However, in a democratic society, the moral and legal consequences of restricting rights obstruct the battle against terrorism. It is usually challenging to put national security above the interest of citizens. At the same time, it would be risky to compromise national security. Hence, there is a need for a viable balance between the two.[146]However, the next section of this chapter will attempt to identify and elucidate some significant aspects of national security in search of an expansive definition of national security.

145 ibid; E. Reed, *Civil Liberties, National Security and Prospects for Consensus: Legal, Philosophical and Religious Perspectives* (Cambridge University Press, New York 2012), 440

146 A. Megan, et al., 'National security and Human rights' (2006) Woodrow Wilson International Center for Scholars <www.wisoncenter.org/kennan> accessed 19 July 2012), 8

3.3 IDENTIFIED ASPECTS OF NATIONAL SECURITY

3.3.1 NATIONAL SECURITY AND ANTI-TERRORISM

The attack popularly referred to as 9/11 prompted an extraordinary empathy for the United States. It also led to series of peculiar legal actions. For instance, NATO activated Article 5 of its founding treaty to bring all member states to the aid of the United Nations; the United Nations Security Council both recognised the inherent right of individual and collective self-defence in conjunction with the attacks and passed series of resolutions to coordinate global action in the fight against terrorism.[147] The fight against terrorism has become a global concern and most countries are working together in the campaign.

This subsection will answer the question: 'How far can the fight against terrorism go in stabilising the security of a nation?' Regional bodies such as the European Union, the African Union, and the Arab League enthusiastically joined in the business of structuring frameworks for fighting terrorism and requiring member states to adhere. Terrorism was criminalised by the member states of the regional bodies. They blocked terrorism financing and increased vigilance on immigration issues. The response, speed and commitment given to the anti-terrorism campaign attracted the admiration of internationalists. For instance, Kofi Anan the former United Nations Secretary-General with respect to the creation of Global Security Law stated, "...the work of the Counter-Terrorism Committee and the cooperation it has received from Member States has been unprecedented and exemplary".[148]

Even though terrorist acts could be described as acts against humanity, the fight against terrorism should not constitute a fight against rule of law. For instance, it is public knowledge that the United States declared that international law was to be no barrier to US action if its self-interests were at stake.[149]Similarly, other sovereign states have taken actions, which may be considered contrary to the principles of international law such as the ECHR in the bid to protect

147 K. Schepple, 'Global Security Law and the Challenge to Constitutionalism after 9/11' (2011) vol 2 Public Law 353-377

148 ibid; K. Roach, The *9/11 effect: Comparative Counter-terrorism* (Cambridge University Press, New York 2011), 42

149 ibid; D. Stephen, et al, *Counterterrorism Law* (Aspen Publishers, New York 2007), 523

their national security. The following cases will show some measures adopted by states in their fight against terrorism and how the courts have interpreted issues of national security within the law of the ECHR.

In the case of ***Al-Jedda v The United Kingdom,***[150] the applicant was arrested, stripped off his British nationality and subjected to internment for three years by the Multi-National Force in Iraq. He was alleged to have been recruiting terrorists outside Iraq with a view to the commission of atrocities there; for facilitating the travel into Iraq of an identified terrorist explosives expert; for conspiring with that explosives expert to conduct attacks with improvised explosive devices against coalition forces in the areas around Fallujah and Baghdad; and for conspiring with the explosives expert and members of an Islamist terrorist cell in the Gulf to smuggle high tech detonation equipment into Iraq for use in attacks against coalition forces.[151]

Hence, the Multi-National Force perceived such activities as a threat to the stability and national security of Iraq.[152] The applicant argued that his internment was unlawful and in breach of Article 5 of the ECHR. He submitted that the requirement to hold him in internment was not an obligation of the United Kingdom even though the Security Council empowered her to do so. He referred to a Namibian case where the International Court of Justice (ICJ) stated: "...the language of a resolution of the Security Council should be carefully analysed before a conclusion can be made as to its binding effect..."[153]

Thus, as the situation demands, the Security Council may require states to embark on particular action. For example, the case of ***Kadi and Al Barakaat International Foundation v Council of the European Union and Commission of the European Communities*** involved the freezing of assets under European Community Regulations adopted to reflect United Nations Security Council (UNSC) Resolutions 1267(1999), 1333(2000) and 1390(2002),

150 Al-Jedda v The United Kingdom (2011) ECHR 27021/08 Grand Chamber

151 ibid., Para.,11

152 ibid; A. Allawi, *The Occupation of Iraq: Winning the War, Losing the Battle* (Yale University Press Publication, Finey 2008), 288

153 ibid, para 49; M. Bailliet, et al., *Promoting Peace Through International Law* (Oxford University Press, United Kingdom 2015), 283; K. Larsen, *The Human Rights Treaty Obligations of Peacekeepers* (Cambridge University Press, New York 2012), 29

which dictated that all states were to take measures to freeze the funds and other financial assets of individuals and entities associated with Osama bin Laden, the Al-Qaeda network, and the Taliban.[154] In this case, states had "*...no autonomous discretion*", with respect to freezing the assets of the designated persons or impounding the aircraft operating from the Federal Republic of Yugoslavia.[155]

The applicant in ***Al-Jedda's*** case stressed that the language of Resolution 1546 and the letters annexed to it clearly stated that the Security Council should authorise the Multi-National Force to:

> "Take measures that it considered necessary to contribute to the maintenance of security and stability in Iraq. It did not require a State to take action incompatible with its human rights obligations, but instead left a discretion to the State as to whether, when and how to contribute to the maintenance of security."[156]

He further argued that if the Security Council's intention were to impose an obligation on the British forces, which would amount to a breach of the United Kingdom's International Human Rights obligation, the language would have been clear and unequivocal.[157]In response to the applicant's alleged breach of Article 5(1) of the ECHR, the Government reiterated her obligation to detain the applicant, pursuant to UNSC Resolution 1546. The Government contended that the operation of the British forces was derived from the law of belligerent occupation, as modified by the UNSC in Resolutions 1483 and 1511. Thus, the preamble to Resolution 1483 in terms recognised the specific authorities, responsibilities and obligations of the Occupying Powers, including those under the Geneva Conventions of 1949.[158] Customary international law, as contemplated in Article 43 of The Hague Regulations, requires the occupying power to take all

154 ibid, para 51; International Monetary Fund, *Maldives: Detailed Assessment Report on Anti-Money Laundering and Combating the Financing of Terrorism* (International Monetary Fund Publication Services, Washington D.C 2012), 68

155 ibid, para 93

156 ibid; C. Akrivopoulou, et al., *Digital Democracy and the Impact of Technology on Governance and Politics: New Globalised Practices* (IGI Global, Pennsylvania 2013), 214; C. Murphy, *EU Counter-terrorism Law: Pre-Emption and the Rule of Law* (Hart Publishing Ltd, Oxford 2012), 85-86

157 ibid

158 ibid., para 50

the measures in its power to restore and ensure, as far as possible, public order and safety in the occupied territory.[159]

The ICJ in ***Democratic Republic of Congo v Uganda*** described this as including a duty "to protect the inhabitants of the occupied territory against acts of violence and not to tolerate such violence by any third party".[160] The Government argued that broad powers were conferred on the occupying powers. For example, by virtue of Article 7 of the Fourth Geneva Convention, the occupying power had a responsibility to take steps to protect the civilian population against all acts of violence or threats thereof. A general obligation was also placed on the occupying power by Article 68 to secure the orderly government of the occupied territory, which included the power to protect its forces and administration from acts of violence. It had powers of compulsion and restraint over the population of occupied territory and Article 78 of the Fourth Geneva Convention recognised the power to 'detain', where the occupying power considers it necessary, for imperative reasons of security, to take safety measures concerning protected persons.[161]

Hence, the Government in its submission maintained that specific authorities, responsibilities and obligations of an occupying power, as identified in United Nations Security Council Resolution 1483, included the power to detain persons in occupied territory on security grounds. The Government also submitted that Paragraph 10 of the Resolution specifically provided the Multi-National Force with "...authority to take all necessary measures to contribute to the maintenance of security and stability in Iraq in accordance with the letters annexed to this resolution..." [162].

---

159 ibid; P. Minnerop, et al., *World Court Digest 2001-2005* (Springer, New York 2005), 437; A. Clapham, et al., *The Oxford Handbook of International Law in Armed Conflict* (Oxford University Press: Oxford 2014), 194

160 ibid; P. Couvreur, *The International Court of Justice and the effectiveness of International Law* (Koninklijke Brill nv Incorporates, Netherlands 2016), 213; M. Langford, et al, Global Justice, State Duties: *The Extraterritorial Scope of Economic, Social and Cultural Rights in International Law* (Cambridge University Press, New York 2013), 168

161 ibid; F. Saulnier, et al., *The Practical Guide to Humanitarian Law* (Rowman & Littlefield Publishers, New York 2008), 343

162 ibid., para 88

The text of Resolution 1546 clearly depicts that the annexed letters were intrinsic to it and defined the scope of powers conferred by the Security Council. Colin Powell, the United States Secretary of State, in his letter expressly referred to 'internment' as one of the tasks, which the Multi-National Force was to continue to perform. Hence, the Government opined that Resolution 1546 could not have been clearer in terms of authorising the Multi-National Force to use: "...preventive detention where necessary for imperative reasons of security in Iraq".[163]

Furthermore, the Government stated that Resolution 1546 and the annexed letters evidently portrayed that what was authorised by the Security Council was a 'regime of detention' modelled on the specific authorities, responsibilities and obligations that had existed during the period of occupation.[164] The Government further submitted that Article 25 of the United Nations Charter established an obligation for United Nations Member States to accept and carry out decisions of the Security Council. Consequently, the operation of Articles 25 and 103 of the United Nations Charter displaced the application of Article 5 of the ECHR to the extent that Article 5 of the ECHR is discordant with such legal regime.[165]

The Government contended that the principle applied by the European Court of Justice in its judgment in **Kadi's** case is dissimilar from that applied in ***Al-Jedda's*** case. Therefore, the applicant's reliance on **Kadi's** judgment in this present case is erroneous.[166] More so, the judgment in ***Bosphorus Hava Yolları Turizmve Ticaret Anonim Şirketi v.Ireland*** [GC] showed that there was no violation of the ECHR. The argument by the applicant that the ECHR recognised a limit on the protection of human rights, applicable in this case was also contended by the Government.[167]

In view of the meaning of national security given in ***Al-Jedda's case,*** the House of Lords approached national security from a wider perspective. The judges held

163 ibid; Hague Yearbook of International Law-Annuaire De La Haye De Driot International (Koninklijke Brill NV Incorporates, The Netherlands 2012), 238

164 ibid; M. Feinberg, *Sovereignty in the Age of Global Terrorism: The Role of International Organizations* (Brill Nijhoff, Boston 2016), 154

165 ibid., para 91

166 ibid., para 92

167 ibid

that Article 103 of the United Nations Charter had authority over resolutions of the Security Council, even in relation to human rights agreements. Hence, Lord Bingham explained that the UK as an occupying power in Iraq had, "...to take necessary measures to protect the safety of the public and its own safety". He pointed out that where a person is deemed to be a threat to public safety or the occupying power, an obligation arises to detain such a person.[168]

According to Lord Bingham, considering the importance of national security, such obligation could not be abated because the occupying power was no longer present in the turbulent region. As long as no improvement has been experienced in the local security conditions, the pre-existing regime should remain in force until the local security conditions are restored. For example, in ***Al-Jedda case***, the appellant's detention was not during the period of occupation, but the prevailing circumstance in Iraq warranted the continuation of the pre-existing regime.[169]

He observed that although the word used in Resolution UNSCR 1511 and 1546 is 'authorisation' and not 'obligation', the significance of the maintenance of peace and security in the world can scarcely be exaggerated, which is the pursuit of the UN. Hence, the UN's interest in Iraq is geared towards such goal, after the recurrent determinations that the situation in Iraq continued to constitute a threat to international peace and security.[170]

Thus, Justice Bingham said:

> "...it is of course true that the UK did not become specifically bound to detain the appellant. But it was, I think, bound to exercise its power of detention where this was necessary for imperative reasons of security. It could not be said to be giving effect to the decisions of the Security Council if, in such a situation, it neglected to take steps which were open to it."[171]

168 ibid; Department of Public Information United Nations (1995), 344

169 ibid; G. Slapper, et al., *The English Legal System* (Routledge Taylor & Francis, New York 2017), 387

170 ibid; N. Boschiero, et al., *International Courts and the Development of International Law* (T.M.C. Asser Press, Netherlands 2013), 659

171 ibid; S. Peer, et al., *The EU Charter of Fundamental Rights: A Commentary* (Hart Publishing, Oxford 2014), 136

Conclusively, Lord Bingham contended for balance between the 'power' and 'duty' to detain, exercisable on the express authority of the Security Council and, on the other hand, a fundamental human right, which the UK had undertaken to secure to those (like the appellant) within its jurisdiction. He said:

> "...there is in my opinion only one way in which they can be reconciled: by ruling that the UK may lawfully, where it is necessary for imperative reasons of security, exercise the power to detain authorised by UNSCR 1546 and successive resolutions, but must ensure that the detainee's rights under Article 5 are not infringed to any greater extent than is inherent in such detention."[172]

Lord Bingham adopted a broad approach to the issue of Iraq's security, and consequently, the maintenance of international peace and security, while also recognising that a detainee's fundamental human rights ought to be respected.[173] Baroness Hale agreed with the other Law Lords but approached the issue of security narrowly. Hence, she said:

> "...it is not immediately obvious why the prolonged detention of this person in Iraq is necessary, given that any problem he presents in Iraq could be solved by repatriating him to this country and dealing with him here. If we stand back a little from the circumstances of this case, this is the response which is so often urged when British people are in trouble with the law in foreign countries, and in this case, it is within the power of the British authorities to achieve it."[174]

The other Law Lords in this appeal saw the appellant's internment as one of the measures available to the Multi-National Force as prescribed by the resolution to maintain peace and stability in Iraq. Lord Bingham in his broad approach to security matters said that:

---

172 ibid; H. Cuyckens, Revisiting the Law of Occupation (Koninklijke Brill NV Incorporates, The Netherlands 2017), 67

173 ibid

174 ibid

> "...in a situation such as the present, obligations in Article 103 should not in any event be given a narrow, contract-based, meaning. The importance of maintaining peace and security in the world can scarcely be exaggerated, and that...is the mission of the UN. Its involvement in Iraq was directed to that end, following repeated determinations that the situation in Iraq continued to constitute a threat to international peace and security."[175]

Baroness Hale opined that the appellant ought to have been repatriated to Britain for his case to be handled there, just as is usually the case when British citizens are in trouble in foreign countries. However, Lord Bingham perceived the maintenance of peace and security in Iraq as an integral part of the maintenance of peace and security in the world. Hence, to reduce the extent of the appellant's chance of being a threat to international peace and security, his repatriation was not contemplated, but he was stripped off his British citizenship, which he did not appeal against. Therefore, the House of Lords held that there was no breach of Article 5(1) of the ECHR.[176]

However, most of European Court of Appeal judges adopted a narrow approach in holding that Article 5(1) of the ECHR was violated. They held that there was no express obligation on the United Kingdom to 'intern' the appellant and refute the notion that international humanitarian law places an obligation on an occupying power to use indefinite internment without trial. Thus, they referred to the judgment of the International Court of Justice in the case of ***Armed Activities on the Territory of the Congo,*** which stated:

> "...this obligation to protect the inhabitants of the occupied territory from violence, including violence by third parties, did not place an obligation on the Occupying Power to use internment..."[177]

However, Justice Poalelungi partially dissented from the opinion of the majority in the European Court of Appeal. He asserted that Article 103 of the UN Charter

175 ibid

176 ibid

177 ibid; M. Schmitt, et al., *Yearbook of International Humanitarian Law* (Cambridge University Press, United Kingdom 2011), 243

must be given priority where a member state takes up an 'authorisation' to maintain international peace under a Security Council mandate.

The fight against terrorism is a significant aspect of national security. Accordingly, post 9/11, the United States of America embarked on the training of security professionals in specific security areas such as airport security and ground security.[178] Legislations are either enacted or existing ones are revised to contend with security challenges; for instance, the Prevention of Terrorism Act of 2006 and the USA Patriot Act 2001. Such legislations criminalise some acts or omissions, which might endanger a nation or the world at large. For example, classes of new criminal offences proposed to aid the police in confronting terrorism were enshrined in Part 1 of the Terrorism Act of 2006 (such as encouragement of terrorism).

3.3.2 SUMMARY

In summary, the inference that could be drawn from the above-mentioned cases is that national security can be ***defined*** as such measures (like repatriation, deprivation of citizenship, internment, passing of new legislations and revising existing ones where necessary) taken by nations to protect their inhabitants and territorial sovereignty from violence. The implementation of such measures must not necessarily be an express obligation on a nation. It might be an implied obligation where a nation stands a risk of any form of violence or threat. Hence, in ***Al-Jedda v United Kingdom***, Justice Poalelungi said:

> "...Internment is a frequently used measure in conflict situations, well established under international humanitarian law, and was, moreover, expressly referred to in the letter of Colin Powell annexed to Resolution 1546. I consider that member States were authorised to continue interning individuals where necessary."[179]

Evidently, the fight against terrorism is not devoid of challenges. However, the effect of the fight against terrorism on a nation or globally cannot be

178 T. Winkler, et al., *Combating Terrorism and Its Implication for The Security Sector* (DCAF & The Swedish National Defence College, Stockholm 2005), 5

179 ibid; G. Oberleitner, *Human Rights in Armed Conflict: Law, Practice,* Policy (Cambridge University Press, Cambridge 2015), 298

overemphasised. Notably, it can lead to loss of safe haven for terrorists. For example, Al-Qaeda has lost its safe haven in Afghanistan.[180] The fight against terrorism attempts to decentralise the terrorists' networks and their command structure.[181] To some extent, it frustrates terrorist support and creates a hostile environment for them. For instance, by virtue of part 1 of the Anti-terrorist, Crime and Security Act of 2001, most of the terrorists' bank accounts are frozen. The fight against terrorism might facilitate the killing or capturing of terrorists to make nations and the world at large a safer place. For instance, most of the culprits of the 9/11 attacks including the plot's mastermind Khalid Shaykh Muhammad have either been captured or killed.[182]

It keeps nations on alert against threats (imminent or anticipatory) and hence, births new security strategies. For instance, since the agonising attacks of 9/11, the Congress has passed legislations revamping the national intelligence effort; made information-sharing a prerogative, modified the electronic-surveillance law to reflect technological developments while upholding the requirement of a judicial warrant, and established the Department of Homeland Security.[183]The essence of counterterrorism measures cannot be overstressed considering the after-effects of a terrorist attack. Thus, the subsection below will discuss the protection of lives and property as an element of national security.

3.4 PROTECTION OF INDIVIDUAL LIVES AND PROPERTY AS PART OF NATIONAL SECURITY

The upsurge of violence against civilians has persisted, irrespective of states' renewed undertaking to adhere and ensure respect to the rules of international humanitarian law. States seem to be more inappropriate agents for the implementation of humanitarian rules, particularly around internal armed conflicts.

180 D. West, et al., *Reality check: The unreported good news about America* (Regnery Publishing Inc, Washington DC 2008),104

181 A. Guiora, *Top ten global justice law review articles* (Oxford University Press, New York 2008), 88

182 S. Aubrey, *The new dimension of international terrorism: Strategie und konfliktforschung* (VdfHochschulverlag, AG 2004),186

183 F. Patel, et al., 'What went wrong with the Fisa Court—Brennan Court for Justice' (2015) <*https://wwwbrennancentre.org/.../what_went_%20wrong* _with_The_FISA. Court.p....> accessed 13 December 2017

States' involvement in internal conflict situations has not only compromised their responsibility of guaranteeing the protection of their citizens but has also created doubts concerning their relevance in generating protection for civilians at the international level.[184]The United Nations Secretary Kofi Anan in his Millennium Assembly Report wrote:

> "International conventions have traditionally looked at states to protect civilians, but today this expectation is threatened in several ways. First, states are sometimes the principal perpetrators of violence against the very citizens that humanitarian law requires them to protect. Second, non-state combatants, particularly in collapsed states, are often ignorant or contemptuous of humanitarian law. Third, international conventions do not adequately address the specific needs of vulnerable groups, such as internally displaced persons, or women and children in complex emergencies."[185]

This subsection will address the question: 'Does national security embrace the protection of individual lives and property or is it just limited to the protection of territorial sovereignty?' It is the responsibility of states as the most important agents of humanitarian protection under international legal instruments, such as the ECHR, to ensure that military operations are restricted to military targets and that populations in need receive adequate relief assistance and protection. National security can be viewed from the perspective of people's security. Hence, Claude Bruderlein in her journal 'People's Security as a New Measure of Global Security,' wrote:

> "Human security is about recognising the importance of the peoples' security needs side by side with those of States, minimising risks, adopting preventive measures to reduce human vulnerabilities and taking remedial action when preventive measures fail."[186]

---

184 C. Bruderlein, 'People's Security as a new measure of Global Stability' (2001) vol 83 (842) International Review of the Red Cross 353

185 ibid; R. Thakur, et al., *International Commissions and The Power of Ideas* (United Nations University Press, New York 2006), 223

186 C. Bruderlein, op. cit.

Article 8(1) of the ECHR provides, "Everyone has the right to respect for his private and family life, his home and his correspondence".[187]

Such right could be derogated from by virtue of S.8(2) of the ECHR under certain circumstances such as national security, public safety or the economic well-being of the country, for the prevention of disorder or crime, for the protection of health or morals, for the protection of the rights and freedoms of others.[188]

In the case of ***Esmukhambetov and Others v Russia***, to prevent terrorist attacks (violence) and suppress the criminal activities of illegal armed groups in the village of Runnoye, military officials launched a missile strike in the village leading to the loss of lives and properties. The first, second, third, thirteenth, and twenty-second applicants argued that the Government failed to account for the applicants' relatives' deaths.[189] They argued that the operation of the military personnel in Runnoye on 12th September 1999 evidently amounted to a violation of Article 2 of the ECHR.[190] They questioned the planning, control and measures taken to condense the risk to the lives of civilians during that operation, and the specific directives given to the pilots of the SU-25 planes who had bombed the village.[191]They contended that the presence of the civilians in Kogi at the time of the military missile strike was well-known to the Government. Hence, the preferred means used by the authorities had obviously contradicted the Convention's strict proportionality test.[192]

As such, the lethal force used had been asymmetric to the purpose pursued by the federal military forces, as the village had in fact been subjected to 'indiscriminate bombing'. The applicants further contended about the vague and inadequate legal framework concerning the use of force and firearms by military personnel in Russia. The Government failed to offer adequate safeguards to

187 European Convention on Human Rights 1950

188 ibid; D. Ehlers, *European Fundamental Rights and Freedoms* (De Gruyter Recht, Berlin 2007), 68

189 Esmukhambetov and Others v. Russia (2011) ECHR 23445/03 Strasbourg para 102

190 ibid., 132

191 ibid., para 131

192 ibid., para 132

forestall the arbitrary deprivation of life and satisfy the requirement of protection by law of the right to life secured by Article 2 of the ECHR.[193]

In response to the applicants' contention, the Government argued that the use of lethal force, which led to the death of the applicants' relatives, had been justified for the purposes of Article 2 (2) (a) and (b) of the ECHR.[194] The Government argued that domestic investigation revealed that illegal armed groups had been showing violent armed resistance to the authorities, thereby constituting a danger to local residents, other persons and the public interest.[195] Thus, the Government submitted:

> "...that danger could not have been eliminated by any other means, and it was impossible to use ground troops near Kogi (Runnoye) ... the federal servicemen, both commanding officers and their subordinates, had acted in full compliance with national legislation and regulations for securing the safety of the civilian population, as well as those relating to the use of lethal force."[196]

The Government submitted that the commanding officers had reliable and sufficient information on the exact site of the terrorist base, on the concentration of illegal fighters at that base and the preparation by them of large-scale terrorist attacks. Hence, the planning and control of the operation in question was not in breach of any legal requirement.[197] The Government alleged that it was clear in the circumstances of the case, the military targets situated near Kogi (Runnoye), their designation and the intensity of the danger they had posed for, inter alia, residents of the nearby Republic of Dagestan, and, as a result, the need for their destruction was apparent.[198]

193 ibid., para 135

194 ibid., para 136

195 ibid

196 ibid; C. Walker, *Terrorism and The Law* (Oxford University Press, New York 2011), 16-17

197 ibid; V. Ramraj, et al., *Global Anti-Terrorism Law and Policy* (Cambridge University Press, Cambridge 2012), 122

198 ibid., para 137

The Court, in its assessment, found that there had been a violation of Article 2 of the ECHR. It adopted a broad approach to the issue of national security in the present case. The Court did not only limit national security to the protection of the nation (Russia, particularly the Republic of Dagestan), but construed the obligation placed on the Government by Article 2 of the ECHR to protect its citizens' right to life as part of national security. It is therefore not enough for the Government to take drastic measures to abate violence in its territory without due considerations of such measures on the existing citizenry.

Terrorism is defined in the Code of Federal Regulations as the unlawful use of force and violence against persons or property to intimidate or coerce a government, the civilian population, or any segment thereof, in furtherance of political or social objectives (28 C.F.R. Section 0.85).[199]Arguably, based on such definition, an act does not necessarily constitute a terrorist attack merely because it was carried out by an armed group. The Government, in such case, can be classified as terrorists considering the model and instrument of attack on its citizenry (unlawful use of force). It is immaterial from where and from whom an attack emanates, provided some elements of terrorism characterise such attack. In other words, the acts of the military in the present case can be described as a 'terrorist attack', as the citizenry who the Government was meant to protect were 'intimidated' and 'coerced' by the military attack. There ought to be a meeting point between peoples' interest and state's interest. Terrorism may not always be external. It can be internal too (domestic terrorism). Thus, a balance needs to be struck between the after-effects of such drastic measures on the existing citizenry and the anticipatory danger from the illegal fighters.

Irrespective of the fact that the Government contended "the lethal force had been used in defence of persons from unlawful violence".[200] The Court was struck by the means chosen by the Russian authorities to get rid of the so-called 'illegal fighters' in Kogi, since there was a village settlement there with women and children. Hence, the Court deemed that the use of lethal force had been "grossly disproportionate to the purpose of effecting the lawful arrest of a person".[201]

199 P. M, et al., Homeland Security: Principles and Practice of Terrorism Response (1st edn Jones and Bartlett Publishers LLC, Maryland 2011), 3

200 ibid., para 147

201 ibid., para 146

Thus, the Government failed in the obligation placed on it by Article 2 of the ECHR. The Court considered the submissions of the Government insufficient and unpersuasive. For instance, the Court held that there should be evidence from the Government to corroborate their submission that reliable and sufficient information was received with respect to the presence of illegal fighters near Kogi (Runnoye) at the relevant time.[202]

The Court concluded that the authorities failed to exercise proper care in the organisation and control of the operation of 12th September 1999. Thus, it asserted that:

> "It does not appear that the authorities had considered comprehensively the limits and constraints on the use of indiscriminate weapons within a populated area.[203] There is also no evidence that at any stage of the operation any measures were taken to avoid, or to minimise,[204] the risk to the lives of the residents of Kogi (Runnoye). It does not appear that the authorities took any steps with a view to informing the villagers of the attack beforehand and to securing their evacuation."[205]

Analytically, on grounds of national security, the authorities may not have given the villagers a prior notice of the attack to avoid being taken unawares by the 'terrorists'; but they out of necessity must have considered the foreseen consequences of the attack (the destruction of lives and properties of the villagers) before carrying out the missile attack in that village. It follows that the measure to be taken at any time for enhancement of national security should not be more than is absolutely necessary for the achievement of the set purpose.

The applicants alleged a violation of Article 8 of the ECHR after the destruction of their properties. The Government acknowledged that the attack of 12th September 1999 had resulted in the destruction of many residential and non-residential buildings in the village of Kogi (Runnoye). They further argued that the attack was necessary to suppress the criminal activities of members of illegal

202 ibid., para 145

203 Isayeva v Russia (2005) ECHR 57950/00 Strasbourg para 189

204 McCann and Others v United Kingdom (1995) ECHR 18984/91 Strasbourg para 194, 201

205 ibid., para 149

armed groups and prevent the terrorist attacks they had been preparing.[206] The Court found no legal basis for such a radical interference as the destruction of an individual's building and property. The Court further observed that no document specifically authorised the operation of the Federal Servicemen. Hence, the interference with the applicants' rights was not lawful within the meaning of Article 8 of the ECHR and Article 1 of Protocol No. 1. Therefore, the applicants' rights under Article 8 of the ECHR were violated by the Government.[207]

Conversely, in the case of ***Secretary of State for Home Department v AP*** a control order was imposed on the appellant—an Ethiopian national—under the Prevention of Terrorism Act of 2005. He came to the UK with his siblings and mother in 1992. In 2005 he travelled to Somalia and Ethiopia. Being a suspected terrorist, he was detained in Ethiopia. The control order confined the appellant to a 16-hour curfew, electronic tagging and restrictions on his right of association and communication, which are usually imposed in such cases.[208]

A modification of the control order required the appellant to live in a town in the Midlands, which was 150 miles from the London address where he lived with his family and friends. The appellant appealed against the modification in the High Court, which held as follows:

> "...that although the interference with AP's rights to private and family life under Article 8 of the Convention was justified and proportionate—on grounds of national security—the overall effect of the curfew and AP's social isolation constituted a deprivation of liberty within Article 5."[209]

On appeal in the Court of Appeal, the necessity for the control order was not in dispute, but only its terms. The Court of Appeal quashed the High Court's decision. It held that the judge had been wrong in treating the Article 8 factors

206 ibid., paras 170, 171

207 ibid., para 179

208 Secretary of State for Home Department v AP (2010) UKSC 24; D. Anderson, Control Orders in 2011: Final Report of the Independent Reviewer on the Prevention of Terrorist Act 2005 (The Stationery Office, London 2012), 18; B. Emmerson, et al, *Human Rights and Criminal Justice* (3rd edn Sweet and Maxwell, London 2012), 521; Great Britain Parliament, House of Lords, *Journals of the House of Lords Volume 240* (HM Stationery Office, London 2006), 948

209 ibid; D. Webber, *Preventive Detention of Terror Suspects: A New Legal Framework* (Routledge Taylor & Francis, New York 2016), Ch. 5

as determinative of the issue under Article 5 regarding whether there had been a deprivation of liberty.[210]

The Secretary of State expressly argued that the Judge should disregard everything that depended on the individual circumstances of the subject's family while assessing the weight to be given to the restrictive effects of a condition such as the one in the present case.[211] The appellant appealed against the Court of Appeal's decision, requesting the Supreme Court to consider the following issues:

- Whether conditions, which were proportionate restrictions upon Article 8 rights, could tip the balance in relation to Article 5?
- Whether the judge could consider subjective or person-specific factors, such as particular difficulties of the person's family in visiting him, when considering whether a control order amounted to a deprivation of liberty?
- Whether, and on what grounds, the Court of Appeal could interfere with the judge's determination?[212]

Unanimously, the Supreme Court allowed the High Court's decision, disregarding the Court of Appeal's decision.

The Supreme Court referred to the case of ***Secretary of State for the Home Department v JJ***.[213]Here the House of Lords held:

> "...that deprivation of liberty might take a variety of forms other than classic detention in prison or strict arrest. The court's task was to consider the concrete situation of the particular individual and, taking account of a whole range of criteria including the type, duration, effects and manner

210 ibid; C. Macken, *Counter-Terrorism and The Detention of Suspected Terrorist* (Routledge Taylor & Francis Group, New York 2013), 34-39

211 ibid; J. Beckman, *Comparative Legal Approaches to Homeland Security and Anti-Terrorism* (Routledge Taylor & Francis Group, New York 2016), 120

212 ibid; M. Amos, *Human Rights Law* (Hart Publishing, Portland 2014), 95

213 Secretary of State for Home Department v JJ (2008) 1 AC 385

> of implementation of the measures in question, to assess their impact on him in the context of the life he might otherwise have been living."[214]

In response to the first issue under consideration, Lord Brown held that Article 8 of the ECHR was capable of being a decisive factor if its restriction was a relevant consideration in determining whether a control order breached Article 5 of the ECHR. The weight to be given to a relevant consideration can only be challenged on grounds of irrationality, which could have been contended in the present case. Lord Brown disregarded the Secretary of State's submission that in assessing the weight to be given to the restrictive effects of a condition, (for instance, the one imposed on the appellant to reside in the Midlands), the judge should disregard all that depended on the individual circumstances of the family. The Secretary of State failed to submit that the appellant's family behaved unreasonably in failing to adequately overcome the practical difficulties they encountered in visiting the appellant on a more regular basis. Rather, the Secretary of State argued that their practical difficulties should have been ignored. The Supreme Court considered this to be an erroneous analysis and held that it could not be accepted. However, Lord Brown said:

> "Plainly the family could not be allowed to thwart what would otherwise be an appropriate residential requirement by unreasonably failing to take opportunities open to them to visit AP and save him from social isolation."[215]

The Supreme Court held that in such circumstance, it should be the families' unreasonable conduct in failing to use the opportunity available to them to visit the appellant to save him from being socially isolated and not the residence condition, which was the operative cause of the appellant's isolation. Finally, the Supreme Court held that there was no contradiction in the High Court's decision, having considered its various parts.[216]

214 Secretary of State for Home Department v AP, op. cit.

215 ibid; L. Herik, *Counter-Terrorism Strategies in a Fragmented International Legal Order* (Cambridge University Press, Cambridge 2013), 40

216 ibid; G. Letsas, et al., *Current Legal Problems* (Oxford University Press, New York 2010), 184

The Supreme Court's decision in the present case is narrow and contradictory. The right under Article 8(1) of the ECHR is not an absolute right. The decision is contradictory in the sense that the Supreme Court upheld the High Court's decision that rejected AP's case under Article 8 of the ECHR on the ground that interference with his family life was justified and proportionate in the interests of national security, but decided that the overall effect of a 16-hour curfew and AP's social isolation (particularly through his being separated from his family) constituted an Article 5 ECHR deprivation of liberty.

The Government's interference with the appellant's private and family life is in itself a deprivation of liberty. Liberty connotes freedom from any form of restriction. Hence, it will be contradictory to justify the interference with the appellant's family life on national security grounds, while at the same time declaring the overall effect of the interference a deprivation of his liberty.

The right to liberty is an embodiment of so many other rights in the sense that its deprivation might wholly or partly affect the enjoyment of some other rights such as the right under Article 8 of the ECHR. The Supreme Court adopted a narrow approach in separating the rights under Articles 8 and 5 of the ECHR respectively, in the present case. Even on grounds of proportionality, the appellant's family was not precluded from visiting him. The argument was only on the difficulties they encountered while embarking on such visits. Thus, he was not socially isolated if national security issues were contemplated. The facts of the case showed that the control order was a necessity, which implied that the appellant was a security threat. It therefore follows that the appellant's right under Article 5 of the ECHR may not have been violated. The security status of the appellant should also have been one of the grounds in determining whether his right under Article 5 of the ECHR was violated.

On the other hand, the nature of the confinement can also determine whether a person's right to liberty has been violated.[217] In the present case, it can be argued that the modification was not necessary since the appellant had the electronic tagging, which can dictate his whereabouts. The question is: Can such equipment restrain an individual from any activity capable of destabilising a nation's security?

---

217 M. Macovei, *The Right to Liberty and the Security of the Person: A Guide to the implementation of Article 5 of the European Convention on Human Rights* (Council of Europe, Germany 2004), 7

Nevertheless, the applicants in the case of ***Esmukhambetov and Others v Russia*** further alleged a violation of Article 3 of the ECHR on grounds that they had suffered severe mental distress and anguish in connection with the attack on their village, deaths of their close relatives, and destruction of their houses and other properties. The Court found no violation of Article 3 ECHR with respect to other applicants in this case. It held that the violation of Article 2 ECHR would be sufficient for them. However, it recognised a violation of Article 3 of the ECHR with respect to the first applicant. Thus, it stated:

> "...having been an eyewitness to the instantaneous deaths of his two young sons and his wife, the first applicant experienced a shock of such intensity that he suffered from a temporary loss of memory. The suffering ... was of such severity for the authorities' acts resulting in the deaths of the first applicant family members to be categorized as inhuman treatment within the meaning of Article 3..."".[218]

Similarly, in the case of ***Huseyn and Others v Azerbaijan*** in view of national security, the military personnel in Baku arbitrarily applied excessive force against persons who were present in the turbulent area within Baku. Thus, the applicants were convicted by the Assize Court for organising public disorder and acts of violence against state officials. On appeal, the Appeal Court held that there had been a violation of the applicants' rights under Article 6 of the ECHR.[219] Hence, in protecting a nation from violence, a balance ought to be struck between issues of national security and human rights.

3.4.1 SUMMARY

In summary, simply put, national security can be ***defined*** as 'peoples' security. By implication it does not only protect the state's interest, but also the citizenry's personal interest to the extent of their lives and personal belongings (property). For instance, the facts in ***Esmukhambetov's case*** revealed that Kogi was a peaceful village and no rebel fighters ever lived there. The Government failed in her responsibility to protect her civilian population from the military

218 Esmukhambetov and Others v Russia, op. cit., para 190

219 Huseyn and Others v Azerbaijan (2011) ECHR 35485/05, 45553/05, 35680/05 and 36085/05 Grand Chamber para 11

attack. There was an arbitrary attack on the population, which led to loss of lives contrary to the spirit of Article 2 ECHR (right to life). The civilian population was not only displaced from their residential homes, but their farmlands were also destroyed, which is contrary to Article 14 of the Protocol. Arguably, there might not be national security in the absence of people's security.

The relationship between human security and national security is synergetic. In essence, peoples' security is complementary rather than competitive. There ought to be a shift from state's security to peoples' security. Without the human element there cannot be a state. A major source of human insecurity is an extrinsically aggressive and intrinsically oppressive regime. The Government and its parastatals are the instruments of national security. Therefore, peoples' security cannot be achieved without sufficient national security strategies put in place. It behoves on the Government to ensure the protection of people's well-being and the hindrance of great harm. Thus, the security dilemma comprises, "Why, when, and how to intervene to protect people and prevent egregious human suffering"?[220] Critically, one of the ways through which the Government can ensure people's security is through effective immigration control. Consequently, the subsection below will explore immigration as an aspect of national security.

3.5 NATIONAL SECURITY AND IMMIGRATION

International travel can be described as a way of life. People travel by air, sea or land for tourism, new life, work, environmental change, study and, at other times, for terrorism. The incidence of global terrorism has made effective immigration policies and border control crucial in pursuit of national security.[221] The diversity of terrorist attacks makes immigration one of the channels of such attacks.[222] The porosity of a nation's border has the potential of leading to the infiltration of illegal immigrants (terrorists inclusive) into the nation.

---

220 M. Manwaring, *Strategic Studies Institute Monograph: The Strategic Logic of the Contemporary Security Dilemma* (Strategic Study Institute, US Army War College 2011), 10

221 C. Rudolph, National *Security and Immigration: Policy development in the United States and Western Europe since 1945* (Stanford University Press, California 2006),1-10

222 J. Hayworth, et al., *Whatever it takes: Illegal Immigration, Border Security and The War on Terror* (Regnery Publishing Inc., Washington DC 2006), 6

The number and migration of foreigners into a nation impliedly stirs a sense of national security.[223]

Accordingly, it is settled in the case of ***Üner v The Netherlands*** that as a matter of well-established international law and subject to its treaty obligations, including those emanating from the Convention, a contracting State has the right to control the entry, residence and expulsion of aliens.[224] However, the absolute nature of Article 3 of the ECHR limits such right. In the case of ***Sufi and Elmi v United Kingdom,*** the first and second applicants were served with deportation orders to Somalia by the respondent for conducts considered dangerous to the community. They contested their deportation orders on grounds that the deportation will lead to the violation of Articles 2, 3 and 8 of the ECHR.[225]

The Court deemed it fit to consider the case of the applicants within the context of Article 3 of the ECHR.[226] The Government submitted that the application was clearly ill-founded.[227] Nevertheless, the Court considered the application admissible and held that the deportation of the applicants to Somalia violated their rights under Article 3 of the ECHR.[228] The activities of the applicants in the United Kingdom portrayed 1them as threats to national security. For instance, the first applicant had about eight convictions in the UK from October 2005 to July 2009,[229]while the second applicant had about nine convictions from June 1992 to June 2004.[230] The absolute nature of Article 3 of the ECHR is a challenge to national security since the severity of an individual's conduct is immaterial if

223 D. Haris, 'Immigration and National Security: the illusion of safety through local law enforcement action' (2011) vol 28(2) Arizona Journal of International and Comparative Law 383

224 Uner v Netherlands (2006) 54 ECHR 46410/99 para 54; Abdulaziz, Cabales and Balkandali v United Kingdom (1985) 9214/80; 9473/81 para 67; Boujlifa v France (1997) 122/1996/741/940 para 42

225 Sufi and Elmi v United Kingdom (2011) 8319/07, 11449/07 Strasbourg para 15, 22, 196

226 ibid., para199

227 ibid.provide the first page of the article article, para 201

228 ibid., para 211

229 ibid., para 14

230 ibid., para 21

he faces a real risk of torture, inhuman or degrading treatment in the receiving country.[231]

Section 3(5) of the Immigration Act of 1975 empowers the Secretary of State to deport non-British nationals, whose presence in Britain is not conducive to the public good. However, such power can only be exercised where the applicants fall within the confines of Article 2(e) of the Qualification Directive, which defines persons eligible for subsidiary protection as those who would face a real risk of suffering serious harm if returned to their country of origin. The Court considered various reports, which showed that the applicants stood a real risk of their rights being violated if deported to Mogadishu.[232] Therefore, a nation's strength to expel aliens who are threats to national security weakens when such expulsion would violate the provisions of Article 3 of the ECHR. Ultimately, what will be the fate of the nationals of the expelling country whose security is at stake because of the acts of the persons being considered for deportation, but cannot be deported because of the violation of their rights under Article 3 of the ECHR?

Similarly, in ***Auad v Bulgaria*** the applicant was issued an expulsion order and was also barred from entering or residing in Bulgaria for ten years by the Head of the State Agency for National Security on grounds that his previous and current activities posed a threat to Bulgaria's national security.[233] The applicant alleged a violation of his right under Article 3 of the ECHR, if he were to be expelled to Lebanon.[234]

The Government countered such allegation, but affirmed that such expulsion must, out of necessity, be subject to S.44(a) of the Aliens Act 1998, which prohibited the expulsion of an alien on grounds of national security or public order to a country where his or her life or freedom would be in danger or where he or she would face a risk of persecution, torture, inhuman and degrading

231 Chahal v United Kingdom (1996) 22414/93 Strasbourg para 79; Saadi v Italy (2008) 37201/06 Strasbourg para 127, 138

232 Sufi and Elmi v United Kingdom., op. cit., para 250

233 Auad v Bulgaria (2011) 46390/10 Strasbourg para 14

234 ibid., para 89

treatment.[235] The Government's contention was based on the fact that the situation in Lebanon would be reviewed and ascertained before any expulsion took place. All the same, the Government argued that the applicant stood no risk of torture upon expulsion to Lebanon. On the contrary, the Court concluded that the applicant stood a real risk of being subject to ill treatment if expelled to Lebanon, after a due consideration of the applicant's circumstance and the situation in Lebanon.

Basically, a nation's power to control an alien's entry, exit and expulsion is not only limited by a real risk of ill treatment or death of the deportee in the receiving country as provided for by S.44(a) of the Aliens Act. S.4(3) of the Asylum and Refugee Act of 2002 also has a similar provision. Such power is also limited where a deportee has also been granted humanitarian protection as provided for in S.67(2) of the Asylum and Refugee Act. Nevertheless, by S.4(4), an alien who poses a threat to a nation's national security cannot benefit from the provision of S.4 (3) of the Asylum and Refugee Act. The Court in the case of ***Saadi v Italy*** recognised the 'imperative duty' of contracting States to protect their citizens against terrorist attacks and to ensure they live without fear of danger to their lives and properties. However, the Court maintained that: "States are not allowed to combat international terrorism at all costs. They must not resort to methods which undermine the very values they seek to protect".[236]

It is difficult to determine whether a court adopted a broad or narrow approach on the issue of national security in a situation where an alien contends that his deportation or expulsion by an expelling country will give rise to a violation of Article 3 of the ECHR, since the focus of the court is not on the conduct of the alien, but on the determination of the likelihood of the alien being subjected to a real risk of torture or ill and degrading treatment in the receiving country. The practicability of a nation's power to control the entry, residence and expulsion of aliens becomes an illusion. It is therefore a challenge to reconcile the provisions of Article 3 of the ECHR with the implications of national security where a deportee faces a real risk of torture or ill and degrading treatment in the receiving country.

235 ibid., para 38

236 G. Gentili, 'An absolute ban on deportation of foreign citizens to countries where torture or ill treatment is a genuine risk' (2010) vol 8(2) International Journal of constitutional Law 311

Deportation is one of the 'pursuits' and 'preventive' measures adopted by nations to counter terrorism.[237] It is a form of immigration control. The Court's decision in ***Chahal's*** case marked a turning point in deportation cases where an allegation of a likelihood of violation of Article 3 of the ECHR is made. The ECHR has remained obstinate in its position that governments are precluded from striking a balance between national security and a real risk of ill treatment of a deportee in the receiving country. Governments have found themselves in a dilemma since often diplomatic assurances are not recognised by the ECHR as a sufficient guarantee for safeguarding deportees, as was seen in the case of ***Saadi v Italy.***[238]

It is an established fact that immigration control is one of the main aspects of a state's sovereignty with respect to which states must be allowed a considerable measure of freedom. On the contrary, the question of sovereignty in recent times perhaps could be regarded as theoretical[239] since, certain categories of people are shielded from deportation under international law such as the ECHR. Hence, a nation's power to control the entry, exit and expulsion of aliens who are alleged to pose a threat to a nation's national security can be limited by the implication of some international human rights, such as the one discussed above (Article 3 of the ECHR) and the provisions of Article 8 of the ECHR, which provide for respect to private and family life.[240]

The ECHR has expanded its understanding of 'family life' to include the relations of the applicant with their parents and siblings. Even in some circumstances where deportation involved a whole family (in which case, the effect of the deportation is not such that will separate the family), the Strasbourg Court has held that their deportation will amount to a violation of Article 8 of the ECHR. This was the situation in the case of ***Slivenko et al. v Latvia*** where the Court not only recognised the fact that the entire family will still be together if

237 E. Mylonaki, et al., 'An Assessment of UK anti-terrorism strategy and the human rights implications associated with its implementation' (2011) Journal on terrorism and security analysis 66

238 B. Middleton, 'Rebalancing, Reviewing or Rebranding the treatment of terrorists' suspects: The counterterrorism review 2011' (2011) vol 75(3) Journal of Criminal Law 225

239 W. Sidhu, et al., *The United Nations and Regional security: Europe and Beyond* (Lynne Rienner Publishers Inc, London 2003), 22

240 Y. Ronen, 'The ties that bind: Family and private life as bars to the deportation of immigrants (2012) vol 8(2) International Journal of Law 283

the deportation order was enforced, but also considered the length of time the deportees had spent in Latvia (from birth). The Court argued that the network of their personal, social and economic relations, which are the major constituents of every human being's private life, would be shattered if the deportation took place. Hence, the Court held that the applicants' removal will amount to interference in their 'private life' and 'home' within the purview of Article 8(1) of the ECHR.[241]

Section 3(5) (a) of the Immigration Act 1971 empowers the Secretary of State to deport an individual if it is deemed to be conducive to public good. Often, the invocation of Article 8(1) of the ECHR determines the extent to which the Secretary of State will exercise its right as stipulated above, since the deportation order stands the risk of violating the right to private and family life of the applicant. Thus, in ***KB (Trinidad and Tobago) v Secretary of State for Home Department,*** the applicant was to be deported on grounds of public good as he had committed some serious criminal offences (serious class A drug offences). He contended a violation of his right to private and family life. On appeal, the Asylum and Immigration Tribunal held that deportation would violate the applicant's right under Article 8(1) of the ECHR as the applicant still had a subsisting family life even while in prison.[242] Clearly, Article 8 of the ECHR is not an absolute right as opposed to Article 3 of the ECHR, but there were circumstances under which the Court quashes a deportation order to forestall Article 8 ECHR violation.

No doubt, the movement of people in and out of a nation is a security issue. A proportionality test is imperative in the determination of deportation cases where the violation of the private and family life of an applicant is alleged. Perhaps, the court ought not to nullify the deportation order of an applicant whose conduct is a threat to national security merely because it will result in a violation of his right under Article 8(1) of the ECHR. Unlike the implication of Article 3 of the ECHR, by virtue of Article 8(2) of the ECHR, the right to private and family life is not absolute. Immigration control is a prerogative of the executive, not the judiciary.

241 D. Thym, 'Respect for private and family life under article 8 of ECHR in immigration cases: A human right to regularize illegal stay?' (2008) 57 (1) International and Comparative Law Quarterly 87

242 C. Nielson, 'Preventing disorder and protecting private and family life: Case comment' (2011) vol 70 (1) Cambridge Law Journal 12

3.5.1 SUMMARY

In summary, national security in view of immigration can be ***defined*** as that part of government policy, which focuses on the control, exit and expulsion of aliens. It is that part of the policy, which regulates the movement/migration of people in and out of a nation. The implication of Articles 3 and 8 of the ECHR makes the full practicability of a county's power over immigration a 'mirage'. The word 'torture' is elastic in the sense that it may not always be 'physical'; it can largely be 'mental'. It might be safe to say that there is a gross imbalance in the consideration of deportation cases where an applicant alleges a real risk of 'torture' if deported to the receiving country as ECHR judges tilt more towards the protection of an applicant's rights under Article 3 of the ECHR. The question is: 'What happens to the rights (such as right to life) of the citizens of a contracting country where the activities of an applicant significantly pose a threat to national security, but cannot be expelled to a receiving country because of the likelihood of a violation of his right under Article 3 of the ECHR?' The severity of the 'torture' to be suffered by a whole population could be more as most of them will be 'mentally or psychologically tortured' because of the feeling of insecurity.

It is a big irony for a person who has had previous convictions and has been involved in activities manifestly classified as 'terrorist acts' in a contracting state to preclude a nation from expelling him on grounds of likelihood of torture, without a proportionate consideration of national security; the threat of which has the potential of resulting in a massive violation of the rights of the citizenry such as the right to life (Article 2 of the ECHR). What happens in a situation where there is no allegation of a violation of Article 3 of the ECHR by an applicant who is to be expelled? Will the position of the court change in favour of national security? If the answer is in the positive, then there is an urgent need to strike a viable balance between national security and Article 3 of the ECHR. Immigration issues, so to speak, involve either regional or global connections. As a result, the subsection below will consider regional security as an essential part of national security.

3.6 REGIONAL SECURITY (INTERNATIONAL SECURITY) AS NATIONAL SECURITY

Terrorism was declared as one of the most serious threats to international peace and stability in the 2005 World Summit.[243] It has now become expedient for the challenge of terrorism to be addressed by the international community within the confines of rule of law. Thus, Vincent Joel Proulx advocates Lord Denning's advice "...terrorism involves the international community as a whole...terrorism...must be combated multi-nationally".[244] As a result, regional, international and multi-national organisations assist in fostering mechanisms for countering terrorism.[245] The foundation of modern day insecurities is diverse and perhaps could be traced to social, environmental, religious and political factors. Conceivably, such insecurities are progressively transcending state borders and having global repercussions such as international terrorism. For humans and nations to be secure, they must be free from pervasive threats and violence. The protection of their rights and safety needs to be assured.[246]

This subsection will try to answer the question: can nations single handedly fight national security? Terrorism may sometimes manifest issues of transnationality, antecedents, concomitants or successions to terrorist crimes, which further complicate national security issues and necessitate international cooperation.[247] The global "war on terror"—pursued by the United States and its allies after the attacks of 9/11—goes beyond national borders. As opposed to most past anti-terrorist actions whose characters were hinged on internal law enforcement operations carried out by governments within their own territory; post 9/11, operations in the "war on terror" transcend national borders of the states embarking on the campaign. The integration of individual states in response

243 N. Asif, 'United we stand, divided we all: Terrorism as an international crime versus terrorism as a transnational crime' (2016) vol1(1) Birmingham Student Law Review

244 EU Focus, Stronger EU action to tackle violent radicalization leading to terrorism (2016) vol 345 EU Focus

245 ibid; J. Maher, *The Europa World Yearbook 2008* (Taylor and Francis Group, New York 2008), 167

246 C. Bruderlein, op.cit.

247 M. Fillipino, 'Terrorist crimes and International co-operation: Critical Remarks on the Definition and Inclusion of Terrorism in the Category of International Crimes' (2008) vol 19(3) European Journal of International Law 536

to threats to safety and security is incidental to the complexities of such transnational threats.[248]

National security is a concept that extends beyond sovereign territory to target external threats and embrace international relations.[249] In other words, a link exists between international security, regional security and national security. The interdependence between such levels of security affects national security. The existence of a threat, risk or lack of security in one nation state may have security implications in another state or region. Therefore, regional or international security is the collective interest of various regional or international actors respectively, since the security of parts of the system is inseparably interwoven.[250]

By implication, the successful management or elimination of regional threats also enhances national security. Hence, it was held in ***Shafiq Ur Rehman v Secretary of State for the Home Department*** that:

> "A risk to national security did not have to represent a direct threat to the United Kingdom, nor were the interests of national security limited to actions that could be said to be targeted at the United Kingdom. National security was threatened if the state targeted by the individual in question, by illegal means or a coup, would in consequence threaten the United Kingdom".[251]

National security embraces and extends the temporal shift to pre-crime along the same axis as security. Beyond this, however, national security, more than security generally, also advocates and advances an additional shift, beclouding the boundary between foreign and domestic and between law enforcement and military action.[252] A lacuna in a nation's national security is sufficient to have

248 A. Boin, 'Managing Transboundary Crisis: What Role for the European Union' (2008) vol10 (1) International Studies Review 1

249 J. McCulloch, 'Pre-Crime and Counter-Terrorism: Imagining Future Crime on the 'War on Terror'' (2009) British vol 49(5) Journal of Criminology 628

250 P. Mbote, *Gender, Conflict and Regional Security* (Heinrich Boll Foundation, Nairobi 2004), 83

251 Shafiqur Rehman v Secretary of State for the Home Department (2001) Human Rights and Public Law

252 ibid

an adverse effect on the peace and security of the entire world. For instance, the situation in Iraq posed a continued threat to international peace and security as was seen in the case of ***Al-Skeini and others v The United Kingdom***, and as such a coalition of armed forces under a unified command piloted by the United States, United Kingdom, Australia, Denmark and Poland evaded Iraq for the disarmament of Iraq's weapons of mass destruction (WMD) and means of delivery.[253]

Similarly, in ***Al-Jedda v The United Kingdom***, the intention of this analysis is not to consider the violation of the applicant's right to liberty as provided for under Article 5 of the ECHR nor the accuracy of the intelligence concerning the presence of WMD, rather it sets out to highlight national security in view of regional security. The suspicion of Iraq's possession of WMD necessitated a coalition of armed forces under a unified command led by the United States to carry out a huge combat operation in Iraq to search and disarm Iraq of its WMD. The coalition forces also eliminated all terrorist infrastructures within Iraq and ensured that terrorists and their groups were denied safe heaven.[254]

Through regional bilateral/multilateral agreements, agencies work with each other across jurisdictional boundaries. To strengthen regional operational and liaison agreements, agencies such as the US Federal Bureau of Investigations (FBI) post liaison officers within a region. Such arrangements enhance the exchange of criminal intelligence between the relevant countries, which promote excellent opportunities for bilateral and multilateral cooperation; thereby, enhancing national security.[255] Again, the creation of regional organisations accelerates cooperation of member countries through common institutions. Regional organisations focus on proffering solutions to peculiar regional problems and the development of specific strategies for countering external and internal threats.[256] For instance, the North Atlantic Treaty Organisation (NATO) remains a very strong force in fostering national security. This is evidenced in the Operation Unified Protector carried out in Libya, which ended Colonel

253 Al-Skeini& others v The United Kingdom (2011) ECHR 55721/07 Grand Chamber

254 Al-Jedda v The United Kingdom (2011) ECHR 27021/08 Grand Chamber

255 J. McFarlane, Regional and international cooperation in tackling transnational crime, terrorism, and the problems of disrupted states (2005) vol 12(4) Journal of Financial Crime 301

256 A. Mikhaylova, 'Region in The National Security System of Russia' (2015) vol 1(1) Social and Economic Geography 9-15

Muammar al-Qaddafi's regime in 2011.[257] The people of Libya rebelled against Qaddafi in February 2011 shortly after the uprising in Tunisia and Egypt. Many spectators thought that what happened in Tunisia and Egypt would replicate itself in Libya. However, to the surprise of many, Qaddafi launched an aggressive counter-attack leading to the death of many Libyans. As a result, the international community responded immediately with the Security Council (SC) placing sanctions and an arms embargo against Libya in late February 2011.[258] The SC also froze Libyan assets and brought in the International Criminal Court in Hague to review and prosecute Qaddafi's war crimes.[259] The Arab League followed suit and suspended Libya's membership from its body urging the SC to impose a no-fly zone against Libya.[260] The Arab League's request was honoured by the SC on March 17 when the body authorised "all necessary measures" to protect civilians.[261] United States coordinated the international response by further freezing $32 billion of Libyan assets, which encouraged other countries to do the same.[262] Further, the US led a coalition to launch air strikes against Qaddafi forces freeing the people of Benghazi and destroying Libya's air defence system. Following such success, President Obama reached out to NATO to take over command and control of the operation, which ultimately led to the rebels capturing and killing Qaddafi.[263]

The African Union (AU), which replaced the Organisation of African Unity (OAU), was launched in Durban, South Africa in July 2002.[264] Shortly after

---

257 I. Daalder, et al., op. cit.

258 I. Daalder, et al., 'NATO's Victory in Libya: The Right Way to Run an Intervention' (2012) vol 91(2) Foreign Affairs 2-7

259 ibid; M. Byers, *War Law: Understanding International Law and Armed Conflict* (Atlantic Books, London 2007), 97

260 ibid; C. Chivas, et al., *Libya after Qaddafi: Lessons and Implications for the Future* (Rand Corporation, Boston 2014), Ch 2

261 ibid; S. Bernstein, The Responsibility to Protect After Libya: Humanitarian Prevention as Customary International Law (2012) vol 38(1) Brooklyn Journal of International Law 306

262 ibid

263 ibid; E. Balabanova, *The Media and Human Rights: The Cosmopolitan Promise* (Routledge Publishers, London 2014), 81; A. Heywood, *Global Politics* (2nd edn Palgrave Macmillan, England 2014), 331; M. Schmitt, et al., *Yearbook of International Humanitarian Law 2011*(Cambridge University Press, Cambridge 2012), 178

264 O. Imoedemhe, 'Unpacking the tension between the African Union and the international criminal court: A way forward' (2015) vol 23(1) African Journal of International and Comparative Law 123

launch, the AU embarked on several peace mission initiatives to foster national security. For example, in 2003, it conducted a peace operation in Burundi, dubbed the African Union Mission in Burundi (AMIB), which allowed a broader UN peace operation.[265] The AU also provided peace initiatives in Côte d'Ivoire, and Darfur.[266] Association of Southeast Asian Nations (ASEAN) has also been instrumental in enhancing national security in Southeast Asia. Six of the ten Southeast Asian states founded the ASEAN in 1967. The countries include Brunei, Indonesia, Malaysia, the Philippines, Singapore and Thailand. By 1999, other states in the region joined the Association, with the addition of Cambodia, Laos, Myanmar, and Vietnam.[267] Since the Vietnamese intervention in Cambodia ended in 1991, Southeast Asian states have not experienced any interstate wars among the original founding states, which is a stark irony to post-World War II era–Vietnam war, Vietnam with China (1979), and Vietnam with Cambodia (1978–1991).[268] Similarly, the newer member nations–Cambodia, Laos, Myanmar, and Vietnam–have not been involved in interstate wars since they joined the Alliance in 1989, although Thailand and Myanmar had a border post conflict in 2001-2002.[269] Southeast Asian nations resolved all their remaining territorial disputes through diplomacy.[270]

Such regional organisations are not devoid of challenges. For instance, notwithstanding the fact that ASEAN nations have avoided interstate wars, some of the member states have experienced separatist insurgencies (opposition from the minority). The insurgencies stem from dissatisfaction with their lack of political

265 T. Murithi, 'The African Union's Evolving Role in Peace Operations: The African Union Mission in Burundi, The African Union Mission in Sudan, The African Union Mission in Somalia' (2008) vol 17(1) African Security Review 70

266 Ibid; A. Orakhelashvili, *Collective Security* (Oxford University Press, New York 2011), 301

267 N. Ripsman, et al., *Globalisation and The National Security State* (Oxford University Press, New York 2010)

268 ibid; A. Guan, *Singapore, Asean and Cambodia Conflict 1978-1999* (National University of Singapore Press, Singapore 2013), 22; B. Womack, *China and Vietnam: The Politics of Asymmetry* (Cambridge University Press, Cambridge 2006), 192

269 ibid; P. Pongsawat, *Border Partial Citizenship, Border Towns, and Thai-Myanmar Cross Border Development: Case Studies at the Thai Border Towns* (University of California Berkeley Press, Berkeley 2007), 280

270 ibid; N. Ripsman, et al., *Globalization and the National Security State* (Oxford University Press, New York 2010), 101; S. Shen, *Multidimensional Diplomacy of Contemporary China* (Rowman and Littlefield Publishers Inc, Maryland 2010), 47; J. Eisenman, et al., *China and the Developing World: Beijing's Strategy for the Twenty-first Century* (M. E Sharpe Inc, New York 2007), 164

autonomy and economic opportunities. The region has also seen the rise of terrorist organisations in the predominantly Muslim states.[271] NATO, faces some challenges too. For instance, some member nations have more military power and often incur most of the financial cost of the conflict relative to other member nations with less military force.[272] Ideally, the cost burden should be shared equitably. Regardless of the initial successes, the AU's experience in its peace missions revealed some shortcomings and lack of resources to execute its own decisions.[273]

Terrorism is borderless. As a result, member states and actors at local, national and regional levels are charged with the responsibility of tackling issues of violent radicalisation. Different regional organisations are charged with different goals geared towards the enhancement of security.

3.6.1 SUMMARY

In summary, national security can be ***defined*** as 'external security'. It can also be defined as cooperative security since protective or preventive measures put in place transcend national boundaries and involve external actors. The dynamics of modern-day terrorism may strengthen the fact that national security may not be attained exclusively without the collaboration of regional actors. This demonstrates the fact that the political machinery of cooperation based as it is on nation states, must take account of the wider dimensions of security challenge. Essentially, regional organisations could be one of the right institutional architectures for national security. Transnational issues of various kinds (such as terrorism) may be settled regionally, as states may not handle such challenges single-handedly. Regional actors adopt the principle of cooperative security: security dialogue and conflict management, new forms of military cooperation, democracy and human rights, economic integration and wider non-military security agenda.[274]

---

271 ibid

272 I. Daalder, et al., op. cit.

273 T. Murithi, 'The African Union's Evolving Role in Peace Operations: The African Union Mission in Burundi, The African Union Mission in Sudan, The African Union Mission in Somalia' (2008) vol 17(1) African Security Review 70

274 A. Bailes, et al., 'Regional Security Cooperation in The Early 21st Century' (1992) In Conference on Interaction 202

It might be safe to say that regional cooperation is a distinctive attribute of national security where partners co-manage security threats to bring them under control. Regional arrangements allow those, whose values are threatened, to participate considerably in the decision-making process. Thus, sovereign states in geographical proximity tend to foster more security interaction amongst states. At the same time, regional security intervention is not limited to geographical proximity. Hence, states that are not directly affected by an issue such as terrorism may collaborate to ensure regional cooperation on issues important for them.[275] For instance, NATO can span through incongruous geographical locations.[276] Having said this, regional security cooperation cannot completely replace national security measures. Therefore, regional security is complementary to national security.

3.7 INTELLIGENCE SHARING AND NATIONAL SECURITY

The efficient management of security threats within and outside a nation can be done through intelligence sharing. It is one of the essential mechanisms employed by nation states for the collection and analysis of timely and accurate intelligence. Intelligence sharing brings the security services of member states together as they share, collect and disseminate intelligence on threat towards themselves, respectively; for example, organised crimes and terrorism.[277]

This subsection will answer the question: Does intelligence sharing have any effect on the security of a nation?' The 9/11event traumatised both professionals in defence policy and non-professionals into a new sense of insecurity. Information is fundamental to national security. Intelligence sharing avails information concerning an imminent and future threat to a nation's security. Hence, one of the mechanisms for investigation, detection, monitoring and reporting of

275 A. Krickovic, '"All Politics Is Regional": Emerging Powers and The Regionalisation of Global Governance' (2015) vol 21(4) Regional Governance 557

276 D. Jividen, 'It Takes a Region: A Proposal for An Alternative Regional Approach to UN Collective Force Humanitarian Intervention' (1999) 10 United States Air Force Academic Journal of Legal Studies 125

277 J. Walsh, 'Intelligence Sharing in the European Union: Institutions are not enough' (2006) vol 44 (3) University of North Carolina 625

anti-security activities or issues is intelligence sharing.[278] Intelligence sharing is one of the ways through which national security could be implemented. At the same time, national security could be narrowly defined in terms of intelligence sharing.

A library function of national security is provided by the intelligence community who keeps track of all sources, secret or open, and assembles them in a logical form whenever non-professionals require them.[279] Hence, there might be need for states to share information amongst themselves for national security, as well as for international peace and order. In the case of ***Binyam Mohammed v Secretary of State for Foreign and Commonwealth Affairs,***[280] national security was considered in the light of intelligence sharing where the Secretary of State in his public interest immunity (PII) certificate pointed out: "that intelligence sharing is essential to allies such as the United States and the United Kingdom. It is vital to the national security of the United Kingdom such that it saves lives".[281]

In ***Al Hanchi v Bosnia and Herzegovina,*** the intelligence report received by the Aliens Service on 19th May 2009, declared the applicant a threat to national security. His deportation was ordered, and he was constrained from re-entering the Republic of Bosnia and Herzegovina for a period of five years. The Ministry of Security and the State Court respectively upheld the deportation order after the assessment of the secret evidence.[282] The Asylum service also disallowed the applicant's asylum claim on grounds of national security, the decision of which was subsequently upheld by the state.

The Court adopted a broad meaning of national security. They were not persuaded by the fact that the applicant averred that he will be subjected to ill treatment as provided for under Article 3 of the ECHR, if deported to Tunisia.

278 A. Chau, 'Security Community and Southeast Asia: Australia, the US and ASEAN's Counter-Terror Strategy' (2008) vol 48(4) University of California Press 630

279 R. Betts, *Enemies of Intelligence: Knowledge and Power in American National Security* (Columbia University Press, New York 2007)

280 Binyam Mohammed v Secretary of state for Foreign and Commonwealth Affairs (2008) EWCH 2048

281 A. Tomkins, 'National security and the due process of the law (2011) vol 64 (1) Current Legal Problems 215

282 Al Hanchi v Bosnia and Herzegovina (2011) ECHR 48205/09 Grand Chamber

However, pursuant to Article 25 of the Law No.49/06 on the Protection of Personal Data in Bosnia and Herzegovina, the applicant was entitled upon a written request to the Controller, to demand for his personal data.[283] The applicant did not contest the content or the quality of the intelligence report against him; rather, he concentrated on the deportation order. Hence, national security involves a nation's capacity to hijack information and employ data, which often assists in detection, investigation and prosecution of terrorist cases.

The complexity involved in terrorist networks require a similar if not a higher level of sophistication in the strategies adopted in combating threats to national security. Technological advancement provides devices employed by terrorists to receive and gather information as well as appropriate advanced armoury. Intelligence sharing, and knowledge is one of the schemes applied by security agencies in fighting threats to national security.

However, there are circumstances in which there might not be any intelligence,[284] or an intelligence report on an individual might be inaccurate[285] or there might be a case of mistaken identity. What becomes the fate of national security if the intelligence report is not reliable on grounds of its inaccuracy? On the other hand, where lies the confidence of the citizenry in a democratic society if the rights of an individual in a nation are restricted (for example, the right to private and family life), based on an inaccurate intelligence report, bearing in mind that the protection of the citizenry is also at the core of national security?

Hence, in ***Rotaru v Romania,*** the applicant was persecuted on political grounds based on false and defamatory information provided by the Romanian Intelligence Service (RIS). The applicant instituted an action against the RIS for damages and an amendment of the false information held by RIS. The Bucharest Court of Appeal allowed a review of the information held about the applicant but made no order regarding damages or cost.[286]

---

283 The Protection of Personal Data in Bosnia and Herzegovina Law No.49/06

284 M. Day, 'Frankfurt airport shooter shouted 'AllahuAkhbar' before opening fire' (2011) <*http://www.telegraph.co.uk/news/worldnews/europe/Germany/8359759/Frankfurt-airport-shooter-shouted-Allahu-Akhbar-before-opening-fire.html*>accessed 19 July 2016

285 R. Kline, et al., *Intelligence and The National Security Strategist: Enduring Issues and Challenges* (Rowan and Littlefield Publishers Inc, Maryland 2006), 11

286 Rotaru v Romania (2000) ECHR 28341/95 Strasbourg

National security will be at greater risk where intelligence reports are made up of inconsistencies. Intelligence sharing constitutes an integral aspect of national security but must be characterised with a high degree of accuracy in its reports. Most legislation provide for the secrecy of intelligence reports. For instance, section 45 of Law No. 14 of 24th February 1992, on the organisation and operation of the Romanian Intelligence Service, provides that: "...documents, data and information belonging to the Romanian Intelligence Service shall not be made public until forty years after they have been archived...".[287]

Similarly, in the case of ***CIA v Sims,*** the US Supreme Court declared that secrecy is implicit to the integrity of the intelligence process. Without secrecy, the Court stated, 'the CIA would be virtually impotent".[288]In further explaining such concept, the Court quoted President George Washington where he wrote that,

> "the necessity of procuring good intelligence, is apparent and need not be further urged... For upon secrecy, success depends in most Enterprises of the kind, and for want of it they are generally defeated".[289]

The applicant knew about the false information held by the RIS against him through a letter submitted to the Court by the Ministry of Information. Where a data subject is not aware of the intelligence report about him, he could pay the price of what he is ignorant of, which is contrary to the spirit of national security.

3.7.1 SUMMARY

In summary, one aspect of national security can be ***defined*** as the collection and assessment of secret intelligence reports with the aim to prevent or stop an impending threat to a nation's security. It connotes the collection and analysis of raw information, which is open, publicly available, or secret, with the goal to reduce the uncertainty about a security policy problem.[290] It includes

287 ibid., para 31

288 CIA v Sims (1985) 471 U.S. 159, 170

289 ibid

290 J. Walsh, op cit

the protection of certain privileged information within the purview of a nation or nations, which is usually not disclosed to the suspect in view of security concerns.

National security entails a requirement for states to maintain the intelligence sharing relationship that exists between them to enable them to safeguard the source of the information, as well as the information within their reach for national security. However, intelligence sharing can constitute a procedural obstacle especially in a democratic state. For instance, in ***Binyams case***, he claimed that his confession was secured by torture, but the US Government declined to make available the information needed, making it impossible for the case of torture to be proved or disproved. The UK Government conceded that the applicant had an arguable case, but in view of security considerations the UK Government endorsed the US Government's position that the disclosure of the said information will impair intelligence sharing between both countries.[291]

3.8 NATIONAL SECURITY AND SELF-DEFENCE

The right to self-defence is a natural right, which is recognised from time immemorial. It is not only available to individuals, but also to states as sovereign entities. Self-defence could be either anticipatory or pre-emptive. The question regarding the legal status of the latter is another issue for consideration. Anticipatory self-defence connotes that something is certain and bound to happen and needs to be responded to. This implies that there is a high intensity for occurrence and a very low chance for miscalculation. In view of national security, anticipatory self-defence comes into play to abort any impending danger.[292]

On the other hand, Professor Reisman defines pre-emptive self-defence as,

291 D. Mckeever, 'The Human Rights Act and Anti-Terrorism in the UK: One Great Leap Forward by the Parliament, but are the Court able to slow the steady Retreat that has followed?' (2010) vol 110 Public Law Journal 116

292 N. Shah, 'Self Defence, Anticipatory Self-Defence and Pre-emption: International Law's Response to Terrorism' (2007) vol 12(1) Journal of Conflict and Security Law 95

> "a claim of authority to use, unilaterally and without international authorisation, high levels of violence to arrest a development that is not yet operational and hence is not yet 'directly' threatening, but which, if permitted to mature, could be neutralised only at a high, possibly unacceptable, cost."[293]

Hence, the danger need not be imminent; the essence is to 'prevent' 'more generalised threats from materialising.

In the case of ***Uzunget & Others v Turkey,*** the applicants alleged that their rights to freedom of thoughts, expression and assembly were violated by the police through their unjustified interference in the applicants' meeting, as provided under Article 11 of the ECHR (freedom of assembly and association).[294] The Government argued that the meeting organised by the applicants was unlawful. They contended that Article 11(2) of the ECHR placed limitations on the applicants' right to peaceful assembly for the prevention of public disorder (a legitimate aim). The Court held that there was a violation of Article 11 of the ECHR. It reiterated that:

> "An interference will constitute a breach of Article 11of the ECHR unless it is 'prescribed by law', pursues one or more legitimate aims under paragraph 2 and is 'necessary in a democratic society' for the achievement of those aims".[295]

The Court maintained that the legal basis of the interference was justified by section 22 of the Assemblies and Marches Act (Law No.911) and therefore, prescribed by law within the purview of paragraph 2 of Article 11 of the ECHR. In determining whether the interference was 'necessary in a democratic society', the Court pointed out that there was an onus on the authorities to ensure the peaceful conduct and safety of all citizens in the event of lawful demonstrations by taking appropriate measures. The Court added that states must also refrain from applying unreasonable indirect restrictions upon the right prescribed under Article 11 of the ECHR.

---

293 ibid

294 Uzunget & Others v Turkey (2009) ECHR 21831/03 Strasbourg Para 39

295 European Convention on Human Rights 1950

The Court opined as follows:

> "Where demonstrators do not engage in acts of violence, it is important for the public authorities to show a certain degree of tolerance towards peaceful gatherings if the freedom of assembly guaranteed by Article 11 of the Convention is not to be deprived of all substance."

Hence, the Court held that in the present case, the forceful intervention of the police officers was disproportionate and was not necessary for the prevention of disorder within the meaning of the second paragraph of Article 11 of the ECHR.

Critically, the Court adopted a narrow approach to the issue of national security in the instant case. The right prescribed under Article 11 of the ECHR is not absolute. In view of Article 11(2), such rights could be restricted in so far as:

> "The restriction is 'prescribed by law' and is necessary in a democratic society for national security, public safety or the prevention of disorder... or the protection of the rights and freedoms of others."

In determining whether there is a violation of Article 11 of the ECHR, some of the relevant domestic laws of Turkey will be considered. As at the time the protest took place, Article 34 of the Constitution empowered:

> "Everyone to hold unarmed and peaceful meetings and demonstration marches without prior permission. ... the formalities, conditions, and procedures governing the exercise of the right to hold meetings and demonstration marches shall be prescribed by law."[296]

It is evident from the facts of the case that the applicants organised a demonstration in a 'public place' without a prior permission. However, the issue for consideration was whether the formalities, conditions and procedures regulating such a demonstration had been complied with by the applicants. Section 10 of the Meetings and Demonstration Marches Act provides as follows:

296 Article 34 of the Turkish Constitution

> "In order for a meeting to take place, the governor's office or authorities of the district in which the demonstration is planned must be informed, during opening hours and at least seventy-two hours prior to the meeting, by a notice containing the signature of all the members of the organising board..."[297]

The above section of the law stipulates the formalities, conditions and procedures that govern such a demonstration. None of such formalities were complied with by the applicants. The applicants gathered in protest in a public park while Section 22 of the Meetings and Demonstration Act:

> "Prohibits demonstrations and processions on public streets, in parks, ... and buildings in which public services were based. Demonstrations organised in public squares had to comply with security instructions and not obstruct individual movement or public transport."[298]

If the applicants had obtained permission from the authorities prior to the protest, the Ankara Police would have had prior knowledge of what the protest was all about, and some security instructions would have been given to the applicants ahead of time for their safety and that of the public. Obtaining a prior permission does not amount to 'interference' in the applicant's right under Article 11 of the ECHR. In view of national security, such permission is necessary in a democratic society for protection of the public at large.

The Court observed that the protest was initially peaceful, and no evidence showed that the group posed a danger to public order, but the police officers intervened and asked the group to disperse. Subsequently, the police dispersed them by force when they refused to adhere to the police order.

The Court went on to observe that:

297 Meetings and Demonstration Marches Act, Law No. 2911

298 ibid

> "...the forceful intervention of the police officers was disproportionate and was not necessary for the prevention of disorder within the meaning of the second paragraph of Article 11 of the ECHR."[299]

Analytically, the fact that the protest appeared peaceful at the initial stage was not a guarantee that it would end peacefully, because the issue under protest was a delicate one (protest F-type prisons regime and the violent clashes that had occurred in Bergama Prison). The applicants had protest banners in their hands and the police 'warned' them to disperse before they intervened. The intervention could be described as 'pre-emptive' 'self-defence' to prevent a more generalised threat from manifesting. Section 24 of the Meeting and Demonstration Act provides that:

> "Demonstrations and processions which did not comply with the provisions of this law would be dispersed by force on the order of the governor's office and after the demonstrators had been warned."[300]

Also, section 6 of Law No. 2559 on the Duties and Powers of the Police provides that,

> "In cases of resistance by persons whose arrest is necessary or by groups whose dispersal is necessary or of an attack or threat of an attack, the police may use violence to subdue these actions."[301]

In view of national security, the intervention was prescribed by law and did not amount to a violation of Article 11 of the ECHR. Based on the facts of the case, the police did not disrupt the demonstration at the onset. They 'warned' (as prescribed by law) the applicants to disperse on grounds that the demonstration was 'unlawful'. The police arrested 24 persons with the applicants inclusive, after they ignored police warning. The police need not wait to see an imminent danger before they can abate it. They acted in self-defence.

---

299 Uzunget and Others v Turkey, op.cit.

300 Meetings and Demonstration Act, Law No. 2911

301 Duties and Powers of the Police, Law No. 2559

3.8.1 SUMMARY

In summary, national security can be ***defined*** as 'anticipatory' and 'pre-emptive' measures taken by a nation for safeguarding against 'threat' and 'violence'. Considering the devastating effect of the 9/11 attack (massive loss of lives and property), national security can be defined as 'anticipatory self-defence', which embraces any pre-emptive use of force to forestall future attacks within territorial sovereignty.[302] Thus, John Negroponte notified the UN that:

> "in response to these [9/11] attacks, and in accordance with the inherent right of individual and collective self-defence, United States armed forces have initiated actions designed to 'prevent' and 'deter' further attacks on the United States."[303]

Customary international law authorised a state to prevent an 'imminent' attack, giving it a right of anticipatory self-defence. Professor Yoram Dinstein uses the term 'interceptive' to signify that the attacker has embarked upon an irreversible course of action. Derek Bowett held that: "Self-defence [h]as, under traditional international law, always been anticipatory". This means its exercise was valid against imminent as well actual attacks or dangers. Indeed, the Caroline case is itself the classical illustration of this.[304]

3.9 CONCLUSION

This chapter set out to assess how the courts defined national security and if national security has a generally acceptable judicial definition. It did this by analysing some cases where it found that: First, national security has not been expressly defined by Judges rather inferences could be drawn from the context in which a Judge perceives as threatening national security in a case. Second, that national security could be perceived either from a narrow or wide perspective. Hence, in the bid to enhance national security, some rights have suffered

302 F. Sperotto, 'The use of force against terrorists: a reply to Christian J. Tams (2009) vol 20(4) European Journal of International Law 1043

303 ibid

304 ibid

flagrant violation by sovereign states. For example, freedom of expression. Third, there is need for a viable balance between national security and human rights. Fourth, national security does not connote a disregard or a violation of human rights by the government. Rather it involves a due consideration of the protection of individual lives and property together with territorial sovereignty. National security is not a replacement of human rights protection. The human element is intrinsic to national security. Fifth, the conduct of a terrorist suspect is immaterial where there is a likelihood of Article 3 ECHR violations in a receiving country. It is a challenge to create a balance between Article 3 ECHR and the implications of national security. Sixth, intelligence sharing is one of the elements through which national security could be defined and at the same time, it is one of the indispensable measures for the implementation of national security. Seventh, there are occasions where national security may not be achieved without regional or global security. However, regional security cannot possibly replace national security.

An understanding of the concept of national security is integral in the fight against terrorism. There is no singular definition of 'national security'. It remains a challenge to identify a generally acceptable definition because what constitutes a national security issue or measure in one nation may vary from that of another. It may be perceived from different contexts as seen above. On the grounds of these findings, this book recommends a comprehensive definition of national security, which will embody a shift from the traditional concept of national security.

CHAPTER 4

A CRITICAL DISCUSSION AND ANALYSIS OF THE IMPACT OF DIFFERENT ASPECTS OF "NATIONAL SECURITY" ON CONCRETE ANTI-TERRORISM LEGISLATION APPLICABLE IN NATION STATES.

4.1 INTRODUCTION

The preceding chapter of this book looked at national security as a legal idea. It espoused some aspects of national security like anti-terrorism, peoples' security, immigration, regional security and intelligence sharing. It established the fact that the concept of 'national security' has been widened. It has deepened beyond the conventional focal point of external and forceful threats to a nation's sovereignty and territorial integrity. The human rights cases analysed showed that there seems to be a conflict between human rights and national security when the latter is to be protected. However, the fact remains that national security and human rights are intertwined. By implication, national security will be threatened if one is prioritised over another. The preceding chapter also espoused the divergent aspects of national security through the analysis of some case laws, from which definitions of national security were either derived or, at least, inferred.

However, this chapter will look at national security not as a legal concept or general idea, but rather as a practical organisational activity and practice by governmental agents/agencies vis-a-vis a concept. It will investigate the pragmatic nature of the practice of national security. The purport of this chapter stems from the necessity to identify the implications of some of the identified aspects of 'national security' on the actual practice of national security. This is for enhanced policy decisions and recommendations. In which case, some such identified aspects of national security could be policy aspiration by governments to sustain the security of their nation states or even perhaps as a "moral goal", on the basis that meeting security needs is a good thing.

This chapter will examine relevant case laws to develop a critical analysis of some practical effects of the identified aspects of the idea of 'national security' on the empirical practice and activity of national security. This chapter concludes by suggesting possible ways of enhancing national security, understood as a method for meeting the basic human need "to feel secure from threat", such as effective intelligence sharing. The effects highlighted in this chapter are representative, but not exhaustive. Specifically, this chapter will address the question: 'Do the different aspects of 'national security' identified in this book have some practical impacts on national security, and if so what impacts and where and under what conditions?'

The uncertainty bred by international terrorism on national, regional and global security is such that it mandates stringent anti-terrorism measures to provide the attention it deserves. As a result, sovereign states are obligated to adopt proper measures to safeguard the lives of individuals within their jurisdiction.[305] The implementation of such measures creates an unconducive environment for terrorists and their organisation. However, while implementing such measures, people's security should occupy a protective place. The protection of the lives and property of individuals is not excluded from the national security scene. Hence, people's security has a symbiotic relationship with national security. This chapter will be divided into subsections in the following order: anti-terrorism measures, people's security, immigration, regional security and intelligence sharing.

A comprehension and the analysis of the effects of different aspects of the meaning of national security will, to a large extent, contribute to an understanding of ways to counter national security threats within and outside a nation. "The nation" will be able to expressly prioritise its national security interests, as well as ascertain areas of its vulnerability and state of preparedness for challenges to such anticipated interests. Such comprehension also plays a crucial role in the drafting of national security policies for the preparation of potential future trends. Realistically, every risk might not be spotted; but the alertness to potential risk is a major security requirement. Considering the current trend

305 Y. Takahashi, *The margin of appreciation doctrine and the principle of proportionality in the jurisprudence of the ECHR'* (Oxford University Printing Press, New York 2002), 216; E. Gross *The struggle of democracy against terrorism: Lessons from the United States, United Kingdom and Israel* (University of Virginia Press, Charlottesville 2006), 27

of international terrorism, is the actualisation of national security a complex matter? Do nations of the world face diverse and complex threats from different sources ranging from terrorism, cyber-attacks, nuclear weapons, tremendous accidents and natural disasters? Or are security threats universally the same? All such threats have implications for national security. The world has become "a global village"; the events and security of nations are either directly or indirectly connected throughout the globe. Essentially, the subsequent sections will explore the effects of the various aspects of national security (identified in chapter 3) on the practice of national security.

4.2 EFFECTS OF ANTI-TERRORISM MEASURES ON NATIONAL SECURITY

The threat posed by terrorism is global, borderless, dispersed and may be centralised in its networking system. The challenge posed by such threat emanates from its peculiar nature. For example, its agents are mostly independent and self-starting and often reside and operate in the country they target.[306] The maturation of international terrorism embodies a broad spectrum of activity that goes beyond carrying out the actual attack. It encompasses education and research, recruitment, radicalism, creation of terrorist cells, training, planning, financing, communications, coordination and the acquisition of materials. Essentially, Al-Qaeda is a recognised terrorist organisation, yet some individuals and small groups are inspired and enthused by Al-Qaeda, but have no operational ties to it. Some terrorist groups paraded themselves as Al-Qaeda, while no history of violence could be traced to them.[307] All these factors together constitute an acute challenge for nations in the fight against terrorism.[308] It therefore remains uncertain when the fight against terrorism will end, since it is also perpetrated by some unknown groups and splinter factions of known groups.

This sub-section will critically analyse the effect of anti-terrorism measures on national security. It will evaluate the freezing of terrorists' funds as an

306 B. Hoffman, 'Rethinking terrorism and counterterrorism since 9/11' (2002) vol 25(5) Studies in Conflict and Terrorism 303

307 W. Shepard, *Islam: The E-book* (Journal of Buddhist Ethics Online Books Ltd, Utah 2009), 286-287

308 D. Prieto, 'War about terror: Civil liberties and national security after 9/11' (2009) <*www.cfr.org/content/publications/.../Civil_Liberties_WorkingPaper*> accessed 1st December 2017)

anti-terrorism measure. By way of contrast, it will also examine some anti-terrorism practices, which are strictly speaking anti-security.

Anti-terrorism simply refers to acts countering terrorism. The hallmark of anti-terrorism measures is to enable nations to strategise on how to demobilise terrorists and their organisations to deter them from carrying out terrorist attacks. The catastrophic incident of the 9/11 attack introduced a new dimension of terrorism, which spurred law enforcement and governmental strategists into the action of crafting responses to terrorism.[309] Democratic societies are faced with challenges furnished by terrorism; especially as it relates to the prevention and punishment of conceptually motivated violence without such states themselves encroaching on civil liberties and engaging in counter-violence that plays into the hands of terrorists themselves.[310] It is incumbent on governments to endow their agencies with prerequisite legal authorities and adequate resources. This is needed for the prevention of terrorism whenever possible and to prosecute it, at least if such legal response is not itself counterproductive.[311]

The threat from terrorism, both national and international, is an enduring one. Countering terrorism is one of the defences for many, if not all, of the national security interest already discussed. There is a radical difference in kind between securing a nation against 'intentional' or 'organised' attacks and those which are better considered 'accidental' or 'natural' attacks, such as flood and famine. Nations use the promulgation of national security policies and legislations as anti-terrorism measures. However, some such measures strain the foreign relationship amongst nations. There have, for example, been disagreements between the United States and some of its allies regarding some anti-terrorism measures. For example, the European Union has disagreed severally with the United States on issues of privacy and intelligence sharing. The insistence of the US Department of Homeland Security to have more access to passenger name record information from European Airlines made a Dutch member of the European Parliament to worry that "we cannot accept this excessive appetite

309 N. Ridley, et al., 'Combating terrorists financing in the first decade of the twenty first century' (2012) vol 15(1) Journal of Money Laundering Control 38

310 A. Bhoumik, 'Democratic responses to terrorism: A comparative study of the United States, Israel and India' (2004) Paper 287 Bepress Legal Series

311 D. Cole, et al., *Terrorism and the constitution: Sacrificing civil liberties in the name of national security* (3rd edn, The New Press, New York 2006), 1

for personal data without any kind of protection against mistakes and abuse from public authorities."[312] More so, public disagreements abound in the international community concerning some detention measures such as the treatment of detainees in Guantanamo Bay and the Abu Ghraib prisons.[313]

It can be argued that some anti-terrorism measures frustrate terrorism. This has a positive implication on national security.[314] For example, in the case of ***Nada v Switzerland,*** the applicant did not contest the grounds upon which his assets and funds were frozen with the European Court of Human Rights, but rather contested a violation of his rights under Articles 8, 13 and 5 of the ECHR. This case sets out to portray some of the antiterrorism measures taken by government to forestall terrorist activities. The effect of freezing terrorist funds is key to national security. For instance, even though in the present case the investigation carried out on the applicant proved to be unsubstantiated, if on the other hand the applicant was linked to terrorist funding, the freezing of his assets, possessions and funds would have hindered, disrupted or delayed a terrorist act to a certain extent, as terrorists need funds for operations, no matter how small.

Persons whose assets and funds are frozen have their names enlisted in the UN sanctions list by Resolution 1333 (2000). The country of an applicant's citizenship or residence lacks the capacity to delist the applicant's name from the sanctions list upon the conclusion of the investigations on such applicant, in view of the Security Council Resolution 1730 (2006). In the present case, precisely on the 27th of April 2005, the proceedings against the applicant were discontinued on the grounds of uncorroborated evidence. However, his name was not removed from the sanctions list until 23rd of September 2009.[315] If the applicant had an alliance with terrorist funding, by implication the sanctions placed on his access to his funds and assets were still operative even though the proceedings against him were discontinued until the deletion of his name from the UN sanctions list. This is part of the stringent measures put in place to ensure proper scrutiny

---

312 D. Prieto, op.cit

313 ibid; Criminal Justice Handbook Series, *Handbook on Criminal Justice Responses to Terrorism* (United Nations Publication, New York 2009), 104

314 K. Jaishankar, et al., Global Criminology: Crime and Victimization in a Globalised Era (Taylor and Francis Group LLC, London 2013), 73

315 'In the name of security: Counterterrorism laws worldwide since September 11' (2012) *<https://www.hrw.org/.../name-security/counterterrorism-laws-worldwide-> (accessed* 3 January 2017)

before delisting any name from the sanctions list. Delayed delisting implies a delayed access to the frozen funds, consequently disrupting an attack if it was dependent upon access to such frozen funds and assets.

The security of a nation is enhanced when measures such as the one mentioned above are put in place to trap threats before they manifest themselves. The direct cost of mounting individual attacks and maintaining a terrorist's network is done through terrorist funding. The maintenance of terrorism infrastructure poses "a significant drain on resources", which is a national security issue.[316] Al-Qaeda was funded approximately $30 million annually. Approximately, $400,000-$500,000 was spent on the 9/11 attack. The 'hawala' system— a system of informal financial network largely used by terrorists and their organisations—records transactions of over $2 trillion annually. If such volume of financial transactions is channeled to 'legal' business transactions, it will obviously contribute significantly, not only to the country's economic growth where the business transaction is based, but to the world at large, because of globalisation.[317]

On the other hand, there are circumstances under which anti-terrorism measures might affect a country's national security policies adversely, especially where it negates a country's foreign policy influence and projection of its soft power and moral authority. For instance, humanitarian ideals are greatly rooted in the US Constitution, which guides and persuades the actions of American leaders. Hence, George Washington authorised enemy prisoners to be treated with "humanity (so they) have no reason to complain of our copying from the brutal example of the British Army in their treatment of our unfortunate brethren."[318] The deviation from a commitment to secure individual liberties through anti-terrorism measures and programmes has the potency of endangering foreign policies related to a country's national security. It decreases the possible legality and legitimacy of anti-terrorism efforts, eliminates the trust of allies and sections of the public at large, hinders cooperation and support from

316 Y. Danziger, 'Changes in methods of freezing funds of terrorist organizations since 9/11: A comparative analysis' (2012) vol 15(2) Journal of Money Laundering Control 210

317 ibid, I. Abubakar, *Anti-Money Laundering and Counterterrorism Financing: Law and Practice in Nigeria* (Malthouse Press Limited, Nigeria 2015), 73-74

318 D. Prieto, op.cit

allies, and supplies weighty propaganda ammunition for extremists to radicalise new followers and recruit terrorist operatives.[319]

National security is not a fight against humanity. It is accepted that the 9/11attack had a catastrophic effect, not only on the United States, but on the world at large.[320] However, there have been far greater tragic losses of life in other parts of the world every few months since then; without them being characterised in such intense way. Further, anti-terrorism efforts can only be sustainable and lasting if the measures applicable will not work contrary to the very subjects they expressly set out to protect. Viable foreign policies are crucial to national security. Therefore, it is pertinent that anti-terrorism measures adopted by nations are such that they will maintain foreign relationships, since terrorism is also a global affair. For instance, the Middle East attacks on the United States Embassies, such as the US Consulate attack in Benghazi[321], required the immediate cooperation of Libya where the embassy was situated, for safeguarding United States' diplomats and property. The embassies of nations are an extension of their geographical jurisdiction. Thus, if foreign relations amongst nations are not cordial, it might be difficult for them to respond accordingly when the need arises. Anti-terrorism measures, to a large extent, have national, regional and international implications on security.

Ironically, some counterterrorism measures embarked upon by nations could be considered 'anti-security'. For example, within the UK and pursuant to the Anti-Terrorism, Crime and Security Act 2001, detainees suspected of international terrorism have the option of ending their detention by agreeing to leave the country to a place of their choice.[322] Arguably, it becomes contradictory to national security as to how such detainees could be given the liberty of leaving the UK to go to a place of their choice to shorten their detention. The word 'international' is key in the fight against terrorism. It connotes that terrorist attack transcends national boundaries. Hence, it will be antithetical to national

319 ibid

320 P. Smith, *Terrorism and Violence in Southeast Asia: Transnational Challenges to States* (Taylor and Francis Group, London 2015), 3

321 S. Tucker, *US Conflicts in the 21st Century: Afghanistan War, Iraq War and the War on Terror* (Praeger Publishers, California), 154

322 A and Others v The United Kingdom (2009) 3455/05 Strasbourg para 11

security to allow suspected 'international terrorists' to go to a country of their choice.

Hence, in the case of ***A and Others v The United Kingdom,*** where the applicants alleged violations of article 3, 5 and 6 of the ECHR respectively, the second and the fourth applicants agreed to leave the UK to go the places of their choice (Morocco and France, respectively); to end their detention as suspected international terrorists. The question is: 'Did the United Kingdom notify the Morocco and French Governments, respectively that the second and the fourth applicants were a 'security risk'; since they were suspected of being 'international terrorists'?' The security of a nation could be at risk through an external attack. By virtue of Resolutions 1368 (2001) and 1373 (2001), the UNSC recognised the 9/11 attack as a threat to 'international peace and security'.[323] By Resolution 1373 (2001), the UNSC, acting under Chapter VII of the UN Charter, which refers to actions relating to threats to peace, breach of peace and acts of aggression, 'required all States to take measures to prevent the commission of terrorist attacks, including denying safe haven to those who finance, plan, support or commit terrorist attacks'.[324] It could be argued that the practice of allowing alien nationals to end their detention by choosing to leave the UK to go to a place of their choice is 'anti-security,' considering the fact that 'national security' is also, or presupposes some measure of safeguarding 'international security' in a wider sense.[325]

If the second and the fourth applicants in the present case were international terrorists, nothing would preclude them from recruiting terrorists from other parts of the world to launch a terrorist attack against the UK. The second applicant was not alleged to be a member of any terrorist organisation; rather, he was alleged to be a member of a terrorist 'network', which is more 'dangerous'. Hence, considering the sophistication of information technology, the second applicant was not limited in his contacts with terrorists and had the capability of recruiting terrorist operatives for an attack against the UK through his network, since this nation state was already the target. On the other hand, the

323 ibid; J. Koh, *Suppressing Terrorist Financing and Money Laundering* (Springer, Germany 2006), 82

324 ibid; N. Ryder, *The Financial War on Terrorism: A Review of Counter-Terrorists Financing Strategies Since 2001* (Routledge, New York 2015), ch 2.4

325 ibid; B. Magsig, *International Water Law and the Quest for Common Security* (Routledge, New York 2015), 11

fourth applicant could mobilise or incite members of the GIA (an Islamic terrorist group) of which he was alleged to be a member, to launch an attack against the UK; since terrorism is group-organised political violence, outside the rules of the liberal democratic game, by those who reject such game in favour of the values taken to be of higher-religious calling.[326]

Notably, it is not in every circumstance that a strict anti-terrorist policy in one nation evokes a negative response from others. For instance, two countries whose terrorist targets are at par (like the US and the UK) might not respond negatively towards each other's strict counterterrorism policies, since their terrorist targets are within close range. For example, Switzerland can comfortably neglect the United States' counter-terrorist decision-making, but UK politicians cannot. By implication, a country's anti-terrorism measures like a pre-emptive policy, which sets out to dismantle terrorist training grounds, will exert a positive effect on the security of such countries suffering the same terrorist threat.[327] Hence, such countries appear as functional alternatives to international terrorist groups. Considering the economy's role in national security, one nation's counterterrorism measure might be cost effective for another nation who shares the same national security interests and whose terrorist targets are the same or similar. Thus, a nation's anti-terrorism strategy has the capability of having a comparative advantage for another country facing a similar terrorist threat. This reinforces not only national security, but also international security.

4.2.1 SUMMARY

In summary, some anti-terrorism measures have the tendency of hindering terrorism like the freezing of terrorist funds as discussed above. However, some anti-terrorism practices, could be anti-security such as the one espoused in the case of ***A and others v The United Kingdom*** (allowing international terrorist suspects to leave the UK to go to a place of their choice). If the UK government excludes terrorist suspects from UK soil, it becomes imperative for the government to notify their 'security status to nation states where such 'international

326 P. Wilkinson, *Terrorism Versus Democracy: The Liberal State Response* (3rd edn Routledge, Abingdon Oxon 2011), 4

327 M. Epifanio, et al., op.cit

terrorist suspects' have chosen to go. Nation states need to be more pragmatic in the formulation of anti-terrorism policies.

Some anti-terrorism measures have the tendency of becoming counterproductive by advancing the likelihood of terrorism and acts associated with it. The legality of some measures might be questioned. Some infringe on international law, posing a threat to democracy. Some others violate fundamental human rights, even though they may seem effectual in practice.[328] For instance, the Anti-Terrorism, Crime and Security Act of 2001 allowed the British Government to deport non-British suspected terrorists without trial. The 2001 Act also empowered the British Government to hold "suspected terrorists indefinitely without charges or trial", while also restricting their right to judicial review.[329] Hence, the UK has adopted a law enforcement approach to counterterrorism, whereby the UK police can detain and interrogate terrorist suspects in anticipation of violence rather than in response to such action.[330] A significant number of Muslims have been arrested for terrorism violations, but were handed over to immigration without prosecution of the alleged terrorist offence. Increased police powers resulting from antiterrorist Acts have particularly targeted Muslims.[331] Some costly mistakes have been made by sovereign states in pursuit of national security. For instance, two Bangladeshi Muslims were shot by the London police; but it was later found they had nothing to do with terrorism. Many Muslims have been arrested followed by release, without explanation.[332] Perhaps, this may arouse the feeling of racial discrimination, social alienation and deprivation among the British Muslim community thereby making them

---

328 S. Sottiaux, *Terrorism and the limitation of rights: The ECHR and the US Constitution* (Hart Publishing USA, Portland 2008), 405

329 Q. Wiktorowicz, *Radical Islam rising: Muslin extremism in the West* (Rowman & Littlefield Publishers Inc., Lanham 2005)

330 A. Meyerrose, 'Possible cause for the increased susceptibility of radicalization among British and American Muslims' (2012) Department of International Studies Rhodes College Memphis Tennessee; M. Innes, A Destructive Influence? "Prevent-ing" Problems and Countering Violent Extremism Policy in Practice (2017) vol 51(2) 252-281

331 ibid; K. Jaishanka, et al., *Global Criminology: Crime and Victimization in a Globalised Era* (Taylor and Francis Group, London), 73; B. Spalek, *Ethnicity and Crime: A Reader* (Open University Press, England 2008), 88-89; T. Caine, *Stamping out Rights: The Impact of Anti-Terrorism Laws on Policing* (A Report of the International Advisory Commission of the Commonwealth Human Rights Initiative, 2007), 31

332 M. Sageman, *Leaderless jihad: Terror networks in the twenty-first century* (University of Pennsylvania, Philadelphia 2008)

susceptible to radicalisation. An understanding of the modus operandi of terrorists, the identification of 'immediate' and 'prospective' threats, particular targets, as well as a full awareness of the damage and aftermath of the acts of terror, is the hallmark of counterterrorism, both nationally and globally.[333]

However, the question that arises thereafter is whether 'indulging' in counterterrorism measures has the potential for curbing terrorism, considering the latter's current structure and pattern. Additionally, it can be argued that it is not democratic to infringe upon the civil liberties of terrorists. However, at the same time, the question could be asked: 'What is democratic about the acts perpetrated by terrorists?' Terrorism destabilises public order in a democratic society, where political goals are sort for by a group of people through undemocratic means.

4.3 THE EFFECT OF THE PROTECTION OF INDIVIDUAL LIVES AND PROPERTY ON NATIONAL SECURITY

It is, perhaps, 'traditional' to perceive national security as military security or as security for the state. States cannot exist without individuals. The primary goal of every government should hinge on the security of the nation, as well as members of the public at large. Therefore, national security strategies should not only be state-centred in the abstract but should also be people-oriented. People's security could be considered a condition for the sustainability of national security in a country. Hence, it is arguable that the protection of individual lives and property is at the core of any viable notion of national security. Thus, the deprivation of life must be in accordance with Article 2(2) of the ECHR, which provides:

> "Deprivation of life shall not be regarded as inflicted in contravention of this article when it results from the use of force which is no more than absolutely necessary: (b) ... to effect a lawful arrest or to prevent the escape of a person lawfully detained;"

333 Y. Alexander, *Counterterrorism strategies: Successes and failures of six nations* (Potomac Books Inc, Washington DC 2006), 190

By implication, people's security connotes safety for people from violent and non-violent threats and takes seriously the interests, needs and rights infringed by, for example, acts of terrorism. It is also typified by "freedom from" extensive threats to people's rights, their safety, and lives. There is also an implied positive obligation on sovereign states to adopt preventive measures to safeguard individuals whose lives are threatened by the criminal acts of others.[334] Thus, rather than putting 'territorial security' into the spotlight, people's security ought to be an equally important point of reference. Human security demands taking preventive action for reduction of vulnerabilities, which the citizenry might be exposed to; as well as taking remedial action, where prevention fails.[335]

This subsection stems from the necessity for governments of nation states to put the protection of individual rights into due consideration in the formulation and implementation of anti-terrorism measures for the promotion of national security. It will critically address the question: 'In what ways can people's security have an impact on national security?' It will analyse cases involving indiscriminate loss of lives of individuals caused by governmental agencies in the 'fight against terrorism'.

"The security of the State is not an end in itself but is a means of ensuring security for people..."[336] It may be widely believed that people's security and national security are mutually exclusive paradigms, which are competitive, not complementary. A dichotomy has been established between state-centered national security and people centered-human security.[337] However, the purport of people's security is far from rejecting the importance of state-centric arguments and the essence of protecting the state against external military violence. Nevertheless, it postulates that considerations of national security must, out of necessity, bring people's security into limelight. Arguably, the indivisibility of security and human rights is at the centre of people's security. The people's

334 D. Ehlers, et al., *European fundamental rights and freedoms* (Hubert & Co Gottingen, Germany 2007), 35

335 L. Axworthy, 'Human security: Safety for people in a changing world' (2007) Centre for Peace and Development Studies

336 H. Mahmud, 'Human security or national security: The problems and prospects of the norm of human security' (2008) vol1(4) Journal of Politics and Law 67

337 D. Chandler, *Critical perspective on human security: Rethinking emancipation and power in international relations* (Routledge publishing limited, New York 2011), 2

security disquisition maintains that there is an absence of security in a nation if the lives of individuals are being threatened by, for example, their government or a military occupier. In the same way, a widespread sense of security is also typically absent when individuals are deprived of their fundamental rights (such as their right to life and property) by the government or foreign military occupier. Obviously, the infringement of fundamental human rights depicts the existence of 'insecurity' if security also implies "protection from harm". People's security acknowledges the multidimensionality of the sources of harm. For instance, there could be military and non-military perpetrators of harm, national and transnational, private and public. Harm can also constitute the result of an 'intentional' act.[338]

It is arguable that national security is also a conduit for people's security. Nevertheless, experience has shown that there is no surety that the realisation of national security necessarily, in practice, provides security for the individuals of a nation. Hence, there can be a discrepancy between the principal political value of national security, and the principal moral value of people's security.[339] For instance, it has become the order of the day for law enforcement agencies in some nations to engage in human rights violations, notably, murders, indefinite detention and disappearances.[340] For instance, it was reported that from 2002-2011, between 9 to 19 individuals fell victims to forced disappearance each year in Ingushetia.[341] National security cannot be achieved in a nation without the prevention or elimination of conditions that heighten the vulnerability of individuals. Hence, a reduction in the level of vulnerability ought to be the heartbeat of national security.

A nation's security could be destabilised through public/civil unrest, where citizens lack confidence in the ability of their government to protect their lives and property—a weak, ineffective state, or one that is corrupt, undemocratic in

338 Ibid., page 21

339 R. Coupland, 'Security, insecurity and health' (2007) 85 Bulletin of the World Health Organisation 181

340 F. Londras, Detention *in the war on terror: Can human rights fight back*? (Cambridge University Press, New York 2011), 192; S. Dadwal, et al., *Non-traditional Security Challenges in Asia: Approaches and Responses* (New Delhi: Routledge Taylor & Francis Group 2015), 232

341 Amnesty International, *The Circle of injustice: Security operations and human rights violations in Ingushetia* (Amnesty International limited, London 2012), 16

practice if not in theory. In the case of ***Umarovy v Russia*** the applicant's relative (Ramazan Umarov) was arrested with two others (Mr. S.S. and Mr. M.R.) in the same flat on the 28th of April 2007. The three were handcuffed and taken to the Department of Fight Against Organised Crime (the UBOP) of the Dagestan Ministry of Interior (the Dagestan MVD), but in different vehicles. The authorities commenced criminal proceedings against Mr. S.S. and Mr. M.R. on that same day under Article 222 of the Russian Criminal Code (Illegal Possession of Firearms). However, Ramazan disappeared while in detention. After a fruitless effort to ascertain Ramazan's whereabouts by the applicants for four years, the applicants alleged a violation of Articles 2, 3, 5, 13 and 41 of the ECHR. Nevertheless, for the purpose of this analysis, the focus will be on Articles 2 and 3 of the ECHR: namely, the right to life and the right not to be tortured or subjected to inhuman or degrading treatment or punishment.[342]

The applicants invoked Ramazan's right under Article 2 of the ECHR. Article 2(1) of the ECHR states:

> "Everyone's right to life shall be protected by law. No one shall be deprived of his life intentionally save in the execution of a sentence of a court following his conviction of a crime for which his penalty is provided by law."

They alleged that Ramazan has been deprived of his life by State agents and that no effective investigation has been carried out by the authorities. The government contended that no evidence showed that Ramazan was dead, nor that he had been abducted by any of the State agents. In response, the applicants argued that upon Ramazan's arrest on the 28th of April 2007 by representatives of State agents, he disappeared for several years without any reliable news about his absence. Therefore, he should be 'presumed dead'. The applicants further argued that the investigation began with a significant delay and was then protracted. The officers who arrested Ramazan on the 28th of April 2007 had not been identified and questioned.[343] The Court found that Ramazan's death could be attributed to the State. Hence, there was a violation of Ramazan's right under Article

342 Umarovy v Russia (2012) ECHR 2546/08 Strasbourg. paras 11, 12, 13

343 ibid

2 of the ECHR.[344] The action of the government with respect to Ramazan's arrest, detention, loss of property (particularly his car) and disappearance raises some questions: Is the fight against terrorism a fight against the "rule of law"? Does the promotion of national security imply a flagrant violation of people's rights? Is the implication of national security exclusively territorial/state security? Or are government agents above the law?

It is generally recognised by most modern political and constitutional theories that it is the government's responsibility to ensure that the lives and property of its citizens are secure.[345] The national security of a nation may not be sustained if the lives and property of its citizenry are in jeopardy. The present case depicts a dereliction of duty by the government regarding Ramazan's arrest, whereabouts (his disappearance from government custody) and loss of his property (precisely, his car). It cannot be imagined that a special operation (the arrest of Mr. S.S., Mr. M.R. and Ramazan) was carried out by law enforcement agents on a specific day without the law enforcement agency having a record of the officers who carried out the operation. It can be safely argued that the government was responsible for Ramazan's disappearance. Hence, there was loss of his life.[346]

Analytically, pursuant to Article 2 of the ECHR, "...No one shall be deprived of his life intentionally". The word 'intentionally' is a major ingredient of the 'right to life'. There are so many instances in the present case, which showed that the government authorities 'intentionally' took Ramazan's life. For instance, the second applicant opined that Ramazan (her brother) had been arrested without warrant by the police, who suspected him of terrorist activities, and that the latter had also taken Ramazan's property (his car).[347] Consequently, the facts of the case revealed that although Ramazan was arrested along with two others on the 28th of April 2007 by the State agents, they were taken to the UBOP, but in different cars. This could be considered an intentional arrangement by the authority to carry out its plan of 'extrajudicial execution' on Ramazan without drawing the attention of the other two arrestees. On that same day, criminal proceeding was instituted against Mr. S.S. and Mr. M.R. without Ramazan. Mr. S.S.

344 ibid

345 ibid

346 ibid

347 Ibid., para 30

and Mr. M.R. stated in their evidence that Ramazan was arrested together with them. It could be argued that this was 'intentionally' done by the government authorities to thwart any move to trace Ramazan, since the court records could have confirmed that Ramazan was arrested by the law enforcement agency if he was prosecuted along with the other two. [348]

The government had significant clues to trace Ramazan, but they were 'passive' about his disappearance. For instance, on the 9th of May 2007 the second applicant received a call notifying them that Ramazan was in a penal institution in Gudermes, Chechnya after been picked up 'unconscious' in a forest.[349] On the 14th of May 2007 two Chechnyan men collected 20,000 Russian roubles from the applicant's friend for information from a police officer (a senior police officer in Gudermes), who was meant to reveal Ramazan's whereabouts and was also meant to secure his release. The police officer's name was also disclosed.[350] The applicants provided the Dagestan prosecutor with details of the phone conversations they had between 9th–15th May 2007 concerning Ramazan and the telephone numbers from which they received the calls. The security guards of a car park confirmed to the investigators of the present case that Ramazan's car disappeared from the car park few days after it was searched by two police officers, who also took away some documents from the car. Overall, the investigation of Ramazan's whereabouts lacked professionalism and was unnecessarily protracted.

Impliedly, the sequence of events shows that the police authority was responsible for whatever happened to Ramazan's life. The facts of the case reveal that, on the 14th of April 2007, Ramazan's car was parked in a car park. On the 27th of April 2007, two police men with their service identity documents spent the whole day waiting for someone.[351] It can be argued that if a government agency (precisely, the law enforcement agency, as in the present case) is unable to trace police representatives, who carried out an arrest as well as the 'disappearance' of someone in its custody, one will begin to question the fate of the common man in such community. Even if Ramazan was a suspected terrorist, the police

348 Ibid., para 12

349 Umarovy v Russia., op.cit., para 15

350 Ibid., para 19

351 Umarovy v Russia., op.cit

authority should bring him under the jurisdiction and processes of the established law.

The government owed Ramazan legal and moral responsibility to protect his life and property, even as a suspected terrorist. His arrest and detention should have taken the course of law. The way and manner of the government's investigation into Ramazan's disappearance from its custody could be considered 'unlawful' and a gross violation of his right under Article 2(1) of the ECHR. If an individual's 'right to life' is not guaranteed because of the 'acts' or 'omissions' of the government, every other right provided by law becomes an illusion. Deterioration in public safety is an essential feature of insecurity. Hence, the UN Human Rights Committee identifies right to life as the "supreme right" of human beings.[352]

By Article 2(2) (b) of the ECHR, as stated above, if Ramazan was deprived of his life through a lawful arrest or in a bid to prevent him from escaping during lawful custody, it could be said that his loss of life was in one sense prescribed by law. However, the facts of the present case never showed that the arrest was itself 'lawful', since no warrant of arrest was produced by the law enforcement agents who arrested Ramazan. Neither was there evidence that Ramazan ever attempted to escape from detention. The law enforcement agency of any nation is a government parastatal and therefore, a representative of the government. If such agency fails in its duty to enhance the protection of the lives and property of members of the public, then the government also fails. Analytically, there could be a collective protest from the public. This can disrupt national security if the public feels a high sense of insecurity and lack of confidence with government agencies, such as the police. For instance, in the present case, the applicants can 'incite' the public against the government, which may destabilise national security as the consequence/s of such protests is/are usually unpredictable.

Furthermore, the applicants alleged a violation of Article 3 of the ECHR: "No one shall be subjected to torture or to inhuman or degrading treatment or punishment." They submitted that they had endured "mental suffering" as a result of both their relative's disappearance, and the government's failure to investigate it effectively. The government countered such submission by arguing that the investigation did not reveal that the applicants were subjected to "inhuman or

352 Human Rights Committee., 'General Comment No. 6 Article 6 (the right to life) (1982) para 1

degrading treatment", as provided for under Article 3 of the ECHR. However, the Court held that there had been a violation of Article 3 of the ECHR, considering the closeness of the relationship between the applicants and the arrestee (Ramazan), as well as the government's reaction and attitude towards the situation.

No doubt, the applicants were tortured mentally by the way the government handled and investigated their case. They suffered severe "mental pain". It could be argued that there was no investigation at all. Arguably, in the present case, the applicants had been subjected to 'severe mental suffering' stemming from the enforced disappearance of their close relative, coupled with years of 'inefficient' and 'fruitless' search for their relative purportedly held in government custody.

However, Article 3 of the ECHR is one of the rare circumstances, or rights, which cannot be derogated from. As defined by the UN Convention Against Torture, torture is not only 'physical pain'. 'Mental' and 'psychological pain' comprise an integral aspect of 'torture'. In my opinion, the applicants were subjected to inhuman and degrading treatment by the law enforcement agents, not because they were 'physically tortured', but because of both the height of 'disregard' and the 'depth of laxity' adopted by the authorities towards their complaints for so many years. If the relationship between Ramazan and the applicants was a distant one, such submission would have been different. However, the relationship is recognised as a very 'close' one (paternity).

Similarly, in the case of ***McKerr v The United Kingdom,*** Gervaise McKerr (the applicant's father) and two others were shot to death, while the car was in motion, by a specially trained mobile support unit of Royal Ulster Constabulary (RUC). The applicant alleged that his father's death was because of the unnecessary and disproportionate use of force by the RUC officer, and that his father was a victim of a "shoot-to-kill policy"—then being operated by the UK government in Northern Ireland.[353] The applicant further submitted that no effective official investigation was carried into the killing of his father. Hence, there was a violation of his father's right under Article 2 of the ECHR.[354]

353 Mckerr v The United Kingdom (2001) ECHR 28883/95 Strasbourg paras 100

354 Ibid., para 103

In response, the government contended that it will be wholly inappropriate on grounds of national security for the court to seek to determine the issues of fact emanating from substantive issues of Article 2 of the ECHR.[355] The government further contended that the procedural aspect of Article 2 of the ECHR was satisfied by the combination of procedures available in Northern Ireland, namely, the prompt and thorough police investigation, which was supervised by the Director of Public Prosecutions (DPP), the criminal trial, the inquest proceedings and civil proceedings. Hence, the available procedure provided the necessary effectiveness, independence and transparency.[356] The court held that the obligation of states to protect the right to life under Article 2 ECHR, if read in conjunction with Article 1 of the ECHR also requires, in effect, some form of effective investigation when individuals have been killed because of the use of force, not just the availability of procedures. Thus, there was a violation of the right to life under Article 2 of the ECHR, as there has been a practical failure of compliance with the procedural obligation under Article 2 of the ECHR.[357]

Arguably, it is accepted that right to life under Article 2 of the ECHR is not an absolute right. Nevertheless, it is incumbent on the state to protect the right to life of individuals, and thereby ensure their right to life secures their life as reasonably possible. A consideration of Article 2(2) of the ECHR reveals that an individual's right to life could be taken away, but this is subject to a circumstance that such killing is 'absolutely necessary'. For instance, as provided under Article 2(b) of the ECHR, "... to effect a lawful arrest or to prevent the escape of a person lawfully detained".[358] Thus, a careful look at Article 2(2) (a) (b) (c) (d) of the ECHR depicts that the applicant's father's death is 'unlawful', as the loss of his life fell out of the ambit of Article 2(2) of the ECHR. The facts of the case show that the applicant's father and two others were 'unarmed'. According to the established facts, the car was still in motion when the police officers fired 109 rounds into the car.[359] By implication, it could be argued that the RUC officers were on a mission to 'intentionally' take away the lives of the deceased, as they believed that the deceased had set out to commit a murder. There was

355 Ibid, para 104

356 Ibid, para 106

357 Ibid, para 161

358 ibid

359 Ibid., para 19

no sign of an attempted arrest. Neither was there a sign of any form of resistance of arrest by the deceased persons. There could have been a positive shift towards the act of the RUC officers, if the number of rounds they released into the car of the deceased were far fewer than what was released (109 rounds). In such circumstance, the action of the RUC officers was not 'absolutely necessary'. Conversely, if the deceased were armed and the RUC officers fired 109 rounds into their car as they were still in motion, the provisions of Paragraph 9 of the UN Force and Firearms Principles, which states, inter alia, that the "intentional lethal use of firearms may only be made when strictly unavoidable to protect life", could have favoured the RUC officers; since they alleged that they acted under the premise that the deceased had set out to commit a murder.

On the other hand, the position would have been different if the deceased were actively resisting arrest. Also, if the deceased were 'armed', Section 3 of the Criminal Law Act (Northern Ireland) 1967 could have offered legal protection to the RUC officers under the purview of "the prevention of crime".[360] However, even in such circumstance, the use of force still has to be 'reasonable'. The RUC officers could not also invoke self-defence, as no attack or opposition had ensued from the deceased.

By implication, Article 2 of the ECHR places an obligation on the government to carry out an effective investigation in an event where the loss of life is because of the use of lethal force. Paragraph 9 of the United Nations Principles on the Effective Prevention and Investigation of Extra-legal, Arbitrary and Summary Executions (UN Principles on Extra-legal Executions), adopted on 24 May 1989, provides, inter alia:

> "There shall be a thorough, prompt and impartial investigation of all suspected cases of extra-legal, arbitrary and summary executions, including cases where complaints by relatives or other reliable reports suggest unnatural death in the above circumstances. ..."[361].

It could be argued that the investigation into the use of lethal force on the deceased by the RUC officers failed standards of procedural diligence. Some

360 Criminal Law Act (Northern Ireland) 1967

361 ibid., para 95

basic elements of "effective investigation" were absent in the present case. Since there is loss of life through unnatural means, such elements are pertinent in the investigation. It is not sufficient for such type of investigation to merely be prompt; it must be 'thorough' and 'impartial' too. The element of 'thoroughness' relates to the effectiveness of the investigation, while the element of 'impartiality' hinges on the independence of the investigation, which incorporates the element of public scrutiny. Paragraph 11 of the UN Principles on the Effective Prevention and Investigation of Extra-legal, Arbitrary and Summary Executions (UN Principles on Extra-legal Executions) specifies as follows:

> "...Governments shall pursue investigations through an independent Commission of inquiry or similar procedure. Members of such a Commission shall be chosen for their recognised impartiality, competence and independence as individuals. They shall be independent of any institution, agency or person that may be the subject of any inquiry..."[362]

It is accepted that investigation into the death of the deceased commenced immediately after the incident. However, the investigation was carried out by the RUC. The officers who carried out the operation (the death of the deceased) were RUC officers. Therefore, the effectiveness of the investigation is bound to be questioned on the grounds of bias. For instance, the Stalker investigation (one of the investigators) reported that the investigation carried out by RUC was uncoordinated as the investigating officers never spoke to each other to coordinate their findings. The investigation files were merely a collection of statements with no resemblance to a murder investigation file. Even when there was need for an independent investigation to be conducted, the appointment was still done by the Chief Constable of RUC. Hence, the report of the investigation by the Stalker/Sampson investigation was required to be submitted to RUC. How then can there be transparency in the investigation? Some vital evidence was withheld from the Stalker investigation and upon request for such evidence, though some documents were later handed over to Stalker, he was removed from the inquiry by the RUC Chief Constable immediately thereafter. Overall, the investigation into the death of the deceased comprised anti-national security, because it failed procedural diligence.

362 ibid., para 96

Ideally, RUC should not have been part of the investigation in any way (appointment of independent investigators inclusive). The inquest that was carried out ended up not fulfilling its purpose, as it was seized with prolonged adjournments (some adjournments lasted for four years), irregularities in RUC files and lack of access to material evidence in RUC custody. Hence, the Coroner stated: "I am satisfied that my aim in deciding to hold inquests for the reason I expressed to the jury when I opened the inquest into the death of Mckerr, Toman and Burns is no longer achievable."[363]

According to the Stalker/Simpson investigation, around the time the deceased were killed, similar killings involving RUC took place in Armagh. The facts of the case revealed that the deceased in the subsequent cases were also unarmed.[364] Could it be said that such method of killing was the modus operandi of RUC? Or is it that the intelligence on the deceased in each of the cases was inaccurate? Or is the practice of such a killing a counterterrorism measure? Whatever is the case, such mode of killing has the potential of being counterproductive for national security, because of the obvious feeling of insecurity amongst the citizenry. On the other hand, the majority might be pleased and feel more secured if they hear that those identified as terrorists have been killed. Many would have welcomed such decision given the polarised, para-militarised society. Nevertheless, in my opinion, the citizenry might engage in organised violence against the government if they continuously feel that the government is working 'against them' instead of 'for them' in the fight against terrorism, due to the indiscriminate killing of individuals by governmental agencies.

National security is not merely a political concept. Rather, it is a compendium of different aspects of security, out of which protection through various state initiatives and practices, of lives and property of individuals (people's security), in the society in question is an integral part. The rate, at which innocent lives are lost or are unaccounted for, in the fight against terrorism, is increasingly turning counterterrorism activities into a 'fight' against 'humanity' (this will be further discussed in the next chapter). Ideally, there ought to be some streamlined elements of 'terrorism' or 'terrorists'. The pattern of enforcement of national

363 ibid., para 61

364 ibid., para 21

security through the "war against terror", especially post 9/11, seems to baptise every violent act, no matter how negligible, as a 'terrorist act'.

4.3.1 SUMMARY

In summary, the government is the custodian of the rights and security of its citizens. The promotion of human dignity is a crucial element of people's security. Freedom from fear of insecurity is also an element of national security. Hence, an explanation of the causes of terrorism and the war against terrorism could be traced to human insecurity. An expression of violence by the government towards its citizens through its flagrant violation of human rights has the capacity of stimulating violence amongst the citizenry; only if citizens themselves are 100% signed up to all human rights agenda. Thus, violence begets violence. If the experience of the applicants in the present case is the order of the day in Dagestan, there is a likelihood for members of the public to revolt against the government on the grounds of 'fear' or 'insecurity'.

People's security is not devoid of challenges. One such challenge is the failure of governments to respond accordingly to the security needs of their citizens. This extends to the government's failure to decipher the fundamental cause/s of people's insecurity and assist to ensure their future safety. The beauty of national security is the mutual reinforcement it has with human security. Ironically, people have lost their lives, properties and have had their fundamental human rights violated either directly or indirectly by the acts or omissions of their own governments. Hence, people's security has been threatened by governments in view of national security. This is antithetical to the spirit of 'national security'. A nations' security will remain porous, until it achieves a high level of people's security. The government cannot function without human beings. Therefore, the security of citizenry demands a place of priority in national security policies. The provision of human security should be the primary role of government. What happens when the government fails to carry out such role? What if the government is not willing to provide human security? What becomes the fate of the common man? There is an urgent need for partnership between the government and its citizenry for people's security to be enhanced in the state. Analytically, co-operation between individuals and the government regarding issues of people's security may help reduce frictions on issues, which positively impact national security.

4.4 THE EFFECTS OF IMMIGRATION ON NATIONAL SECURITY

Immigration does not necessarily connote migrating to a country to remain there permanently. Once there is movement from one country to another, migration has taken place. Simply put, migration can be defined as the movement of people across borders, irrespective of the length of time. The implication of immigration on national security has been a thing of great concern.[365] Hence, the 1995 bombings of the Paris metro system by Algeria's Armed Islamic Group, the Kurdistan Workers' Party attacks in the 1990s on various Western states and the fact that nineteen alien hijackers entered, lived and trained in the United States of America to prepare for the 9/11 attack, reinforced such concern.[366]

This sub-section will address the questions: 'How does immigration affect the security of a nation? Is immigration, one of the conduits for terrorism, itself understood as a national security challenge? Are there challenges encountered by states when trying to deport alien terrorist suspects?'

In recent times, immigration has posed an outstanding feature in the economic, social, and political landscape of most European countries. States are not against migration; rather, they are interested in having exclusive control over the entry, permanent residence and naturalisation of foreigners in their nation. Although not all migrants are terrorists, immigration could be viewed as one of the channels for terrorism in the sense that most of the terrorist attacks in North America and Europe were carried out by aliens. Hence, a report published by the Nixon entre declares that: "Immigration and terrorism are linked; not because all immigrants are terrorists but because all or nearly all terrorists in the West have been immigrants."[367] Rohan Gunaratna claims in the same report that, "All major terrorists' attacks conducted in the last decade in North America and Western Europe, with the exception of Oklahoma city, utilised immigrants."[368] Most of

365 J. Krishner, *Globalization and national security* (Routledge Taylor and Francis Group, New York 2013), 63

366 F. Adamson, 'Crossing borders: International Migration and National Security' (2006) vol 31(1) International security 165

367 F. Adamson, op.cit

368 ibid; P. Ghosh, *Migrants, Refugees and the Stateless in South Asia* (Sage Publications, California 2016), 293

the terrorists involved in the suicide bombings of the London Transport system on July 7th, 2005 were men born and bred in Britain in immigrant descended communities. Also, some of the would-be bombers of London transport in July 21st, 2005 originally came as asylum seekers who became naturalised British citizens.[369] The threat posed by immigration to national security is heightened when it becomes a challenge to extradite, remove or expel persons who are terrorist suspects or people posing threat to public good, especially in a situation where there is an allegation of a tendency to violate article 3 of the ECHR in a receiving country.

Hence, in the case of ***Othman Abu Qatada & others v United Kingdom,*** the applicant had a series of convictions in absentia in Jordan. He was convicted for conspiracy to cause explosions, in a trial known as the "reform and challenge" case. He was alleged to have conspired to carry out bombings in Jordan, which gave rise to successful attacks on the American school and Jerusalem Hotel in Amman in 1998. The applicant was involved in the 'millennium conspiracy' case in the autumn of 2000, where he was alleged to have conspired to cause explosions at Western and Israeli targets in Jordan to coincide with the millennium celebrations.[370]

However, on the 11th of August 2005, the applicant (a radical cleric) was served with a notice of intention to deport by the United Kingdom's Secretary of State on the grounds of national security.[371] The applicant was granted asylum in the UK before the UK Secretary of State discovered that he was a 'security risk'. By virtue of the asylum granted, the applicant had become a legal immigrant in the United Kingdom. However, it could not have been a coincidence that the applicant constituted a threat in Jordan and in the United Kingdom, subsequently. Perhaps, it shows that he had a criminal tendency, which is a security issue. By implication, he was a threat not just to the United Kingdom, but to the world at large; since terrorism is a global affair. The allegations against him in Jordan showed that he was a 'good motivator'. Hence, the potential to motivate others is often an inherent feature that manifests whenever the occasion arises. The applicant was a 'motivator' whose opinions legitimised acts of violence;

369 J. Hampshire, et al., op.cit

370 Othman (Abu Qatada) v United Kingdom (2012) ECHR 8139/09 Strasbourg

371 ibid

therefore, he could influence vulnerable residents in the UK towards terrorist activities.[372]

Analytically, the effect of migration on national security has been a thing of great concern, but the difficulty encountered by states in protecting their population against terrorist violence, especially when the threat is internally generated by foreigners who are residents in the contracting country, is of greater concern. For instance, there is all likelihood of an allegation of a violation of Article 3 of the ECHR in an event of an expulsion or a deportation order of an alien to a receiving country. Therefore, the principle espoused in the case of ***Üner v. The Netherlands,*** which states that,

> "As a matter of well-established international law and subject to its treaty obligations, including those emanating from the Convention, a Contracting State has the right to control the entry, residence and expulsion of aliens,"[373] is not easily applicable in most cases.

The signing of a memorandum of understanding (MOU) between a contracting and a receiving country does not alleviate the difficulties encountered by states when expelling or deporting foreign nationals, who constitute a threat to the national security of a contracting state either. The fact that a contracting state signed an MOU with the receiving country is also not a condition precedent that the deportation of an applicant will be allowed under international law. Often when assurances are signed, the deportee contests its reliability.

In the case of ***Othman (Abu Qatada) v. United Kingdom***, although a reliance on the MOU in this case was allowed, the applicant contested the reliability of the MOU because it undermines the long-standing international legal mechanism for the prohibition of torture. It therefore became needful for the Court to determine the general human rights situation in Jordan and the quality of assurances given in addition to the possibility of compliance with the assurances

372 ibid; L. Jarvis, et al., Anti-terrorism, Citizenship and Security (Manchester University Press, Manchester 2015), 87

373 Uner v Netherlands (2006) 54 ECHR 46410/99

based on the previous practices in Jordan. The determination of all these was 'time' and 'resource' consuming.[374]

Where there are high human rights violations in the receiving country, such as evidence of gross ill treatment of detainees or torture, the MOUs are not usually recognised by the international community. Thus, in **Suresh v. Canada (Minister of Citizenship and Immigration)** the Court stated:

> "... We would signal the difficulty in relying too heavily on assurances by a state that it will refrain from torture in the future when it has engaged in illegal torture or allowed others to do so, on its territory in the past. This difficulty becomes acute in cases where torture is inflicted not only with the collusion but through the impotence of the state in controlling the behaviour of its officials."[375]

Mike Blakemore, Amnesty International's UK spokesman, asserts that such assurances are not worth "the paper they were written on." Also, Manfred Nowak, the UN special rapporteur on torture, observes, "...the very fact that such assurances are sought reveals that the UK government perceives a serious risk of torture or ill treatment."[376] In **Chahal v United Kingdom,** the applicant was an Indian national who migrated to the United Kingdom. His position as a leading Sikh leader made his continuous presence in the United Kingdom unconducive to public good on grounds of national security and the international fight against terrorism. The Sikh group showed evidence of violence and human rights abuses.[377] Pursuant to the applicant's deportation order, the diplomatic assurances were rejected by the European Court of Human Rights because the applicant still stood a chance of real risk of torture if returned to India, considering the persistent violation of human rights in India and the Punjab territory.[378]

---

374 Othman (Abu Qatada) v United Kingdom., op cit

375 Suresh v Canada (Minister of Citizenship and immigration) (2002) 1 SCR 3

376 J. Hampshire, et al., 'Migration, Integration and Security in the UK since July' (2006) <*www.migrationinformatiom.org/USFocus/display.cfm?ID=383*> accessed 21 August 2012

377 Chahal v United Kingdom (1996) ECHR 22414/93 Strasbourg

378 ibid, para 14-16

Hence, nations face the challenge of being 'trapped' with alien nationals who constitute 'security risk' but cannot face deportation because of the risk of torture in the receiving country. Deportation is an aspect of a nation's immigration policy applied as a device for the removal of instantaneous threats from a nation. However, the power to deport a 'perceived threat' is limited and poses a challenge where the deportee stands a real risk of torture in the receiving country. The use of diplomatic assurances has also become widely unpopular, so much that it cannot be guaranteed that the Court, as the case may be, will authorise its application in any event of deportation. More so, human rights advocates posit that diplomatic assurances are not sufficient to prevent torture. They are neither treaties nor legally binding.[379]

On the other hand, national security has also been threatened by home-grown terrorists. Experience has shown that terrorists need not be foreign nationals. There could be 'enemies within' (people born and bred in a nation). They need not visit an actual military training camp or interact directly with terrorist organisations such as Al-Qaeda. They rely on terrorist training manuals, internet chat forums, audio and video recordings. Hence, without having formal contacts with any terrorist organisations, home-grown terrorists can become visual associates of terrorist organisations by cautiously studying their online knowledge base and executing terrorist attacks against their enemies.[380]

The economic strength of a nation is a security issue. Immigration management is capital intensive. After the attack of 9/11, most nations of the world embarked on capital intensive programmes or strategies to enhance their border and immigration control. For instance, in 2004, the USA invested 1.8 billion USD on immigration services. Also, 49 million CAD was committed to the Citizenship and Immigration Canada (CIC) as part of the Canadian Government's anti-terrorism plan. The essence of such investments is to abate irregular movements, the impact of criminal groups on such movements and to lessen security

379 A. Scheonholtz, et al., 'The immigration control of terrorism and the prevention of terror' (2009) Institute for the study of International Migration, Walsh school of Foreign Service Georgetown University

380 E. Kohlmann, 'Homegrown terrorists: Theory and cases in the war on terror's newest front' (2008) vol 618(1) The ANNALS of the American Academy of Political and Social Science 95

weaknesses in the migration sector.[381] Considerable budgets are spent on immigration matters to ensure that the entry and exit of foreigners are controlled. The extra resources invested on immigration can be geared towards other areas of national development.

Advanced industrial countries spend fortunes in asylum applications. For instance, in 1980, 180,000 people submitted asylum applications.[382] Generally, this increased to 923,000 applicants in 2001.[383] In the 1990s, approximately 6,000,000 asylum applications were made in advanced industrialised countries.[384] Ironically, only a small percentage constituted authentic asylum seekers. The office of the United Nations High Commissioner for Refugees' annual budget is far less low than what the advanced industrial countries spend on asylum applications. Records show that advanced industrialised countries spend approximately $10 billion on asylum applications annually.[385] Such degree of expenditure has the capacity of adversely affecting national security as such resources could be channeled to other sensitive areas like intelligence sharing.

Paradoxically, skilled and unskilled immigrants can help to boost a nations' labour market, which may enhance its financial security. The mobility of skilled labour is popularly seen as a "good thing" in the EU. The implication of a nation's economic clout on national security was brought into limelight by the tragic collapse of the Soviet Union and the Eastern bloc.[386] Countries run programmes in specific sectors of their economy for attracting foreign labour to complement the existing domestic work force. For instance, Australia, Canada and New Zealand have a point based system that encourages the migration of skills to meet the specific needs of their domestic labour market. 56% of the individuals admitted in 2005 by Canada entered through economic category,

381 International Organization for Migration, *'World Migration 2005: Costs and benefits of international migration'* (Academic Foundation press, India 2006), 349

382 F. Adamson, op.cit

383 ibid; P. Legrain, *Immigrants: Your Country Needs Them* (Princeton University Press, Princeton 2014), 9

384 ibid

385 ibid; K. Bem, et al., A Price Too High: The Cost of Australia's Approach to Asylum Seekers (2007) Oxfam Australia 29

386 D. Kerwin, 'The use and misuse of 'National Security' rationale in crafting US refugee and immigration policies' (2005) vol 17(4) International Refugee Law 749-763

68% in Australia and New Zealand.[387] Hence, David Held and his co-authors stated: "There is now almost no state or part of the world that is not importing or exporting labour".[388] States that declared that they were "not countries of immigration" have amended long lasting migration and citizenship policies to fit into the realities of current migration flows.[389]

Vigorous policies for the recruitment of skilled and highly skilled workers have been supported by most countries of the Organisation for Economic Co-operation and Development (OECD). For instance, young alien professionals could work in France conditional to annual quotas based on a series of bilateral agreements entered by France. The Czech Republic initiated a project referred to as the 'active selection of qualified foreign workers', permitting willing, highly-skilled professionals to remain permanently in the country. A green card specifically focused on IT professions was also introduced by Germany. Immigration flows are tremendously correlated to economic growth.[390] The spurring growth of the US economy in the 1990s was traced to migration flows and an increase in foreign-born labour force.[391] The rationale behind such programmes is to obtain the talents needed to fill up the skill shortages in some areas in a systematic way.[392] A restricted admission of foreign-born students, entrepreneurs, scientists, scholars and inventors has the potential of diminishing a nation's economic strength, which might, in turn, have a national security implication.[393]

To some extent, immigration is indirectly an economic issue. The economic power of a nation could be referred to as the backbone of the nation's security. Immigrants have the potential of creating new businesses. The ***'Partnership for a new American Economy'***[394] estimates that immigrant business owners

387 G. Facchini, et al., 'From individual attitudes towards migrants to migration policy outcomes: Theory and evidence' (2008) vol 23(56) Economic Policy 651

388 F. Adamson, op.cit

389 ibid

390 ibid; M. Zhou, *Contemporary Chinese America: Immigration, Ethnicity and Community Transformation* (Temple University Press, Philadelphia 2009), 38

391 ibid; D. Kendall, *Sociology in Our Time* (11th edn Cengage Learning, Boston 2016), 292

392 ibid; G. Borjas, *Immigration Economics* (Harvard University Press, Cambridge 2014), 170

393 ibid

394 D. Nicklaus, 'Immigrant entrepreneurs could help jump start the economy' (2012) www.stltoday.com/...nicklaus/immigrant-enterpreneurs-could-help-start-the-eco... accessed 20 August 2012

employ one in 10 U.S. private-sector workers, and notes that they started more businesses in recent years, in contrast to a decline in start-ups by native-born Americans. The Partnership headed by Michael Bloomberg (a New York Mayor) and News Corp. reported that in 2011, 550 new businesses were formed by immigrants each month for every 100,000 immigrants as opposed to 270 businesses each month per 100,000 people among the native-born Americans. Immigrants' rate of business formation rose by 50% between 1996 and 2011, while the native-born Americans' entrepreneurial proclivity fell by 10%. In 2011, immigrants launched 28% of the all new U.S. firms. Immigrants start more than one-quarter of all new businesses in the economy's fastest-growing sectors, including retail, health care and business services.[395]

It could be argued that terrorists understand the crucial role a nation's economy plays in its national security and internal security and, hence, attack economic targets. Hence, Al-Qaeda must have acknowledged the level of economic activities that go on in the World Trade Centre before they targeted their attack—bearing in mind the devastating effect it would have on not just the United States of America's economy, but also on the world at large. The economic gains of immigration cannot be underestimated. The high and the low skill sectors benefit from migration too.[396]

Immigration is not necessarily an economic burden as the public and policy makers at the destination country often see it, or claim it to be, for internal political purposes. They argue that immigration has the capacity of leading to loss of jobs, heavy burden on public services, social tension and increased criminality. Often immigrants are blamed for a rise in unemployment, but no strong evidence can support such contention.[397] The cumulative implication of immigration on wages in OECD countries has been found to be negligible both in the short and long runs.[398] Moreover, employed immigrants also pay their taxes and contribute to social security, as the case may be. Hence, immigration supports

395 ibid

396 ibid; A Constant, et al., *International Handbook on the Economics of Migration* (Edward Elgar Publishing Limited, Cheltenham 2013), 143

397 D. Papademetriou, et al., 'Migration and economic downturn: What to expect in the European Union' (2009) Transatlantic Council on immigration, Migration Policy Institute

398 S. Longhi, et al., 'A meta-analytic assessment of the effect of immigration on wages' (2005) vol19(3) Journal of Economic Surveys 451

the maintenance of public services. Also, illegal migrants cannot claim welfare benefits, but still pay indirect taxes and sometimes even direct income tax in countries like the USA (less so in the UK). Such taxes help to boost the economic security of a country, which is an integral aspect of national security.

Although the concept of national security has expanded from military security to other aspects of security, like intelligence sharing, and regional security, a nation's military strength still constitutes an important aspect of national security. Foreigners play a prominent role in the provision of technical and intelligence expertise, for instance, in the analysis of and foreign language skills. In the pursuit of military ends, the role played by émigré scientists in the 1930s in the development of US nuclear programme exemplifies immigrants' positive impacts on national security. Nations also draw on the immigrant population when fighting wars. Private contractors are largely used in the US military force. For instance, in 2004 an estimate of 40,000 US non-citizens were recruited into the US military.[399]

Immigration has many appendages, such as border controls. Border control constitutes a major threat to national security. State borders have a direct relationship with immigration and national security. It encompasses ports and transportation networks such as surface, air and maritime networks. National borders occupy a delicate part of the nation. The United Kingdom Border Agency (UKBA's) slogan relates to this and constitutes an entry target for all sorts of security threats. Indisputably, border issues are security issues since legal and illegal entry and exit of human beings and commodities take place at the border. International terrorism requires support (human and financial). Most of the terrorists/criminals are financially sponsored through illicitly organised crimes that take place across borders such as drug, human and currency trafficking.[400] Border security has become indispensable to national security. Thus, mechanisms could be put in place to thwart illegal fundraising activities (like drug and illegal arms trafficking) for terrorists/criminals who transpire across state borders. Perpetrators continually invent new ways of circumventing

399 ibid; P. Ghosh, *Migrants Refugees and the stateless in South Asia* (Sage Publications India Pvt Ltd, New Delhi 2016), 128

400 B. Obama, 'Transnational organized crime: A growing threat to national and international security' (2011) National Security Council, <*www.whitehouse.org/.../eop/nsc/transnational-crime/threat*> accessed 20 December 2012

border security strategies to perpetrate their crimes, which, in turn, makes state borders a major security concern.

Research has shown that drug smugglers from Mexico through the United States border constantly exhibit a high level of creativity in inventing new means of smuggling drugs into the United States.[401] For instance, a carbon dioxide tank was used to power the cannon that propelled dozens of containers of marijuana into the US territory from Mexico.[402] In another example, eighty-five pounds of marijuana with an estimated value of $42,500 were tucked into soup cans and then inserted into larger sealed containers.[403] It becomes a huge problem for border patrol and national security strategists to figure out what the latest means of an organised crime would be. Such uncertainty is one of the things, which make border security a huge threat to national security. Hence, Linwood Estes, a Border Patrol Agent in Yuma, told ABC News that, "The more and more successful we are the more and more unique they become in trying to get the drugs across."[404]

The 'values' and 'culture' of a nation makes it distinct from other nations. Such variables play an important role in national security policies. For instance, the national security policies of a nation where the citizenry is predominantly Muslim will be radically different from that of a predominantly Christian nation, because of the diversities in their respective cultural and religious values. Hence, the migration of a multicultural population can constitute a threat to the traditional models of national security that adopt a unitary prototype of national identity from which a set of national interests can be obtained. The basis of a nation's security can be jeopardised if the nation loses grip of its sovereignty in certain areas. For instance, religious extremism can pose a threat to a country's national security where such religion is traditionally passive.[405]

---

401 T. Hom, 'Drug smugglers shoot drugs across borders with cannon' (2012) America Broadcasting Company Network abcnews.go.com/blotter/drug-smugglers-shoot-drugs-border-cannon/story?id... accessed 12 December 2012

402 ibid; P. Kan, *Drug Trafficking and International Security* (Rowman & Littlefield, Lanham 2016), 2

403 ibid; D. Snow, *National Security* (Routledge Taylor & Francis Group 2017), 351

404 ibid, T. Payan, *The Three US-Mexico Border Walls: Drugs, Immigration and Border Security* (2nd edn Praeger Security International, California 2016), 125

405 M. Lombardi, et al., *Countering Radicalisation And Violent Extremism Among Youths to Prevent Terrorism* (IOS Press Inc, Netherlands 2014), 1-2

4.4.1 SUMMARY

In summary, this sub-section has argued how in one sense, unregulated immigration constitutes a threat to national security, whilst showing that migration can enhance security in some ways. Even when nation states seek to deport some alien terrorist suspects, they are handicapped in some cases because of certain treaty obligations. Although contradictions thrive in the world of immigration, it can also play a vital role in a country's economic security, which is an integral aspect of national security. A nation's population size constitutes one of the main dimensions of its power. Thus, nations can exercise their national interests through their migration polices. The effectiveness of a country's population as the most paramount resource and an instrument of power is dependent on its mobilisation. It is a well-known fact that a country's social security system plays a significant role in the nation's economic stability, especially in times of crisis. Hence, the aging population in most of the industrialised countries needs the mobilisation of young workers for the maintenance of their social security system and adequate competition in the world market.[406]

Advocates of increased immigration enforcement claim that the entry of undocumented immigrants into the United States is a national security risk, irrespective of the fact that none of the 9/11 terrorists entered the United States uninspected. An efficacious border and immigration control is essential for the maintenance of national security. Hence, Senator John Cornyn states that "...in a post 9/11 world, border security is national security."[407] For instance, the 9/11 terrorists were alien nationals who exploited the US border and immigration policy to permeate the nation in order to execute their task.[408] The event of 9/11 has clearly shown that a nation cannot depend solely on the protection of its borders for its total protection and that of its citizenry; even though efficient border control helps to purge a nation of those who pose the utmost danger to national security. However, the fact that immigration has its downsides for a nation's

406 A. Fiona, 'Crossing borders: "International migration and national security"' (2006) vol 31(1) International security 165-199

407 K. Johnson, et al., *Immigration law and the US-Mexico border: Si se puede?* (University of Arizona Press, Arizona 2011), 217

408 C. Rudolph, *National security and immigration: Policy development in the United States and Western Europe since 1945* (Stanford University Press, California 2006), 2

security does not imply that its strong points should be ignored. For instance, California's economy would collapse if all illegal immigrants returned at once.[409]

The incident of 9/11 has shown that terrorism, to a large extent, is a global affair. Therefore, deportation of alien nationals who are perceived as threats to a country's national security may not be an efficient means of countering terrorism, because of the global network of terrorists. It is indisputable that a deportation order might disrupt an 'immediate threat'. However, there could be reinforcement by a terrorist group or organisation in the event of the deportation of a group member if the deportee truly is a terrorist; the reinforcement of which might comprise strategies 'unknown' by the contracting country. Robert Liken argues that "...terrorist organisations view immigration from a strategic perspective using all aspects of the immigration system to gain access to the target states."[410] Again, it is always better to deal with the proverbial devil, you know. Nations can restructure their immigration policies in such a manner that alien nationals who constitute danger to their national security can be prosecuted in the receiving country. If suspected terrorists are allowed to go to a country of their choice, they might migrate to another nation state within the same region to which there is an increased security risk beyond the national level.

4.5 THE EFFECT OF REGIONAL SECURITY ON NATIONAL SECURITY

Activities aiming to ensure "regional security" are imperative to national security, as one nation's national insecurity has the potential of transcending into another nation. Hence, transnational threats jeopardise the fibre of national security. For instance, one country's ineffective border control might constitute a security threat to another country, whereby weapons of mass destruction, drug traffickers, and terrorists/extremists have a smooth sailing into the neighbouring nation.[411] This illustrates the United States' national security interests in the Caribbean as its 'third border' to abridge the vulnerability likely to spring

409 A. Picchi, 'How would deporting undocumented workers affect the US economy?' (2016) *CBS News* <URL> accessed 19 May 2017

410 F. Adamson, op.cit

411 T. Paul, et al., *Globalization and National Security State* (Oxford University Press, New York 2010), 3

from terrorism, illegal immigration, drug and human trafficking, and the smuggling of contraband, chemical, biological, radiological and nuclear materials.[412] Impliedly, a nation's incapability to cater to its security needs might culminate in security challenges for another nation, especially where both countries are connected geographically. For example, the Caribbean's geographic location and construct comprise its most cherished assets. However, it heightens its vulnerability to illicit crimes such as international terrorism and drug trafficking. This constitute a major regional security threat, especially as the Caribbean states express incapacitation around technical and financial resources to combat such crimes with the severity they demand.[413]

This subsection investigates the question: Does regional security have implications on national security? It will refer to some regional organisations like the Shanghai Co-operation Organisation (SCO), the African Union, The North Atlantic Treaty Organisation (NATO) and the Arab League in the promotion of national security. National security cannot be independently achieved by a single nation irrespective of how efficient its national security strategies may appear. To a large extent, a nation cannot sensu stricto allege a stabilised national security where the regional state/s is/are insecure, as regional insecurity might transcend into it. Hence, a nation's security cannot be guaranteed suo moto. For instance, the vulnerability of the United States border is heightened as Mexico creates and maintains illicit corridors for border crossing, which opens up a route for other criminal and terrorist actors or organisations.[414] In such circumstance, can it be said that the United States is secure when its borders are still vulnerable, as a result of the illicit activities of its neighbours, despite the fact that there are some effective national security measures operational within the United States?

Some regional organisations have played positive roles in the promotion of national security. For example, the Shanghai Co-operation Organisation (SCO) is one of the regional organisations established in Central Asia to tackle the three evils prominent in the member states, namely: terrorism, extremism and

412 C. Ward, 'Regional threats: Security capacity imperatives in the Caribbean' (2010) (58) Joint Force Quarterly 27

413 ibid

414 B. Obama, 'Strategy to combat transnational organized crime' (2011) <*www.whitehouse.gov/.../eop/nsc/transnational-crime/threat*> accessed 5th December 2012

separatism. The SCO identifies terrorist organisations and assists in preventing terrorist attacks in the member states. For instance, in one of their regional anti-terrorist structure (RATS) meeting, 14 terrorist organisations were identified as direct threats to the security of member states.[415] The RATS regime was also commended for preventing about 250 terrorist attacks in member states since its inception. Despite the fact that they want to diversify their interests, anti-terrorism remains their primary focus.[416] The SCO also acts as a problem-solving body for both traditional and non-traditional security threats to member states. For instance, it acts as a coordinator in the resolution of disputes pertaining to key waterways and the damage to the Aral Sea, which is a vital regional fresh water source, from Soviet-era misuse.[417]

The African Union (AU) is one of the regional organisations that contribute to the enhancement of national security within the African continent. It established the Union's right to intervene in domestic affairs of member states in cases of war crimes, genocide and crimes against humanity. Such right extends to "serious threats to legitimate order".[418] Article 3(b) of the Constitutive Act of the AU provides that one of the objectives of the Union is to "defend the sovereignty, territorial integrity and independence of its member states."[419] By virtue of Article 4 of the Constitutive Act, the AU can intervene without the consent of the target state.[420] Impliedly, the AU intervenes to restore peace and security within member states and sets out to protect vulnerable populations.[421]

Even though the AU's Constitutive Act had some uncertainties, for instance, it had not yet defined "genocide", "crimes against humanity", or "war crimes",

415 M. Lanteigne, 'In Medias Res: The development of the Shanghai Co-operation Organization as a security community' (2006/2007) vol79(4) Pacific Affairs, University of British Columbia 618

416 ibid

417 ibid., 619

418 B. Moller, 'The African union as security actor: African solutions to African problems?' (2009) Working paper no.59 Regional and Global Axes of Conflict., Danish Institute of International Studies

419 T. Kwasi, et al., 'African union's new security agenda: Is Africa closer to a pax- pan Africana' (2005) vol 60(4) International Journal 937

420 ibid; J. Biswaro, *The Quest for Regional Integration in the Twenty First Century* (Mkuki Na Nyota Publishers, Salem 2012), 341

421 ibid; F. Viljoen, *International Human Rights Law in Africa* (Oxford University Press, Oxford 2012), 165

such Act stands as the first international treaty to establish a right to intervene in a member state for a humanitarian objective.[422] Thus, it can be argued that the AU in its quest to maintain peace and security in member states has people's security as one of its core objectives. Under the AU mandate, where populations of member states are at risk, it intervenes without the state's consent, which is a major national security breakthrough in view of people's security.[423] The AU and the sub-regional organisations have brought relative peace to countries such as Burundi, Sierra Leone, Liberia and Sudan.[424]

NATO is another organisation that acts as a machinery of peace and stability all over the world.[425] It is involved in peaceful settlement of disputes, multilateralism, democracy and human rights promotion in the international sphere.[426] For instance, NATO has assisted in enhancing the security of the Baltic States (Estonia, Latvia, and Lithuania). The quest for regional cooperation and hard security guaranteed by Western allies necessitated the Baltic States to integrate with NATO to satisfy their security concerns. To enhance the national security of the Baltic States, considering their history and geographical location, NATO assisted in shaping the militaries of such States from scratch.[427] The Baltic States lack the capacity to protect their airspace as they have no fighter jets of their own. Hence, NATO contributed to the Baltic air-policing mission, which protects the air space and territories of the Baltic countries; with other allied nations rotating in the mission. This is essential for the Baltic security.[428] The limitation of the Baltic States' armed forces, coupled with their strategic location, make their integration with NATO vital for their security.[429]

---

422 ibid

423 ibid

424 B. Moller, op.cit

425 G. Bush, *The national security strategy of the United States of America* (Morgan James Publishing, New York 2009); D. Bourantonis, et al, *The United Nations in the New World Order: The World Organisation at Fifty* (Macmillan Press Limited, London 2016), 1

426 A. Gheciu, 'Security institutions as agents of socialization? NATO and "The New Europe"' (2005) vol 59(4) International Organization 973

427 S. Shetty, et al., *The Baltic States, NATO and Non-strategic nuclear weapons in Europe* (Stephen Austin and Sons Ltd., United Kingdom 2012)

428 ibid; R. Lugar, et al., *Russia, its Neighbours and an Enlarging NATO: Report of an Independent Task* (Council on Foreign Relations Inc, New York 1997), 33

429 S. Shetty, et al., op cit

A detailed examination of the nexus between regional and national security shows that regional security has the tendency to enhance national security too. For instance, Colombia has succeeded significantly in the reduction of cocaine production and the frustration of illegal armed groups, such as the Revolutionary Armed Forces of Colombia (FARC) that sustain transnational crimes through United States' assistance.[430] National security and in effect international security could be fortified through regional security.[431] Columbia now exports law enforcement and justice sector capabilities, providing assistance and advice to police, prosecutors, protection programmes, judiciary, criminal law and procedure development. All these are a result of the United States' support to Colombian capacity building.[432]

Nevertheless, regional security is not devoid of inherent difficulties. There could be competing and divergent interests within the region. For instance, political tensions might exist amongst regional players who seek to demonstrate their position as the 'regional hegemon'. In effect, such tensions get to the organisational level where regional security decisions take place. For instance, the Arab League is an ethno-cultural regional organisation set up to promote independence and sovereignty of Arab countries, as the colonial powers considered the fate of the territories, they held at the end of World War II.[433] Unfortunately, for the past 65 years, the League has struggled, among other things, with competing loyalties and divergent interests among the Arab countries. This has affected the League's organisational structure, thereby hampering its function as a regional organisation.[434] What constitutes a "security threat" to one state might not receive the same level of attention from another nation state. For instance, it might be surprising to note that some nations within the Western Balkans do not perceive terrorism as an 'imminent danger'.[435] More so, even where there is an agreement regarding regional threats, the method of combating the threats

430 B. Obama, op.cit

431 N. Aloupi, 'The Right to Non-Intervention and Non-Interference' (2015) vol 4(3) Cambridge Journal of Comparative and International Law 566

432 B. Obama, op cit

433 D. Farah, 'The League of Arab States and regional security: Towards an Arab security Community?' (2012) vol 39(2) British Journal of Middle East Studies 1

434 ibid

435 D. Stancic, et al., 'Study on the assessment of regional security threats and challenges in the Western Balkans' (2007) Geneva Centre for the Democratic control of armed forces

might be totally different from the security strategy applied in a nation state, irrespective of the fact that the states are regionally situated.[436] Hence, security dialogue and cooperation is pertinent for the accomplishment of regional security, since more than one player is involved.

It is accepted that regional security can assist in fostering effective national and global security. On the other hand, it can amount to potential threat both to national and global security. For instance, if regional players incorporate themselves with anti-security agents so much so that they conspire to launch attacks on other regions or work against international security policies, it becomes a serious security threat to the world. While the advantage of regional security over national and global security is acknowledged, its side effects should not be taken for granted. More so, if regional security management becomes too self-reliant, it can also represent a potential threat to national security and to a large extent, international security.

Bahrain's Foreign Minister Shaikh Khalid bin Ahmed Al Khalifa reiterated in a major security forum in Manama that Iran is on a dangerous collision course with the region and there is an urgent need to stop her from developing the nuclear weapons.[437] Shaikh Khalid asserted:

> "Iran's decision to continue to pursue a nuclear programme with a lack of sufficient transparency is steering the region to a dangerous collision course, presenting a real and immediate hard challenge to national security."[438] "The threats are many here and the Iranians continue to issue statements threatening vital international trade routes and the sovereignty of the GCC states." [439]

436 K. Jacobsen, et al., 'East Africa: Regional Security organizations and dynamics' (2012) Danish Institute for International Studies

437 M. Singh, 'Tehran, a threat to security' (2012) The Voice of Bahrain: Gulf Daily News <URL> accessed 9 December 2012

438 ibid

439 ibid; S. Kim, et al., *North Korea And Nuclear Weapons: Entering the New Era of Deterrence* (Georgetown University Press, Washington D.C 2017), 3-4

Such outcry from Bahrain's minister cannot be ignored as its national security and those of other Gulf Cooperation Council (GCC) states and the world at large is being threatened, if Iran is not put under check.

In the case of ***Al-Skeini and Others v The United Kingdom,*** subsequent to the UNSC Resolution 1441, Iraq was given a final opportunity to comply with its disarmament obligations and set up an enhanced inspection regime. Iraq incessantly remained in breach of its obligations under previous UNSC Resolutions to disarm and cooperate with UN and International Atomic Energy Agency (IAEA) weapons inspectors. Hence, she was mandated to cooperate instantly, unconditionally and actively with the investigators.[440]

In the present case, although the applicants alleged, amongst other things, a violation of Article 2 of the ECHR, they did not contend the loss of lives of their relatives. Rather, they alleged that the death of their relatives took place within the jurisdiction of the United Kingdom irrespective of the fact that they were on Iraqi soil. However, the purport of such analysis is to analyse the implication of the coalition force (regional security) on Iraq's national security, regional and by implication international security. Iraq posed a threat not only to its national security, but also to regional and international security in a broad sense. The location of nuclear weapons in Iraq poses an unprecedented threat to peace and security. In an event of any explosion, be it accidental or organised, it's devastating effect will not be limited to Iraq alone; but might transcend into the region. On the other hand, Iraq can also use such weapons against other nations of the world outside its region. This has the potential of wiping out populations on a large scale. Iraq can also delve into clandestine business transactions to sell some of the weapons to terrorists in which case, the how, when and where of the use of such weapons will be unknown; which constitutes a greater threat to world security at large.

The presence of the coalition forces in Iraq in the present case illustrates the fact that regional security enhances national security. Apart from the inspection of Iraq for weapons of mass destruction, the coalition forces annihilated terrorist infrastructures and resources within and worked towards ensuring that terrorists and terrorists groups are denied safe heaven. They supported

440 Al-Skeini and Others v The United Kingdom (2011) ECHR 55721/07 Strasbourg para 9

and coordinated demining and related activities.[441] All these are geared towards securing Iraq, its region and the globe.

On the other hand, regional security in certain circumstances poses a threat to national security. It might not be disputed that people's security is at the core of national security. However, considering the issue of cultural dichotomy, regional security might put human security at a high risk. It is customary in Iraq to discharge gunshots at a funeral. This might be strange for the British soldiers, as one of the British commanders shot the first applicant's brother in self-defence; as alleged by him during a patrol where a funeral ceremony was going on and several gun shots were released.[442] Hence, in the present case some of the investigations into the death of the applicants' relative were impeded because of cultural differences. For example, according to the Muslim culture, a dead person is meant to be buried within 24 hours and the body be left undisturbed for 40 days.[443] Thus, in the case of the fifth applicant's son it was practically impossible to ascertain the cause of death, since the boy was buried according to the Muslim practice. Exhuming the boy's body after the 40-day mourning period also could not help the investigation. In view of human security, and in consonance with the procedural requirement of Article 2 of the ECHR, which stipulates the circumstances under which a person's life can be taken away under law, an 'independent investigation' becomes a vital element, whenever an unnatural death takes place, to ascertain whether it occurred within the purview of law.

Language is also a significant aspect of a nation's culture. What if in the present case some interpreters failed to interpret with accuracy, especially with reference to some facts fundamental to an investigation? It is accepted that the coalition forces helped to check terrorism, which is a security threat, but at the same time 'human insecurity' is also a security threat, which ought not to be overlooked. The circumstance under which some of the Iraqis were killed is such that can invoke violence amongst the Iraqi populace.

441 ibid

442 ibid., para 36

443 ibid., para 30

It may also be argued that it will amount to a security risk for a nation to establish or re-establish the security agency of another nation. For instance, in the present case one of the principal obligations of the coalition forces is to re-establish the security forces of Iraq.[444] The question that comes to mind is this: Will the re-established security forces be sustained after the transition period? If the answer is in the affirmative, how safe will a nation be, if its security agency is established or re-established by a coalition government? Impliedly, the coalition government will be seized of the nation's security 'operational tactics' or 'strategies', which ordinarily, no other nation should have the knowledge of, basically on national security grounds. This is a security threat in the sense of a security lacuna.

Analytically, regional security can lead to porosity of a nation's security. For instance, what if the intention of the coalition forces is not strictly security based? What if they also intended to take control of Iraq's natural resources, such as the Iraqi oil? In the present case, the coalition forces could gain access to Iraqi oil, natural gas or get them into an agreement that will make them economically vulnerable with regard to their natural resources. The natural resources of most nations constitute/s their major economic strength. Hence, when they are siphoned illegally or tampered with, it affects the nation's economy drastically, which is anti-security.

Regional insecurity can give birth to national insecurity. Transnational crime networks metamorphose into transnational gangs, which diffuse and ripen into national security threats. For example, there is an increased instability in Central America as it occupies a significant position in the convergence of threats where illegal trafficking in drugs, people, revenue and weapons flow. The opulence of some Central American States is threatened by the accompanying violence resulting from such regional crimes; the consequence of which will cost some Central American States about 8% of their gross domestic product as posited by World Bank.[445] The Balkans has also created an ideal atmosphere for the nurturing and growth of transnational organised crimes. The Balkan-based transnational organised crime groups control major drug and human trafficking routes

444 ibid., para 21

445 ibid; S. Castles, et al., *The Age of Migration: International Population Movements in the Modern World* (5th edn The Palgrave Macmillan, England 2014), 55

and Western European markets as well. The Balkan region provides a channel for Latin American cocaine, a source of synthetic drugs and a transit region for heroin chemical precursors for use in the Caucasus and Afghanistan.[446] It is imperative for this region to be purged of all such menaces; if not, the security of the nation states within the region will remain an illusion.

A region with weak governance is characterised by corrupt officials, who are indifferent to transnational crimes, might have an overpowering effect on the national security of other nation states. Often, transnational crimes are perpetrated through corrupt organised networks. When such networks infiltrate the political circle, their activities become a threat to national security. Other times, such networks stir up political opposition either regionally or nationally. They present themselves as substitute supporters of governance, security, services and livelihood. Transnational crime networks establish alliances with financial institutions, political leaders, law enforcement, and foreign intelligence and security agencies. Hence, stability is threatened. Transnational crimes like terrorism present an extensive challenge to national security and to world security at large. Transnational crimes enhance the diversification of anti-security activities with the implication of converging threats that were previously distinct and currently have explosive and destabilising consequences. The enhancement of the spread of governmental instability and the spawning of significant sums of illicit revenue through criminal control of territory and piracy ransom is exemplified in Somalia.[447]

The effect of regional security on national security could emanate into an 'ambiguous political relationship' if the recipient nation does not tread on the part of caution. For instance, if a nation state is solely dependent on a wealthier nation within its region for security, by implication the dependent state might be treading its path into colonisation, if the wealthier nation state gets politically ambitious. Colonisation in such respect might not necessarily mean 'physical takeover' of the political seat (power usurpation), but it implies the wealthier state having an upper hand in the recipient nation's policy decisions or the signing of some bilateral agreements between the states, which might not be

446 ibid; O. Pavliuk, et al., *The Black Sea Region: Cooperation and Security Building* (Routledge, New York 2016)

447 ibid; M. Shaw, Transnational Organised Crime in Africa: An Overview from Six Governments (Sage Publishers, Los Angeles 2013), 93-115

acceptable by the citizens of the recipient state. This can lead to political instability and public outcry, which stands out as a threat to national security. Hence, President Suharto of Indonesia states: "Military pacts have proven not to be an effective form of defence, as they will weaken our national resilience and identity."[448]

4.5.1 SUMMARY

In summary, the unprecedented effect of national insecurity in certain situations is such that it demands regional/global alliance. Poor economy, weak and corrupt government, as well as inadequate technological know-how pose a serious threat to the capacity of most nations to enhance their national security. By implication, such lacuna transcends into an atmosphere of world insecurity. Hence, George Bush asserted:

> "The events of September 11th, 2001 taught us that weak states, like Afghanistan, can pose as great a danger to our national interests as strong states. Poverty does not make poor people into terrorists and murderers. Yet, poverty, weak institutions, and corruption can make weak states vulnerable to terrorist networks and drug cartels within their borders." [449]

By implication, since such states are not able to secure their nation because of some inherent challenges like those aforementioned, regional cooperation can assist in breaking down vulnerabilities, which constitute threats to the nation, its region and the world at large.

No doubt regional security has a positive impact on national security; for example, Switzerland is very secure because of its position within the EU region. The essence of regional intervention is for the maintenance of national security of an unstable nation (security wise). The place of 'people's security' in national security is such that it cannot be ignored. However, for regional security to

448 S. Tang, et al., *Asia-Pacific Security Cooperation: National Interest And Regional Order* (2nd edn Taylor And Francis Group: London 2015), 75; R. Sukma, Indonesia and regional security: The quest for co-operation security (2002) Institute of Defence and Strategic Studies Singapore (IDSS) *www.propatria.or.id/loaddown/paper%20Diskusi/Indonesia..., accessed 3rd march 2016*

449 S. Rice, 'The new national security strategy: Focus on failed states' (2003) The Brookings Institution Policy Briefs Policy Brief No.116

enhance national security there should be sufficient background back up, such as a basic knowledge of the foreign culture. In the ***Al-Skeini's*** case, the way the British soldiers ended the lives of some Iraqi citizens, such as the first applicant's child, one will begin to doubt the real intention of the coalition with respect to the protection of the lives of the citizenry. Although in most of the cases, the applicants were compensated by the British command, life cannot be monetised. The fact that the British soldiers had authority and control over Iraq at the time does not exclude them from adhering to their obligation under the ECHR and other international agreements such as the International Human Rights Law to ensure the protection of the rights of the Iraqi civilians.

4.6 EFFECTS OF THE PRACTICE OF INTELLIGENCE SHARING ON NATIONAL SECURITY

Terrorism and organised crimes constitute a major challenge to the national security of democratic states. Thus, intelligence sharing enables nations to forecast information about terrorists, potential terrorists, terrorism and criminal actions precisely to strategise regarding the nation's security. The pieces of information from various sources are synthesised into systematic knowledge for the prevention of any act contrary to the stability of a nation's security. Such capability of unraveling and intercepting terrorists' schemes or other violent activities puts intelligence sharing on a high scale in national security strategies. However, some policy makers have argued that national security intelligence is distinct from law enforcement intelligence. The crux of the matter is that both forms of intelligence are geared towards the nation's security through 'strategic information'.[450]

It must be noted that raw information cannot be regarded as intelligence until it is organised, analysed and interpreted with regard to a target.[451] Effective intelligence sharing has the potential of producing analytic policing techniques.[452]

450 S. Loyka, et al., 'Protecting your community from terrorism: The strategies for local law enforcement series' (2005) vol. 4 Police Executive Research Forum, US Department of Justice office of community oriented policing services 12

451 ibid; D. Evans, *Not an Ordinary Life* (Coogee Creations LLC, Florida 2014)

452 ibid; R. Watson, *White House Studies Compendium, Volume 4* (Nova Science Publishers Inc, New York 2007), 83

Hence, intelligence can serve as an instrument for making effective national security decisions. Therefore, threats in an environment can constitute the theme of executive policy consideration. This equates to a situation where a corporation seeks to maintain or increase its market share by collecting information on market fluctuations, consumer trends and their fluctuations.[453] By implication, its expectation is achieved through informed decision-making. Practically, a national security policy made based on the intelligence on the ground has a high level of success if properly implemented since it sets out to target a specific security threat. In view of national security, intelligence sharing could be said to be diagnostic (investigative) in nature, leading to the administration of the appropriate security response.

This subsection will address the question: 'Does intelligence sharing have any implication on the national security interest of a country?' The former Assistant Director of the Central Intelligence Agency Mark Lowenthal has defined intelligence as follows:

> "Intelligence is the process by which specific types of information important to national security are requested, collected, analysed, and provided to policymakers; the products of that process; the safeguarding of these processes and this information by counterintelligence activities; and the carrying out of operations as requested by lawful authorities."[454]

One of the security strategies applied by states for the collation and dissemination of information is intelligence sharing. The main effect of intelligence sharing is for states to obtain such information, which is crucial to their national security interest. Even if no security information was received during an interception, the 'awareness' of the public regarding a possibility of interception of communication network is a security issue. Intelligence sharing often goes beyond a nation to connect other nations of the world. Such network becomes paramount in the war against terrorism as the world has become a global village. By implication, states must, of necessity, connect with each other since a

453 S. Loyka, et al., op cit

454 D. Carabin, 'An Intelligence sharing continuum: Next generation requirements for U.S counter-terrorism efforts' (2011) <oai.dtic.mil/oai/oai?verb=getRecord&metadataPrefix=html...> accessed 5 September 2012

merely internally generated intelligence base might not be sufficient to respond to its security needs. Hence, while discussing terrorism a commentator stated:

> " .... Therefore, for an individual state to make a meaningful assessment of its security situation it needs to process information pertaining to individuals and events existing in far-off places at any given time. No single state has the power to collect and exploit this type and volume of information..."[455]

Additionally, the challenge of 'home-grown' terrorists has also made intelligence sharing imperative to national security. Most such 'home-grown' terrorists are groomed in some violent Islamic ideologies, which have the potency of destabilising the security of a nation. The intentions, strategies and tactics applied by terrorists make intelligence sharing imperative for the enhancement of a nation's security. Intelligence sharing assists governments in monitoring and preventing the activities of such 'home-grown' terrorists in favour of national security.[456]

Through intelligence sharing, member states exchange operational information with respect to actions or movements of terrorist organisations, persons or networks. In effect, this promotes national security. It will be obviously impossible for states to have information (particularly of terrorism related activities) around the world without networking with each other, since no single nation is omniscient. Hence, in ***Chahal v United Kingdom,*** a deportation order was made against the applicant because his continued presence in the United Kingdom is unconducive to public good (national security) and other political grounds such as the international fight against terrorism. The applicant was perceived as a 'threat' to United Kingdom's national security.[457] The intelligence received about him, amongst other things, showed that the applicant had been the principal figure directing the support for terrorism organised by the London wing of Sikhs, which is closely connected to the Sikh terrorists in Punjab, his involvement in the provision of funds and equipment to terrorists in Punjab

455 C. Forcese, 'The collateral casualties of collaboration: The consequence for civil and human rights of transnational intelligence sharing' (2008) <*www.http://ssm.com/abstract=1354022*> accessed 27 August 2012

456 ibid

457 Chahal v The United Kingdom (1996) ECHR 22414/93 Strasbourg

since 1985 and his involvement in planning and financing terrorist attacks in India, United Kingdom and elsewhere. He contended such allegations by denying any involvement in funding and supporting terrorism. However, the intelligence report about him declared him a 'security risk' in the United Kingdom. Through intelligence sharing, the UK had information about the applicant's alliance and support to terrorism. Hence, one of the conduits through which security gaps could be filled not only in a nation, but the world at large, is intelligence sharing.[458]

Often the person alleged to constitute a threat to national security based on the intelligence report on him does not have knowledge of the allegations against him, or the source of the evidence against him. This might sound undemocratic, but the complexities involved in terrorist attacks and organised crimes demand some level of clandestine approach. By implication, the United Kingdom's intelligence agents collected, analysed and shared intelligence on the activities of the applicant to conclude that he posed a 'threat' to public good. Even if the analysis of the intelligence on the applicant's activities is inaccurate, a consciousness is created in the minds of the terrorists and their organisations that they might be under secret surveillance by intelligence agencies known or unknown to them. This will also contribute to the enhancement of national security, although some terrorists in the pursuit of their religious and political objectives accept to sacrifice their lives in the process, if need be.[459]

Intelligence sharing serves as a check on the perpetrators of terrorism. Although such sharing has been used by nations since time immemorial, the 9/11 incident gave it a renewed spark. Information and communication are crucial for the success of any business or act (including terrorist attacks). The advancement of information technology in recent times makes the transmission of all kinds of information possible within split seconds. Therefore, through electronic (telephone, email, facsimile) interception of certain communication in transit, a nation might obtain important information, or clues concerning an 'impending' or a 'remote' attack. The citizenry, are in turn, awake to the fact that their

458 ibid; A. Neal, *Security in a Small Nation: Scotland, Democracy, Politics* (Open Book Publishers, Cambridge 2017), 149

459 D. Carabin, op.cit; M. Grozdanova, *What Motivates Suicide Terrorism?* (Grin Publishing, Germany 2016), 3

communication can be intercepted. Such consciousness serves as a check not only on the perpetrators of terrorism, but also on society at large.

Hence, in the case of ***Liberty & Others v The United Kingdom,*** the applicants alleged before the Investigatory Powers Tribunal that UK's security and intelligence agencies intercepted their email, telephone, facsimile and data communications, including privileged and confidential information, which violated their right under Article 8(1) of the ECHR.[460] The applicant alleged that the procedure for the use and retention of intercepted materials as stipulated under s.6 (1) (2) of the Interception of Communications Act of 1985 (the 1985 Act) did not include an arrangement that gave the public, or individuals, access to ascertain whether the procedure stipulated therein was followed. They asserted that the Tribunal also lacked the jurisdiction to investigate compliance with such procedures. More so, even though the Commissioner was empowered under s.8 of the 1985 Act to review the procedures, he lacked the power to review whether they had been met in individual cases. They also submitted that it would not compromise national security to describe the arrangements in place for 'filtering' and 'disseminating' intercepted material, and that detailed information about similar systems had been published by several other democratic countries, such as the US, Australia, New Zealand, Canada and Germany. Additionally, the applicants argued that the interception of their communication failed to pursue a legitimate aim.[461]

The government replied by contending that if the applicants' communication was intercepted during the period stated by them, then it was done in accordance with the requirements of s.3 (2) of the 1985 Act. It submitted that gathering of intelligence enables governments to take preventive action to safeguard national security, as well as the lives and well-being of its citizens, the failure of which amounts to a dereliction of governmental duties towards citizens.[462] Hence, the provisions of s.3 (2) of the 1985 Act were both proportionate and 'necessary in a democratic society'. According to the Government, a degree of secrecy is pertinent with the method of interception effected.[463]

460 Liberty v The United Kingdom (2008) ECHR 58243/00 Strasbourg

461 ibid

462 Ibid; M. *Lowenthal, Intelligence from Secrets to Policy* (7th edn Congressional Quarterly Inc, 2016), 1

463 ibid

In response to such arguments, the Court held that there was a violation of the applicants' rights under article 8 of the ECHR. It concluded that the domestic law at the relevant time lacked clarity in some aspects of interception of communication. For instance, it failed to provide the public with the accessibility of the procedure to be followed for the selection, examination, sharing, storing and destruction of intercepted material. Hence, the interference with the applicants' rights under Article 8 of the ECHR was not in accordance with law.[464]

Arguably, in view of the provisions of Article 8(1) of the ECHR, which states that, "Everyone has the right to respect for his private and family life, his home and his correspondence", it is an indisputable fact that the applicants have the right to their private life and correspondence as stipulated under article 8(1) of the ECHR. It is also recognised that an 'intentional' interception of communication during its transmission by post, or through a public telecommunication system, is an offence by virtue of s.1 of the 1985 Act. However, s.3(2) of the 1985 Act empowers the Secretary of State to issue a warrant for the interception of communication, whenever he deems it necessary in the interest of national security, for preventing or detecting serious crimes, and for safeguarding the economic well-being of the United Kingdom.[465] It is accepted that the applicants' right to privacy was infringed upon at the relevant time through the interception of their communication. However, such right is not absolute. Article 8(2) of the ECHR states:

> "There shall be no interference by a public authority with the exercise of this right except such as is in accordance with the law and is necessary in a democratic society in the interests of national security..." [466]

By virtue of Article 8(2) of the ECHR, the right under (1) could be derogated from in the interest of national security in a democratic society. By implication, there must have been a security alert that warranted the interruption. However, the

464 ibid; H. Cremer, *Human Rights and the Protection of Privacy in Tort Law* (Routledge-Cavendish, New York 2010), 71

465 ibid; H. Fenwick, *Civil Liberties and Human Rights* (Cavendish Publishing Limited, London 2002), 540-542

466 ibid; M. Colvin, *Developing Key Privacy Rights* (Hart Publishing, Portland 2002), 37

applicants need not know about the security alert if there was one, because it will undermine the essence of intelligence.[467]

Secrecy is one of the vital elements of intelligence sharing. If the procedures involved in the interception of communication are made available to the public, especially in relation to the examination, sharing and storage of intercepted communication, the effect of such interception could be undermined. For instance, if the procedure involved in the examination of an intercepted communication is made public, terrorists have the potential of being able to circumvent such procedure in their subsequent plots, which maintains porosity in national security.[468] Impliedly, national security will be compromised if the public has access to interception procedures such as 'filtering' and 'dissemination' of intercepted materials. Hence, the fact that a procedure worked out successfully in a nation is not a condition precedent that it will be successful in another nation, because of the diversities in the national security interests of nations.

In the present case, although the Court held that the applicants' rights under Article 8(1) of the ECHR were violated, the applicants' awareness of the interception of their communication or a 'possibility' of interception has the potential to deter them from carrying out a plan contrary to the national security of the United Kingdom. Hence, intelligence sharing can serve as a deterrent to anti-security activities.

The implication of an effective intelligence sharing on national and international security cannot be underestimated. The absence of 'proactive' intelligence can cause loss of innocent lives, destruction of property, confusion, suspicion of trust among allies and the disruption of political affairs in general. All these are security issues. For instance, the anti-American attack that broke out on Tuesday 9/11, 2012 was after a TV network broadcast of a short film titled 'Innocence of Muslims'. The ABC News network reported that the US government officials were aware of the 'inflammatory' content of the film, but there was no

467 ibid, H. Born, et al, *Democratic Control of Intelligence Services: Containing Rogue Elephants* (Ashgate Publishing Company, England 2016), 257

468 ibid; C. Bjola, et al., *Secret Diplomacy, Concepts, Contexts* (Taylor and Francis, London 2016), 130

intelligence alert of a possibility of violent attacks on US diplomatic missions in the Islamic world.[469]

Paul Pillar, a top US former intelligence analyst for the Middle East and South Asia, argues as follows:

> "The number of potentially inflammatory things that are said or broadcast every week (is so large) ... that warning about all of them would be useless," "It was "impossible to predict" the kind of violent reaction that occurred in Libya, Egypt and elsewhere.[470]

Analytically, the advent of globalisation makes intelligence sharing a prerequisite for both national and international security. Intelligence is 'diagnostic' (investigative) and 'pre-emptive' in nature. There could have been an intelligence alert on the likelihood of an outbreak of violence after the broadcast on the Al-Nas TV network, considering the tenacity with which some religious extremists react whenever they consider any issue 'critical' of their religion is raised. Such security threat rapidly spread through half a dozen nations of the Middle East within few hours. In the fight against terrorism, no intelligence alert is a waste of time. If a single life is saved because of an alert or even if the intelligence is not apt, such 'intelligence' is worthwhile. The intelligence cannot be taken for granted considering the consequence/s of violent attacks. For instance, the Benghazi, Libya, 9/11, 2012 violent attack, claimed the lives of four Americans on a diplomatic mission (the US Ambassador to Libya inclusive).[471]

4.6.1 SUMMARY

In summary, the importance of intelligence sharing cannot be underestimated in the fight against terrorism. The knowledge of a 'threat' ignites a necessary response. Hence, intelligence sharing is one of the security schemes that reveals

469 M. Hosenball, 'US intelligence agencies didn't issue high alert about Mideast unrest threat' *American Broadcasting Corporation News Network* (2012) Copyright Thompson Reuters <URL> accessed 14 September 2012

470 ibid

471 F. Burton, et al., *Under Fire: The Untold Story of the Attack in Benghazi* (1st edn St Martin's Press, New York 2013), 5; E. Murdock, *Obama Won but Romney Was President: How the Democrats Targeted Electoral College Votes to Win the 2012 President Election* (H.O.T Press, 2012), 219

'when', 'where' and 'how' a terrorist attack or an organised crime will take place or is likely to take place.[472] It also helps to document a threat, determines its likelihood of happening, and ascertains a course of action in response. One of the United States' most critical tools for counterterrorism is the use of intelligence operations: "to detect terrorist activity before it manifests itself in an attack so that proper pre-emptive, preventive, and protective action can be taken."[473] Additionally, time is of essence in intelligence sharing. Hence, effective intelligence sharing demands that analysis and evaluation of intelligence be done in a timely manner for prevention of any threat to security, no matter how insignificant such threat might appear.

Traditionally, intelligence sharing was geared towards the identification and neutralisation of 'external' threats posed by extraterritorial powers, organisations, or transnational actors such as terrorists. However, the current trend of terrorist attacks reveals that an ideal intelligence central point ought not to be 'external' alone; as experience has shown that there could be some 'home-grown' security threats ("enemies within"). In effect, intelligence sharing avails nations the opportunity for the usurpation and prognosis of terrorist activities, which transcends not just 'beyond' their territorial sovereignty, but also 'within' their territorial sovereignty. Hence, an effective and efficient intelligence sharing focused upon gathering, analysing and disseminating intelligence, generated both externally and internally, is the heartbeat of national security.

It must be noted that protection of the source/s and methods of intelligence is also a security issue. Accordingly, 'secrecy' is an inherent aspect of intelligence sharing. Thus, it can be argued that it is not undemocratic not to disclose certain aspects of the 'intelligence' to an applicant, as well as some procedures of intelligence sharing, provided they could protect the security interest of a democratic state against its subversion by anti-democratic forces. On the other hand, an individual is entitled to his right to a fair trial by virtue of Article 6 of the ECHR in a democratic society. Hence, secret intelligence sharing can raise human rights issues in court cases such as deportation cases and possibilities of judicial oversight.

---

472 M. Hosenball, op cit; W. Bloss, *Under a Watchful Eye: Privacy Rights and Criminal Justice* (ABC-CLIO-LLC Press, California 2009), 161

473 J. Samaha, *Criminal Procedure* (10th edn Cengage Learning, Boston 2016), 621; D. Carabin, op.cit

4.7 CONCLUSION

It will be insufficient for this book to identify different aspects and definitions of national security without identifying and analysing practical and policy implications on national security of some of the aspects identified. As there are different aspects and meanings of national security, there are also different threats to national security and a clear and express understanding of the scope and meaning of national security may enable us to better decipher the implications of such various meanings on national security. The effect of which is to strategise regarding how to fight against such threats, either by formulating new security policies or by improving and implementing existing ones. The effective implementation of such aspects of national security meets the essential human need 'to feel secure from threat'.

This chapter set out to investigate the implications of the different aspects of national security identified in this book on the security of a nation. It did this through the evaluation of applicable ECHR case laws for the development of critical analysis of practical implications of the identified aspects of national security on the practice of national security. It analysed the facts of the cases, arguments of parties and court decisions. Thus, it finds that there is a nexus between the aspects identified and national security and such aspects affect national security, either directly or indirectly. For instance, effective counterterrorism measures are needed in the fight against terrorism. However, the implementation of such measures outside the nations where they are formulated might constitute a great challenge since some nations see themselves as a 'low terrorist target' and therefore have different security interests. Analytically, terrorist attacks are uncertain in nature with catastrophic consequences. It is imperative that respect for 'rule of law' and the protection of human rights as enshrined under some treaty obligations such as the ECHR should be borne in mind when formulating counterterrorism measures. Hence, the fight against terrorism is not a fight against humanity and government agents are not above the 'law'. International terrorism is a global issue and therefore requires a global response, as some of the 'low terrorist target' nations could be used by terrorists and their organisations as haven.

However, in the fight against terrorism, the protection of the lives and property of individuals in a nation occupies a significant place in the security of a nation. All security issues revolve around humanity. Therefore, people's security should be a prerogative of the government. Often the protection of individual's lives, and property takes back stage in policy issues, irrespective of International Conventions, Human Rights Laws and domestic laws. This is illustrated in the way and manner government agencies take the lives of individuals in the exercise of their duties as illustrated above, which contradicts the provisions of some International Conventions such as Article 2 of the ECHR. National security will be vague in the absence of people's security. Lack of confidence in the government by the citizenry is sufficient to ignite 'organised violence' in a nation. Therefore, peoples' security plays a complementary role in national security. It remains a misnomer for governments to disparage people's security in pursuit of national security. A 'reassured' population is an 'assured' nation.

Immigration and border control are also major elements of national security. To enhance a nation's security, the passage (entry) of human beings and commodities must be under scrutiny, irrespective of the fact that there are domestic security threats, such as home-grown terrorists. Such 'enemies within' sometimes need external support like financial support; often generated through illicit crimes across national borders.[474] Hence, the hard core is mainly on immigration and border security.

Arguably, without regional security there can be no national security. Such argument stems from the fact that security in the simplest sense connotes 'freedom from fear'. Therefore, if a nation is relatively peaceful, but its region is prone to violence, such nation is invariably insecure, because there could be a proliferation of violence or crime from the region. Transnational organised crimes are on the rise and uncertainty surrounding international terrorism is such that it warrants regional cooperation. It is accepted that regional security has its challenges but, all the same, it plays a significant role in enhancing national security where there is a clear-cut understanding of the security threat to be handled. International terrorism poses a serious challenge to world security and most nations of the world cannot face such challenge mainly because of their financial incapacity and lack of high technology. Regional security sets in to augment national security in this fight against terrorism.

474 B. Obama, op.cit

Contradictorily, regional security in some cases can also constitute a threat to other aspects of national security like people's security. Thus, any regional/international cooperation must consider the peculiar circumstance or nature of the nation they seek to support security-wise before any interference. For instance, there must be an understanding of some vital aspects of the culture and tradition of the recipient nation; like the Muslim tradition that requires a dead person to be buried within 24 hours of his death, with the body to be left undisturbed for 40 days. This will obviously impede independent investigation into the cause of death, where such death is caused by an act or omission of a soldier from a coalition force; as was seen in the case of ***Al-Skeini and Others v The United Kingdom.***[475]

It might be safe to say that without effectual vertical and horizontal information on threats and other security issues, there may not be effective security in a nation. Intelligence sharing connotes the decoding of security threats within, around and outside territorial boundaries. The absence of this makes a nation vulnerable to avoidable attacks or insecurities. In all, time is of essence in intelligence sharing.

Therefore, a nation's security will be enhanced if all the aspects of national security analysed in this chapter are pragmatically put in place. The issue of security is one of the essential needs of mankind. If citizens of a nation state feel that they are free from threat, by implication such nation will be considered relatively safe. Different aspects of national security discussed in this chapter can be grouped into 2 headings. Such aspects of national security have practical implication on a nation's territorial integrity (immigration, intelligence sharing and regional security) and the security of individuals in a nation state especially with respect to the protection of their lives and property. Such implications can only be practicable in a 'democratic society'. These findings will promote policy decisions and counterterrorism proposals.

By examining the implications of the various aspects of national security identified in this book on the practice of national security, the stage is now set for the next chapter to investigate the possibility of creating a viable balance between the competing interests in the fight against terrorism. This might

475 Al-Skeini and others v The United Kingdom., op.cit

assist in avoiding the difficulties associated with counterterrorism. Through the assessment of the practice and implementation of counterterrorism measures of nation states, questions on their suitability and practicality can be resolved. Hence, such assessment allows for theoretical and practical reforms.

CHAPTER 5

AN EVALUATION OF THE POSSIBILITY OF STRIKING A "VIABLE BALANCE" BETWEEN NATIONAL SECURITY IMPERATIVES AND THOSE COUNTERVAILING HUMAN RIGHTS PROTECTIONS THAT ARE DEEMED "NECESSARY IN A DEMOCRATIC SOCIETY".

5.1 INTRODUCTION

The previous chapter elucidated the implications of various aspects, meaning and scope of 'national security' on the practice of the national security of a nation. Hence, it conceptualised national security as an ideal, vis-à-vis a concept that interlinked a certain understanding of security with that of a nation. The analysis of such conception reveals the possibility of acute violations of certain understandings of "human rights" in the course of countering terrorism for the enhancement of national security. The examination of some ECHR violations analysed in the previous chapter raises the question whether national security issues tend to take precedence over "human rights" concerns, especially since the 9/11 attack. However, it is the government's imperative to protect the state and uphold the legal rights of individuals within its territorial sovereignty, and to prevent the subversion of constitutional governance, particularly by means of politically-motivated violence and intimidation. The fact that protection of human rights can be considered a constituent aspect of national security as espoused in the third chapter of this book makes the task of balancing such role during security practices a challenge for the government. There are clearly pitfalls of both overplaying and underplaying the importance of national security, and of giving an excessive and overly narrow role to "human rights" concerns.

Realistically, it can be argued that anti-terrorism measures must infringe on human rights to some extent.[476] This is because of the current type of terrorism such as the 9/11 attack. Hence, this chapter will review the possible violation of

476 J. Piazza, et al., 'Transnational terror and human rights' (2009) vol 53(1) International Studies Quarterly 127

some fundamental human rights as provided under the ECHR that has commonly taken place in the bid to counter terrorism. It actively seeks the possibility of striking a viable balance between promotion of national security on one hand, including those forms that are essential to the practice of democratic self-governance, and protection of "human rights" in the fight against terrorism on the other. Hence, it sets out to answer the question: 'Must the protection of human rights always 'trump' the protection of national security or vice-versa in what may appear to be a zero-sum game in which there can never be any win-win outcomes, but only an almost mechanical trade-off between two apparently incompatible alternative options?'

National security and human rights ought not to be in stark conflict, not least because aspects of the latter are presupposed by the former, including a stable democratic, political and independent legal system free from corruption and intimidation. Ideally, national security policies must not entirely undermine, but rather support aspects of human rights. The protection of human rights does not necessarily have to undermine national security. It can be argued that national security and human rights reinforce each other since a threat to national security of a broadly democratic regime by a terrorist group seeking to impose a theocratic regime by violence, is, to an extent, also a threat to human rights. The concerted and militant institutional defence of democracy against undemocratic practices and aspirations of a terrorist group is also the defence of institutional preconditions for the enforcement and recognition of human rights.

On the other hand, some scholars are of the view that national security takes pre-eminence over the protection of human rights. They discountenance the watering down of governmental anti-terrorism strategies by the judiciary in the name of individual freedoms and liberties as understood by liberalism. They contend that courts lean too heavily on human rights without due contemplation of the severity of imminent terrorist threats on nations.[477]

Post 9/11, most nation states enacted or expanded existing counterterrorism legislation to meet the challenges posed by terrorism. Some such counterterrorism laws are so extensive that they negate some basic legal principles, such as, the right to freedom of expression and association, and the right not to

477 E. Owen, 'State security vs. human rights: Finding a proportionate balance', (2010) <www.e-ir.info/2010/08/28/state-security-v-human-rights> accessed 2nd January 2013

be detained except after a fair trial.[478] For example, Section 1 of the Terrorism Act 2006, which criminalises statements likely to be understood as encouraging terrorism,[479] and Part 4 of the Anti-terrorism, Crime and Security Act 2001 (ATCSA), which empowered the government to indefinitely detain non-citizens suspected of being "international terrorists".[480] Indeed, they have departed from liberal conceptions of the 'rule of law' and also from those broadly liberal conceptions of human rights that to some extent at least, underlie western liberal democracies. The Canadian and Australian Attorney Generals advocate reconceptualisation of counterterrorism legislations to reconcile national security and human rights.[481] However, the challenge between enhancement of national security and human rights protection is not confined to semantics or reconceptualisation of ideas. Rather, it extends to the question of evaluating issues of national security and issues of human rights to ascertain whether a proportionate balance could be created without the core imperatives of each being jeopardised in a democratic society.[482]

Most nations of the world responded to both domestic and international obligations post 9/11 incident. For example, pursuant to Resolution 1373 of the United Nations Security Council of September 28, 2001, states were required to 'take necessary steps to prevent the commission of terrorist acts'. Hence, nations of the world hastened to legislate. For instance, the United States enacted the USA Patriot Act of 2001; the United Kingdom enacted the ATCSA of 2001, New Zealand enacted the Terrorism Suppression Act 2002 and Australia enacted a variety of measures galvanised into several Acts.[483] The enactment of some such measures appeared to plunge human rights protection into a dilemma. In attempting to strike a viable balance between national security imperatives and

478 G. William, et al., 'Balancing national security and human rights: Assessing the legal response of common law nations to the threat of terrorism' (2006) vol 8(1) Journal of Comparative Political Analysis 43

479 S. Ekaratne, 'Redundant restriction: The UK's offence of glorifying terrorism' (2010) vol 23 Harvard Human Rights Journal 205

480 Antiterrorism, Crime and Security Act 2001

481 G. Williams, op. cit.

482 ibid; M. Goodhart, et al., *Human Rights in the 21st Century: Continuity and Change Since 9/11* (Palgrave Macmillan, New York 2011), Ch.9

483 ibid; A. Bandarage, *The Separatist Conflict in Sri Lanka: Terrorism, Ethnicity, Political Economy* (Routledge Taylor & Francis Group, New York 2009), 9

human rights protection, this chapter will evaluate some of the ECHR rights that are commonly violated in the fight against terrorism. Conceivably, it will be beyond the ambit of this chapter to evaluate all the rights enshrined in domestic legislations and international Conventions that could possibly be affected by anti-terrorism measures.

5.2 UNLAWFUL DETENTION AND COUNTERTERRORISM

Arguably, the liberal doctrine of the rule of law has been undermined by the "war on terror" initiated by the US, post 9/11. Thus, sovereign states formulate counterterrorism measures that disregard the rule of law principles. Hence, this has posed substantial challenges for the protection of human rights all over the world.[484] Some such challenges include subjecting people who have not been charged with, or convicted of, any criminal offence to unlawful detention where they have been tortured, abducted or even detained indefinitely.[485] With the collaboration, complicity and acquiescence of the US and other governments, extraordinary rendition is practised. Extraordinary rendition is defined as transfers of suspects from one state to another, which may sometimes take place "extra judicially", i.e. outside the law.[486] This has been employed in the "fight against terrorism", whereby prisoners and terrorist suspects are transferred for interrogation or detention to countries recognised for torture. The purpose of such rendition is to gather evidence by any means whatsoever and exclude detainees from judicial oversight.[487] Such system of clandestine prison, referred to as 'black sites' or secret detention centres, are located in Afghanistan, Guantanamo Bay, Cuba, Iraq, Jordan, Pakistan, Thailand, and Uzbekistan.[488] Hence, unlawful detention could be seen as deprivation of personal liberty characterised by violation of indispensable defence rights, such as access to judicial review and

484 M. Sharma, 'How not to fight terrorism' (2009) vol 44(5) Economic and Political Weekly 10

485 ibid; M. O'Boyle, 'Emergency government and derogation under the ECHR' (2016) Law Society of England and Wales 4

486 M. Barnett, 'Extraordinary rendition: International law and the prohibition of torture' (2008) Law and Government Division Parliament of Canada 1

487 M. Sharma, op. cit.

488 ibid

professional legal advice—in short, a detention that places the detained person *de facto outside* the jurisdiction of the law.[489]

Some nation states, like the USA, have incorporated preventive detention in their counterterrorism policies.[490]Preventive detention is the confinement of a person in a secure facility without a criminal charge to prevent a future criminal or wartime harm.[491]Essentially, unlawful detention such as 'preventive detention' has been widely criticised. Thus, some renowned political individuals, military figures and distinguished journalists contend that Guantanamo Bay detention centre is a 'recruiting tool' for Al-Qaeda.[492] Hence a terrorist expert, R. P. Eddy recognised that President Barak Obama's announcement to close Guantanamo deterred Al-Qaeda's ability to recruit. This is validated by Ayman al-Zawahri's confused, racially-streaked attack on the Obama administration.[493] Mathew Alexandra—the pseudonym of the Air Force Major heard directly from freedom fighters and Sunni Iraqis that Guantanamo was their main motivation to join Al-Qaeda.[494] Preventive detention advocates contend that Guantanamo represents abuse of Muslim prisoners, consequently instigating Al-Qaeda's terrorist recruitment in localities that identify with the victims.[495] Critics of preventive detention also delegitimise detention facilities like Guantanamo by portraying them as 'cage prisons'.[496] Based on photos of cages used in the Guantanamo detention facility, human rights activists have also described the facility as an 'inhumane' place to detain people.[497]

489 F. Geyer, 'Fruit of the poisonous tree: Member states' indirect use of extraordinary rendition and the EU counterterrorism strategy' (2007) Centre for European Policy Studies Working Document No.263

490 G. McNeal, 'The status quo bias and counterterrorism detention' (2011) vol 101 (3) The Journal of Criminal Law and Criminology 862

491 H. Ludsin, *Preventive detention and the democratic state* (Cambridge University Press, India 2016), 33

492 G. McNeal, op cit

493 ibid

494 ibid; G. McNeal, The Status Bias and Counterterrorism Detention (2011) vol 101(3) Journal of Criminal Law and Criminology 862

495 ibid; G. Cornelisse, *Immigration Detention and Human Rights: Rethinking Territorial Sovereignty* (Marinus Nijhoff Publishers, Leiden 2010), Ch.1

496 ibid; G. Fuller, *The Telegraph History of The World: An Anthology of The Telegraphs Finest Reporting* (Aurum Press, London 2015), Ch 4

497 Ibid; D. Rose, *Guantanamo: The War on Human Rights* (New Press, New York 2006), 160

This subsection sets out to address the question: 'To what extent is the practice of unlawful detention acceptable in a democratic society in the context of the fight against terrorism?'

It is admitted that not all rights stipulated in binding international Conventions or domestic laws are absolute. Hence, state parties are entitled to derogate from specific rights contained in the Conventions they have agreed to be bound by, in times of "emergency" threatening the nation's life, or during wartime. However, the lawfulness of derogation is generally predicated upon the fulfilment of other several legal requirements.[498] Hence, Article 5(1-5) of the ECHR provides that everyone has the right to liberty and security. Such right is subject only to lawful arrest or detention, under certain circumstances, such as arrest on reasonable suspicion of a crime or imprisonment in fulfilment of a sentence. The article also provides the right to be informed in a language one understands, of the reasons for the arrest and any charge against them, the right of prompt access to judicial proceedings to determine the legality of one's arrest, detention to a trial within a reasonable time, or release pending trial, and the right to compensation in the case of arrest or detention in violation of this article.[499]

For example, in ***El-Masri v The Former Yugoslav Republic of Macedonia***, a suspicion arose over the authenticity of the applicant's newly issued German passport.[500] He was detained in a hotel for 23 days in Macedonia by armed men in civilian clothes. They interrogated him throughout the detention in English language, despite his inadequate ability in the language.[501] The applicant commenced a ten-day hunger strike in protest of his unlawful detention,[502] before he was handed over to a Central Intelligence Agency (CIA) rendition team at Skopje airport, handcuffed and blindfolded.[503] According to the applicant, his pre-flight treatment was degrading and humiliating[504] and included, among other things, a

498 C. Michaelson, 'Derogating from international human rights obligations in the 'War Against Terrorism'? A British/Australian perspective' (2005) vol 17(1-2) Terrorism and Political Violence 131

499 European Convention on Human Rights

500 El-Masri v The Former Yugoslav Republic of Macedonia (2012) 39630/09 Strasbourg para 17

501 ibid., para 18

502 ibid., para 19

503 ibid., para 20

504 ibid., para

forceful insertion of a firm object into his anus.[505] He was flown to Afghanistan to a CIA-run facility where the unlawful detention and interrogation continued. Thereafter, the CIA agents abandoned him in Albania when they found that he had no links with Al-Qaeda.[506] Hence, the applicant alleged, among other things, a violation of Articles 3, 8 and 5 of the ECHR.[507]

In the present case, the judicial analysis of the extent of legality in a democratic society for a questionable detention with reference to the fight against terrorism, will hinge on the interpretation of the alleged violation of Article 5 of the ECHR. The applicant contended that he was detained by the respondent government unlawfully without an arrest warrant and was kept incommunicado. He alleged that he had not been brought before a judge and the respondent state had not carried out a prompt and effective investigation into his credible allegations. Hence, there had been a violation of his rights under Article 5 of the ECHR.[508]

The respondent government contested the applicant's allegations. The Court acknowledged the importance of his right under Article 5 of the ECHR, and stressed that the deprivation of the right to liberty must not only be carried out in compliance with substantive and procedural requirements of national law but must, of necessity, acknowledge the purpose of Article 5 of the ECHR; namely, to protect the individual from state arbitrariness.[509] The Court maintained that the respondent state failed to comply with their positive obligation to protect the applicant from being detained in violation of Article 5 of the ECHR. They had simply handed him over to the CIA, thereby facilitating his subsequent detention in Afghanistan, irrespective of the fact that they were aware, or ought to have been aware, of the risk of such transfer.[510] The Court found that no effective investigation had been carried out by the respondent state into the applicant's allegation of ill treatment. It pointed out that there has been a breach of the applicant's right under Article 5 of ECHR and that the breach had continued

505 ibid

506 ibid., para 32

507 El-Masri v The Former Yugoslav Republic of Macedonia (2012) 39630/09 Strasbourg

508 ibid., para 224

509 ibid., para 230

510 ibid., paras 239, 240

throughout the entire period of the applicant's captivity.[511] Hence, the Court established that the applicant was subjected to "extraordinary rendition", which entails detention "...outside the normal legal system" and which "...by its deliberate circumvention of due process is anathema to the rule of law and the values protected by the Convention".[512]

The right to liberty and security of a person is an exclusive right, which must be read as a whole. A person's security must be seen in relation to 'physical liberty', which cannot be interpreted as referring to different matters such as the state's duty to give someone personal protection against an attack by others or right to social security.[513] Therefore, the right to liberty and security of a person embraces a nation state's duty to protect individuals against the arbitrary use of authority by itself (i.e. the government) or its agents/agencies. Such right is also provided for under Articles 12 §§ 1, 2 and 4 of the Yugoslav Constitution of 1991(*Устав*). Additionally, by virtue of Article 5 of the ECHR, there is a procedural guarantee for the inhibition of arbitrary detention. Hence, a person can be deprived of his or her liberty, but it has to be carried out in accordance with the procedure prescribed by law; for instance, as stipulated under Article 5 (1-5) of the ECHR. Essentially, the importance and integrity of Article 5 (3) (4) of the ECHR cannot be underestimated as it serves as one of the procedural guarantees against unlawful detention in a democratic society. Logically, the requirement of 'promptness' and 'judicial review' of a detention under such subsections reinforces the early exposure of arbitrary detention.

In the present case, it could have been argued that the applicant's detention fell short of international obligation under the ECHR, as well as the procedural requirement of domestic law. For instance, pursuant to S.188 (3) of the Domestic Criminal Procedure Act 1997 (*Закон за кривичната постапка*), hereinafter referred to as 'the Act', a person can be detained by ministry officials if it is deemed expedient for the determination of the person's identity, for the verification of the person's alibi, or for the collection of information to enable

511 ibid

512 ibid., para 239

513 M. Macovei, 'The Right to liberty and the security of the person: A guide to the implementation of Article 5 of the European Convention on Human Rights' (2002) Human Rights Handbook No. 5

proceedings to be brought against a third party.[514] Implicitly, in the present case, it was not unlawful for the respondent agents to detain the applicant for the purpose of determining the authenticity of his newly acquired German passport. However, it was unlawful for them to have interrogated him in English language, in which he was not proficient and to have detained him for over 24 hours without an opportunity to be brought before a judge. This constitutes a violation of Section 3 of the Criminal Procedure Act of 1997, which provided:

> "...that anyone who was summoned, arrested or detained had to be informed promptly, in a language which he or she understood; a detainee should be brought promptly or, at the latest, twenty-four hours after the detention before a judge who would decide on the lawfulness of the detention." [515]

The arrest of the applicant was allegedly carried out without an arrest warrant. However, an arrest could, in principle, be lawfully carried out by the officers of the Ministry of Interior without a warrant. However, the arrested person must be brought 'promptly' before an investigating judge as stipulated under S.188 (2) of the Act. The applicant was also deprived of communication with other people. For instance, his request to contact the German embassy while he was in detention at the Skopje hotel was refused. He had no opportunity to contact either his family regarding his whereabouts or any other third party, which amounted to violation of Article 3 of the Act.[516] As provided under section 3 of the Act, while in detention from the onset, the applicant was legally entitled to get a lawyer of his choice and have his lawyer present during his interrogation by both the respondent agents and the CIA officers. This was not made accessible to him. Also, the facts of the case did not show that the respondent state obtained any legal assurance or guarantee from the CIA agents indicating that the applicant would not be tortured while in their custody. Hence, they failed to protect the applicant from torture or other ill or degrading treatment.

514 Criminal Procedure Act of 1997 (*Закон за кривичната постапка)*

515 ibid; M. Skerker, *An Ethics of Interrogation* (University of Chicago Press, London 2010), 169

516 ibid; R. Leo, et al., *The Miranda Debate: Law, Justice, and Policing* (North-eastern University Press, Boston 1998), 283

Critically, an allegation of a violation of Article 5 of the ECHR by an applicant necessitates a 'prompt' and 'effective' investigation because of the vulnerable nature of the person facing such violation. The violation of the right to liberty has the potential to result in the violation of other rights as well, such as the right not to be tortured (Article 3 of the ECHR), which is an absolute right, and the right to family and private life (Article 8 of the ECHR) as seen in the present case.

The Court held that there was no prompt and effective investigation into the applicant's allegations of having suffered a violation of Article 5 of the ECHR. Consequently, an internal inquiry was carried out by the respondent state's Department for Control and Professional Standards within the Ministry of the Interior (DCPS) who did not avail the applicant the opportunity to give evidence before it. The applicant was not informed of the outcome of the inquiry; rather the results were communicated to European Union representatives.[517] Hence, no meaningful investigation was carried out by the respondent state about the applicant's allegation of unlawful detention.[518]

In the present case, the applicant was subjected to unlawful detention for the extraction of information regarding whether he was affiliated to any Islamic organisation or Al-Qaeda. Nevertheless, the specific legal question that arose was: 'How credible is any information obtained during an unlawful detention?' What if a terrorist suspect states that he or she accepts that he or she is affiliated to a terrorist organisation, but does so only to end the arbitrary detention? How will such information assist in the fight against terrorism (the enhancement of national security)? It can be argued that information obtained during an unlawful detention is inadmissible on the grounds of unlawfulness of the detention as the detainee may have released such information under duress. To avoid this, suspects cannot be compelled to provide any information against their will.

Also, if the applicant was detained on security grounds, such detention must, out of necessity, be done in accordance with law. The fact that a detention is necessitated by the security needs of a state is not a condition precedent for such detention to be done outside the confines of law. The substantive dimension of

517 El-Masri v The Former Yugoslav Republic of Macedonia., op. cit., para 64

518 ibid, para 242

'arbitrary detention' demands that "detention be proportional to the security justification".[519] In the present case, the applicant's detention was not proportional to the security justification. Hence, it can be argued that on grounds of proportionality, the applicant's detention from the hotel to Afghanistan had no security justification as he was neither declared a security risk by the respondent state agents nor by the CIA.

In 2006, a CIA memo revealed a combined use of interrogation techniques for the purpose of coaxing High Value Detainees (HVD) to provide threat information and terrorist intelligence in a timely manner.[520] Physical and psychological pressures in a comprehensive, systematic and cumulative manner were to be applied to influence HVD behaviour, to overcome their "resistance posture".[521] The CIA memo also mentioned the three interrogation techniques applied in the CIA run detention facilities: Namely (a) the initial condition technique, which involves capture shocks. This contributes to the physical and psychological condition of HVD before the commencement of interrogation. (b) Transition to interrogation technique, which involves rendition, whereby a detainee is medically examined before the flight, during the flight he is securely shackled and deprived of sight and sound through the use of blindfolds, earmuffs and hoods. (c) The interrogation technique, which includes the descriptions of detention conditions (conditioning techniques and corrective techniques).[522] No doubt the events of 9/11 changed the way most nation states react towards the issue of national security, especially in relation to terrorism. The fight against terrorism ignites a persistent and intentional erosion of fundamental rights by state actors. Nation states have subjected apparently innocent nationals to arbitrary detention, as was seen in the present case.

5.2.1 JUSTIFICATION FOR UNLAWFUL DETENTION

Analytically, what if a terrorist suspect does have in fact an affiliation with a terrorist organisation; will his or her detention in violation of the rights already mentioned become lawful in a democratic society? It can be argued that the

---

519 El-Masri v The Former Yugoslav Republic of Macedonia., op. cit.

520 ibid., para 124

521 ibid

522 ibid., paras 124, 125

fight against terrorism or the consequences of terrorism for the rights and interest of others is not in itself a legal justification for unlawful detention in a democratic society. Hence, considering the wording of Article 5 of the ECHR, it can be argued that the word 'everyone' and 'no-one' is imperative in the interpretation of such aspect of the ECHR. By implication, in a democratic society, Article 5 includes people who are caught in the very act of terrorism or crime. Hence, by virtue of the second arm of Article 5(c), such persons can be detained "in order to enhance the security of other persons". Thus, it provides for: "the lawful arrest or detention of a person... when it is reasonably considered necessary to prevent his committing an offence or fleeing after having done so..."[523] However, to prevent unlawful detention (arbitrariness) of persons detained or arrested under Article 5(1) (c) of the ECHR, Article 5(3) of the ECHR requires that they be brought before a judge, or other officer authorised by law, for trial within a 'reasonable time'. Nevertheless, here the phrase 'reasonable time', if given a wide interpretation, could create room for "arbitrariness" since this part of the article did not expressly stipulate what constitutes a 'reasonable time'; although, of course, this can be interpreted as reasonable in all the specific circumstances of the case. Also, it could be argued that the practical implementation of Article 5(4) and 5(3) of the ECHR in the fight against terrorism will be a mirage since, often, the victims of unlawful detention are taken outside the jurisdiction where their detention cannot be reviewed before a judicial authority to ascertain its legitimacy (as was seen in El-Masri's case).

It has been claimed that nation states, such as the UK, have violated Article 5(4) of the ECHR. This article entitles anyone whose liberty has been deprived through arrest or detention to undertake proceedings for the speedy determination of the lawfulness of such detention. The court will order an immediate release if the detention is unlawful.[524] Thus, pursuant to S 25(1) of the Anti-Terrorism Crime and Security Act 2001 (ATCSA), access to judicial review by an international terrorist suspect of the Secretary General's certification, is limited as the certified suspect cannot appeal to a British court of law. However, by the provisions of S. 21(ATCSA), appeal is available to the Special Immigration Appeals Commission (SIAC), which is not a normal court of law incorporated in the standard British Court system. Irrespective of the fact that SIAC has been

523 European Convention on Human Rights 1950

524 ibid

established as an impartial and independent tribunal, having the same status as the High Court and able to exert some level of control; there is doubt regarding whether proceedings before it offers adequate guarantee of judicial procedure.[525]

5.2.2 SIAC AND THE ADVERSARIAL SYSTEM

Detainees in the UK do not fully enjoy the benefits of the adversarial procedure in the SIAC system. An appellant and/or his counsel may be absent during proceedings for the determination of the lawfulness of the appellant's detention before SIAC. The detainee and his legal representative are precluded from seeing all the evidence and are not given detailed information of the reasons for the decisions taken with respect to the detainee. The detainee's legal representative is chosen for him by the Solicitor General. Hence, it is arguable that proceedings before SIAC fall short of adequate guarantee of judicial procedure and it cannot be considered a court within the meaning of Article 5(4) of the ECHR.[526] It can be argued that the SIAC system is against the spirit of Article 5(4) of the ECHR. The requirement of judicial review of the lawfulness of an appellant's detention pursuant to Article 5(4) of the ECHR is hampered under the SIAC procedure, since all the materials available to SIAC with respect to an appellant's case are not made available to the appellant and/or his legal representatives.

The classification of some of the relevant materials as 'closed materials' makes it difficult, if not impossible, for a detainee to satisfactorily have the lawfulness of his detention judicially reviewed since he or she might not have knowledge of some of the crucial contentions and allegations. How then can it be said that 'international terrorist suspects' have the opportunity of having the lawfulness of their detention reviewed as required under Article 5(4) of the ECHR? For instance, in the case of ***A and others v The United Kingdom,*** the main allegations against the first, third, fifth and tenth applicants were provided as 'closed evidence', such that it was not possible for them to challenge the allegations against them; the open evidence was not substantial enough for them to rebut their link to terrorism.[527] Also, special advocates are appointed in the SIAC

525 C. Michaelsen, 'Derogating from international human rights obligations in the 'War Against Terrorism'? A British/Australian perspective' (2005) vol17 (1-2) Terrorism and Political Violence 131; Human Rights Act 1998 (Designated Derogation) Order 2001, No.3644

526 ibid

527 A and Others v The United Kingdom., op. cit.

procedure to make submissions on behalf of appellants.[528] How will the appellants be convinced that the special advocates will represent their interest?

On the other hand, considering the after-effects of a terrorist attack, such as loss of innocent lives, disruption of public order, or destruction of property, it can be argued that the enhancement of national security in response to an emergency cannot be underestimated in the bid to protect an emphatic conception of the meaning and scope of human rights in the fight against terrorism. Hence, the definition of an 'international terrorist' by the ATCSA of 2001 shows that an international terrorist is not just a person involved in the very act of terrorism, but includes a person who has been concerned in the preparation or instigation of acts of international terrorism.[529] By implication, if it is manifestly evident that a person has the potential to prepare or instigate acts of international terrorism, then it becomes incumbent on the government as a core duty to take "necessary steps" to prevent the likelihood of an attack emanating through such a person, or his link. Therefore, the liberty of such a person could be lawfully limited through detention.

Analytically, the deportation of such a person might not guarantee the security of the contracting country, the receiving country or the world at large since terrorist networks can be global. Ben Brandon, a UK legal practitioner opines that the threat to international and national security post 9/11 is entirely different in nature as it is internationalised, amorphous and has the capacity to strike anywhere in the world.[530] Hence, there is a need for prolonged detention of terrorist suspects for the enhancement of international and national security where it is impossible to deport the terrorist suspect. (Terrorist attacks could be described as inhuman treatment on not only the citizenry, but also on the nation itself.)

> "Whilst the terrorist does not forfeit his fundamental rights, the law does recognise that those rights can be restricted or derogated from in particular circumstances. Rights are not only one way. It is not only the rights of suspected persons that are important. The rights and liberties of

528 ibid

529 B. Brandon, 'Terrorism, Human Rights and the Rule of Law: 120 years of the UK legal response to terrorism' (2004) Criminal Law Review 981

530 ibid; S. Ramage, *Privacy-Law of Civil Liberties* (iUniverse Inc. Lincoln 2007), 26-27

> other citizens are important too. Let us not forget that terrorism, by its methods and aims, has the potential to render nugatory all the individual rights that we hold dear."[531]

Arguably, the element of mutuality is paramount in the task of seeking a viable balance between the protection of human rights and enhancement of national security against the background of counterterrorism. No doubt, democracy is predicated upon the rule of law. However, the pattern of modern-day terrorism necessitated the formulation and implementation of certain national security measures and polices to safeguard the nation and its inhabitants. Unfortunately, some such security measures/policies eliminate, encroach upon or limit the enjoyment of fundamental human rights thereby causing a dramatic shift in the observance of an integral principle of a democratic society, namely, respect for human rights. In effect, state governments have been accused of acting arbitrarily in their attempt to counter terrorism.[532] Thus, a significant victim of the struggle against terrorism has been respect for human rights. All those who have laboured to promote human rights, both domestically and internationally, comment on the increase in the incidence of abuse, especially post-9/11.[533] Hence, the pertinent question is: Who is to be blamed? Is it the government who has the responsibility to take necessary steps to enhance a nation's security and, to a wider degree, regional and international security because of the modern-day pattern of terrorism? Or the terrorist who has determined to deprive himself of his fundamental right, such as his right to life, since most of them are suicide bombers as was exemplified in the 9/11 attack, 7/7 suicide attack on London transport network, car bomb attacks in London and Glasgow 2007[534] and who are also determined to deprive a whole community of some of their inalienable rights such as their rights under Articles 2, 3, 8, and 17 of the ECHR. They also kill not only to end lives, but to end a way of life.[535]

---

531 ibid

532 ibid

533 R. Foot, 'The United Nations, Counter Terrorism and Human Rights: Institutional Adaptation and Embedded Ideas' (2007) vol 29 (2) Human Rights Quarterly 489

534 I. Turner, 'A Communitarian Justification for Measures to Prevent Terrorism in the UK' (2016) vol 10(5) Perspective on Terrorism

535 F. Megret, "War'? Legal semantics and the move to violence' (2002) vol13(2) European Journal of International Law 361

Acceptably, it is the responsibility of governments of nation states to enhance national security, which includes the protection of human rights. However, the national security strategy of most nation states took a different turn post-9/11. Nation states embarked upon anticipatory actions to prevent future terrorist activities. Hence, a range of controversial measures were put in place, such as indefinite detention of suspected terrorists, extension of periods of detention prior to charge, and control orders,[536] which constrain the principle of liberalism (liberty and equality of individuals). Accordingly, in the pursuit of some selfish extremist interests, terrorists violate the rights of others, as pointed above. At the same time, governments infringe on human rights, especially in the bid to curb terrorism,[537] even though in most cases most of the counterterrorism measures need to be reviewed for possible adjustments. At the same time, nation states cannot fold their arms and watch terrorists take over their nation, region or the globe. Hence, the UK government plainly considers that an individual's right not to be detained by the state without trial is negotiable.[538]

5.2.3 DEMOCRACY AND SECURITY DILEMMA

Arguably, the 9/11 incident changed the western world. The change was orchestrated not only by terrorism, but also by counterterrorism measures.[539] No doubt, investigation of terrorist offences presents acute challenges to state actors. They include the risk of maltreating the innocent.[540] However, for a viable form of democracy to be maintained in practice, some fundamental values, such as the rule of law, civil liberties and human rights have to be respected unfailingly.[541] On the contrary, a political scientist called Karl Lowenstein argued that democracies must proactively defend themselves from fascist threats through the adoption

536 I. Cram, 'Failing Justice Brennan's quest? Anticipating terrorism risks and the US Supreme Court' (2013) (1) Public Law 30

537 ibid

538 ibid

539 C. Lewis, et al., *Counter-Terrorism and the Post-Democratic State* (Edward Elgar Publishing Limited, Cheltenham 2007)

540 L. Arbour, 'In our name and on our behalf' (2006) vol 55(3) International and Comparative Law Quarterly 511-526

541 C. Michealsen, op. cit.

of militant democracy.[542] This is the fight against radical movements, especially (political) parties and their activities.[543] According to him, in order to destroy democracy, fascists abuse the fundamental rights granted to them by democratic constitutions. Lowenstein maintains that the antidote to defend democracy and defeat fascism is a denial of such fundamental freedoms through temporary restrictive legislation.[544] He maintains that there is need for democracies to apply more robust mechanisms to challenge modern anti-democratic mass movements.[545] According to Lowenstein, emotional mobilisation (for instance, where new elections or referenda are obtained through emotional mass politics) is a vital tool in authoritarian regimes and fascist movements. Hence, emotionalism replaces the rule of law in authoritarian regimes. According to him, nationalist fervour, intimidation and implied threat of physical coercion constitute the most popular strategies of political emotionalism. He reiterates that the major purpose of such movements is the seizure and retention of power at all costs.[546] Lowenstein was pessimistic and apprehensive about fascism.[547]

Accordingly, Article 17 of the ECHR could be invoked in analysing the place of fundamental rights in a democratic society against the background of the fight against terrorism. Hence, pursuant to Article 17 of the ECHR, states are precluded from engaging in acts or activities that are geared towards the destruction of any rights and freedoms provided by the ECHR to an extent greater than what is provided. Essentially, it precludes a nation state from adopting the principles of militant democracy. Such principles advocate for robust mechanisms in curbing anti-democratic activities. Analytically, Lowenstein's views of fascist movements and militant democracy are perhaps comparable to modern day terrorism and some counterterrorism measures/legislation of nation states. It follows that some counterterrorism measures are ab initio unlawful; for instance, detention without charge and trial under the Prevention of Terrorism

542 B. Plache, 'Soldiers for democracy: Karl Lowenstein, John H Herz, militant democracy and the defense of democratic states' (Virginia Commonwealth University Theses and Dissertations Paper 2995, 2013)

543 A. Sajo, Militant *democracy* (Eleven International Publishing, Netherlands 2004)

544 B. Plache, op. cit.

545 A. Sajo, op. cit.

546 ibid, 211

547 B. Plache, op. cit.

Act 2005. Long detention periods without giving a detainee the right to contest his charges are incompatible with the ECHR obligation. Thus, it can be argued that most counterterrorism measures are robust with the aim to fight terrorism. However, the effectiveness of such counterterrorism measures in curbing terrorism could be ascertained from the extent to which terrorism has either increased or decreased today. Consequently, such counterterrorism measures have in certain circumstances encouraged terror violence rather than curbing it, as was seen in some of the testimonies given by some radicalised extremists.[548]

Undeniably, sovereign states have the exclusive right to use force to protect their national security. Nevertheless, states are bound by international humanitarian law that prohibits excessive and indiscriminate use of force and reprisals. Hence, a scholar argues that there is a risk of nation states coming to the level of terrorist organisations; if they fail to adhere to the rules of international humanitarian law in the bid to enhance national security.[549] Some such counterterrorism measures have also, in certain circumstances, alienated the masses.[550] Impliedly, a militant strategy might not solve the problem of terrorism; as this might result in an endless circle of terror. Again, militant democratic values do not synchronise with liberal democratic values. They are antithetic to each other.

Conversely, John Hertz opines that human beings are basically concerned with security dilemmas regarding the understanding that man can inflict violence and death on one another.[551] Hence, man is concerned about his security being attacked, subjected, dominated or annihilated by other groups and individuals. Thus, to obtain security from such attacks, they acquire more power to escape the effect of the power of others. This, in turn, increases the challenge of insecurity as others feel more insecure and prepare for the worst.[552] According to him, despite man's best intention, he must always be suspicious of his neighbour, realising that there could be an outbreak of violence at any time.[553] In sync with

548 ibid

549 P. Wilkinson, *Terrorism versus Democracy: The liberal state response* (Frank Cass Publishers, London 2001), 125

550 T. Tuba, op. cit.

551 J. Herz, 'Idealist internationalism and the security dilemma' (1950) vol 2(2) World Politics 157-180

552 ibid

553 B. Plache, op. cit

the security dilemma, man feels he is exposed to dangers that threaten his life. This leads man into the search for security against such menace. In consequence, man realises that it is impossible for him to totally destroy those who might endanger his existence. At the same time, his dependence is on other men for production and acquisition of necessities of life. Hence, the dilemma; as man relies and is suspicious of his neighbour, the means of security become more competitive. He argues that it is useless to appeal to a higher authority for protection and survival. He maintains that the only way a nation can guarantee his security is by competing with its neighbours. This enkindles a vicious circle of suspicion and counter-suspicion, power competition, arms races and, ultimately, war.[554] However, Hertz maintains that political realism and political idealism has hope for a peaceful future where nations coexist irrespective of their political belief.[555]

Analytically, modern day terrorism has plunged nation states into a frenzied security dilemma in which states are gripped with the fear of potential terrorist attacks. Hence, they have formulated preventive terrorist measures. Such dilemma has led to the continued amendment of some counterterrorism legislations/measures to meet up with security need. For instance, the Terrorism Prevention and Investigation Measures Act 2011 (TPIMS) was replaced by the Counterterrorism and Security Act 2015. Realistically, security threats cannot be expunged completely from any human society. Rather, they can be controlled. Their effective control might not be possible through the adoption of some anti-democratic means, such as unlawful detention. Analytically, if nations understand that it will be impossible to eradicate terrorism or the issue of insecurity completely from human society, they will appreciate and acknowledge the principles of rule of law in their counterterrorism policies. However, a peaceful co-existence could be achieved in view of John Hertz's political realism and political idealism in which case, nations coexist irrespective of their political beliefs. Nevertheless, it could be questioned whether it is possible for nations with different political idiosyncrasies to coexist. Domestic and international terrorism cannot be defeated by anti-democratic means, especially in 'rule of law'

554 ibid

555 ibid

states, unless such states are prepared for Pyrrhic victory.[556]Anti-democratic means are not only illegal but counterproductive too; they may provoke grievances which may, in turn, promote terrorism. Democracy stands for fundamental rights and fair play for all opinions. How could it address itself to curtailing this without destroying the very basis of its existence and justification?[557] Going by the precepts of democracy, namely, rule of law, human rights and civil liberties, will a democratic society that adopts anti-democratic activities still be regarded as democratic? Or will its nomenclature change?

5.3 SUMMARY

Terrorism is both a tactic and a strategy. It involves the intentional maiming and killing of non-combatants for political effect by non-state actors and subnational groups.[558] The US has not been a lone victim of terrorism. Nations such as India, Spain, UK and more have had incidents of terrorism.[559] Thus, some questions could be asked: Should states change their current response towards such modern pattern of terrorism? Can a democratic society have effective control over anti-democratic activities such as terrorism, especially suicide violence, without encroaching upon human rights? Could it be said that present day counterterrorism measures represent militant democracy? Is the modern-day terrorist movement the same as the fascist movements of the 1930s where the movement is described as nationalist, authoritarian and violence is accepted in the struggle for power?[560] What is the place of fundamental human rights in democratic societies predicated upon the rule of law?

Analytically, the aim of terrorists is not limited to the abolition of states and their institutions, but extends to the defeat of the democratic legal order and its

556 T. Tuba, 'War on terror in the US and the UK: An evaluation with regard to civil liberties' (2006) vol2(7) Review of International Politics 111

557 A. Sajo, *Militant democracy* (Eleven International Publishing, Netherlands 2004)

558 R. Art., et al., *Militant democracy and counterterrorism: Lessons from the past* (United States Institute of Peace, Washington 2007)

559 I. Turner, 'Freedom from torture in the war on torture: Is it absolute?' (2011) vol 23(3) Terrorism and Political Violence 419

560 BBC News, 'What is a fascist?' (2009) <news.bbc.co.uk/2/hi/UK_news/magazine/8316271.stm> accessed 14 January 2017

replacement with a theocratic regime contradictory to free democratic order.[561] However, the task and duty of a state to secure its citizens and environment is such that cannot be totally neglected, delegated, privatised or given up.[562] Hence, if an existing legal framework is not sufficient to take care of a threatening situation in a nation; it becomes pertinent for the nation to devise alternative means to take care of such situation.

Nation states whose judicial systems are predicated on liberal conceptions of the "rule of law" should not have recourse or even be passive accomplices to practices such as abductions, extra-legal transfers, secret detentions, or indefinite detentions, as they amount to complete repudiation of law and of the justice system.[563] The rule of law is an ideal that relates to legality. This implies that things are done according to law. Hence, the activities of the government and its agencies are limited by law.[564] The observance of rule of law by no means guarantees the protection of human rights. However, the arbitrary use of power for personal gain, vengeance or favouritism is often manifested in the making of legal orders[565] or policies. Thus, a British pioneer of terrorism studies, Paul Wilkinson asserted that 'the primary objective of any counterterrorism strategy must be the protection and maintenance of liberal democracy'.[566]Above all, the maintenance of democracy demands an enduring respect for three liberal society core values; namely, rule of law, civil liberties and human rights.[567] Hence, to a great extent 'unlawful detention' cannot be considered legal in a democratic society even against the background of the counter terrorism.

---

561 M. Thiel, *Militant democracy principle in modern democracy* (Ashgate Publishing Limited, Surrey 2009)

562 ibid

563 ibid

564 B. Tamanaha, 'The history and elements of the rule of law' (2012) Singapore Journal of Legal Studies 232

565 A. Kavanagh, Arguing *about the law* (Routledge Publishers, Abingdon 2009)

566 ibid; H. Khatchadourian, *The Morality of Terrorism* (Wipf and Stock Publishers 2011), 115; A. Cronin et al., *Attacking Terrorism: Elements of a Grand Strategy* (Georgetown University Press, Washington, D.C 2004),142

567 ibid; A. Staniforth, *Routledge Companion to UK Counter-Terrorism* (Routledge Taylor& Francis Group, London 2013), 269

In view of human rights, it is essential to adhere to fundamental legal principles established in important international treaties, such as the ECHR. Hence, it is incumbent on liberal democratic countries, such as the UK, to uphold such rights even in the event of serious emergencies. It must be recalled that such international treaties also create room for derogation at the instance of any threat to a nation's security, but such derogation must, of necessity, comply with the international legal commitment of such nation. However, after 9/11, anti-terrorism laws of most liberal democracies are inconsistent with their international legal commitments. For instance, under the Australian Security Intelligence Organisation Legislation Amendment (Terrorism) Act, 2002 (ASIO), non-suspects can be detained for the purpose of questioning and intelligence gathering, which is incompatible with Australia's international human rights legal commitment under the ICCPR.[568] Assuming detention for questioning is essential in a particular circumstance; it could have been more reasonable for such detention to be confined to persons who are reasonably suspected of being terrorists or who are involved in terrorist activities.[569] Some questions could be asked: Where is the force of 'rule of law' in the fight against terrorism? What is the actual meaning of national security against the background of counterterrorism? Does national security connote violation of human rights? Does the 'war' context of counterterrorism connote 'vengeance' against terrorists or does it symbolise a campaign for the enhancement of national security? If it sets out to enhance national security as it claims, then counterterrorism legislations/ measures ought to conform to liberal democratic principles and rule of law.[570]

It can be argued that to create a viable balance between the protection of human rights and enhancement of a coherent form of national security practice in anti terrorism measures, the prevailing circumstance in a nation state or globally must be considered. For instance, post-9/11, a state of emergency was declared in the UK as it was perceived that it was a potential target for terrorists because of her close alliance with the US and the presence of some international terrorist suspects on UK soil.[571] Thus, some necessary steps to enhance national security according to the exigencies of the situation needed to be taken. This, in turn,

568 C. Michaelsen, op. cit.

569 ibid

570 P. Wilkinson, *Terrorism and the liberal state* (New York University Press, New York 1986), 125

571 A and others v The United Kingdom., op. cit.

plunged previous understandings of the meaning and scope of human rights into a potential dilemma.

However, a close look at Article 15 of the ECHR shows that it is not sufficient for a nation state to derogate from its obligations under the ECHR merely because 'there is a state of emergency threatening the life of a nation'. Three substantive conditions must be met for a derogation to be valid, one of which is that: the measures taken in response to it must comply with a state's other obligations under international law.[572] Therefore, by implication, 'derogation' on the grounds of a 'state of emergency' ought not to be an opportunity for the violation of treaty obligations or the infringement of fundamental human rights. For example, in ***A and Others v United Kingdom,*** the right of the first, third, fifth and tenth applicants were violated as most of the cases to be answered by them were in the 'closed material'.[573] Hence, they were not aware of the reasons why they were branded 'international terrorist suspects', which is a violation of their right under the second arm of article 6 (3) (a) of the ECHR that entitles them to be informed of the nature and cause of the allegation against them.[574]

Ultimately, the possibility of creating a viable balance between unlawful detention and national security in a democratic society will practically constitute a great challenge, not only for state actors, but for the protection of human rights and society at large. For instance, considering the issue of indefinite detention of suspected terrorists, which is an aspect of unlawful detention, what happens to national security where it is not possible to deport or remove a terrorist suspect to his home country or a third country because of the likelihood of torture or other ill or degrading treatment? Should the terrorist suspect be detained indefinitely pending the determination of his or her security status? Or should he or she be released into the society to enjoy a right to liberty at the expense of other peoples' right to liberty and security, if the determination of his security status cannot be completed within a "reasonable time"?

Arguably, the determination of what constitutes a "reasonable time" should be dependent on the circumstances of a case. Such detention should also be open

572 European Convention on Human Rights 1950

573 A and others v The United Kingdom., op. cit.

574 European Convention on Human Rights 1950

to public scrutiny to serve as a potential check on "arbitrariness". The enhancement of national security entails not only the maintenance of public order, but also the protection of people's security; there might be a 'minimal' deprivation of liberty depending on the circumstance/s of a particular case, which ought not to culminate into a flagrant violation of Article 5 of the ECHR. On the other hand, how will a balance be struck between national security and protection of the right to liberty and security as enshrined under Article 5 of ECHR where a terrorist suspect is abducted (enforced disappearance) in transit and detained unlawfully as was seen in El-Masri's case? How will his detention be reviewed by a judicial authority to ascertain its lawfulness within a reasonable time, given suspects are usually moved out of the protection of law (as in El-Masri's case)? In such circumstance, a democratic society ought to remain democratic (in the sense that it must be cognisant of the implications of the rule of law) even in the case/s of emergency threatening a nation's security.

Article 1(2) of the International Convention for the Protection of All Persons from Enforced Disappearance (CED) provides:

> "No exceptional circumstances whatsoever, whether a state of war or a threat of war, internal political instability or any other public emergency, may be invoked as a justification for enforced disappearance."

Thus, the threat of terrorism, or an actual terrorist attack, ought not to legitimise 'enforced disappearance', which is an aspect of unlawful detention, whether it is for interrogation or preventive detention. Pursuant to Article 2 of the CED, 'enforced disappearance' is:

> "Considered to be the arrest, detention, abduction or any other form of deprivation of liberty by agents of the State or by persons or groups of persons acting with the authorisation, support or acquiescence of the State, followed by a refusal to acknowledge the deprivation of liberty or by concealment of the fate or whereabouts of the disappeared person, which place such a person outside the protection of the law."[575]

---

575 International Convention for The Protection of All Persons from Enforced Disappearance (CED) 2010

Accordingly, in a democratic society, the arrest or detention of a terrorist suspect or a terrorist must conform to international obligations and requirements of domestic law. Thus, by virtue of Article 4 (CED), it is incumbent on state parties to ensure that 'enforced disappearance' constitutes an offence in their respective criminal laws, since it is an aspect of unlawful deprivation of liberty (unlawful detention).[576] To a great extent, the practice of unlawful detention remains an anathema in a democratic society.

5.4 TORTURE AND COUNTERTERRORISM

International human rights law stipulates certain fundamental rights, which individuals should enjoy and proscribes some actions such as torture, cruel, inhuman or degrading treatments by the states and its agents.[577] Torture is virtually universally condemned as barbaric and ineffective, yet it continues in the contemporary world.[578] Article 1 of the United Nations Convention against Torture and other Cruel, Inhuman or Degrading Treatment or Punishment defined Torture as:

> "... any act by which severe pain or suffering, whether physical or mental, is intentionally inflicted on a person for... obtaining from him or a third person information or a confession, punishing him for an act he or a third person has committed or is suspected of having committed, or intimidating or coercing him or a third person, or for any reason based on discrimination of any kind... by or at the instigation of or with the consent or acquiescence of a public official or other person acting in an official capacity..."[579].

By implication, torture is not always physical. The pain or suffering could be mental. It must be inflicted by a public official or a government agent who deliberately inflicts the pain to obtain information or confession. The person tortured

576 ibid

577 D. Bertrand, et al., 'Preventing human rights violations in places of detention: A European initiative' (1995) vol1(3) Health and Human Rights 236

578 P. Miller, 'Torture approval in comparative perspective' (2011) vol 12(4) Human Rights Review 441-463

579 United Nations Convention Against Torture 1984

must not be the culprit. He might be a suspect or might be tortured on behalf of a third person. Torture could take the form of 'intimidation' and 'coercion'. However, to constitute torture, the pain or suffering must be 'severe'. The basis for torture does not have to be for information or confession; it might be based on discrimination. The judgement of a judicial authority cannot constitute torture. Thus, in ***Akosy v Turkey***[580]amongst other things, the detainee was subjected to 'Palestinian hanging'. His hands were tied to his back and he was strung up by his arms. The European Court of Human Rights (ECtHR) considered Palestinian hanging as 'torture', since it was deliberately inflicted with a certain degree of preparation and exertion required to carry it out. The ECtHR held that such treatment could only be intentional with the purpose of obtaining information or admissions from the detainee who did not only suffer severe pain at the time, but also suffered paralysis of both arms thereafter. According to the Court, such treatment was 'severe' and 'cruel'.[581] Similarly, in ***Ireland v UK***[582]the court held that torture involves a certain 'intensity' and 'cruelty', attaching a special stigma to deliberate inhuman treatment causing very 'serious' and 'cruel' suffering.[583] Thus, even though the "five techniques" such as wall-standing, hooding, subjection to noise, deprivation of sleep and deprivation of food applied by the Northern Ireland authorities were systematic; they were not torture as contemplated under Article 3 of the ECHR.[584] Accordingly, for an act to constitute torture, 'severity' and 'cruelty' must be one of its defining elements.

In times of crisis, nations embark on torture for immediate intelligence. Hence, they torture persons suspected of terrorism to obtain information or confessions from them concerning terrorist attacks. Nonetheless, the spirit of international conventions, the European Convention on Human Rights, is such that 'torture' and any form of cruel, inhuman or degrading treatment is an aberration of international human rights law. The right not to be tortured is absolute, unqualified and non-derogable.[585] In effect, it is immaterial whether there is an extreme state

580 Akosy v Turkey (1996) 23 EHRR 553

581 ibid., para 64

582 Ireland v UK (1978) 2 EHRR 25

583 ibid., para 167

584 ibid

585 I. Turner, 'Freedom from torture in the war on terror: Is it absolute?' (2011) vol 23(3) Terrorism and Political Violence 419

of emergency in a nation.[586] The law expressly prohibits the crime of torture. Terrorism is pictured as a danger of substantial magnitude in current counter-terrorism rhetoric.[587] It threatens not only lives, but "our way of lives" and "civilisation..."[588] Thus, former UK Home Secretary affirms "...that we face a real and serious threat from terrorism".[589] In *"The threat to patriotism"*, Ronald Dworkin observed that there is a tendency to think that the gravity of terrorist acts is a reason in and itself to erode the legal protections of suspected terrorists.[590] Thus, detainees are subjected to torture, ill or degrading treatment in detainee black sites such as Guantanamo Bay, Cuba.

This subsection sets out to answer the question: Are there circumstances under which torture is acceptable in the "fight against terrorism"? Torture has been considered "the supreme enemy of humanitarian jurisprudence and of liberalism and the greatest threat to law and reason "by western societies since the 19th century.[591] Unlike other rights and protections that may be curtailed, the prohibition on torture under major international human rights and humanitarian law Conventions is absolute.[592] Hence, Article 3 of the ECHR provides that "no one shall be subjected to torture or to inhuman or degrading treatment or punishment". The absolute ban is deemed universal and has become part of customary international law.[593] Torture is generally criticised as a violation of international law and jus cogent norms.[594] Hence, the right not to be tortured is an international law principle in which no derogation under domestic or international

586 Fiona, 'International decision: Saadi v Italy' (2008) vol 102(3) The American Journal of International Law 616

587 J. Wolfendale, 'Terrorism, security and the threat of counterterrorism' (2007) vol 30(1) Studies in Conflict and Terrorism 75

588 ibid

589 BBC News, 'Three guilty of airline bomb plot' (2009) *<http://news.bbc.co.uk/1/hi/UK/8242238.stm>* accessed 19July 2016

590 J. Wolfendale, op. cit.

591 O. Gross, 'Are torture warrants warranted? Pragmatic absolutism and official disobedience' (2004) vol 88 Minnesota Law Review 1481

592 J. Lokanneta, *Transnational torture: Law, violence and state power in the United States and India* (New York University Press, New York 2011)

593 O. Gross, op. cit.

594 J. Gathii, 'Torture, Extra-Territoriality, Terrorism and International Law' (2004) vol 67 Albany Law Review 335

law is permitted. Nevertheless, despite the absolute prohibition on torture, there are revelations that law enforcement agents or military personnel apply excessive force while interrogating suspects. Often, governments reassure us that such actions are not reflective of any general policy. However, the 9/11 incident and the war on terrorism has opened a new chapter in the story of torture.[595] The Bush administration developed an unprecedented detention system post-9/11, tailored to operate outside any established legal framework. Such detention system has undermined the US' enduring commitment to the prohibition against torture and other forms of abuse.[596]

Some scholars, such as Elshtain Frankly, opine that the use of 'torture lite' and 'torture 2' (forms of coercion that entail moderate physical pressure and do not have lasting physical damage) might be used with regret.[597] She argued that a refusal to endorse the use of such techniques amounts to 'moral laziness'.[598] Logically, for a 'pain' to fall under the threshold of torture it must carry a certain degree of severity.[599] Hence, the issue of 'torture lite' or 'torture 2' might not be considered, strictly speaking, as 'torture' sequel to the definition of 'torture' by most international Conventions such as the UN Convention. In other words, 'moderate' physical pressure can be exerted on a 'suspect' or 'an accused' where it is reasonably believed that he/she has useful information since such pressure cannot cause 'severe physical or mental pain'. It does not also fall within the ambit of 'cruel', 'ill' or 'degrading' treatment as they carry a certain degree of severity of 'pain' and 'suffering'.

However, unlawful and counterproductive practices prevail in law enforcement organisations charged with fighting terrorism.[600] Post-9/11, terrorist suspects

595 O. Gross, op. cit.

596 J. Hafetz, 'Torture, judicial review and the regulation of custodial interrogations' (2007) vol 62(3) NYU Annual Survey of American Law 433

597 J. Waldron, *Torture, terror and trade-offs: Philosophy of the White House* (Oxford University Press, New York 2010)

598 ibid

599 European Convention on Human Rights as amended by Protocols Nos. 11 and 14 supplemented by Protocols Nos. 1, 4, 6, 7, 12 and 13. *"Article 3—Prohibition of Torture. Anti-torture and inhumane treatment."* <*https://Ukhumanrightsblog.com/incorporated-rights/articles-index/article-3-of-the-echr.*> accessed 1st August 2016. R (Adam, Limbuela and Tesema) v Home Secretary (2005) UKHL 66 para.54

600 L. Shetret, et al., 'Promoting organizational change to ensure respect for human rights while countering terrorism' (2012) Center on Global Counterterrorism cooperation; Policy Brief

have been subjected to systematic torture and cruelty such as water boarding, extended sleep deprivation, forced nudity, slamming them into walls, and forcing them into painful, stressful positions for hours at a time.[601] The consequence/s of torture and abuse of suspects during interrogations cannot be ignored. For instance, the constituents of torture perpetrators are put at a greater risk of becoming innocent victims of terrorist acts.[602] Hence, to rationalise the targeting of innocent bystanders, the terrorist who detonated the Edgware Road bomb (London train bombing on 7/7) states as follows:

> "Your democratically elected governments continuously perpetrate atrocities against my people all over the world. Your support of them makes you directly responsible, just as I am directly responsible for protecting and avenging my Muslim brothers and sisters."[603]

Thus, enemies who ab initio were not there are created. Impliedly, torture has the potency of radicalising people who, ordinarily, are not connected to terrorism or acts related to terrorism. Hence, out of sympathy for their religious affiliation or ethnicity, some innocent individuals answer the call to terrorism as they witness or access information concerning the type of treatment (torture) their 'brothers' are subjected to as terrorist suspects. This complicates the terrorism challenge. Also, the interrogator might be given false information. Essentially, if an innocent person is being tortured as a terrorist suspect for the purpose of obtaining information or a confession, his likely response might be to either remain silent, since he knows nothing about terrorism, or to release false information to his interrogator in order to bring the treatment (torture) to an end. There are circumstances under which torture has produced false leads. For instance, the Iraq war was justified through false information obtained from torture.[604] This can result in economic waste. For example, millions of dollars

601 Cole D., 'Where liberty lies: Civil society and individual lies after 9/11' (2012) vol 57 Wayne Law Review1203

602 W. Stritzke, et al., *Terrorism and Torture: An interdisciplinary perspective* (Cambridge University Press, London 2013), 1-18

603 A. Clarke, *Rendition to Torture* (Rutgers university Press, Newbrunswick New Jersey 2012), 91

604 ibid

and innumerable man hours have been wasted while US officials and agents chase multiple false leads.[605]

However, to further discuss freedom from torture, an ECtHR case on torture will be applied as a case study. Hence, in ***El-Masri v The Former Yugoslav Republic of Macedonia***[606]the applicant alleged that his interrogation at the Skopje hotel, repeated threats and prolonged uncertainty amounted to a violation of his right under Article 3 of the ECHR. He alleged that the severe psychological effect of the anguish and stress he was subjected to by the respondent was deliberately orchestrated to break his psychological integrity for the purpose of interrogation. This had been adequate to push the applicant to embark on a hunger strike for ten days. He alleged that the brutal and terrifying treatment he was subjected to by the respondent agents during his transfer to the CIA's custody at Skopje airport was intentionally meant to induce 'capture shock' and to break his will for further interrogation. He alleged that the violence used to transfer him to the CIA plane had been out of proportion to any threat he had posed and had been inflicted for debasing him or breaking his spirit. He submitted that all such treatments amounted to torture. The applicant argued that despite the public evidence of ill-treatment in Afghanistan, the respondent State failed to obtain diplomatic assurances before they transferred him to the CIA. Lastly, he submitted that the investigation into his case was grossly inadequate.[607]

The respondent Government completely denied the applicant's allegations. They conceded that the investigation carried out by the authorities was ineffective, but the ineffectiveness was a result of the late submission of the applicant's criminal complaint and the fact that it had been filed against an unidentified perpetrator.[608] The Court held the respondent state responsible for all the inhuman and degrading treatment suffered by the applicant in the hotel, for his torture at Skopje airport and for the transfer of the applicant into the custody of US

605 ibid

606 El-Masri v The Former Yugoslav Republic of Macedonia., op. cit.

607 ibid; K. Larsen, *The Human Rights Treaty Obligation of Peacekeepers* (Cambridge University Press, Cambridge 2012), 408

608 ibid;

authorities, thereby exposing him to the risk of further violation of his rights under Article 3 of the ECHR.[609]

Analytically, the argument on torture in this book can be approached from three angles: (a) Torture of a 'terrorist suspect' in the "fight against terrorism". (b) Prohibition of torture on a terrorist suspect in the event of deportation or expulsion. (c) Terrorism as 'torture'.

5.4.1 TORTURE OF A TERRORIST SUSPECT

Basically, the offence of torture is usually committed when government officials/agents want to obtain information from 'suspects' or 'accused' persons forcefully. Analytically, for an act to constitute torture, as defined under Article 1 of the UNCAT, it must possess some significant elements. Thus (a) severe mental or physical suffering/pain must be inflicted on the 'accused' or the 'suspect'. According to the Bybee memo(torture memos by US assistant AG), the severity of the pain is such that it is associated with serious physical injury so severe that death, organ failure, or permanent damage resulting in a loss of significant body function will likely result.[610] The memo added that severe mental pain requires suffering, not just at the moment of infliction, but also requires lasting psychological harm such as mental disorder like post-traumatic stress disorder. Thus, the severity of the mental or physical pain that describes torture is higher than the pain emanating from a cruel, inhuman or degrading treatment or punishment.[611]

(b) The act must be intentional. An inadvertent act does not qualify for such element, even if such an act culminates in 'severe' pain or 'suffering'. Pain or suffering arising only from, inherent in or incidental to lawful sanctions such as detention facilities does not amount to torture.[612] The crime of torture warrants a specific intent as opposed to general or basic intent. In such case, the accused

609 ibid D. Zartner, Courts, *Codes, and Custom: Legal Tradition and State Policy toward International Human Rights and Environmental Law* (Oxford University Press, Oxford 2014), Ch.1

610 C. De Vos, 'Mind the gap: Purpose, pain, and the difference between torture and inhuman treatment' (2007) vol 14(2) Human Rights Brief 4

611 ibid

612 O. Hathaway, et al., 'Tortured reasoning: The intent to torture under international and domestic law' (2012) vol 52 Virginia Journal of International Law. 791

must not only intend to inflict pain or suffering but must do so for a purpose prohibited by the UNCAT.[613] By way of contrast, in ***DPP v Morgan,*** Lord Simon explained that in crimes of basic intent, the mens rea does not go beyond the actus reus.[614]

(c) The act must be for the purpose of obtaining information or a confession. Hence in the absence of such element, it is immaterial whether the mental and physical pain suffered is 'severe'. In effect, it is the purpose of such an act that will determine the severity of the pain to be inflicted for the act to amount to torture since cruel, inhuman or degrading treatment can also cause severe pain and suffering, but the defining element between the two is the purpose behind the act. Hence, in ***Keenan v United Kingdom,*** the ECtHR pointed out that it is the purposive element of torture, the intent that motivates the conduct, which basically differentiates it from cruel, inhuman and degrading treatment and not the severity of the treatment itself.[615]

(d) It must be inflicted by someone acting in an official capacity such as a public official or on their behalf.[616] Hence, the crime of torture is committed by the state through its agents. A typical torturer will be a law enforcement officer or a member of a security or intelligence service specifically seeking to obtain, during or in furtherance of his duties, information or confessions.[617] It may be a person without official status acting in collusion with, and to advance the purposes of, public officialdom mostly to cloak the duties of the members of such officialdom. Thus, a perpetrator is not limited to the official who directly inflicts the torture. Hence, there is a tendency for a direct perpetrator of the torture to act in collusion with, and to advance the intentions of, a civilian political authority that might be indifferent to the excesses of law enforcement or security

613 ibid

614 DPP v Morgan (1976) AC 182 at 216-217, 1975 WL 44975

615 Keenan v United Kingdom (2001) ECtHR 27229/95

616 United Nations Convention against Torture and other cruel, inhuman or degrading treatment or punishment

617 N. Rodley, *The definitions of torture in International Law* (Oxford University Press, London 2002), 467

officials.[618] In sum, a public official must be the perpetrator of torture either directly or indirectly for the violation of freedom from torture to be established.

Such elements are obvious in El-Masri's case. Hence, Article 3 of the ECHR provides: "No one shall be subjected to torture, inhuman or degrading treatment or punishment".[619]In effect, pursuant to Article 15 ECHR, the right not to be tortured is one of those rights that cannot be derogated from. Legally speaking, no circumstance can validate torture. By implication, torture is not acceptable. It can be argued that the applicant was subjected to severe mental and physical suffering/pain from men working in their official capacity (respondent government agents and CIA agents). For instance, in Skopje hotel he was watched by a team of nine armed men who intentionally interrogated him throughout his detention in the hotel for the sole purpose of obtaining information or a confession from him. He was intimidated and threatened with a gun pointed at his head when he requested his release. The mere fact that he was watched by strange armed men who interrogated him repeatedly coupled with the uncertainty surrounding the duration of his confinement in a place that was not a legal place for detention, is sufficient to cause him 'severe suffering' and 'pain'.

The applicant was also subjected to degrading treatments before he was handed over to the CIA rendition team at Skopje airport. For instance, amongst other things, he was blindfolded; handcuffed and sodomised (a suppository was forced into his anus).[620] During his flight to Afghanistan two injections and an anaesthetic were administered over his nose. Such actions contravene Article 3 ECHR which expressly prohibits ill, inhuman or degrading treatment. Hence, the forceful insertion of an object into the applicant's anus could be described as a 'degrading treatment'. The facts of the present case reveal that the respondent government agents' interrogation was accompanied by threats, insults, pushing and shouting.[621] Such treatments invoke the respondent state's positive duty to prevent acts of torture as states undertake not to violate freedom from torture. Therefore, the question arises: 'Were positive steps taken by the respondent state

---

618 J. Burgers, et al., *The United Nations Convention against torture: A handbook on the Convention against torture and other cruel, inhuman and degrading treatment or punishment* (MartinusNijhoff Publishers, Dordrecht 1988), 119

619 International Covenant on Civil and Political Rights 1976

620 El-Masri v The Former Yugoslav Republic of Macedonia., op. cit.

621 El-Masri v The Former Yugoslav Republic of Macedonia., op. cit.

to prevent acts of torture, degrading and inhuman treatment on the applicant?' The facts of the case never revealed that necessary steps were taken by the respondent government to prevent torture or degrading, ill and inhuman treatment that was suffered by the applicant. Rather, the respondent's agents actively facilitated torture and the degrading treatment that was given to the applicant.

Essentially, international law attaches great importance to the positive nature of the anti-torture right obliging states to prevent harm to its citizen's.[622] Hence, in ***Osman v United Kingdom,***[623]it was pointed out that state obligation connotes putting in place effective criminal law provisions to deter the commission of offences against the person supported by law enforcement machinery for the prevention, suppression and sanctioning of breaches of such provisions.[624] Thus, Article 142 of the Criminal Code (Кривичензаконик) punishes acts of torture with a prison term of three months to five years. Also, Article 143 of the Criminal Code (Кривичензаконик) makes it an offence for a person acting in his official capacity to mistreat, intimidate, insult or treat another in such a manner that his or her human dignity or personality will be humiliated.

Arguably, the act of preventing, suppressing and sanctioning breaches of freedom from torture through the enactment of the Criminal Code (*Кривичензаконик)* could be seen as one of the ways through which states can prevent the offence of torture. However, a question could be asked: 'How effective will the provisions of such articles be in the prevention of torture, since torture is perpetrated by government/public agents?' Post-9/11, states commit acts of torture with impunity. The provisions of the criminal code (Кривичензаконик)would be a mirage without an effective justice system. Analytically, the positive duty of preventing acts of torture by states extends to taking positive steps to prevent 'impunity' for the sake of justice for victims. Perhaps this might deter or suppress future acts of torture on suspects. Hence, it becomes pertinent for states to maintain an effective and consistent justice system where the rule of law is upheld, and public confidence is guaranteed.[625]

622 I. Turner, op. cit.

623 Osman v United Kingdom (2000) 29 EHRR 245

624 ibid., para., 115

625 El-Masri v The Former Yugoslav Republic of Macedonia., op. cit., para 105

Nevertheless, specific circumstances must ensue before a state would be obliged in law to act, to prevent the violation of a person's right under Article 3 (ECHR). For instance, there must be a particular threat to identifiable victim/s as opposed to a general risk of harm to individuals as with terrorism.[626] The facts in El-Masri's case reveal that El-Masri (an identified victim) was under threat of torture from the time he was unlawfully detained in a hotel for 23 days by the respondent agents, until the time he was transferred to Afghanistan. This was a threat to the applicant's personal capacity as opposed to a threat of terrorism to the Republic of Macedonia. Again, it must be settled that the authorities knew or ought to have known that a 'real' and 'immediate risk' of torture subsists.[627] By virtue of Article 3 of the UNCAT, state parties are prohibited from expelling, returning or extraditing a person to another state where there are substantial grounds for believing that he would be in danger of being subjected to torture.[628] The UN General Assembly Report of the Special Rapporteur of the Commission on Human Rights on the question of torture and other cruel, inhuman or degrading treatment or punishment maintains that states must not surrender persons intended for extradition under terrorist or other charges unless the government of the receiving country has provided an unequivocal guarantee that the right under Article 3 (ECHR) of the persons concerned will not be violated.[629] The receiving country must also put an effective monitoring system in place to ensure that the personal dignity of the persons concerned is respected.[630]

Analytically, the right not to be tortured is one of those rights that come with inherent responsibilities or obligations on nation states such as:

(a) The obligation to obtain diplomatic assurance where there is a likelihood of torture or ill or degrading treatment. Hence, if it is expedient that a suspect or an accused person must be returned to his country or a third country where there is a likelihood of torture, the contracting country must, of necessity, obtain

626 I. Tuner, op. cit.

627 ibid

628 United Nations Convention against Torture and other Cruel, inhuman or degrading Treatment or Punishment Please provide the year

629 UN General Assembly Report of the Special Rapporteur of the Commission on Human Rights on the question of Torture and other Cruel, inhuman or degrading treatment or punishment 2002 (A/57/173)

630 ibid

diplomatic assurance from the returning country. It was not shown in the present case that the respondent government obtained such diplomatic assurance on the applicant's behalf. Neither was it shown that any monitoring mechanism was put in place by the respondent government to ensure the protection of the applicant's personal dignity while in Afghanistan. It is immaterial whether the purpose of the applicant's removal from Macedonia was an 'enforced disappearance'. It was incumbent on the respondent government to provide an effective monitoring mechanism that could shield the applicant from torture, ill or degrading treatment in Afghanistan.

(a) A duty to ensure that an 'effective' and 'independent' investigation is carried out whenever there is an allegation of 'torture' or 'ill' or 'degrading treatment' on an 'accused' or a 'suspect'. It can be argued that the applicant's case was never investigated as the facts of the case reveal that the internal inquiry set up within the Ministry of Interior to investigate the applicant's case never invited the applicant to produce any evidence, nor was he informed of the outcome of the inquiry. Therefore, the facts upon which the inquiry Committee acted were one-sided. Ideally, serious allegations of ill or degrading treatment presuppose rigorous investigation. The effectiveness of the investigation must measure up with certain procedural threshold such as 'fairness' and 'transparency'.

A contracting country is not exempt from its responsibility to carry out an 'effective' and 'independent' investigation over an allegation of torture merely because she obtained a diplomatic assurance from a returning country and put a monitoring mechanism in place to ensure that a deportee's freedom from torture is guaranteed. Hence, in ***Agiza v Sweden***[631] *and* ***Alzery v Sweden***[632]**,** Sweden obtained diplomatic assurance that Agiza and Alzery consecutively, would not be subjected to torture, would have fair trials and would not be subjected to death penalty. The assurances were backed up by regular visits by the Swedish Ambassador and participation by Swedish observers in the trial. The treatment Mr. Alzery was subjected to at the Bromma Airport included acts like he was drugged through his rectum, placed in diapers, blindfolded, hooded and

631 Agiza v Sweden (2005) Communication no 233/2003, UN Doc CAT/C/34/D/233/2003

632 Alzery v Sweden (2006) UN Doc CCPR/C/88/D/1416/2005

barefooted among other things.[633] All this amounted to the violation of Article 7 of the ICCPR, (which is equivalent to Article 3 ECHR) because Sweden had breached its obligation to carry out a prompt, independent and impartial investigation into the events at Bromma airport.[634]

The expansion of state power at the detriment of human rights is an outstanding consequence of adopting a 'war paradigm' in counterterrorism policies of most nation states such as the United States and Britain.[635] However, by virtue of S.3 of the Criminal Procedure Act of 1997 "anyone who was summoned, arrested or detained.... could not be forced to make a statement.... a person accused of an offence had to be clearly informed from the outset of his or her right to remain silent..."[636] By implication, an accused person or a suspect has the right to remain silent and by law should not be tortured to divulge any information or intelligence against his will. However, it could be questioned whether it is legal to apply torture for obtaining information in a circumstance where it is 'reasonably' assumed that a terrorist suspect has some vital information concerning a terrorist attack/threat but is not willing to release it. The provisions of Article 2(2) of the UN Convention reveal that there should be no justification for torture. Therefore, it is immaterial whether there is a state of war or a threat of war, internal political activity or any other state of emergency.[637] In El-Masri's case cited above, the treatment he was subjected to by the respondent government and the CIA agents consecutively, lacked 'legal' and 'moral' justification; even if the applicant had crucial information about a terrorist outbreak in Macedonia at that time or a future terrorist threat against Macedonia. He had the legal right not to disclose it and should not have been coerced to do so.

Arguably, if the rationale behind counterterrorism measures is to enhance national security, it becomes antithetical not to use any available means such as 'torture' to obtain an important 'intelligence' from an individual who is 'reasonably' suspected to have such information. Hence, five days after 9/11 the US

633 ibid., para 3.11

634 El-Masri v Republic of Macedonia., op. cit., para 109

635 J. Hafetz, 'Redefining state power and individual rights in the war on terrorism' (2012) vol 46(3) Valparaiso Law Review 843

636 Criminal Procedure Act of 1997 (*Закон за кривичната постапка*)

637 United Nations Convention, op. cit.

Vice President, Dick Cheney said, "...a lot of what needs to be done here has to be done quietly without any discussion... it's going to be vital for us to use any means at our disposal basically to achieve our purpose."[638] Analytically, for the purpose of enhancing national security, which also includes the protection of fundamental rights of the citizenry, this book advocates three major factors that should be present before a terrorist suspect could be tortured. (a) 'Reasonable suspicion': This excludes factors such as 'racial profiling'. Hence, if the activities of a 'terrorist suspect' point to the fact that he/she poses a significant threat to others and to the society at large, and it is reasonably believed that he/she has useful information concerning a terrorist attack but is reluctant to release such information, it becomes an obligation on the nation state to use available means such as a systematic interrogation technique to extract such information; considering the fact that one of the duties of a nation state is the promotion of national security, (which includes protection of human rights such as protection of the right to life).

However, to ensure that the need to 'torture' is not abused by the government or its agents, there must be sufficient proof to show that the suspect truly has useful information about an imminent terrorist attack. (b) Material information: For a terrorist suspect to be tortured in such circumstance, the information in his possession must be 'material' to a terrorist threat or it must be such that will assist in frustrating an impending danger if extracted, but he is not willing to release it. (c) Test of proportionality: This simply refers to the application of 'torture' as it is proportional to the circumstance. Hence, the level of torture should be proportional to the urgency of the situation. For instance, the level of torture to which a terrorist suspect who has vital information about an 'imminent' terrorist threat is subjected to should vary from the level of torture suffered by a terrorist suspect with information about a 'future' terrorist threat. By implication, torture in such circumstances is based on the premise that the person in question is in possession of information, which is 'material' to a terrorist threat/attack (imminent or future threat) but is reluctant to release it.

638 W. Stritzke, et al., op. cit.

5.4.2 PROHIBITION OF TORTURE ON A TERRORIST SUSPECT IN THE EVENT OF DEPORTATION OR EXPULSION

Contracting states have the right as a matter of well-established international law, and subject to their treaty obligations, including the ECHR, to control the entry, residence and expulsion of aliens.[639] However, the exercise of such right may give rise to an issue under Article 3 of the ECHR. Hence, in international human rights law, it is an anomaly for states to transfer individuals to countries where there is a real risk of torture or ill treatment. In ***Chahal v United Kingdom,*** the applicant was given notice of intention to deport as his continued stay in the UK was deemed unconducive to public good in view of national security and the fight against international terrorism. The applicant contested such notice because he will be subjected to torture if deported to Punjab.[640] The court held that Article 3 of the ECHR obliged states not to move a person to another state where he would face a real risk of torture or inhuman or degrading treatment or punishment (hereinafter, "torture"), notwithstanding any threat to public safety or national security.[641]

In effect, Article 3 ECHR makes it a challenge for nation states to expel terrorist suspects who cannot be convicted of criminal offence/s and with regard to whom vigilance or constraint on their movement might be insufficient to protect public safety. Hence, the focus is on the protection of the 'single' right of a terrorist suspect not to be tortured vis-a-vis the innocent citizenry living in 'torture' as a result of 'intense fear' of insecurity (terrorism). Critically, the non-derogatory nature of Article 3 of the ECHR to some extent frustrates the enhancement of national security. For instance, although the applicant in the present case had the freedom of assembly and association pursuant to Article 11 of the ECHR to join the Sikh movement, his exercise of such right should not encroach into the rights of others; neither should it negate the interest of national security.[642] The facts of the case reveal that the applicant was a leading figure in the Sikh community. The Sikh movement advocated the use of

639 Chahal v United Kingdom., op. cit.

640 ibid

641 Chahal v The United Kingdom., op. cit.

642 European Convention on Human Rights 1950

'violence' for the achievement of its vision. Hence, the Sikhs in London reacted with 'horror' to the storming of the Golden Temple in India (the holiest Sikh shrine). The applicant assisted in the organisation of a demonstration in London in protest of the Indian Government's actions. He was also convicted of assault and affray after disturbances in London. Amongst other violent activities of the Sikh in India was the killing of a senior Indian police officer in the Golden Temple and the assassination of the former Indian Prime Minister, Mrs Indira Gandhi, by her two bodyguards who were Sikh members.[643] The applicant might not have been a terrorist in stricto sensu; but overall it could be argued that he had violent tendencies, which can disrupt the peace of the community.

Also, in the event of any demonstration by the Sikh movement in the UK, other clandestine vulnerable or terrorist groups in the UK might have taken advantage of such demonstration to launch a terrorist attack in the UK, even if the Sikh movement was not a terrorist movement. Undoubtedly, the court considered the prevailing circumstances in Punjab in its decision. Nevertheless, one questions the reasonability of retaining someone whose activities or tendencies pose a threat to public order all in the name of the observance of his right not to be tortured. National security as analysed in this book incorporates people's security (human rights), which implies not only the security of a 'single' individual but the security of all. In complying with the absolute nature of the right under Article 3, we must also lend credence to the fact that the safety of people is the first law.[644]

Considering some of the effects of terrorism, such as loss of lives, it can be argued that the absolute nature of the right not to be tortured indirectly waters down the observance and full enjoyment of some other fundamental rights such as the 'right to life'. Thus, if a person who poses a security risk cannot be moved to another country in compliance with his right not to be tortured, to what extent is the 'right to life' of the masses in the contracting nation protected in view of the uncertainty that characterises terrorist networks and attacks respectively? In this vain, are we looking at the absolute nature of the right not to be tortured in relation to its practicability or are we concerned merely with the

643 ibid

644 M. Ignateiff, *The lesser evil: Political ethics in an age of error* (4th edn, Princeton University Press, New Jersey 2004), viii

compliance of such provision of international human rights law in isolation to life occurrences? Hence, the question could be asked: 'What is the rationalisation of the right not to torture someone whose activities manifestly show that he is a potential security risk when often most terrorists are suicide bombers, as was seen in the 9/11 incident? Which is the greater evil, torture or murder?'

Ultimately, if a terrorist suspect is not deported or expelled on grounds of the protection of his right under Article 3 ECHR, his continuous detention has the tendency of culminating into unlawful detention (indefinite detention); often arbitrary detention creates an environment for the offence of torture. Therefore, in the long run, the terrorist suspect who could not be deported in observance to his right not to be tortured is still caught up with the same evil in the contracting country while in detention.

5.4.3 TORTURE AS TERRORISM

On the other hand, legally speaking, as pointed out above, the absolute nature of the right not to be tortured is such that even if the applicant is caught in an act of terrorism he cannot be subjected to torture or any ill or degrading treatment or punishment for obtaining information. Its absolute nature persists, even in emergency situations. Hence, it is immaterial whether a nation's security is threatened by terrorism. However, terrorism, like torture, instigates intense fear (anxiety) and terror in human beings. Realistically, the mechanism and goal of torture are same as that of terrorism. The means by which torture is thought to achieve its objective is by instilling an overpowering sense of debility (weakness), dependency and dread in the victims.[645] In terms of terrorism, the intense fear and anxiety provoked by the threat of coercion is more devastating than the sensation of real physical pain.[646] Moghaddam defined terrorism as:

> "Politically motivated violence perpetrated by individuals, groups, state-sponsored agents intended to instil fear and helplessness in a population to influence decision making and to change behaviour".[647]

---

645 W. Stritzke, et al., op. cit.

646 ibid; K. Morrison, et al., *International Handbook of War, Torture, and Terrorism* (Springer, New York 2012), 7

647 ibid; M. Basoglu, *Torture and its Consequences: Current Treatment Approaches* (Cambridge University Press, Cambridge 1992), 207

Comparatively, the provocation of 'intense fear' is also the principle objective of torture to obtain information. The goal of terrorists is not only the infliction of 'pain' and 'suffering' on individuals, but they also aim to diffuse fear among nation states and ruin the entire sense of personal and national safety. Accordingly, instilling debilitating fear is mutual to both terrorism and torture as a means of achieving political ends.[648] In such sense, torture ought to remain unacceptable as a counterterrorism measure and legally prohibited. Probably, the prohibition of torture should assume a 'war paradigm' as is the case with 'terrorism' since, despite the absolute nature of the right not to be tortured, nation states are still caught in acts of torture. However, a question may be asked about how far the adoption of a 'war paradigm' would go in the eradication of torture. Conceivably, a comparative analysis of the adoption of a 'war paradigm' in countering terrorism has shown that it aggravates the problem rather than curtailing the persisting challenge of terrorist acts. For instance, some people get radicalised when they see the level of torture terrorist suspects are subjected to, especially people from the same religious faith.[649] Hence, torture is part of a failing logic in reducing the threat of terrorism and bringing terrorists to justice.[650]

It could be asked how productive torture is as a means of obtaining intelligence. It could be said that torture is not only illicit or immoral but is ineffective in generating authentic intelligence. Bin Laden's case can be considered in answering such question. The detainee who released the information, which eventually helped to capture Bin Laden, was never tortured.[651] The most crucial intelligence obtained from him concerning the main Al-Qaeda facilitator, his role in Al-Qaeda and his relationship with Bin Laden was gained through normal non-coercive means.[652] This is opposed to the false information given by another detainee who

648 ibid; F. Allhoff, *Terrorism, Ticking Time-Bombs and Torture: A Philosophical Analysis* (The University of Chicago Press, Chicago 2012), 12

649 A. Clarke, op. cit.

650 ibid

651 J. McCain, 'Bin Laden's death and the debate against torture' (2011) *http://www.washingtonpost.com/opinions/bin-ladens-death-and-the-debate-over-torture/2011/05/AFdimdsG_story.html*, accessed 2nd December 2017

652 ibid; G. Solis, *The Law of Armed Conflict: International Humanitarian Law in War* (Cambridge University Press, New York 2016), 632

was subjected to intensive interrogation techniques.[653] Nevertheless, it cannot be denied that the abuse of prisoners sometimes produces useful intelligence; but often it produces false intelligence as the detainee might intentionally give false information in order to end the torture.[654]

The criminal offence of torture is complicated in nature in the sense that it incubates in other offences such as arbitrary detention, enforced disappearance, complicity in intelligence sharing, and extrajudicial killing. States are complicit of torture in the war against terrorism. Complicity in torture by states or their agents is deemed unlawful under general principles of international law of state responsibility for internationally wrongful acts. Internationally wrongful conduct often emanates from collaboration of two or more states as opposed to one state.[655] For instance, British airspace and airport facilities have been in use for rendition and torture. The UK government has been complicit in torture through her intelligence sharing. The British intelligence services obtain information knowingly and with reasonable suspicion that such information is obtained through torture. For example, Binyan Mohammed was subjected to torture by Moroccan interrogators in order to extract confessions from him based on information furnished by the British M15.[656] The British intelligence services have also passed unreliable intelligence to intelligence services of other countries, which formed the basis for detention, abuse and torture of detainees.[657] Arguably, if torture is deemed illegal and unacceptable as a counterterrorism measure, its proceeds (intelligence) should also be regarded as such.

The exploration of the nature of torture depicts that torture destroys the individual, leaving in its place only meat, bones and blood.[658] Hence, "a society that thinks it has to torture will become as it tortures, something no longer

---

653 ibid; E. Holtzman, et al., *Cheating Justice: How Bush and Cheney Attacked the Rule of Law, Plotted to Avoid Prosecution and What We Can Do About It* (Beacon Press, Boston 2012), Ch 3

654 ibid; J. Stone, *Interrogation: World War II, Vietnam, and Iraq* (NDIC Press, Washington, D.C 2010), 3-6

655 Great Britain Parliament: House of Lords, House of Commons, Joint Committee on Human Rights., Allegations of UK complicity in torture (2008-09) Twenty-third report of session

656 ibid

657 A. Qureshi, 'Fabricating terrorism 111: British complicity in renditions and torture' (2011) <*www.therenditionproject.org.uk/documents/eur-comlicity.html*> accessed 10 March 2014

658 M. Davis, 'The moral justifiability of torture and other cruel, inhuman and degrading treatment' (2005) vol19 (2) International Journal of Applied Philosophy 161-178

recognisable as a human society."[659] This, in effect, will rubbish the very essence of human security which, on a wider scale, encompasses national security. Torture constitutes grave human rights violation whose effect on the victim is both physical and psychological.[660]To obtain confession, pain is inflicted on terrorists or terrorist suspects. Thus, Maurice MerleauPonty argues that,

> "body and mind possess an intimacy that is undeniable... the mind's higher functions, including perception, cognition, memory and wanting, are 'anchored in the body' and when one undergoes torture, these capacities are altered."[661]

Although torture is declared illegal by most national, regional and international laws and treaties, it continues to occur around the world. The flagrant violation of the right not to be tortured under international human rights law ignites some questions: What has gone wrong? Were peculiar circumstances (such as international terrorism) not considered, before the laws on 'torture' were enacted? Or do states that ratified international treaties on torture not perceive international law as 'law' in strict sensu? Realistically, the offence of torture, ill, inhuman or degrading treatment or punishment is predominant in cases of arbitrary detention such as secret detentions, enforced disappearance, or extraordinary rendition. Such offences are peculiar, though not limited to, the search for intelligence in the bid to counter terrorism. Practically speaking, such provisions of international Conventions become illusory since acts of torture are often committed by states that are expressly obligated through rules of international human rights law to comply with its jus cogent norm. On the other hand, logically, the degree of compliance with rules of international human rights law in relation to 'torture' would have been encouraging if the offence of torture is committed by individuals in their personal capacity. In such circumstance, the enforcement of law will be by a superior (state actor) over a subordinate (non-state actor). The situation becomes cumbersome where the enforcement of a law is meant to be carried out by the violator (in this case state actors).

---

659 R. Brecher, op. cit.

660 J. Jadhav, et al., 'Views of medical students on torture in Ahmadabad city' (2013) vol 5 (7) International Journal of Current Research and Review 61

661 M. Flynn, *Screening torture: Media representations of the state of torture and political domination* (Columbia University Press, New York 2012)

5.5 SUMMARY

In summary, one of the fundamental values of a democratic society is enshrined in the prohibition of torture. The prohibition of torture is inseparably linked to the concept of human rights. Human rights have gained low priority post-9/11, especially for such states that feel justified in ignoring their obligations. Hence, they respond with policy shifts or alterations in law that restrict fundamental rights. Therefore, they prioritise torture in the face of terrorism.[662] Torture constitutes one of the strongest bases of community grievance against state authority.[663] However, the task of creating a balance between 'torture' and 'terrorism' is problematic. Torture is a two-sided coin in the sense that in certain circumstances it has the potential of stimulating terrorists or potential terrorists into action (terrorist attack) in a bid to get revenge for any treatment considered by them as torture, ill or degrading to their counterparts. For instance, those responsible for the London bombing of July 2005 claimed that they were motivated by the attendant atrocities done by the UK government during their bombing and occupation of Iraq.[664] A British foreign secretary "... warned that the camp was as much a radicalising and destabilising influence" as it was an aid in the "war on terror".[665] Hence, a senior Pentagon analyst stated, "Quite frankly I'd have thought that if they weren't terrorists before they went to Gitmo (Guantanamo Bay) they would have been by the time they came out".[666]

On the other hand, since the issue of torture has attracted worldwide attention through information technology post-9/11, it can be argued that torture also has the potential of serving as a deterrent to potential terrorists. Perhaps, torture, ill or degrading treatment accounts (such as water boarding) of terrorist suspects can serve as a discouraging factor to some potential terrorists. It might not deter a huge number of potential terrorists from engaging in future terrorist attacks, especially those who have the tendency of suicide bombing. However, to some

662 C. Moore, 'The world spins madly on: How the P5 caused a paradigm shift in norm diffusion' (2013) Social Science Research Network

663 W. Stritzke, op. cit.

664 R. Brecher, *Is the use of coercive interrogation or torture permissible and effective as a counterterrorism model:Contemporary debates on terrorism* (Routledge, Oxon 2012), 132

665 M. Beckett, 'Beckett admits Guantanamo camp should be shut down', (2006) <*http://news.independent.co.uk/uk/politics/article/1868066.ece.*> accessed 17 February 2014

666 S. Levinson, *Torture: A collection* (Oxford University Press, New York 2004), 291

degree it can discourage a percentage of them from terrorism. In such sense, to a lesser degree, it can be reasoned that torture indirectly serves as a counterterrorism measure.

For the purposes of clarity, this book does not advocate torture or other cruel, ill or degrading treatment; but it is critical of the 'non-derogatory' nature of the right not to be tortured. The possibility of creating a viable balance between torture and terrorism might be vague considering the absolute nature of the right not to be tortured. Under international law, a nation state cannot expel or deport an individual to his country or to a third country where there is likelihood of him being tortured or subjected to cruel, ill or degrading treatment. Impliedly, a nation state cannot deport or expel a person who is 'reasonably suspected' of terrorism to a country where he might be tortured even when his activities in the contracting state pose a risk to national security. Hence, one queries what the moral or legal justification is for a deportee not to be tortured, since his personal 'activity' or 'terrorist tendency' amounts to torture to the nation and its citizenry as they stand at risk of a terrorist attack.

5.6 FREEDOM OF EXPRESSION AND COUNTERTERRORISM

The right to freedom of expression is provided for under Article 10(1) of the ECHR, which provides:

> "Everyone has the right to freedom of expression. This right shall include the freedom to hold opinions and to receive and impart information and ideas without interference by public authority and regardless of frontiers..."[667]

Unlike Article 3 of the ECHR, this right is not an absolute right. It is limited to the thoughts, opinions and intentions that are not proscribed by law. Hence, freedom of expression does not guarantee a truly free expression in the sense of being wholly unrestricted. This is because, in a democratic society, freedom comes with duties and responsibilities towards the rights, duties and need of

667 European Convention of Human Rights, op. cit.

others. In exercising the right to freedom of expression, it will therefore be inimical to perceive the right as one with unrestricted permissiveness.[668] The restriction of such right can be on moral, ethical, private or national security grounds.[669] However, even where restricted such right plays a vital role at every level (individual and state levels). It enhances individual dignity and facilitates state-related decision making. Arguably, the level of implementation of the right to freedom of expression depicts the level of legal awareness in a society and exhibits the existence and quality of a proper democracy in a state. Therefore, freedom of expression constitutes one of the most crucial civil liberties and an integral element of a constitutional foundation of any state.[670]

Freedom of expression is one of the fundamental human rights that constitute an intrinsic aspect of a democratic society.[671] It constitutes one of the basic conditions for its progress and for every individual's self-fulfilment.[672] Freedom of expression, in addition to its synonymous concept, freedom of speech, depicts an essential aspect of civil rights and liberties. Freedom of speech guarantees political rights of people to express their opinions and ideas without governmental restriction, whereas freedom of expression goes a step further to cover seeking, receiving[673] and communicating information, opinions or ideas through any form of communication and media.[674] From a liberal perspective, freedom of expression is a crucial requirement for a healthy society since optimal solutions to problems are obtained through open debates.[675] Freedom of expression is not limited to the rights to freely express thoughts and opinions, but embraces

---

668 E. Gordon, 'Freedom of expression and its limits in blogs as means of contemporary communication' (2013) vol 37(4) Teme: CasopiszaDrustveneNauke 1779

669 S. Aaronson, 'Internet governance or internet control: How to safeguard internet freedom' (2013) <*www.cicerofoundation.org*> accessed 29 April 2014

670 E. Gordon, op. cit.

671 ibid

672 K. McGuire, et al., 'State of the union report: A road map addressing reform possibilities based upon a comparative analysis of the legal regulation of hate speech and hate crime' (2013) Central Lancashire online Knowledge

673 G. Nick, 'Enforcing the London 2012 airspace restrictions: Lessons arising from the "lethal force option' (2014) vol 2 European Human Rights Law Review 142

674 E. Gordon, op. cit.

675 J. Balkin, Digital speech and Democratic culture: A theory of freedom of expression for the information society (2004) vol 79(1) New York University Law Review 1

the right to share such information through various information channels and communication media such as newspapers, radio, television and the internet.[676]

This subsection sets out to answer the question: 'Are there circumstances under which the restriction on the right to freedom of expression is necessary to prevent or inhibit terrorism?'

The use of information and communication technologies became subjects of in-depth discussion post-9/11, as new technologies started posing their challenges in the exercise of the right to freedom of expression. For instance, television, the internet, mobile phones and computers have both positive and negative consequences. In reality, nation states face challenges and possibilities from the use of the internet and the increased interconnectedness of the world, as individuals are connected through the social media, internet forums and email. In addition, a single data stick can store millions of pages of top-secret documents. At the same time, the use of the internet and other platforms of communication have made it possible for states to identify, survey and control information distributed through such media.[677]

From a militant liberal ideological position, the importance of freedom of expression cannot be underestimated in any society.[678] However, individuals and governments vary in the value they place on it. Ultimately, through freedom of expression, individuals debate key issues to achieve a common good. An interviewee argues that in a democratic society, poisonous views ought not to be hidden from the public; rather they ought to be contested in the open. He reiterates that doctrines which we do not subscribe to ought to be tolerated, but must be contested through debate.[679] Hence, from such liberal perspective, the basis of freedom of expression is the protection of the ability of the people as a whole to ascertain their own fate and permit true self-determination.[680] Some

676 E. Gordon, op. cit.

677 C. Bollingtoft, et al., 'Under the guise of national security: Surveillance, Snowden and the challenges to democracy' (2014) Roskilde University: Department of Society and Globalization

678 J. Mill, *On Liberty* (Broadview press, Canada 1999)

679 M. Buerk, 'What are the limits of freedom of expression?' (2014) <*www.bbc.co.uk/podcast/series/moralmaze*> accessed 3rd July 2014

680 J. Raikka, 'The argument from truth as a basis for legislation concerning freedom of speech' (2003) vol 7(4) Trames 249

liberal scholars posit that freedom of expression is predicated upon the existence of a free society. Hence, its limitation by law will result in the contradiction of self-government and the limitation of our basic rights.[681] They contend that governmental restriction should not encroach on freedom of expression. Hence, one scholar posits that tolerance for hate speech strengthens society.[682] They argue that freedom of speech is more essential than censoring speech content. Thus, if speech is restricted, it silences those who will largely benefit from its expression.[683]

However, there is a degree of risk (the risk of human rights violation) in a democratic society. As a result, we have a responsibility to uphold the principles of democracy. Ideally, democracy needs to have tools to protect it. Article 10(2) of the ECHR could be one (of) such tool. Hence, the right to freedom of expression has some boundaries. For instance, hate speech ought to be restricted by law as it has the potential to brew violence.[684] Expressions are not viruses.[685] They do not infect your mind, but pass through the brain or mind and as such can poison our minds. Some vulnerable individuals can be radicalised through such expressions. In such circumstances, it becomes safer not to access such information. It will be illusionary to say that certain expressions do not incite certain people to violence. Some expressions could be more lethal than others. Not everyone can cope with some dangerous ideas.[686]

From such perspective, undoubtedly, freedom of expression is one of the essential ingredients of a democratic society.[687] However, we must not ignore the fact that unrestricted enjoyment of the right to freedom of expression has the potential of giving legal effect and legitimacy to the abuse of rights. For instance, in

681 D. Downs, et al., 'Predicting the importance of the freedom of speech and the perceived harm of hate speech' (2012) vol 42(2) Journal of Applied Social Psychology 1353

682 L. Bollinger, *The tolerant society: freedom of speech and extremist speech in America* (Oxford University Press, New York 1986)

683 D. Downs, op. cit.

684 S. Foster, Are we becoming afraid of free speech (2013) vol 18(1) Coventry Law Journal 92-99

685 M. Buerk, op. cit.

686 ibid

687 C. Marino, 'Freedom of expression and the internet' (2013) Inter American Commission on Human Rights

B.H., M.W., H.P. and G.K. v Austria,[688] the applicants' right under Article 10 of the ECHR was restricted, as its unrestricted enjoyment had the capacity of encroaching into others' right under Article 14 of the ECHR namely; prohibition of discrimination. The applicants were punished for their membership and leading functions within two right wing political organisations. Their activities were inspired by national socialist ideas, which included the preparation and promotion of publication pamphlets suggesting that the killing of six million Jews was a lie. Additionally, one of the party programmes was based on an ideology, which included the alleged biological differences between individuals, peoples and races.[689] Thus, the European Commission on Human Rights maintained that National Socialism is a totalitarian doctrine incompatible with 'democracy' and 'human rights', whose adherents seek the type of aims referred to in Article 17 of the ECHR. As a result, the Commission declared the applicants' complaints based on violation of their right under Article 10 of the ECHR as manifestly ill founded.[690] Accordingly, the exercise of a person's freedom of expression is not a guarantee for the violation of other peoples' rights under the ECHR; hence, there is need for its restriction. However, it is pertinent that such restriction is carried out within the confines of rule of law and as is "necessary in a democratic society". To discuss this further, it is necessary to examine ECHR case law on such phrase and how it fits into the legal qualifications to freedom of expression.

In **Saygili and Falakaoglu v Turkey,**[691] the applicants were the owner and editor of a newspaper, respectively. The newspaper published an article entitled "Abductions are on the increase". Subsequently, the newspaper also published another article concerning the issue of forced disappearances in south-east Turkey. The applicants were charged with the disclosure of the identities of public officials who were involved in the fight against terrorism, thereby exposing such persons as targets to terrorist organisations. The prosecutor alleged that the articles had endangered the life of Colonel L.E. (a public official).[692] The applicants maintained that the article in question was a news item of public

688 B.H., M.W., H.P. and G.K. v Austria (1989) European Commission 12774/87

689 K. McGuire, et al., op. cit.

690 ibid

691 Saygili and Falakaoglu v Turkey (2008/09) Strasbourg 39457/03

692 ibid., para 8

interest, which they communicated in a manner consistent with their obligations and responsibilities.

The Court acquitted the applicants in respect of charges concerning the second article but convicted them in respect of charges concerning the first. The Court contemplated that the first article was written under the pretext of news with the purpose of presenting Colonel L.E. as a target for a terrorist organisation as the Colonel's name was expressly mentioned in the first article.[693] On appeal, the Court's judgement was upheld. The applicants contended that the conviction amounted to a violation of their right to freedom of expression.

Acceptably, the outstanding role of the press in a state governed by rule of law cannot be ignored; for instance, the responsibility of imparting information and ideas on political questions and on other matters of public interest.[694] As stated above, the right to freedom of expression is not an absolute right. Hence, in such case, in exercising their right to freedom of expression, the applicants must ensure that they comply with formalities, conditions, restrictions or penalties prescribed by law and are necessary in a democratic society for prevention of disorder or crime or for protection of the reputation or rights of others.[695] In such a case, it could be argued that the applicants exceeded the limits of their rights to freedom of expression. Obviously, it is not the intention of Article 10 of the ECHR to bring about disorder in society. Hence, the express mention of Colonel L.E.'s name in the first article published by the applicants had the capacity to incite the public into an unlawful attack against the Turkish government or against Colonel L.E. or both. Thus, pursuant to S. 6 of Turkey's Prevention of Terrorism Act of 1991 it is an offence for the identity of civil servants involved in anti-terrorist operations to be revealed in any publication or for any person to be marked as a target.[696] Nevertheless, it will be consistent with the rights and responsibilities of an individual in a democratic society if such articles or information are made available to the public in such a manner where the identities of persons involved in the incidents in question are not expressly mentioned, but

693 ibid., para 10

694 ibid., para 22

695 ibid

696 The Prevention of Terrorism Act (Law No 3713 12 April 1991)

at the same time the appropriate message is conveyed to the audience without being watered down.

By virtue of S.3 of Turkey's Press Act of 1950, an article will be said to have been published if it is exposed, displayed, distributed, sold, offered for sale or subjected to emission in a place where it can be accessed by the public or by anyone.[697] A consideration of the second part of S.3 of this Act shows that the applicants would not have committed an offence if the article was not published, except where the article is unlawful.[698] By implication, it is immaterial whether the article is published. The law forbids the existence of an article, if it is unlawful. Hence, a critical examination of the last part of S.3 of the Press Act reveals that even if an article is not published, it will still constitute an offence if such an article is in itself unlawful. An analysis of Article 10 of the ECHR shows that a publication will be unlawful if it has the potential of bringing disorder or leading to crime in society or impinging on the reputation or rights of others. Thus, unlawful materials/articles are parallel to the intention of the right to freedom of expression. Impliedly, although article 10 of the ECHR empowers individuals to express their opinions in various ways such as the publication of materials, it does not empower them to publish materials, which will destabilise national security or impair the reputation of others. Such publications are not acceptable (illegal) under law; for example, provocative materials (materials related to religious or political extremism). Essentially, if an article is unlawful because of its contents it is ab initio inconsistent with the spirit of freedom of expression.

Logically, freedom of expression does not connote freedom to express every piece of information within one's ambit. It must be accepted that such right is not absolute. However, when an individual is legally mandated to filter the information he or she seeks to express, such an individual cannot always freely express personal account of incidents that took place in the society. Where then is the core of the right to freedom of expression? Often the information individuals are prevented from publishing is such that touches on national security, or such that touches on the reputation of those in authority, as was seen in the present case. In such circumstance, can it be said that the right to freedom of expression is actively operational in a democratic society? Arguably, what will

697 ibid

698 The Press Act (Law No 5680 15 July 1950)

be the essence of the right to freedom of expression if one cannot publish his opinion or information in the form or manner as he or she perceives it? If a person is prohibited by law from publishing his opinions, ideas or information in their raw state, freedom of expression is as good as being non-existent. More so, the right to freedom of expression automatically involves two parties; the communicator and the receiver. Analytically, the receiver's right to freedom of expression is also curbed as such right extends to the reception of information (freedom to receive information), which is one of the constitutive elements of freedom of expression.

Critically, the significance of the right to freedom of expression in a democratic society cannot be undermined without damaging democracy itself. Freedom of expression can assist in curbing the possible excesses of a government and executive power. For instance, the newspaper article entitled "abductions are on the increase" by the applicants had the potential of reducing the rate of forced disappearances in Turkey. This was because the government recognised the fact that a greater awareness of such abductions has been created in the public domain. Analytically, once such consciousness is created or enlarged within the public domain and, also in government circles, it may serve as a check on the latter. In such respect, it is immaterial whether the information is true.[699]

On the other hand, the legal restriction on the right to freedom of expression may to a great extent assist in checking terrorism, thereby enhancing national security. As a result, the issue is not one of maximising either freedom of expression or national security within a balance or zero-sum game. In exercising their right to freedom of expression, persons both private and public can become aware that certain formalities, conditions and restrictions must be met. Therefore, it is legally settled that certain information and opinions cannot be expressed and certain materials cannot be published. Hence, freedom of expression does not apply to such expressions that will ignite insecurity in the society (both private and national insecurity) or destabilise public order; for example, incitement to violence, defamation, espionage, subversion, sedition, and genocide, glorification of terrorism or hate crime. Accordingly, the potential of an expressed opinion or a published material to cause 'harm' to others can be seen, even if a classic liberal ideological position stemming from J S Mill is provided as

699 Saygili and Falakaoglu v Turkey., para 23

a justification for the restriction on the right to freedom of expression.[700] Or, is it simply on a less absolutist reading that freedom of expression does not apply and therefore is not limited here at all?

The right to hold opinion is one of the embodiments of freedom of expression. For example, the radical opinion that Britain and USA need to be transformed into Islamic theocratic states by whatever means necessary to achieve this, including politically motivated paramilitary violence, could be interpreted as being outside the acceptable limit of Article 10 of the ECHR. Thus, as soon as an opinion is expressed or communicated in any manner or medium, it becomes of concern to others (private persons, the public, nations, groups, organisations), as the case may be. The expressed opinion has the potential to affect the receivers of such opinions either positively or negatively and the issue of "radicalisation" of potential terrorists needs to be thought of in such context too. Ultimately, the restriction is on the expression of the opinion and not on holding the opinion as such, because there is no reasonable premise for interfering with the freedom of thought.[701] Nevertheless, laws imposing political or religious censorship or laws ensuring governmental control over the media and muting nonpartisan or critical voices or practices for example, the intimidation of journalists, are contrary to the spirit of the right to freedom of expression.[702]

Considering the legal restrictions on the right to freedom of expression, could it be said that terrorism is under an effective control vis-a-vis the exercise of the right to freedom of expression? The world has "gone digital".[703] The internet is a product of globalisation, defined as a type of global information infrastructure consisting of computer hardware and software that is characterised as both 'general' and 'open'.[704] It is general in the sense that it was not designed for a particular set of services. Impliedly, many of the currently available services, such as the direct, real-time interaction, had not been conceived when the internet was designed. The internet is open in that all the specifications required to

700 M. Tushnet, et al., Handbook of Constitutional Law (Rutledge Publishing, London 2013)

701 ibid

702 ibid

703 R. Peterson, et al., op. cit.

704 R. Peterson, et al., 'Exploring the implications of the internet for consumer marketing' (1997) vol 25(4) Journal of the Academy of Marketing Science 329

use it are publicly available; anyone who observes certain protocols can access and traverse it.[705] It is possibly the most common medium of communication by means of email, Skype, Facebook and the like. The very technologies that empower us to create and build empower to disrupt and destroy.[706]

Cyber war has become the order of the day.[707] The inherent characteristics of the internet, such as affordability, anonymity, security and the fact that it is not geographically bound and is mostly an unregulated channel for communication, has, on one hand, provided its users with an unprecedented marketplace for the exchange of ideas. On the other hand, it has, amongst other things, created an environment for communication among criminal co-conspirators.[708] It has become increasingly clear that terrorist organisations in the exercise of their freedom of expression have availed themselves of the opportunity provided by the internet to recruit, train adherents and foot soldiers, and plan and execute (cyber) attacks.[709] Amongst other things, the internet facilitates information sharing and information gathering for terrorism.[710] Through the internet, terrorists and their organisations engage in publicity, propaganda and psychological warfare. There is increased publicity for terrorism through the internet. This can come in form of historical information, profiles of leaders, or manifestos. At the same time, terrorists use the internet for disinformation, delivering threats and disseminating horrific images.[711] Considering the unique nature of the digital world (geographically unbound), such expressions are released around the globe within seconds. Hence, the internet permits fast dissemination of violent beliefs and ideas as well as the encouragement of glorification of violent hate crimes.[712]

---

705 ibid

706 N. Sah, et al., Cyber-attack armed attack? The implications and challenges (2013) vol 19(8) Computer and Telecommunications Law Review 226

707 R. Jody, Cyber war v Cyber stability (2009) Paper for the 42nd Session World Federation of Scientists International Seminars on Planetary Emergencies 97-103

708 T. Hinnen, The cyber front in the war against terrorism: Curbing terrorist use of the internet (2004) vol 5(5) The Columbia Science and Technology Law Review 1-42

709 ibid

710 M. Conway, 'Terrorists "use" of the internet and fighting back' (2006) vol19 Information and Security 9

711 M. Conway, Terrorism and the internet: New Media-New threat? (2006) vol 59(2) Parliamentary Affairs 283

712 K. McGuire, et al., op. cit.

The support of communication technologies has made societies into organised networks of integrated or "wired" individuals. The media communication system operates as a connection between organisations, institutions and communities of "networked" individuals.[713] Individuals and groups of individuals spread all kinds of information around the world with the advent of the internet and some of them are related to the actuality or reality of acts of terrorism or beliefs and plans connected with such acts and their incitement or glorification. Arguably, the way information is generated, processed and transmitted in the network system constitutes its defining element.[714] Hence, Rebecca Blood proposed, "... the weblog's greatest strength—its uncensored, unmediated, uncontrolled voice—is also its greatest weakness."[715] A web host once stated:

> "...our service is designed to let internet users freely express any ideas and opinions without us censoring or endorsing them... However, you may also find the occasional blog that offends you...we will not shut down blog because they are offensive."[716]

Undoubtedly, the free and open architecture of the World Wide Web constitutes a challenge to freedom of expression and national security.[717] The level of control of such right in the web is not such that it will reduce or eliminate the level of abuse of the right to freedom of expression to its bare minimum. Similarly, the level of control of the exercise of the right to freedom of expression in the web is such that it cannot enhance national security. Hence, in exercising their right to freedom of expression, the internet is used by terrorists as an "information weapon" for the increase of their visibility and publication of their activities,[718] thereby terrifying their targets through psychological warfare.[719] Ultimately, materials posted are not monitored or controlled. Realistically, society cannot

713 C. Bollingtoft, et al., op. cit.

714 ibid

715 E. Gordon, op. cit.

716 ibid

717 B. Kyrgyzstan, *Capacity building in the fight against terrorism* (Netherlands IOS Press BV, Amsterdam 2013)

718 ibid; T. Johnson, *Power National Security, and Transformational Global Events* (CRC Press, New York 2012), 6

719 ibid; D. Ventre, *Information Warfare* (Iste Ltd.& John Wiley and Sons Inc, New York 2016) Table 4.7

depend on the propriety of bloggers to ascertain that only 'decent' and 'security friendly' materials will be posted. Terrorists can be bloggers. Terrorists and their groups or alliances might recruit loyalties through the internet or they may use the internet to educate the public on terrorism. Undeniably, offenders could be punished under state laws. However, practically speaking, the wide use of the internet in recent times will show that the proportion of unpunished internet offenders will outweigh such offenders who are punished.[720] It is immaterial whether such right is under an effective control offline through the media such as television, radio, or newspapers. The level of control on the right to freedom of expression in the web constitutes a major challenge to national and international security.

The impact of such blogs on national security cannot be disregarded in any discussion on the exercise of the right to freedom of expression. Bloggers have the potential to influence their readers who have specifically subscribed to them out of personal interest, and even becoming their opinion leaders as their readers can also communicate with them.[721] Analytically, the importance of the role of information technology, such as the internet, in the exercise of the right to freedom of expression cannot be overlooked in a contemporary society. At the same time, arguably, it constitutes a major threat to national security. For instance, most web hosts exempt themselves from the responsibility of the contents of materials posted on their websites. For example, the following text is found in each web host:

> "All content whether publicly posted or privately transmitted is the sole responsibility of the person who originated the content. We may not monitor or control the content... and we cannot take responsibility..."[722]

Logically it will be inappropriate for a web host to be held responsible for another person's act of expression, merely because the information is made public through his or her web service, as the thought expressed in the information is not that of the web host. However, it can be argued that the information

720 ibid; B. Ganor, et al., *Hypermedia Seduction of Terrorist Recruiting: NATO Science for Peace and Security Series* (IOS Press, Amsterdam 2007), 47

721 E. Gordon, op. cit.

722 ibid

was expressed at the time it was transferred from the originator to the web host for publication and not when it is posted on the internet. Arguably, it is immaterial whether the web host is just a single individual. Once two parties are involved; the communicator and the receiver, expression could be deemed to have taken place. To such extent, it is possible that the legal restriction on the right to freedom of expression as provided under Article 10 of the ECHR has not done much to prevent terrorism.

Conversely, an examination of Article 10 of the ECHR depicts that freedom of expression is not limited to the 'reception' of information. It extends to the 'impartation' of information. Thus, it can be argued that it is in consonance with the intention of Article 10(2) of the ECHR for a web host to take responsibility of the contents of the materials that will be published through his websites, since 'publication' is an element of 'impartation of information' irrespective of the fact that the web host is not the originator of such material. This could be seen as one of the formalities, which qualify the right to freedom of expression in a democratic society. On the other hand, it could be argued that the censorship of a material by a web host who is not an originator of such a material could possibly amount to an interference with the owner's right to freedom of expression; especially where the expression is 'contentious', but at the same time is within the purview of Article 10. Individuals differ in the way they perceive issues. It is possible for a web host to perceive a 'contentious' expression as 'provocative'. In effect, this might alter the main substance of such material if it is being censored by the web host. Perhaps, such censorship should pursue a legitimate aim such as prevention of crime or disorder. Accordingly, the spirit of Article 17 of the ECHR is such that will not allow a web host to censor a material to a degree greater than is allowed under law.

Freedom of expression issues can also arise in the context of decisions by individuals to express support for organisations accused of being terrorists or using terrorist methods. Here, the clear and present danger test propounded by Justice Oliver Wendell Holmes could be applied. According to him:

> "...the question in each case is whether the words are used in such circumstances and are of such a nature as to create a clear and present

danger that they will bring about... substantive evil... It is a question of proximity and degree".[723]

By implication, this refers to expressions, either through word of mouth or through other channels such as leaflets or pamphlets, which are released in circumstances where it could be manifestly seen to brew violence or has an imminent possibility of destabilising the social and/or political order in society.[724] Thus, in ***Gul and Others v Turkey,***[725]the Turkish public prosecutor charged Ms Zehra Delikurt (Ms Z) with membership of an illegal organisation. The public prosecutor alleged that Ms Z had shouted slogans in support of the TKP/ML-TIKKO (a Turkish armed illegal organisation) during the May Day demonstrations in 1997 and 1999, as well as the demonstration on 2nd July 1998.[726] It was also alleged that she had written TKP/ML-TIKKO slogans on school walls in Ankara. She was suspected of having sold the periodical 'ÖzgürGelecek',[727] which was owned and published by the 'TKP/ML-TIKKO'.[728] The other applicants were charged with aiding and abetting members of an illegal organisation, under Articles 168 and 169 of the former Criminal Code respectively.[729] Hence, the applicants complained that their conviction and sentence constituted a breach of their right to freedom of expression. The government maintained that the conviction of the applicants was not based on the fact that they expressed their opinion, or participated in a meeting, but for aiding and abetting an illegal organisation, pursuant to Article 169 of the Criminal Code.[730] The ECHR held that there had not been a violation of Article 10 of the ECHR.[731]

723 T. Torres, 'How national security limits speech in four Anglophone states' (Seton Hall Law eRepository 2013)

724 K. Poling, 'Protecting freedom of expression in times of terrorism: A comparison of United States, Germany and South Korea' (Law School Student Scholarship Paper 546, 2014)

725 Gul and Others v Turkey (2010) Strasbourg 4870/02

726 ibid., para 11

727 ibid., para 11

728 ibid., para 6

729 ibid

730 ibid

731 ibid

Here, it can be argued that the ECHR adopted a narrow view in its decision. Accordingly, the enjoyment of the right to freedom of expression is linked to other important rights; the right to freedom of thoughts, conscience and religion, belief and opinion.[732] Analytically, often the right to freedom of expression is also linked to freedom of assembly and association. Patently, the applicants have the general legal right under Article 11 of the ECHR to form and join trade unions or organisations of their choice for the protection of their interests, provided they were themselves lawful. However, they do not have the right to exercise such freedom beyond the ambit of positive law (established law). Implicitly, they must consider national and private interests of others in the exercise of such right. Hence, in the case of the first applicant, she was precluded by law from joining an 'illegal' organisation as the interest of such organisation could be contrary to national security interests or public safety.

Pursuant to Article 10 of the ECHR, the applicants were precluded by law from making any expression that had the propensity to destabilise the security of the nation or encroach upon the rights of others. Thus, shouting, writing, showcasing a poster/picture and selling of propaganda materials are all elements of expression, since they entail the 'impartation of information'. The facts of the case revealed that the first applicant shouted slogans in support of an illegal organisation during a demonstration. For instance, she shouted: "We are the brave voice of the workers and peasants; we are the public's bullet lodged in the barrel of a gun".[733] Similarly, the other applicants also shouted some slogans such as: "Revolt against fascism; the leader is Partisan". "Workers, peasants and youth, we are all united in the people's war." "It is the barrel of the gun that will call to account."[734]

Obviously, such slogans could be regarded as 'provocative' and imply propaganda for essentially violent and undemocratic forms of changing government policy or modes of governance or even social organisations. Thus, considering the circumstance under which such statements were made in the course of a political demonstration, it could be alleged that they have the potential to incite

732 Office of the United Nations High Commissioner for Human Rights, 'Human rights, Terrorism and Counterterrorism' (2009) <*www.ohchr.org/Documents/Publications/Factsheet32EN*> accessed 14 April 2014

733 Gul and Others v Turkey., para 11

734 ibid

the public to violence against the elected government, or they might create an opportunity for a different illegal group/organisation (whether terrorist or otherwise) to launch an attack against an opposition party, as the case may be. Nonetheless, in such context, it is arguably immaterial whether the demonstration in which such statements were made is "peaceful" in the literal sense of the term of an absence of physical violence.[735] Conversely, in view of the fact that Turkey faced 'enemies within' in the shape of domestic terrorists, it cannot be ruled out that such statements might be inimical to the defence of national security and various clusters of rights resting in practice upon such security.

Again, the effects of such statements could be 'unpredictable'. Such statements could be described as 'non-deterministic' in nature, in the sense that there is no automatic relation between a statement as a "cause" and violent terrorist acts as an "effect". Impliedly, it is uncertain whether such statements would always have the potential of actually inciting the public to violence. However, at such point, we must also remember that attempted incitement can itself be a crime. In such respect, within the USA at least, public anxiety has taken a new turn post-9/11 as it becomes interconnected with terrorism. "Normal" expressions are now more likely perceived as "exceptional threats" by associating them with actions of terrorists. Such anxiety compels states to formulate policies or enact legislations that restrict human rights, such as the right to freedom of expression in the quest to enhance national security and for promotion of public order.

As pointed out above, in view of the 'clear' and 'present' danger test as promulgated by Justice Oliver Wendell Holmes, it could be argued that the slogans shouted by the applicants were 'clear' and capable of presenting chaos in the society, since they were expressed during a demonstration.[736] Hence, the 'degree' and 'proximity' between where the slogans were released and the place where the demonstration took place was such that could lead to public unrest.[737] The first applicant was also alleged to have written the following slogans on school walls: "IBO is alive, TIKKO is fighting". "Long live our party TKP-ML, TIKKO." "Guerrillas don't die; long live the people's war." "The martyrs of the party and

735 A. Buyse, 'Dangerous expressions: ECHR, violence and free speech' (2014) vol 63(2) International and Comparative Law Reform 491

736 T. Torres, op. cit.

737 ibid

revolution are immortal." "TKP-ML, TIKKO, workers and peasants hand in hand, towards democratic revolution."[738]It can be argued that such words have the potential of provoking terror in society and can serve as a recruitment instigator for such citizens who feel oppressed and think they need support for the protection of their interest outside the government.

The first applicant was also suspected of having sold the periodical *ÖzgürGelecek*.[739] The facts of the case did not show whether the periodical contained propaganda statements. However, a holistic scrutiny of Article 10(2) of the ECHR shows that the proper exercise of the right to freedom of expression can avert public disorder. Hence, by virtue of Article 10(1) of the ECHR, the first applicant has the general right to disseminate information. Notably, the dissemination of information takes various forms, which include the selling of reading materials such as periodicals. Nevertheless, such right precludes the selling of unlawful materials. Therefore, under the spirit of national security, which also embodies the protection of many of the rights of private persons, it will be contrary to the intention of Article 10 of the ECHR and Article 169 of the former Turkish Criminal Code, respectively, if the selling of the periodical was geared towards the facilitation of the operations of an illegal organisation. In exercising their right to freedom of expression, it will also constitute an offence under s.7(2) of the Turkish Prevention of Terrorism Act of 1991 for any of the applicants to disseminate propaganda in favour of any terrorist organisation.[740]

The right to freedom of expression faces substantial challenges after some counterterrorism efforts. Hence, to some extent, the wide range of anti-terror enactments, especially post-9/11, criminalises some acts of expression. Thus, the UK enacted the Terrorism Act of 2006, which empowered the government to prosecute individuals for encouraging terrorism or for disseminating terrorist publications, as well as to proscribe terrorist organisations that glorify terrorism.[741] Some critics have argued that the UK Terrorism Act of 2006 is overly broad and encroaches into the right to freedom of expression. Ideally, a consideration

738 Gul and Others v Turkey., para 11

739 ibid

740 Prevention of Terrorism Act (Law no 3713 of 12th April 1991)

741 E. Parker, 'Implementation of the UK Terrorism Act 2006-The relationship between counterterrorism law, free speech and the Muslim community in the United Kingdom versus the United States' (2007) 21 Emory International Law Review 711

of the circumstance in the UK before and after the July 7th bombing could be a justification for the enactment and implementation of the UK Terrorism Act of 2006. For instance, the UK has the challenge of dealing with home grown terrorists. Prior to the July 7th bombing, London became an anchorage for radicals and a place for calls to jihad.[742] Consequently, London became a home base for potential terrorists where funds were raised, new members were recruited, and inspirations were drawn from militant messages and images. Hence, international terrorists considered London their home base too.[743] Accordingly, the protection of public order and national security necessitated the restriction in the exercise of the right to freedom of expression as such right is a potent force to repression, war and conflict.[744]

Again, the challenge of Islamic terror escalated following the July 7th bombing. For instance, in an interview in September 2006, Abu Abdullah a radical Muslim cleric "...called the September 11th attack a 'deserved punch in the nose' for United States and described President Bush as a scalp that needs to be taken".[745] Arguably, the "glorification" of terrorism by some radical Muslims in the UK necessitated, or at least justified, the inclusion of the encouragement of terrorism offence in the 2006 Act. For example, a radical cleric Sheik Omar Bakri Mohammed called for a jihad against the United Kingdom and instigated young Muslims to become part of the insurgency in Iraq.[746] However, critics have also argued that the encouragement of terrorism offence criminalises speech based on its *contents alone.* Analytically, under part 1(1) (a) (b) of the Terrorism Act of 2006, in considering whether a statement "encourages terrorism"; the totality of the statement in addition to the circumstance and the manner of its publication will be contemplated.[747] Hence, the statement will not be dealt with in isolation as the intention of the speaker will also be inferred as stipulated under part

742 E. Sciolino, et al., 'For decade, London thrived as a busy crossroads of terror' New York Times (2005) New York Times

743 E. Parker, op. cit.

744 Article 19 global campaign for free expression., 'The impact of UK anti-terror laws on freedom of expression' (Please provide the *Website's name,* date April 2006) <*www.article* 19.org/pdf/.../terrorism-submission-to-icj-panel.pd...> accessed 23 April 2014)

745 E. Parker, op. cit.

746 E. Sciolino, op. cit.

747 Z. Akhtar.,'Malicious communications, media platforms and legal sanctions' (2014) 20(6) Computer and Telecommunications Law Review 179

1(2) (b) (i) before he or she will be considered to have committed an offence. By implication, in practice mere 'content' of an expression is not a sufficient premise in the determination of provocative expressions. A holistic consideration of such expression is paramount. Hence, in ***R.A.V. v City of St. Paul,*** the Court maintained that certain types of speech are proscribable including 'fighting words'. However, it is unconstitutional to regulate speech based on its content. The Court stressed that unless a regulation is necessary to stop violence that flows from the fighting words; such a regulation is "presumptively invalid". [748]

It can also be argued that the contents of some statements manifestly show that they are contrary to the intention of freedom of expression as provided for under Article 10 of the ECHR and under other Conventions and domestic legislations. For instance, five hundred people attended a sermon in 2004 where Mohammed vowed that, "If western governments did not change their policies, Muslims would give them a 9/11 day after day after day..."[749] Such statement could be seen as a clarion call to terrorism/violence. To such degree, it could be argued that the provisions of Article 10 of the ECHR and other counterterrorism legislations are commensurate to the level of threat the society is subjected to as a result of incitement to terrorism. However, it is legally clear that not all statements glorify terrorism. The inclusion of some conditions in some of the anti-terrorism legislations strengthens the contention that although the right to freedom of expression is generally crucial in a democratic society, it is not an absolute right and becomes qualified by other factors related to national security and the defence of democracy. To such extent, the restriction on the right to freedom of expression also serves as a check on the incitement of terrorism.

Anticipatory action geared towards the obstruction of future terrorist attacks has become fundamental to counter terrorism strategies of democratic states. The CONTEST strategy (prevent, pursue, protect, prepare) has validated strikes against 'enemies of the state'. Hence, anticipatory strikes against freedom of expression also feature in the arsenal of disruptive tools. Counter-radicalisation policies have been put in place by nation states to restrict positive acts of

748 R.A.V v City of St. Paul (1992) 505 US 377, 420-21

749 E. Parker, op. cit.

expression.[750] For instance, the UK has adopted the complementary and controversial technique of criminalising the failure to disclose information to the police concerning suspected terrorist activities. In effect, this has led to coercive incorporation of family members and friends in issues of risk anticipation.[751]

Analytically, freedom of expression is a personal right. It should be seen as a right that ought to be exercised in an individual's personal capacity. Hence, it would be antithetical for nation states to compel individuals, such as terrorist suspects, to exercise such right against their will only for the extraction of terrorism related information in pursuit of counterterrorism policies. On the other hand, even a cursory look at Article 10(2) of the ECHR reveals that the right to freedom of expression may be exercised under certain conditions such as national security, public safety or the prevention of crime. On such premise, and against the background of counterterrorism imperatives, is it legally justified for a terrorist suspect to be compelled to exercise his right to freedom of expression in the name of national security? Thus, Article 10(1) of the ECHR expressly posits that such right should be exercised 'without interference by public authority and regardless of frontiers. In effect, legally speaking, governments are stopped from intruding into the exercise of a terrorist suspect's right to freedom of expression irrespective of the interest such as national security. Legally, national boundaries should not also hinder the exercise of such right.

It must be noted that full enjoyment of the right to freedom of expression is principle for achieving full enjoyment of some other fundamental rights (such as the right to freedom of assembly and association), as well as the healthy functioning of democracy.[752] Hence, in restricting freedom of expression, precautions should be taken not to encroach upon the enjoyment of other rights. Pursuant to Article 17 of the ECHR, it is unlawful for a right, which is guaranteed by the ECHR to be restricted merely because the restriction of another right in the

750 I. Cram, 'Failing Justice Brennan quest? Anticipating terrorism risks and the US Supreme Court' (2013) (1) Public Law 30-51

751 ibid

752 Article 19 global campaign for free expression., 'The impact of UK anti-terror laws on freedom of expression' (2006) <*www.article* 19.org/pdf/.../terrorism-submission-to-icj-panel.pd...> accessed 23 April 2014

ECHR is required. Freedom of expression is the 'life blood of democracy' without which the rule of law is impracticable.[753]

5.7 SUMMARY

In summary, in the bid to fight terrorism, nation states have revised their legislations and policies post-9/11. New laws have been adopted, old laws have been revised, policies and practices have been changed. The powers of the government to fight terrorism have been expanded by most such revisions. Often, controls on such powers are inadequate.[754] Freedom of expression is an essential right of all citizens in a modern and democratic society. Democracy depicts equal participation of all. Hence, the masses should be capable of expressing their opinions and stand up for what they believe in. Situations could be approached from different dimensions when there is an open flow and exchange of ideas and information, which leads to good representation of people's needs.

The possibility of striking a viable balance between freedom of expression and national security constitutes a challenge. Thus, a critical examination of Article 10 of the ECHR depicts that the right to freedom of expression is a 'right' that ought to be exercised by everyone (the government inclusive). The limitation of public access to information invariably limits the public's right of thought and opinion since the expression of an opinion, to some degree, is predicated on received information. Hence, the right to freedom of expression is not limited to the holding of opinions. It extends to 'receiving' and 'imparting' information. Often, governments of nation states, such as the UK, limit public access to information under the guise of national and people's security. They come up with rules and regulations (such as the Local Government Act 2000, Freedom of Information Act 2000) or invoke 'official secrecy' whereby the public have very little access to local government information and meetings,[755] thus depriving them of their freedom to receive information. How then can there be a balance between the right to freedom of expression and national security when there is no full enjoyment of such right by the masses? The restriction on the right

753 A. Bailin, 'Criminalising free speech' (2011) 9 Criminal Law Review 705

754 D. Banisar, 'Speaking of terror' (2008) Media and Information Society Division, Council of Europe

755 A. Draper, et al., 'Media in the UK' (2013) Hong Kong University, Faculty of Social Sciences

to freedom of expression is one-sided (on the public), instead of on both sides (government and the public). Open exchange of ideas is integral to a nation's security. Obviously, the root cause of insecurity in a nation could be ascertained through the expression of ideas and opinions between state and non-state actors. Ideally, the public must not have full access to all government information, but, to create a balance, the restriction ought to be not more than necessary as public input in certain issues might be beneficial to national security.

A further scrutiny of Article 10 of the ECHR depicts that responsibilities, duties, restrictions and formalities attached to the exercise of the right to freedom of expression are also attributable to 'everyone'. By implication, this includes the government. However, in practice the mechanisms or structures of restrictions are set up by the government. In the quest to strike a balance between national security and human rights, the question arises: how will there be an effective restriction of the right to exercise freedom of expression in a situation where the government is in default (having exceeded the acceptable limit or having failed to exercise the right, especially when it is for the benefit of the public at large)? Or is the government above the law? Ultimately, it can be argued that the only means through which the public can compel the government to release certain information, which might be beneficial to society at large through public debate, is through the 'effective' exercise of the right to freedom of expression that entails equal right of expression for all.

Often, if the government fails to release certain information to the public, the latter cannot compel them (the government) to effect the release of such information. On the other hand, under counterterrorism measures, individuals are compelled by the government to disclose information, which they claim is in favour of national security. For instance, the United Kingdom adopts complementary and controversial techniques of criminalising failure to disclose information to the police about suspected terrorist activities. Thus, it is assumed that the public has a legal responsibility to disclose certain information in the exercise of their right to freedom of expression. Nevertheless, is the government not included in such responsibility? Accordingly, a report of the Joint Congressional Committee inquiry into the incident of 9/11 condemned the failure of the FBI and the CIA respectively to share relevant intelligence.[756] The intelligence community was

756 The New York Times, 9/11 Congressional Report Faults F.B.I-C.I.A Lapses (2003) *www.nytimes.com/2003/07/24/.../9-11-congressional-report-faults-fbi-cia-lapses.html*, accessed 18/10/2017

aware that from 1994, the Islamic terror group was contemplating using aircrafts as weapons, yet the possession of such information did not lead to a specific assessment of the threat.[757]

Analytically, the intelligence community might argue that such information is strictly 'state secret' and therefore should not be expressed in public domain. Realistically, if such information is made available to the public, to some extent it will destabilise the orchestrators of such attack. They (the terrorists) will see that their scheme is known. The worst-case scenario for the terrorists might be to devise another means of attack. In essence, a fresh scheme of attack will take some time, which might enable the intelligence community to know what the new strategy is, thereby giving another opportunity for it to be thwarted. In the long run, such chains of events help to enhance both national and international security, as the case may be. Thus, the publicity of the strategy (mode of attack) of non-state actors might go a long way towards thwarting their plan or disrupting their scheme.

The uncertainty and sophistication, which characterise modern forms of terrorism and globalisation due to information technology, respectively, also make the task of striking a balance between national security and the right to freedom of expression a challenge. It is interesting to note that such expressions, which seem 'contentious' and 'offensive' ought to be the ones that require legal protection. However, in practice they are the ones that are deemed illegal and outside the legal covering of the right to freedom of expression. How can there be a balance since there is a misconception of expressions, which are deemed to destabilise national security; whereas in the actual sense they are expressions, which ought to reassure the citizenry that their right to freedom of expression is protected and guaranteed? Logically, such expressions in a democratic society should not be conceived as 'prejudicial'; but should be regarded as expressions that create awareness amongst the citizenry of the occurrences in the society. Hence, the right to freedom of expression is not only limited to 'complimentary' expressions. It extends to 'contentious' and 'offensive' expressions. Hence, the media and public at large have the right to express and receive such opinions. Nevertheless, it is of utmost importance that the expression of such opinions

757 S. Atkins, The 9/11 Encyclopedia (2[nd]edn ABC-CLIO, California 2011), 674

(contentious and offensive opinions) must be done in a manner that is consistent with the spirit of democracy and national security.

Paradoxically, it might be argued that it is safer to err on the part of excess than being taken unawares by terrorists or other violent groups. Thus, the wide restriction given to the exercise of the right to freedom of expression post-9/11 could be considered commensurate to the 'uncertainty' of modern-day terrorism. Analytically, 'contentious' and 'offensive' opinions expressed in the media or during a lawful demonstration might provoke violence in society. Thus, such expressions might influence the minds of people negatively. Terrorists or other illegal groups/organisations might also capitalise on the prevailing opportunity to launch an attack. Therefore, which is the way forward?

The foregoing analysis has shown that human rights must be violated to some degree in the fight against terrorism. Nevertheless, the violation must be done within certain acceptable legal standards such as derogation. Also, the law has imputed some limitations on the exercise of certain fundamental rights such as those delineated under Articles 8-11 of the ECHR. Hence, it becomes expedient if possible, to distinguish derogations from ECHR and limitations on national security grounds particularly in the Articles 8-11 context.

5.8 DISTINCTION BETWEEN DEROGATION FROM THE ECHR AND LIMITATIONS ON NATIONAL SECURITY GROUNDS PARTICULARLY IN THE ARTICLES 8-11 ECHR CONTEXT

Distinctions persists between derogations from the ECHR and limitations on national security grounds especially in the Article 8-11 context. Even though, one of the circumstances permitting derogations from the ECHR is also one of the grounds for possible limitation, derogations differ from limitations in character and scope, in the situations in which they may be imposed, and in the methods by which they are implemented. Derogations in times of emergency are clearly aimed to have a temporary character. On the contrary, limitations can be permanent. Limitations on guaranteed rights must be provided by law. Whereas, no such requirement exists for temporary derogations.[758]

Derogations from the ECHR permit the complete suspension of rights while complying with the conditions under the ECHR.[759] Limitations of rights are allowed even under conditions of 'normalcy' whereas derogations are justifiable only in a 'state of emergency'. Articles 8-11 of the ECHR include clauses on the grounds warranting limitations to rights, and some clauses clearly invoke security grounds such as 'national security' or 'public safety'. On the other hand, derogation (temporary suspension of rights) in time of war or other public emergency threatening the life of the nation is enshrined under Article 15 of the ECHR. Notably, states of emergency are justified only by security exigencies. Also, a state of emergency may involve empowering the executive at the expense of the legislature and adjourning democratic and judicial control of security organs.[760]

Certain concepts such as 'national security', 'public safety', 'territorial integrity' and the 'prevention of disorder'/'protection of public order' are prominent within the Articles 8-11 ECHR context. These concepts are devoid of the same meaning but are inter-connected with each other. They do not also have a generally acceptable meaning. For instance, In the case of CG and others v Bulgaria, the ECtHR states:

> "it is true that the notion of 'national security' is not capable of being comprehensively defined...it may, indeed, be a very wide one with a margin of appreciation left to the executive to determine what is in the interest of security, however that does not mean that its limits may be stretched beyond its natural meaning...".[761]

758 H. Shelton, et al., *International human rights: Problems of law, policy and practice* (5th edition Aspen Publishers United States, New York 2011)

759 S. Peers, et al., *The European Union Charter of fundamental Rights: politics, law and policy* (Hart Publishing United States, Portland Oregon, 2004), 170

760 K. Touri, *European constitutionalism* (Cambridge University Press United Kingdom, Cambridge 2015), 270-271

761 L. Doswald-Beck, *Human rights in times of conflict and terrorism* (Oxford University Press United States, Oxford 2011), 76

Essentially, national security is a permissible ground for restricting the exercise of rights under Articles 8-11 ECHR. National security may be invoked to justify measures limiting these rights only when they are taken to protect the existence of the nation or its territorial integrity or political independence against force or threat of force.[762] National security cannot be invoked merely for imposing limitations to prevent local or comparatively isolated threats to law and order nor can it be used as a ground for imposing vague or arbitrary limitation. Arguably, the word 'national' excludes restrictions solely in the interest of a regime, government or power group.[763] Also, if the limitation is purposed to prevent riots or other disturbances or to frustrate revolutionary movements which do not threaten the life of the entire nation, national security cannot be invoked. Such grounds for restriction may sometimes fall within the ambit of 'public order' or 'public safety' but not 'national security'.[764] However, national security might be invoked when a democratic society is threatened by highly sophisticated forms of espionage and terrorism.[765] National security may also allow limitation on the rights of members of the armed forces.[766]

On the other hand, public safety is a permissible ground for limiting the exercise of freedoms enshrined under Articles 8-11 of the ECHR. Public safety generally refers to security of the public or their freedom from danger; the safety of the community from external or internal danger.[767] According to Daes, it implies the existence of a set of provisions, intended to ensure, within a country, public peace, social harmony, respect for just law and the legitimate decisions or orders of public authorities.[768] According to Kiss, the protection of public safety may justify restrictions as a result of police rules and security regulations intended to protect the safety of individuals in areas such as transportation, vehicular traffic,

762 N. Jayawickrama, *The judicial application of human rights law: National, Regional and International jurisprudence* (Cambridge University Press United Kingdom, Cambridge 2001), 193

763 ibid

764 ibid

765 B. Rainey, et al., *Jacobs, White and Ovey: The European Convention on Human Rights* (7th edition Oxford University Press United Kingdom, Oxford 2017), 349

766 N. Jayawickrama, op cit

767 ibid, 194

768 ibid

consumer protection or the regulation of labour conditions.[769] Also, public order ordinarily implies, prevention of disorder or crime. Public order supersedes the ordinary maintenance of law and order and is synonymous with public peace, safety and tranquility, an absence of violence and public disorder.[770] Public order permits a state to rescind specific terms of international covenants and treaties to which it is a signatory, but which it considers unacceptable given its own legal system, values and norms. Public order relates to national sovereignty and the laws of particular state. It differs pursuant to time and place. As a result, there is no singular way 'public order' is defined in practical terms; its articulation is contingent upon the principles, values and laws that a nation state considers as vital to its sociopolitical composition and collective identity.[771] While Territorial integrity refers to national borders. it is associated with issues of national security. Thus, in CG and others v Bulgaria, where the applicants were involved in unlawful trafficking of narcotics. The court said that it cannot be categorized as a crime under 'national security'. On the other hand, the court did accept that the notion of national security can cover the need to preserve territorial integrity and of public safety to prevent crime.[772]

Basically, the concept of national security is broad. In the sense that it covers a wide spectrum of concepts such as territorial integrity, public safety, prevention of disorder and protection of public order. Ultimately, 'public order' is broader than 'public safety' but both are connected. 'Public safety' also includes but is broader than 'prevention of disorder/crime'. Ultimately, the interpretation of these "legally permissible" categories of exception depends on the nation state and the values and norms it deems fit for protection.

5.9 CONCLUSION

This chapter set out to review some of the fundamental human rights as provided under the ECHR that are violated in the fight against terrorism. It sought

769 D. Vitkauskaite-Muerice, "The scope and limits of the freedom of religion in international human rights law" (2011) vol 18(3) Jurisprudence 849

770 N. Jayawickrama, op cit, 195

771 S. Mahmood, *Religious difference in a secular age: A minority report* (Princeton University Press United States, New Jersey 2015), 164

772 L. Doswald-Beck, op cit

the possibility of striking a balance between promotion of national security on one hand and the protection of human rights in the fight against terrorism on the other. It did this through the analysis of relevant case laws for the advancement of essential arguments geared towards the possibility of striking a balance between the competing interests in the "fight against terrorism". Hence, it finds that human rights must be violated in the bid to counter terrorism because of the method of terrorism in recent times (such as the 9/11). International terrorism and human rights are at crossroads. Post-9/11, counterterrorism measures have tested the tensions that exist between such two areas. The tragedy of 9/11 sparked off many questions about the relationship between the individual and the state.[773] The issue of creating a balance between national security and individual personal rights and freedoms remains unresolved and controversial. Nation states have different degrees of security threats. Hence, they enact laws and formulate policies that infringe upon human rights. Human rights have been impaired for the sake of security. For instance, detentions have been unlawful, torture has been rationalised, and freedom of expression has been restricted.[774]

Obviously, the right to liberty and security of persons (Article 5 of the ECHR) is not an absolute right. Hence, there are legal conditions which must be complied with for such right to be derogated from to prevent arbitrariness. Consequent to President Bush's declaration of the "War on terror" in his speech to Congress in 2001, individuals have been detained without charge at various locations around the world; the most apparent being Guantanamo Bay, Cuba, and Afghanistan. The detention policies at Guantanamo Bay have been described by scholars and commentators as "a deliberate attempt to place detainees in a legal vacuum.[775] Categorically, by virtue of Article 5 of the ECHR, unlawful detention is illegal. If a person's detention is not legally justified, they have the right to be released.[776]

An act which is not only unlawful in itself, but which by its nature clearly leads to the propagation of other unlawful acts cannot ab initio become lawful because of a peculiar circumstance such as the 'war against terror'. Analytically, the

773 ibid

774 ibid

775 T. Eatwell, 'Selling the pass: Habeas corpus, diplomatic relations and the protection of liberty and security of persons detained abroad' (2013) vol 62(3) International and Comparative Law Quarterly 727-739

776 ibid

violation of Article 5 of the ECHR often culminates into the violation of other fundamental human rights. Unlawful detention is an embodiment of indefinite detention, abductions, extra-legal transfers, and secret detentions. Such forms of detentions usually take a suspect outside the jurisdiction of law. Hence, it erodes a terrorist suspect of some of his defence rights such as his right of access to judicial review and legal representation. Thus, to some extent, his right to legal representation under Article 6 of the ECHR is violated. Besides the violation of Articles 3, 8 and 6 of the ECHR respectively, unlawful detention in its essential characteristics manifestly violates Article 5 of the ECHR. Consequently, one unlawful act (unlawful detention) leads to the violation of four fundamental human rights. Ultimately, to a large extent, unlawful detention cannot become lawful in a democratic society under any circumstance including the "war against terror".

The formulation and implementation of counterterrorism measures is one of the ways through which states' compliance with human rights laws and policies are tested. The right not to be tortured is also one of the rights that have been widely abused in the "fight against terrorism". Thus, the terrorist suspect is debased mentally, physically, emotionally, psychologically and sometimes morally (as was depicted in El-Masri's case). The systematic mechanism of contemporary terrorism makes the practicability of the absolute nature of the right not to be tortured vague. In principle, nation states condemn the use of torture during interrogations of terrorist suspects, but, practically, most of them have mixed records in their efforts in the war against terrorism.[777] Individuals in many countries encourage strong implementation of security measures in response to domestic terrorism threats despite the criticism of torture and inhuman practices.[778] In considering the absolute prohibition of torture, it is pertinent to recognise the fact that most of the international treaties or domestic laws that prohibit torture absolutely were enacted or ratified before the 9/11 attack. For instance, the ECHR was entered into force in 1953.[779] Hence, it could

777 A. Williams, et al., 'The psychological impact of torture' (2013) vol 7(2) British Journal of Pain 101-106

778 J. Davis, et al., *International handbook of war, torture and terrorism: Perspectives of torture in Great Britain, Northern Ireland, United States, Canada and Australia* (Springer New York, New York 2013) 551

779 European Convention on Human Rights as amended by Protocols No.11 and 14., Supplemented by protocols 1, 4, 6, 7, 12 and 13, <*www.echr.int/.../Convention-ENG.pd...*> *accessed* 7 February 2014

be argued that different circumstances/scenarios, under which torture might be considered, were not put under consideration at the time such laws were promulgated. Although 9/11 did not usher terrorism into the world, the mechanism of its implementation plunged the world into a historical dilemma. Thus, a holistic reconsideration of the absolute nature of the right not to be tortured might go a long way in providing a viable balance between human rights, and national security in the "war against terror", particularly in relation to the expulsion or deportation of terrorist suspects whose activities significantly show that they are a security risk in the contracting state, but cannot be moved to their countries or a third country as a result of torture or its likelihood. Thus, the question could be asked: If the modern form of terrorism was in place at the time the right not to be tortured was made an absolute right, galvanised into domestic laws and international Conventions; would torture still have been made an absolute right? Or would the situation have been different?

It could be contended that the right not to be tortured is reinforced by various provisions of domestic law and articles of international conventions. Arguably, the right to remain silent is connected to the right not to be tortured. This follows from the fact that the offence of torture is most often committed when state actors claim that they are in need of information to counter terrorism for enhancement of national security. Considering the main purpose of torture in the war against terrorism is reception of intelligence, it can be argued that the recognition of the right to remain silent is reinforcement of the legality and acceptability of the right not to be tortured in a democratic society. Hence, a study has revealed that post-9/11, progress against terrorism has stemmed from securely grounded police work within a rights-driven criminal justice system as opposed to war (torture) and its rhetoric, which has proved counter-productive in fighting terrorism.[780] Analytically, torture ignites a feeling of injustice amongst non-state actors which results in the radicalisation of some extremists. The adoption of a war paradigm in countering terrorism suspends the values and effective operation of a criminal justice system, which initiates a balance between the rights of an accused or a suspect and a nation's right to security.

Some counterterrorism measures create disruptions and variances in the circulation of information from government agencies to the citizenry and amongst

780 W. Strikzke, op. cit.

the public, respectively. Hence, recourse to counterterrorism measures has engendered intense domestic and international debates on the tension between such measures and human rights vis-a-vis national security. The concentration of most of the debates is on issues related to criminal procedures such as detention and torture. Issues concerning incitement to terrorism have also taken up front lines in counterterrorism debates. Thus, the prevention of incitement to terrorism through international initiatives, to some extent, has restricted some human rights such as the right to freedom of expression.[781] As pointed out above, freedom of expression goes beyond the expression of thoughts and opinions. It stretches into the right to share information through various information channels such as the internet. Thus, one of the greatest challenge individuals have encountered with the exercise of their rights to freedom of expression in the "fight against terrorism" is in the area of sharing their information (opinions and ideas). Often, the expression of certain ideas and opinions by the citizenry are regarded as 'anti-security' either against public officials (government) or against the nation itself. Hence, individuals are restricted from fully enjoying their right to freedom of expression. However, it can be argued that the legal restriction on the exercise of such right to some extent helps to prevent or reduce public disorder. For example, in ***Saygili and Falakaoglu v Turkey***[782]**,** the express mention of the name of a public official in a newspaper article had the potential to brew violence as that could be described as an act infringing upon the 'reputation of another'. The issue is not about the accuracy of the information, rather the issue is hinged on the capability of the expressed information to destabilise national security. Hence, the observance of legal restrictions helps to maintain public order in the society.

On the other hand, against the background of counterterrorism, could it be said that the restriction has assisted in the prevention of terrorism? Analytically, the wide use of information technology constitutes a great challenge to national security as terrorists (terrorist groups/organisations) and potential terrorists post all kinds of information on the web. Nevertheless, to some extent the restriction of such right has helped to prevent terrorism as nation states censor information online. The fact that the world has become a global village strengthens such

781 Y. Ronen, Incitement to terrorist acts and international law (2010) vol 23(3) Leiden Journal of International Law 645-674

782 Saygili and Falakaoglu v Turkey (2008/09) Strasbourg 39457/03

censorship. Notwithstanding, the effectiveness and efficiency of the censorship is another issue for consideration. Therefore, to a great extent, the restriction has not done much to prevent terrorism. Again, it can be argued that the way and manner in which governments have restricted such right post-9/11(restriction of positive acts of expression) is undemocratic and repugnant to the principles of international human rights law.

Ultimately, the proportionality test is paramount in any endeavour to strike a viable balance between enhancement of national security and violation of human rights in the fight against terror. Certain restrictions on fundamental rights might be pertinent to maintain or enhance a nation's security. Nevertheless, such restrictions must be proportional to the exigencies in that particular circumstance. Hence, the restriction must not be such that will be manifestly unjust in a democratic society putting every prevailing circumstance (such as terrorism) into consideration. It must be noted that the issue of human rights in the "fight against terrorism" must not always trump national security issues and vice versa. Essentially, the task of striking a possible balance remains a dilemma. Hence, the question that begs to be answered is: Pragmatically post 9/11, can the required security be maintained or achieved in countering terrorism without derogating from human rights? Perhaps, a possible answer to this puzzle might emanate from the formulation of an extensive definition of national security which is different from existing scholarship. Hence, the next chapter will attempt to expand, the meaning, scope and rationale of national security comprehensively against the background of counterterrorism.

Chapter 6

Comprehensive definition of National Security shown to be contextually appropriate for anti-terrorism measures And the theory of 'Preservative Legitimacy'

6.1 INTRODUCTION

The previous chapter elucidated conceivable violations of some of the fundamental human rights as provided under the ECHR, which have habitually taken place in the bid to counter terrorism. It embarked on a viable balancing exercise between the enhancement of national security on one hand, and the protection of "human rights" in the "fight against terrorism" on the other. The task of creating and justifying such balance revealed that international terrorism and human rights are currently at an intersection. Hence, the issue of creating a feasible balance continues to be unsettled and, perhaps, inherently contentious. The variation in the degree of perceived security threats of nation states as opposed to terrorist attacks adds to such contention. Thus, counterterrorism laws and policies that infringe on human rights policies are enacted and formulated to meet such threats. Consequentially, such laws perpetrate "unlawful" detentions, justify torture and hamper freedom of expression and other rights.[783]

The analysis from the previous chapters of this book suggests that enhancement of national security inevitably includes breaches of, and potential threats to, people's security. The flagrant violations of human rights in the fight against terrorism make the balancing exercise a 'must', especially in relation to the requirements of a democratic society. Post-9/11, democratic societies perhaps have traded their democratic nature in the bid to counter terrorism, as most counter terrorism legislations have shifted from the principles of 'the rule of law.' The 'rule of law' is defined as compliance with the following six legal principles: (a)

783 C. Moore C, op.cit

Legality, which implies a transparent, accountable, democratic and pluralistic process for enacting laws; (b) Legal certainty (transparency and predictability of the law); (c) Prohibition of arbitrariness of executive powers; (d) Independent and impartial courts; (e) Effective judicial review including respect for fundamental rights; (f) Equality before law.[784] Such principles ought to be adhered to irrespective of the circumstance. The critical evaluation of such balancing exercise sparks the need for a comprehensive and revised definition of "national security" outside the existing scholarship, which could be shown to be contextually appropriate for anti-terrorism measures. The basis of such definition is anchored in the outcome of the analysis of judicial interpretation of human rights cases examined in the third chapter of this book, where national security was considered as a legal idea vis-à-vis as an ideal. Hence, it was seen partly as a concept.

The third chapter of this book identified and explored different aspects of national security through the analysis of various ECHR case laws relevant to anti-terrorism legislations, where it was found that sovereign states embarked on some measures contrary to the principles of rule of law. In contrast, this chapter will develop a comprehensive definition of national security based on the findings from the third chapter. Such definition will incorporate those aspects of national security into a comprehensive whole to formulate a definition that will surpass other definitions existing in the current constitutional scholarship. The goal is to expressly supplement existing academic literature in ways that will be seen as resolving difficulties within it.

The traditional concept of security tends to focus on military threats emanating from other nation states. However, there has been a major shift since 1983 when Ullman defined a security threat as:

> "An action or sequence of events that (1) threatens drastically...to degrade the quality of life for the inhabitants of a state or (2) threatens significantly to narrow the range of policy choices available to a government of

784 D. Kochenov, et al., 'Monitoring and enforcement of the rule of law in the EU: Rhetoric and reality' (2015) vol11(3) European Constitutional Law Review 512-540

a state, or to private, nongovernmental entities (persons, groups, corporations) within the state."[785]

This definition was criticised by realists, who maintained a narrow focus on the constituents of security threats. They argued that widening the concept of security will render it superfluous by making it all-embracing and watering down its main assignment of analysing military threats and inter-state conflicts.[786] However, such widening conceptions of security maintain that military threats are not the only threats that states, people and the world at large encounter. Hence, the concept of security traditionally confined to military threats by (and directed to) states has increasingly stretched to cover a much wider set of phenomena and actors. The understanding of security has become more inter-subjectively defined and less self-evidently 'objective' in its essence.[787]

6.2 COMPREHENSIVE DEFINITION OF NATIONAL SECURITY

Terrorist activities are not new in international arena. However, there are different types of terrorist attacks. The most critical and contentious are large and ongoing. They are usually targeted against one or more nation states or an important portion of their population.[788] They have perpetrated tremendous grievous harm on many human beings and threaten to continue doing so.[789] Terrorism is an anathema that has destabilised national security and, to a large extent, the international community. Measures have been adopted by nation states to counter such terrorism, which has eaten deep into the fabric of many of our societies. The current constitutional scholarship contains various definitions, but not a comprehensive, coherent and viable one. The existing definitions of national security have not, for example, successfully articulated various

785 P. Hough, *Understanding global security* (3rd edn, Routledge Publishers, Abingdon 2013)

786 ibid

787 S. Lucarelli et al., *The EU and multilateral security governance* (1st edn, Routledge Publishers, New York 2013)

788 C. Wellman, 'Terrorism and counterterrorism: A moral assessment' (2013) vol 9 Springer Briefs in Law

789 ibid

elements of national security into a comprehensive whole. They only contain fragments of national security (see chapter 1 and 2).

It has been accepted that national security needs of sovereign states differ. Nevertheless, Chapters 1 and 2 of this book have shown that national security go beyond military security, as the protection of human rights have the potency of posing security challenges in certain circumstances. Hence, while national security issues can be external (such as international terrorism), they can also be largely internal (such as protection of individual lives and property). The task of countering terrorism necessitates the formulation of a comprehensive definition of national security with general applicability capable of addressing its transnational dimensions. The definition will need to articulate not only the vital elements of national security in a sovereign state, but also potentially regional dimensions (see chapter 3). If such elements are properly articulated, then they can also contribute towards effective measures or strategies for countering terrorism. Although the formulation of a comprehensive definition of national security is not a conclusive mechanism for countering terrorism, it is a vital starting point to delineate the field towards which law enforcement and wider policies concerned with "security threats" can be directed. Based on the analysis of different aspects of national security and the evaluation of several national security schools of thought in this book, in consonance with the liberal communitarian school of thought, national security is comprehensively defined in this work as:

> "A systematic protection against undesirable intimidation. It is a concept predicated upon the principles of the rule of law which is inherently linked to respect for democracy and fundamental human rights. It comprehensively connotes those 'anticipatory' and 'pre-emptive' measures (self-defence[790] and anti-terrorism[791]) that a nation embarks upon in their sovereign capacity to protect the personal, group and collective interest of its citizens (people's security[792]), its territorial sovereignty, the entry and exit of aliens (immigration[793]) and the collection as well as the

790 Chapter 1.,1.2.7

791 ibid., 1.2.1

792 Chapter 1., 1.2.2

793 Ibid., 1.2.4

> assessment of secret intelligence reports (intelligence sharing[794]) for safeguarding against 'threat' and 'violence' within and around (outside) its domain (regional security)." [795]

Such concept of national security is multi-dimensional. It comprises both 'security' and 'national' aspects of "national security". Thus, the quest for security defined in such or similar terms, is one of the most integral aspects of humanity. The demand for security strives for fulfilment in every area of life, including political, financial, personal or social.[796] The main goal of any modern nation state, especially post-9/11, is the maintenance of national security, defence from external enemies and preservation of internal peace, order and prosperity. However, the distinct "security element" of national security is not limited to the detection and assessment of external security threats, such as international terrorism. It also encompasses enhancement of internal security for destabilisation of domestic threats such as home-grown terrorists, organised crime, and human rights violation by state and non-state actors. Essentially, strict compliance to the rule of law, detection of security threats, and maintenance of domestic harmony and accumulation of resources necessary for safeguarding against potential enemies constitute the major responsibilities of a state.[797] The imperativeness of national security, stability and integrity makes them particularly appropriate devices for validating actions that threaten and violate the very things they claim to protect.[798] History abounds with examples of abuse of liberty, rights and security carried out by state actors in an attempt to protect 'national security'. Unavoidable conflicts have arisen between the security demands of sovereign states and their citizens, nations and sub-groups, national sovereignty and global community.[799] Hence, security issues have been contested vigorously, especially post-9/11, as people vary in their opinions concerning both the place and constituents of security in society.

794 Ibid., 1.2.6

795 Ibid., 1.2.5

796 Hobbes Thomas., *Leviathan or the matter, form and power of a common-wealth ecclesiastical and civil* (Andrew Crooke, London 1961), 66

797 A. Kyi, *Empowerment for a culture of peace and development: Freedom from fear and other writings* (New edn, Penguin Book Publishers, London 2010), 264

798 Ibid

799 C. Gibbs, 'Securing the nation: Radicalism and security in 1970s Britain' (2013) Research Paper, University of York

The challenge pertaining to traditional security studies has touched three major areas: the objectivity of the threat, the source of the threat and the actors involved.[800] Security threats have begun to be politically and socially identified in phenomena that have been first politicised, and later securitised; for instance, in the environment, economy and social phenomena such as migration. It is undisputable that security threats could be non-military in nature.[801] The extended security environment embraces international and transnational groups, individuals, and national agencies. Even human security has been introduced, as human beings are perceived as potential referents of trans-boundary risks. Thus, both traditional state actors and non-traditional and non-state ones are contained in such broadened security environment.[802]

Additionally, the distinctly "national" aspect of national security in this book is viewed from the perspective of state sovereignty. Hence, it recognises a nation as a distinct political entity within a distinct, territorially bound form of sovereignty. However, in defining national security, this book sees a nation state as a distinct corporate collective entity, but one whose security, to some extent, is connected with regional and international (global) security. The 9/11 incident, categorically, is a clear indication of the fact that the security of a nation is, to a large extent, extended to regional and international security, even though every sovereign state has its own different security needs as distinct sovereign entities. Hence, in a 2004 hearing of the full International Relations Committee, Governor Tom Kean stated:

> "Our Commission came to the judgment pretty quickly that the United States cannot win this war against terrorism without friends and allies. In every area we talk about, we need strong international partnerships. If our activities are to be successful, they must take place in the context

800 S. Lucarelli, et al., op.cit

801 ibid; J. Youde, *Global Health Governance* (Polity Press, Cambridge 2013), 1980; M. Chatterji, et al., *Conflict and Peace in South Asia* (Emerald Group Publishing Limited 2008), 74; D. Smith, *The Baltic States and Their Regional: New Europe or Old?* (Rodopi, Amsterdam 2005), 295

802 ibid

> of strong government-to-government relationships and sustained international cooperation."[803]

Interestingly, attendees of the joint hearing on September 14th, 2014 also acknowledged terrorism as a global problem – a global threat that cannot be fought successfully by one country, irrespective of its military strength. Excerpts of the transcript of the joint hearing state:

> "The world-wide reach of terrorist networks implies that the effort against global terrorism cannot be fought effectively solely by military means; comprehensively only on one's home soil; nor successfully by any one country alone. To be successful, the entire tool box of policy, as noted by the 9/11Commission, must be utilised."[804]

It is not surprising then why the President of the United States, George W. Bush, assembled a 'Coalition of the willing' shortly after the 9/11 incident to topple the Taliban government and pursue Al-Qaeda.[805] The transatlantic and regional cooperation was very effective post-9/11 in combatting terrorism and pursuing Al-Qaeda.

Agreeably, regional and international security play an important role in the security of any nation and should not be overlooked or ignored. The 9/11 attack gave rise to a chain of events that, unavoidably and directly, involved NATO, whose members, for the first time collectively, invoked a basic principle of the Alliance (Article V North Atlantic Treaty of 1949), which clearly states, "An attack on one member shall be considered an attack on all and that each member nation has an obligation to assist the attacked member by any means possible."[806]

803 'US-European cooperation on counterterrorism: Congressional hearing' (2004) <*http://0-Congressional.proquest.com.library.ggu.edu/congressional/docview/t29.d30.hrg-2004-hir-0109?accountid=25283*> (accessed 29 December 2015), 1

804 ibid. page2

805 B. Harrison, *Power and Society: An Introduction to The Social Sciences* (12th edn, Cengage Learning, Wadsworth 2010), 407

806 T. Warren, 'ISAF and Afghanistan: The impact of failure on NATO's future' (2010) Research Project, USAWC

Hence, NATO declared that the 9/11 attack was an atrocity on all 19-member states.[807] They agreed that a terrorist attack by a non-state actor should activate NATO's collective self-defence obligation. In the spirit of global security, the Alliance charged itself to make countering terrorism an enduring NATO mission. For instance, it started the operations 'Active Endeavour and Eagle Assist' as part of its military operational involvement in the war against terror.[808] Also, NATO practicalised an element of collective self-defence by deploying forces from many NATO states in Afghanistan.[809] In Afghanistan, the allies exhibited powerful political homogeneity and NATO was used as a pedestal for the integration of capabilities and assets.[810]

For the EU, the terrorist attacks of 9/11 were a factor that led to the growth of judicial and police co-operation in Europe. Additionally, all subsequent policies developed by the EU have been influenced in various ways by the fight against terrorism as evidenced by the European Capabilities Action Plan (ECAP) formed soon after 9/11.[811] Under such capacity, a policy of willingness was developed at the EU level, and within a few years, most of the objectives linked to the fight against terrorism were attained.[812] Member states agreed on specific measures under the ECAP:

> "Under the ECAP the member states agreed to 'mobilise voluntarily all efforts, investments, developments and coordination measures, both nationally and multi-nationally....'"[813]

---

807 B. Goderis, et al., 'Human rights violation after 9/11 and the role of constitutional constraint' (2012) vol 40(1) The Journal of Legal Studies 13

808 R. Mathieu, 'Defence against terrorism: What kind of co-operation between NATO and the EU?' (2006) vol X11(23) Agenda Internacional 136

809 M. Ruhle, 'NATO after Prague: Learning the lesson of 9/11' (2003) vol 32(2) Parameters 89

810 R. Mathieu, op cit

811 R. Mathieu, 138

812 ibid

813 G. Quille, *The Nordic countries and the European Security and Defence Policy: The impact of EU capability targets and operational demands on defence concepts and planning* (1st edn, Oxford University Press, New York 2006), 127

Undisputedly, the independence of states, their supremacy at home and their freedom pertaining to external affairs is cardinal to the issue of national security.[814] By implication, a nation state may not enhance its national security effectively without acquiring a sovereign status. Sovereignty ascertains the position of particular political entities. It qualifies a nation state for basic international rights.[815] Thus, under international law, there is a possibility for sovereign states to take advantage of certain substantial rights; which include diplomatic and sovereign immunity, jurisdiction over legal matters domestically and internationally, a right to declare war and conclude peace treaties and protect national citizens travelling abroad.[816] Sovereignty also attracts political responsibility for governing, defending and promoting the welfare of a human community.[817]

Generally, sovereignty is addressed and explained at two levels: internal and external. Internal sovereignty is a principle, which legalises domestic political organisation or control as opposed to external sovereignty, which is a mechanism for the enhancement of international security.[818] Hence, the enhancement or maintenance of a nation's security is enforced through government agencies controlled by a sovereign authority (a political entity). Internal sovereignty centres upon population, territory and a recognised authority. In effect, nation states are at liberty to pursue their internal affairs without external interference, other than those which it has voluntarily submitted through interstate treaties or which arise from state practices to form customary international law. However, internal sovereignty is not limited to the right to control but extends to the capability to exercise control. Such control must, out of necessity, recognise and respect the welfare of the citizenry (people's security), which is an integral element of national security—as identified in this book.

814 J. Bunck, et al., *Law, power and the sovereign state: The evolution of and the application of the concept of sovereignty* (University of Pennsylvania State University Press, Pennsylvania 2010)

815 Ibid E. Weisband, et al., *Political Culture and The Making of Modern Nation-States* (Paradigm Publishers, Colorado 2015), 82; M. Hunt. *Using Human Rights Law in English Courts* (Hart Publishing, Oxford 1997), 4

816 Ibid M. Graber, *A New Introduction to American Constitutionalism* (Oxford University Press, New York 2015), 138

817 ibid

818 S. Makinda, 'Sovereignty and global security' (1998) vol 29(3) Sage Journals 281

Post-9/11, governments of sovereign states became more concerned about the lacuna in their efforts to neutralise potential terrorist threats. For instance, most of the finishing plans of 9/11 were engineered in the US. Probably, the attack could have been forestalled with better mechanisms and policies, which could have discerned, analysed and acted on such 'concluding plans' within the US, eventually uncovering the plot.[819] Thus, in line with the definition of national security formulated in this book, sovereign states embark on anticipatory or pre-emptory actions geared towards the destabilisation of future terrorist attack/s.[820] They emphasise on preventing and preparing for potential terrorist attacks. Such potential attacks are not limited to 'transnational terrorists', but also include "home-grown terrorists", who have increasingly manifested themselves within the borders of sovereign states.[821] As a result, national security mechanisms provide anticipatory and pre-emptive measures to thwart such plots and disorient terrorists. Such measures are orchestrated to create inhospitable environments for terrorism-related activities.[822] Essentially, it is pertinent that such measures are in sync with the principles of the rule of law, especially in a democratic society. Hence, some anticipatory and pre-emptive counterterrorism measures implemented by some sovereign states will be discussed below.

6.3 EVALUATION OF SOME ANTICIPATORY AND PRE-EMPTIVE COUNTERTERRORISM MEASURES ADOPTED BY SOME SOVEREIGN STATES IN THE FIGHT AGAINST TERRORISM

Unlike other regimes, democratic regimes are in existence because of their citizens and for them.[823] Unfortunately, after the shocking incident of 9/11, sovereign

819 M. Waxman, 'Police and national security: American local law enforcement and counterterrorism after 9/11' (2009) (3) Journal of National Security Law & Policy 377

820 I. Cram, *'Failing Justice Brennan's quest? Anticipating terrorism risks and the US Supreme court'* (2013) vol 1Public Law 30-51

821 G. Kelling, et al., 'Policing terrorism: Civic bulletin' (2006) <*http://www.manhattan-institute.org/html/cb43.htm*> accessed 7 May 2015

822 ibid

823 E. Gross, *The struggle of democracy against terrorism: Lessons from United States, United Kingdom and Israel* (University of Virginia Press, Charlottesville 2006), 27

states embarked on some robust measures;[824] some of which will be considered below. As shown in ***chapter 3*** of this book, some of these measures are elements of national security which constitute integral parts of the definition of national security crafted in this book. Impliedly, intelligence sharing and some of the pre-emptive measures in this book fall under matters of how national security is defined ***(section 6.2).*** At the same time, as will be seen all through the ***sub-sections of 6.3***, intelligence sharing and other pre-emptive strikes demonstrate how national security is implemented. Accordingly, this section will first examine deportation as a counterterrorism measure; different types of detention such as indefinite detention, pre-charge detention and extraordinary detention as practised in the "war against terror"; intelligence sharing, and thereafter it will examine the theory formulated in this book, namely, the ***theory of 'preservative legitimacy'.***

6.3.1 DEPORTATION

The definition of national security formulated in this book reveals that nation states in their sovereign capacity tend to develop measures to obviate terrorist attacks for the protection of the personal interest of the entire people and their territorial sovereignty.[825] For instance, states have adopted deportation as one of the measures employed by them to exclude persons whose presence may threaten, or appear to threaten, the security of their nation. In the exercise of their sole and exclusive authority regarding internal governance and external inter-state relations,[826] sovereign states assert near absolute and unrestricted autonomy to regulate entry to, residence within, and expulsion from state territory, where they exercise effective control and authority.[827]

Nation states typically perceive that majority of terrorist threats emanate from foreign nationals, particularly such nationals of states defined as or potentially hostile during, for example, war. Such perception of threat has significantly

824 M. Crenshaw, *The consequences of counterterrorism* (Russell Sage Foundation, New York 2012), 17

825 *R(Wellington) v Secretary of State for Home Department* (2008) UKHL 72 (2009) 1 A.C 335; RB(Algeria) and another v Secretary of State for the Home Department (2009) UKHL 10; Ben Khemais v Italy (2009) ECtHR application no. 246/07 Grand Chamber

826 S. Benhabib, 'Borders, boundaries and citizenship' (2005) vol 38(4) Political Science and Politics 673

827 H. King, 'Extraterritorial human rights obligations of state' (2009) vol 9(4) Human Rights Law Review 521-556

influenced counterterrorism measures of most government states. For instance, the UK government's policy has been to deport such foreign nationals whose presence in UK is interpreted as threatening national security since, with respect to intercept evidence (recordings or transcript from intercepted communications), they might not be prosecuted under the UK criminal justice system.[828] Furthermore, sovereign states have been generally reluctant to deal with cases involving suspected terrorists by means of their criminal justice system. For example, the UK government maintains that it is barely possible to prosecute terrorist suspects, because intercept evidence should not,[829] and cannot,[830] be applied in criminal proceedings in order to not compromise intelligence sources. This narrows the circumstances under which terrorist suspects could be charged with criminal offences. As a result, the government resorts to means other than incarceration following conviction to deal with the threat perceived to be posed by terrorist suspects.[831]

However, there is a non-refoulement principle of international law, which prohibits states from rendering, transferring, sending or returning a person where there are substantial grounds for believing that he or she would be in danger of being subjected to torture or ill-treatment. Such principle has put a major snag on deportation of foreign terrorist suspects.[832] In order to side-track such principle, sovereign states have promoted the use of diplomatic assurances, with the goal that such assurances will make lawful such deportations, which ordinarily might be precluded by Article 3 of the ECHR.[833] For instance in ***Chahal v United Kingdom,*** the applicant received notice of an intention to be deported on the grounds that his continued presence in England was non-conducive to public good for reasons of national security and the war against international terrorism.[834] He contested the deportation based on the likelihood of a violation of his right under Article 3 of the ECHR. Nevertheless, the home secretary

828 ibid

829 *Ramzy v Netherlands* (2010) 25424/05 Strasbourg para 126

830 Regulation of Investigatory Powers Act 2003

831 M. Elliot, 'United Kingdom: The "war on terror" UK style-the detention and deportation of terrorist suspects' (2010) vol 8(1) International Journal of Constitutional Law 131-145

832 *Chahal v United Kingdom.*, op.cit

833 M. Elliot, op. cit

834 *Chahal v United Kingdom.*, op. cit para 25

sought and received assurance from the Indian government with the intention that such assurance will circumvent the prohibition on deportation based on Article 3 of the ECHR.[835]

Again, in ***Soering v The United Kingdom,*** the US government requested the extradition of the applicant pursuant to the Extradition Treaty of 1972 between the US and UK.[836] However, the British government addressed a request to the US government seeking a diplomatic assurance:[837]

> "...that, in the event of Mr Soering being surrendered and being convicted of the crimes for which he has been indicted ..., the death penalty, if imposed, will not be carried out. Should it not be possible on constitutional grounds for the United States Government to give such an assurance, the UK authorities ask that the US undertake to recommend to the appropriate authorities that the death penalty should not be imposed or, if imposed, should not be executed."[838]

Accordingly, human rights organisations condemn the use of diplomatic assurances.[839] They contend that diplomatic assurances concerning the rights of suspects are 'unenforceable promises', whose breaches by sovereign states might not attract severe consequences[840]. They also maintain that often it constitutes a great challenge to ascertain when a breach has occurred.[841]

Basically, Article 1(1) (c) of Protocol No.7 of the ECHR states that a non-national can be expelled from a contracting country, where such expulsion is "necessary in the interest of public order" or is grounded on "reasons of national security". Also, the Immigration Act 1971 permits the deportation of those who are a threat

835 ibid., para 37

836 *Soering v The United Kingdom* (1989) 14038/88 Strasbourg para 14

837 ibid., para 15

838 ibid

839 C. Michaelson, 'The renaissance of non-refoulement? The Othman (Abu Qatada) decision of European Court of Human rights' (2012) vol 61(3) International and comparative Law Quarterly 750-765

840 'Not the way forward: The UK's dangerous reliance on diplomatic assurance' (2008) <*http://www.hrw.org/sites/default/files/reports/uk1008web.pdf&gt*> accessed 27 April 2015

841 ibid

to national security in cases where there is insufficient admissible evidence for prosecution.[842] Hence, legally speaking, a sovereign state reserves the right to deport anyone who is perceived as a threat to national security. However, such right does not empower either the contracting or the receiving governments to arbitrarily violate the rights of anyone who might be subject to deportation. Nevertheless, often deportees allege a violation of Articles 3, 5, 6 and 8 of the ECHR. Practically speaking, the violation of the rights provided for under such Articles could be described as the natural consequences of deportation in the war against terror. Thus, any sovereign state that adopts deportation, extradition or expulsion as a counterterrorism measure will probably encounter issues relating to such articles (3, 5, 6 and 8 respectively).

Evidently, in the fight against terrorism, many deportations before ECHR reveal flagrant violations of Article 3 of the ECHR, irrespective of the diplomatic assurances obtained from the receiving country. For instance, in ***Agiza v Sweden,*** the Committee found an infringement of Article 3 of the Convention Against Torture in Agiza's deportation based on persistent and large scale practice of torture against detainees in Egypt; in addition, it identified a greater tendency of torture for 'detainees held for political and security reasons'.[843] The Committee maintained that diplomatic assurances procured were not adequate to shield Agiza from the manifest risk of torture in Egypt.[844] Similarly, in ***Alzery v Sweden,*** the Committee considered the whole situation of human rights in the state. They acknowledged the existence of diplomatic assurances, their contents and mode of enforcement in their decision.[845] They held that Alzery's expulsion amounted to a contravention of Article 7 of the ICCPR, as Sweden did not show that diplomatic assurances obtained were enough to eradicate the risk of ill treatment to a level commensurate with the provision of Article 7 of the ICCPR[846], which states that, "No one shall be subjected to torture or to cruel, inhuman or degrading treatment or punishment."[847] Which is an equivalent of Article 3 ECHR.

---

842 Immigration Act 1971

843 *Agiza v Sweden* (2005) communication No 233/2003 UN DOC CAT/C/34/D/233/2003para 13.4

844 ibid

845 *Alzery v Sweden* (2006) Human Rights Committee Communication No 1416/2005, CCPR/C/88/D/1416/2005para 11.3

846 ibid., para 11.4

847 International Covenant on Civil and Political Rights 1966

Essentially, as pointed out above, some of the counterterrorism measures adopted in the war against terror have led to the flagrant violation of Article 5 of the ECHR. Hence, different forms of arbitrary detention characterise the national security strategy of most sovereign states in the fight against terrorism, some of which will be discussed below as pre-emptive measures.

6.3.2 INDEFINITE DETENTION

Sovereign states have also adopted different forms of detention, such as indefinite detention, control orders, pre-charge detention, and extraordinary rendition as anticipatory measures.[848] Sovereign states have detained terrorist suspects indefinitely in circumstances where they could not deport them, because of the risk of them being subjected to torture, inhuman or degrading treatment and where such person cannot be put on trial for a criminal offence because of intercept evidence.[849] For instance, UK responded locally by enacting the Anti-Terrorism Crime and Security Act 2001 (hereinafter called the 'Act'). Some civil liberties of alien non-nationals suspected of terrorism were curtailed by the Act.[850] For instance, Part 4 of the Act allowed the Home Secretary to certify any non-British national whom he or she suspected "to be a terrorist" and detain them indefinitely pending deportation, even when such a deportation would be prohibited.[851] Hence, under Section 23 of the Act, suspected international terrorists must be detained irrespective of the fact that their removal or departure from UK is prevented by international law.

The meaning of national security in this book values and respects 'equally' the rights of everyone in the society.[852] In other words, it upholds non-discriminatory counterterrorism measures. It abhors unequal treatment between citizens and aliens. It recognises rule of law's principle of equality before law in a

848 F. Londras, *Detention in the 'war against terror': Can human rights fight back?* (Cambridge University Press, New York 2011), 76-116

849 Regulation of Investigatory Powers Act 2003

850 V. Henning, 'Anti-terrorism Crime and Security Act 2001: Has the United Kingdom made a valid derogation from the European Convention on Human Rights' (2002) vol 17(6) American University International Law Review 1263

851 Anti-terrorism, Crime and Security Act 2001

852 C. Marong, 'Protecting the public? Challenging the indefinite preventive detention of non-citizens' (2014) vol 3(1) Journal of Law and Jurisprudence 115

democratic society. It acknowledges the fact that aliens, as well as citizens, could be involved in terrorism or terrorism-related activities. Hence in ***Secretary of State for Home Department v A,*** the House of Lords held that indefinite executive detention of non-citizens was unlawful, as its discriminatory operation rendered it inappropriate as a means of combating the risk of terrorism.[853] Nevertheless, subsequent to the House of Lords' judgment in ***Secretary of State for Home Department v A***, a new scheme of control orders was introduced through the Prevention of Terrorism Act 2005 (PTA), which sought to replace Part 4 of the Act. The PTA permitted extensive series of conditions on the movement of suspected persons with constraints in the form of house arrests. This time, the provisions of the PTA apply to both alien and non-alien nationals who are suspected of terrorism.[854] Hence, pursuant to S.2 (1) PTA, on the confirmation of the court, the Home Secretary reserves the right to issue either a 'derogatory' or a 'non-derogatory' control order to an individual who the Secretary reasonably suspects to be involved in any terrorism-related activity,[855] or the Secretary could make a control order imposing obligations on an individual for the protection of the members of the public against any risk of terrorism.[856] However, the issue of determining the compatibility of control orders with Article 5 of the ECHR has given rise to some case law challenges.

Hence, in ***Secretary of State for Home Department v JJ,*** the respondents were subjected to an 18-hour curfew in a one bedroom flat. They were mandated to wear electronic tags and restricted to movements within 72 square kilometres of their residence. They were not permitted to meet unauthorised persons and their premises could be searched at any time.[857] The House of Lords concluded that the obligations imposed by the control order on the respondents violated their right under Article 5 of the ECHR.[858] Lord Bingham concluded that the respondents' lives were wholly controlled by the Home Office as a prisoner's life would be. He

---

853 *Secretary of State for Home Department v A* (2004) UKHL 56; (2005) 2 A.C 58 (HL)

854 C. Lumina, 'Counterterrorism legislation and the protection of human rights: A survey of selected international law practice' (2007) vol 7(1) African Human Rights Law Journal 35-67

855 Prevention of Terrorism Act 2005

856 ibid

857 S. Dominik-Bachmann, et al., 'Control orders post 9/11 and human rights in the United Kingdom, Australia and Canada: A Kafkaesque dilemma' (2010) vol 15(2) Deakin Law Review 139

858 ibid., 140

further concurred with Sullivan J.'s earlier judgment that the restrictions were "the antithesis of liberty and equivalent to imprisonment".[859] Sullivan J. relying on a prior judgment in ***Gizzard v Italy***[860] stated that the obligation imposed by the order was very severe so as to constitute a deprivation of liberty amounting to a violation of Article 5 of the ECHR.[861] The court in the present case pointed out that it amounted to more than a mere restriction on the right to freedom of movement.[862] Nevertheless, Lord Hoffmann opined that deprivation of liberty must involve 'actual imprisonment' or any circumstances relatively close to an actual imprisonment.[863] However, the majority of the House of Lords held that general social isolation to which the controlees were subjected, amounted to 'solitary confinement'; because of the duration of the curfew (18 hours) and the absence of liberty to interact with the outside world.[864] Lord Bingham expressed how bleak the fate of the controlees was as they had no opportunity to communicate with others or access entertainment facilities as those in an open prison would. Hence, the Lords quashed the control order on the grounds of its incompatibility with Article 5 of ECHR and the fact that the defects of the control order could not be corrected by altering specific obligations.[865]

Arguably, the case of JJ illustrates that the court adopted a narrow approach to Article 5 of the ECHR in relation to acceptable curfew periods. Thus, the UK government disallowed the 12-hour curfew period recommended by the Joint Committee on Human Rights.[866] Lord Brown adopted the position that a 16-hour curfew period would only restrict a suspect's liberty of movement as opposed to deprivation of his right to liberty. He opined that the Strasbourg Court would most likely declare a 16-hour curfew period as a deprivation of liberty.[867] He

859 ibid

860 *Guzzardi v Italy* (1980) A/39 ECHR 7367/76 ECtHR

861 S. Dominik-Bachmann, et al., 140

862 ibid., page 139

863 ibid., page 141

864 ibid; L. Webley, et al., *Complete Public Law: Texts, Cases, and Materials* (Oxford University Press, Oxford 2015), 670

865 ibid; J. Caselia, et al., *Hell is a very small place: Voices from solitary confinement* (New Press, London 2016), 81-82

866 ibid., page 142

867 ibid., page 143

concluded by leaving the challenge of determining a curfew period compatible with the spirit of Article 5 of the ECHR on the floor of the Parliament and the Strasbourg Court, respectively. In any case, it can be argued that the question of determining the length of a curfew period should be predicated upon the degree of risk, which a suspect constitutes to national security (this includes other people in the society). A curfew period might lose its essence if the controlee still has his liberty to operate without restriction, like any other member of the society. The length of a curfew period might not necessarily constitute a deprivation of liberty, but the restrictions attached to the control order might amount to the 'actual' deprivation of liberty. The length of a curfew period should be such that will enhance national security. Hence, the consideration of a legally acceptable length of curfew period should, perhaps, be determined on a case-by-case basis.

For instance, in ***Secretary of State for Home Department v E,*** the controlee was not placed on any geographical restriction during the daytime.[868] His control order was between the hours of 7pm-7am (a 12-hour period) and as such, he was not deprived of any social network.[869] Having considered the time, duration, effects and manner of the implementation of the order, the Court of Appeal held that there was no deprivation of liberty under Article 5 of the ECHR.[870] Returning to ***Secretary of State for Home Department v JJ,*** Lord Brown adopted the position that a 16-hour curfew period would not constitute a deprivation of liberty under Article 5 of the ECHR.[871] Hence, looking at ***JJ*** and ***E's*** cases respectively, it seems that curfew periods of 16 hours or less are not seen as being antithetical to Article 5 of the ECHR.

On the contrary, in ***Secretary of State for Home Department v AP,*** the Supreme Court declared a 16-hour curfew period together with some restrictions to constitute a deprivation of liberty under Article 5 of the ECHR.[872] Basically, the courts' refusal to endorse long period curfews confining individuals to their place of residence, puts the government in a tight situation. If the

868 *Secretary of state of home department v E & S* (2007) EWCA 459 para 231

869 ibid., para 231

870 ibid., paras 62, 63, 64

871 S. Dominik-Bachmann, et al., 143

872 ibid, 146

courts allow only limited curfews, such as the one seen in ***E's*** case above, the reason for the restriction of movement could be defeated as some desperate suspects might elope or perhaps, in one way or another, engage in terrorist-related activity. Obviously, the courts and the government may continue facing a deep-seated challenge of balancing the sphere of protection granted by Article 5 of the ECHR in relation to control orders and the difficult task of enhancing the nation's security.[873] However, it could be argued that a genuine effort to provide a more commensurable response to terrorism led to the enactment of the UK Terrorism Prevention Investigation Measures 2011 (TPIM). This was evident in Lord Hoffmann's conclusion of the case when he stated that the right to liberty can only be violated by 'literal physical restraint.[874] Lord Brown pointed out that the right to liberty should be 'absolute in its terms', both in peace time and times of emergency.[875]

Comparatively, TPIM had more relaxed measures than the 'Act' and PTA, respectively. For instance, the TPIM regime terminated the forced relocation of suspects from their home base to another place, to interrupt their likely involvement in terrorism related activity. Constraints on geographical movement were also loosened up, while individuals were only excluded from foreign travel and tightly defined places.[876] The TPIM also shortened the duration of curfews, replacing them with an overnight residence supported by electronic tagging.[877] Nonetheless, the TPIM has been described by critics as 'control orders lite'. They pointed out that it could have been more productive for UK to reconstruct its security measures into a form that more "proportionately" affects individual freedoms positively.[878] This begs the answer to the question of what is and is not "proportionate", a notoriously elastic and indeterminate conception that

873 ibid, 146

874 ibid; P. Tripathy, *Contemporary Social Problems and the Law* (A.P.H Publishing Corporation 2000, New Delhi), 238

875 ibid; V. Ramraj, *Global Anti-Terrorism Law and Policy* (Cambridge University Press, Cambridge 2012), 487

876 B. Middleton, 'Terrorism prevention and investigation measures: Constitutional evolution not revolution?' (2013) vol 77(6) The Journal of Criminal Law 562-582

877 Terrorism Prevention Investigation Measures 2011 Schedule 1., para 1

878 C. Walker, 'The reshaping of control orders in the United Kingdom: Time for a fairer go, Australia!' (2013) vol 37(1) Melbourne University Law Review 143

presupposes that the person making the judgment has full and reliable knowledge of both sides of the issue, which in security matter is not likely.

The jurisprudence of the ECHR has continually declared that states have overstepped the limits of permissible action. The enduring threat of both terrorism and the need for well-articulated anti-terrorism legislations has been sustained as a pragmatic prospect for nation states.[879] For instance, the British government formulated extraordinary measures to handle terrorism due to the increased consciousness that UK has become a terrorist target, partly because of its close relationship with the United States and military intervention in Iraq. The UK government also affirms that a public emergency exists, which necessitates the employment of "extraordinary measures" to detain suspected "international terrorists" for the enhancement of national security.[880] However, a pertinent question arises: is national security antithetic to the rule of law? Or is the "war against terror" a war against human rights? Or is there still a state of emergency?

It could be argued that the declaration of a state of emergency in nation states might warrant the adoption of some counterterrorism policies contrary to the rule of law. However, such measures ought to be temporary measures in the sense that they ought to be discontinued as soon as the state of emergency ceases. For instance, UK declared a state of emergency immediately after the 9/11 attack.[881] The state invoked the spirit of Article 15(1) of the ECHR to derogate from Article 5 of the ECHR, in order to validate the detention of some terrorist suspects, as was seen in the case of ***A and others v The United Kingdom***.[882] However, considering the strategies and schemes of modern terrorism and persistence of terrorists in their course of action today, some pertinent questions arise. Using UK as an example, did the state of emergency in UK end with the 9/11 incident? Or does the state of emergency still exist in UK? Such questions could be attributed to other nation states too in relation to terrorism. If answers to such questions are in the affirmative, it implies that the implementation of counterterrorism measures by nation states might perhaps be a continuum.

---

879 C. Walker, 'The reshaping of control orders in the United Kingdom: Time for a fairer go, Australia!' (2013) vol 37(143) Melbourne University Law Review 143

880 V. Henning, op cit

881 *A and Others v United Kingdom* (2009) 3455/05 Strasbourg para 10

882 ibid., para 11

Hence, the former Australian Prime Minister, Julia Gillard stated, "Terrorism is an ever-present threat and the review of our laws is important to ensure that our laws remain necessary and provide effective powers for our police and agencies."[883]As a result, counterterrorism laws will also remain ever-present. If modern terrorism has come to stay, does it imply the world has been plunged into the realm of perpetual state of emergency as no one knows how, when and where the next unprecedented terrorist attack will be launched? Does it also imply that there will be a perpetual erosion of some supposedly "fundamental" human rights, since many of them may be violated during periods of state of emergency? Where are we now? Where are we going with national security?

Terrorism is an aspect of political violence, which expressly contradicts and specifically rejects the rule of law. Nevertheless, the meaning of national security in this book clamours for democratically accountable counterterrorism policies and legislations. It raises a flag for sovereign states to take due care in the formulation of counterterrorism instruments to avoid impacts, which may impair the founding principles of a democratic society as highlighted above. Hence, national security measures must comply with the rule of law requirements of 'transparency' and 'pluralism' (pluralistic process for enacting laws) for proper democratic scrutiny.[884] Also, the element of 'legal certainty' becomes pertinent in the "fight against terrorism". In other words, the conduct of individuals involved in terrorism or terrorism-related activities needs to be regulated by clear and predictable counterterrorism measures.[885] For instance, in the spirit of democracy, terrorist suspects ought to know and understand counterterrorism measures they are or will be subjected to. Again, the meaning of national security in this book precludes the government from acting arbitrarily in the bid to counter terrorism. Hence, in the exercise of its executive powers it must act within the confines of law.[886] As such, individuals should be entitled to adequate judicial protection of their fundamental rights and freedom. This includes independent and effective judicial review of cases involving flagrant violation of human rights in the "fight against terrorism".

883 C. Walker, 'The reshaping of control orders in the United Kingdom: Time for a fairer go, Australia!' (2013) vol 37(143) Melbourne University Law Review

884 D. Bigo, et al., The EU counterterrorism policy Responses to the attacks in Paris towards an EU security and liberty agenda (2015) No 81 CEPS Paper in liberty and security in Europe

885 *Amministrazione delle Finanze dello Stato v Salumi* (1981) ECR 2735 para 10

886 Hoechst v Commission (1989) ECR 02859 para 19

Terrorism invokes very compelling emotional and contradictory responses. However, the definition of national security in this book argues that enhancement of national security should hinge on the principles of the rule of law. By implication, counterterrorism measures of nation states ought to comply as such. Thus, the meaning of national security in this book maintains the truism that sovereign states have an intrinsic obligation to protect the rights of their respective citizens and residents. Accordingly, the protection of the rights of individuals in a nation state is integral to national security. The fact that sovereign states are at liberty to enact counterterrorism measures, which are in consonance with their peculiar local circumstances, does not preclude them from complying with their obligations under international law and the basic obligation to protect the rights of everyone devoid of discrimination of any kind.[887] Hence, Article 5 of the ECHR protects the public against unjustified detention by prohibiting state intrusions into individual liberty and security.

Clearly, the 9/11 attack ignited support and sympathies for the United States from other nation states. This metamorphosed into swift evaluation of their security strength and enactment of new anti-terrorism legislations for enhancement of national security. Most anti-terrorism legislations such as the ones mentioned above on detention have generated concerns within the rule of law. Thus, Lord Hoffman stated, "the real threat to the life of the nation, in the sense of a people living in accordance with its traditional laws and political values comes not from terrorism but from such laws." Most of the detainees in the fight against terrorism are merely 'terrorist suspects', who are suspected for engaging in activities connected to terrorism. This erodes the requirement of proving their case beyond reasonable doubt. Accordingly, it is unacceptable that indefinite restrictions on liberty are placed on the grounds of reasonable suspicion of involvement in terrorism-related activity, as against proof beyond reasonable doubt.[888] Hence, detention is predicated upon 'suspicion' as opposed to 'investigation'. As a result, persons who have nothing to do with terrorism or terrorism-related activities suffer innocently, as was seen in chapter 4 of this book (***Elmasri's case***). National security as defined in this book does not only

887 C. Lumina, 'Counterterrorism legislation and the protection of human rights: A survey of selected international law practice' (2007) vol 7(1) African Human Rights Law Journal 35-67

888 Middleton B., op.cit

recognise sovereignty, but also recognises the protection of people's personal interest in a sovereign nation.

On the other hand, in the spirit of national security, if a person is evidently known to be involved in terrorism-related activity, but cannot be prosecuted immediately because of inadmissible evidence; for instance, evidence from non-compellable foreign sources, then what will happen? Should he be left in the society until his case is proven beyond reasonable doubt or should he be subjected to some form of detention in order to deter insecurity? Legally speaking, preventive detention is permitted and encouraged under international law of war. Clearly, terrorism may not be categorised as armed conflict. For instance, in an armed conflict, hostilities cease at the end of the war.[889] In addition, the removal of combatants from the battlefield is seen as a way of assisting in ending the hostilities. However, hostilities against terrorist organisations are distinct, as the US has adopted the position that such hostilities may continue. Thus, invariably, in the "fight against terrorism", preventive detention could continue, legally, indefinitely.[890] Notably, the essence of preventive detention as a counterterrorism measure is to accurately assess the threat of the moment and protect against it effectively and efficiently. Hence, the outstanding element in preventive detention is 'risk' to national security, as opposed to 'justice' or 'retribution'.[891] Fundamentally, the anticipatory and pre-emptive measures employed by sovereign states in the enhancement of their national security, especially within the sphere of the fight against terrorism, ought to strike a balance between the personal welfare of people and its rule of law principles. In essence, the authority of a sovereign state under international human rights law to deprive individuals of their liberty is strengthened by a moral obligation not only to treat detainees humanely, but also extends to the limitation of their confinement to that which is essential to realise legitimate objectives.[892] Thus, it will be contrary to the rule of law, repugnant to natural justice, equity and

889 M. Eppinger, 'Reality check: Detention in the war on terror' (2013) vol 62(2) Catholic University Law Review 325

890 ibid

891 ibid

892 J. Hafetz, 'Detention without end? Re-examining the indefinite confinement of terrorism suspects through the lens of criminal sentencing' (2014) vol 61University of California Los Angeles Law Review 326

good conscience for individuals to be warehoused and detained without being charged and convicted of any crime.

6.3.3 PRE-CHARGE DETENTION

States have also practised pre-charge detention as a form of preventive detention. Pre-charge detention is a period where an individual is held and questioned by the police before being charged with an offence.[893] It is where a defendant is detained without bail, pending trial.[894] Pre-charge detention as a counterterrorism measure could be counterproductive. CIA detention facilities are potential environments for radicalisation. Thus, arbitrary detentions such as pre-charge detention might lead to societal alienation and aggravation of radicalisation considering the mental, emotional and psychological states of an innocent detainee, who may have been detained for a long time without charge. Again, realistically, a nation cannot exist without a people. Impliedly, there cannot be national security in the absence of people's security. Thus, protection of a nation's geographical boundary will be meaningless without an efficient and effective security of its inhabitants, which includes respect for their personal well-being. Analytically, pre-trial detention could be preventive and protective, but ought not to be punitive. Realistically, there is a thin line between such three types of detention, particularly in the "fight against terrorism". Unlawful detention of terrorist suspects poses exceptional conflicts between the need for security and protection of human rights. The true meaning of national security as espoused in this book clamours for compatibility with the principles of the rule of law, which prohibits arbitrariness of executive powers.

6.3.4 EXTRAORDINARY DETENTION PROGRAMME

Furthermore, nation states such as the US government adopt the 'high value detainee programme' (HVD Programme) as a counterterrorism measure. Such programme is also referred to as the 'rendition detention interrogation programme' (RDI Programme) or the extraordinary rendition programme where suspected terrorists are subjected to a special interrogation and detention

893 T. Chen, et al., *Cyber terrorism: Understanding, assessment and response* (Springer Publishing Company, New York 2014), 208

894 M. Bove, et al., *Pre-trial detention in 20th and 21st century common law and civil law systems* (1st edn, Cambridge Scholars Publishing, London 2014), 235

programme. Under such programme, the CIA is granted extended competences related to its clandestine actions, such as its authority to detain terrorist suspects and establish secret detention facilities outside the US in collaboration with the governments of the nations concerned.[895] Hence, in the case of ***Al Nashiri v Poland***[896], the applicant was captured in Dubai and transferred to a CIA-run detention facility. Subsequently, he was transferred to a secret CIA facility in Afghanistan called 'salt pit'. From here, the applicant was taken to another secret CIA prison in Bangkok code-named 'Catseye', where he was subjected to enhanced interrogation techniques.[897]

Under the HVD programme, government agents from one country detain terrorist suspects in another country, kidnap them and deliver them to another country to be subjected to enhanced interrogation techniques. The CIA set up black sites, established and operated in the Middle East and Europe.[898] Such type of rendition is distinct from 'irregular rendition', even though irregular rendition is also problematic as it evades internationally established processes for acquiring control of citizens of another country. In extraordinary rendition, terrorist suspects are detained from any part of the world before they are turned over to the CIA agents, who transfer the suspects to a black site where they are subjected to complete control of Americans.[899] Such detainees are subjected to three phases in the black sites: (a) the initial condition phase, where they are photographed naked and evaluated; (b) the transition to interrogation phase where, the interrogators try to ascertain the detainees' responsiveness towards the release of information—the degree of the detainees' readiness to release information may lead to an intense level of interrogation; (c) the full blown interrogation phase, where interrogators employ different kinds of techniques to achieve their goals. Detainees are subjected to white noise; sleep deprivation, prolonged nakedness,

---

895 *Al Nashiri v Poland* (2014) 28761/11 Strasbourg

896 *Al Nashiri v Poland* (2014) 28761/11 Strasbourg paras 47, 48

897 ibid., paras 83, 84, 85, 86

898 K. Tucker, 'Abduction, torture, interrogation: An argument against extraordinary rendition' (2014) vol 10(2) Brazilian Journal of International Law 141

899 ibid

constant light during interrogation, electric shock treatments, walling, slaps, sexual torture threats, wall standing and cramped confinement.[900]

Obviously, some counterterrorism measures orchestrate tensions in the society. The adherents of extraordinary rendition prioritise national security and anchor their support for extraordinary rendition on the prevention of terrorist attacks. They posit that extreme interrogation techniques adopted in black sites have the capacity to prevent terrorist attacks. However, a pertinent question could be asked: since extraordinary rendition became public knowledge, especially post-9/11, is terrorism on the increase or has it declined? Arguably, severe interrogation techniques adopted in black sites coupled with the way people are abducted, transferred and detained in such black sites, could be a source of incubating hostility in the world. Perhaps, this might aggravate terrorism.

Illustratively, some tourists have been abducted and transferred to black sites as in ***El masri's case***. Such hostility filters into regions and sovereign states respectively, especially through extremists and the media. In addition, the world might see the perpetrators of the HVD programme as the real enemy of security. Conceivably, the HVD programme has the tendency of instilling the feeling of insecurity and aggression globally. Again, the fact that such HVD interrogators are shielded by the US government from being prosecuted by detainees or other interest groups such as the civil liberties groups provokes loss of confidence in the security of the world.[901]Accordingly, the Obama administration publicly promised the CIA that CIA agents would not be prosecuted. Obama threatened Spain with many sanctions if they did not cease their investigations of two criminal complaints filed by detainees and civil rights groups against the US government official responsible for HVD interrogation.[902] In essence, high value detainee programmes could be inimical to national security and, to a large extent, global security.

However, in line with the definition of national security formulated in this book, national security extends the geographical boundaries of a nation. It is

900 ibid; M. Danner, *Spiral: Trapped in the Forever War* (Simon & Schuster Paperbacks, New York 2017), 60-61

901 S. Cooper, et al., *Psychology serving humanity: Proceedings of the 30th international congress of psychology*, vol 2 Psychology Press, UK 2014), 54

902 ibid

incumbent on sovereign states to enhance security not only within their territorial jurisdiction, but also regionally and, to a large extent, globally. Arguably, the abduction of terrorist suspects by a sovereign state through its cooperation with other sovereign states in extraordinary rendition may have a counter-effect on security. While it is the responsibility of sovereign states to safeguard their domain from threats and violence, it is also their responsibility to ensure that people's personal interests (this protection is not exclusive to nationals) within their territories are protected. Hence, the implication of Articles I and 3 of the ECHR, when read conjunctively, requires sovereign states to take necessary measures to ensure that individuals within their jurisdiction are not subjected to torture, inhuman and degrading treatment or punishment, as well as ill treatment administered by private individuals. Analytically, a sovereign state who allows its territory to be used for CIA rendition could be deemed to have had prior knowledge of the nature and purpose of the activities to be carried out in its domain by another nation's agent. It is immaterial that torturous activities on a detainee were carried out by another country's agent; when the 'host' sovereign state acquiesced in the preparation and execution of the rendition. Logically, if an act is antithetical to national security ab initio, the course of such act cannot enhance national security. Ultimately, if extraordinary rendition is inimical to national security in this respect, it follows that the activities there from cannot be seen to be congenial to national security. Hence, the flagrant abduction, transfer and detention of individuals labelled as 'high value detainees' in unknown detention facilities plunges the world into a further realm of global insecurity.

The definition of national security in this book emphasises the importance of nation states fulfilling their obligation under international law and at the same time, achieving victory in the "fight against terrorism". Thus, it is compelling on states to take measures structured appropriately to guarantee that individuals within their jurisdiction are not unlawfully detained and subjected to any form of torture, inhuman or degrading treatment/punishment. Undeniably, the effect of the high value detention programme on national security cannot be over emphasised. For instance, it has been reported that some of the released detainees become recidivists (reoffenders) after release.[903] For example, Othman Al Omaira, a Yemen citizen, was repatriated to Saudi Arabia in 2006, where

903 M. Denbeaux, et al., 'National security deserves better: "odd" recidivism numbers undermine the Guantanamo policy debate' (2013) vol 43 Seton Hall Law Review 643

he was put through a rehabilitation programme. He soon disappeared, and, in 2009, was included as one of the eleven former Guantanamo prisoners on the Saudi most wanted militant list. In May 2009, an Al-Qaeda video highlighted Al Omairah, distinguishing him as an 'operational commander'.[904] Furthermore, the department of defence claims that sixty-one former detainees had returned to the fight.[905] In 2009, the department of defence claimed seventy-four former detainees had re-engaged.[906] In addition, the House Armed Services Committee stated that 150 detainees had re-engaged in terrorist or insurgent activities.[907]

Arguably, the extraordinary interrogation techniques perhaps make detainees become 'anti-society' upon their release from the 'black sites'. The ill treatments during detention toughen such detainees, making them more 'hostile' than they were prior to being taken into the 'black sites'. Additionally, such ill treatments also have the proficiency of making 'innocent' detainees (such terrorist suspects who had nothing to do with terrorism but were erroneously captured and detained) hostile to the society upon their release. In the long run, the application of extraordinary interrogation techniques on detainees at the black sites has a double jeopardy (counterproductive effect) on national security and to a large extent global security.

Critically, the nature of terrorist attacks creates the prospects for arbitrary military detention. Evidently, the "war on terror" is a war that lacks the features of a traditional international armed conflict. For instance, it is not a war between state actors; there is no clear battle zone where the enemy combatants engage in warfare. In a traditional international armed conflict, there is a clear geographical space in which combatants engage in warfare and detainees are captured for detention.[908] There is a distinction between active combatants and civilian pop-

904 ibid; H. Krieger, *The Kosovo Conflict and International Law: An Analytical* (Cambridge University Press, Cambridge 2001), 235

905 ibid; R. Johnson, et al., *Battles and Leaders of The Civil War: The Tide Shifts* (Castle Books, Tullamarine 1985), 752

906 ibid; H. Metzler, *County Reports on Terrorism 2007*(Nova Science Publishers, Incorporated, Hauppauge 2010), 328

907 ibid; T. Veldhuis, *Prisoner Radicalization and Terrorism Detention Policy: Institutionalized fear or evidenced-based policy making?* (Routledge, New York 2016), Ch.1

908 L. Blank, 'A square peg in a round hole: Stretching law of war detention too far' (2011) vol 64(1) Rutgers Law Review 1169

ulation in traditional international armed conflict. Such observable attributes help with the identification of enemy combatants and create the possibility for only enemy combatants to be detained.[909] Additionally, the authority to detain enemy combatants in a traditional armed conflict extinguishes at the time the conflict ends.[910] All such discernible characteristics of traditional international armed conflict help to eliminate, or reduce considerably, erroneous detention. On the contrary, terrorist attacks lack obvious attributes of a typical international armed conflict, such as the ones mentioned above. Terrorists carry out their attacks anywhere in the world and at any time.[911] They are not constrained to a geographical battle zone, as their operations are transnational. Obviously, the absence of a clear-cut battle zone in terrorism makes it difficult for terrorists to be distinguished from individuals who have no affiliations with terrorism.[912] As a result, people are arrested indiscriminately, detained and often detained erroneously and indefinitely in the "fight against terrorism".

6.3.5 INTELLIGENCE SHARING

Another area of grave concern is the issue of 'intelligence' for enhancement of national security. The definition of national security in this book recognises intelligence sharing as an indispensable tool in countering terrorism.[913] Essentially, the need to maintain a reliable and steady intelligence network amongst sovereign states of the world and the need for states to maintain reliable and consistent intelligence sharing within the various levels of government in the state is crucial for enhancement of national security. Since 2001, USA and UK have devoted serious attention to the cultivation of intelligence sharing with countries within such regions, which controlled and developed security networks. Intelligence sharing is fundamental in countering terrorism, whether the terrorist threat is within the state or transnational. Hence, in situations of

909 C. David, et al., *"Jousting at windmills": the laws of armed conflict in an age of terror-state actors and nonstate elements* (Columbia University Press, New York 2011), 67-84

910 K. Hammond, National defense authorization Act and the unbound authority to detain: A call to congress (2013) vol 22 Southern California Interdisciplinary Law Journal 193

911 M. Dudziak, *Wartime: An idea, its history, its consequences* (Oxford University Press, New York 2012)

912 M. Waxman, 'Administrative detention of terrorists: Why detain, and detain whom?' (2009) vol 3(1) Journal of National Security Law and Policy

913 B. Brooks, 'Law enforcement's role in US counterterrorism strategy' (2010) vol 83(2) The Police Journal 113-125

emergency, states fall back on their closest partners for support. In September 2001, UK's first move in relation to enhanced counter-terrorism co-operation involved efforts to restore some of the institutional linkage between UK and USA and the EU member states, which had deteriorated since the end of the Cold War.[914] The definition of national security in this book recognises the role of intelligence sharing nationally, regionally and globally in safeguarding against threat and violence.

However, the issue of intelligence sharing has in some circumstances, infringed on the right to a fair trial Article 6(1) of the ECHR. Thus, nation states such as UK have adopted the 'closed material procedure' in control order cases to assert preventive counter terror measures, which seemed to rest on the perception of creating an overall fairness without complying with the rigid rules of procedure.[915] This is one of the procedures in control order cases, where the case against an applicant could be contained as closed material, concealed from him and his legal representative. In effect, the security service information is protected, in addition to the sources of information and methods of procuring the information.[916] Against the background of counterterrorism, counsels and judicial officials have maintained, in most control order cases, that failure to disclose any detail of a case is compatible with Article 6(1) of the ECHR because Article 6 of the ECHR must be interpreted flexibly, where the interest of the public demands non-disclosure. They argued that general interest of the community must be balanced against the rights of a single individual.[917] Thus, governments that adopt closed material procedure maintain that it encourages intelligence sharing amongst allies and agents of nation states to foster national, regional and global security, as the source and contents of the intelligence is not disclosed to the public.

Practically speaking, intelligence sharing network functions with maximum levels of clandestineness. In effect, the fundamental elements of intelligence sharing such as the participants, the modus operandi and the agreements themselves

914 C. Murray, 'Out of the shadows: The courts and the United Kingdom's malfunctioning International counter-terrorism partnership' (2013) vol 18(2) Journal of conflict and security law 193-232

915 H. Fenwick, 'The Human Rights Act or a British Bill of Rights: Creating a down-grading recalibration of rights against the counter-terror backdrop' (2012) Public Law 468-490

916 ibid

917 ibid

stay classified[918]. Accordingly, intelligence producers establish ethics and norms that members must comply with.[919] They call for the enforcement of set rules for the handling and storage of shared intelligence as every piece of shared intelligence risk disclosure of its sources and its methods, which jeopardises future intelligence.[920] Principally, shared intelligence must be kept confidential and not disseminated further without the sender's permission. For instance, in ***A and Others v The United Kingdom,*** the case against the applicants was contained in both open and closed materials, but the determination of their appeal was founded on the closed evidence available to the tribunal. The appellants never had access to such closed materials. As a result, the tribunal relied on the open materials, which comprise general issues most of the time.[921] Often, the open material might not be extensive, as was seen in the case of the third appellant in ***A and Others v The United Kingdom.*** This put the appellants in a disadvantaged position, as the evidence against them was largely contained in the closed material and as such, they did not have knowledge of the substantive aspect of the case against them.

Disputably, the adoption of 'closed material' procedure as a counter terror measure is not compatible with the definition of national security in this book. Acceptably, sovereign states have an absolute obligation to protect the source of intelligence received by them on an individual. At the same time, it could be done in a way that will reduce the feeling of lack of confidence in the system; as such, feeling could enhance hostility in the society. In the closed material procedure, individuals are deprived of a fair opportunity to challenge the case against them. Ideally, it would be fair for a terrorist suspect to have an opportunity to know the case against him. However, even though decisions are made based on the 'open' and the 'closed' evidence before the tribunal, the decision is predicated upon the evidence that is unknown by the applicant and therefore uncontested by him. Impliedly, the case is sustained by the closed evidence.[922]

918 J. Richelson, *The US intelligence community* (4th edn, Westview Press, Colorado 1999), 294

919 S. Chesterman, 'The spy who came in from the cold war: Intelligence and international law' (2007) vol. 27(4) Michigan Journal of International Law 1071

920 B. Muller-Willie, 'For our eyes only? Shaping an intelligence community within the EU' (2004) vol 50 European Union Institute for Security Studies <*http://www.iss.europa.eu/upload/media/occ50.pdf*> accessed 27 February 2015

921 *A and Others v United Kingdom.*, para 31

922 ibid., para 48

Arguably, the closed material procedure is intentionally orchestrated to evade 'open' and 'public' analysis of the respondent's case[923]. Ironically, s.25 (2) (a) of the 2001 Act empowers the Special Immigration Appeals Commission (SIAC) to cancel a certificate, if it considers that there are reasonable grounds to believe that the appellant is an international terrorist. Critically, it might be safe to say that s. 25(2) (a) of the 2001 Act is a mere formality; as an appellant does not have access to the intelligence against him and as such cannot contest it with SIAC.

Justifiably, an allegation of a threat to national security, terrorism, or membership of a terrorist organisation against an individual requires a defence from the part of the accused, especially in a democratic society. Acceptably, the protection of the source of intelligence is crucial, especially in a situation where the intelligence originated from an external source, but at the same time the measures nation states adopt for enhancement of national security ought to carry a 'human face'. Perhaps, the SIAC procedure could have availed appellants the opportunity of knowing the case (intelligence) against them without the disclosure of the source of the evidence (intelligence) against them. Ultimately, there is a crucial need for rule of law-compliant counterterrorism measures. Against the background of national security, a considerable measure of procedural justice should be accorded to a controlee.

Some advocates have argued that a strong state serves as a best guarantor for human rights.[924] As a result, it is imperative for sovereign states to understand the need and role of human security in national security. More so, respect for human rights will also assist nation states to understand why individuals engage in terrorism. This will also deter states from formulating aggressive counter terrorism measures, notably such that negligently result in greater incidence of terrorism.[925] Hence, in ***Saadi v Italy,*** Judge Myjer pointed out that,

> "States are not allowed to combat international terrorism at all costs. They must not resort to methods which undermine the very values they

---

923 ibid., para 55

924 M. Bassiouni, 'Challenges facing a rule of law-oriented world order' (2010) vol 8(1) Santa Clara Journal of International Law 1

925 I. Kfir, 'A regime in need of balance: The UN counterterrorism regimes of security and human rights' (2013) vol 4 University of Miami National Security and Armed Conflict Law Review 7

> seek to protect. And this applies the more to those "absolute" rights from which no derogation may be made in times of emergency..."[926]

In essence, the definition of national security as propagated in this book advocates for such anti-terrorism measures that synchronise with the principles of the rule of law.

Terrorism could be a strategy adopted by a group of people to achieve a specific goal or ideology. Accordingly, it is natural for sovereign states to react through the formulation and implementation of counterterrorism measures after a terrorist attack; especially the 9/11 incident, which was unprecedented in its ramifications. Thus, it could be argued that terrorists can foresee that the level of their attack would be such that it would compel sovereign states to overreact to forestall future terrorist attacks. Subsequently, there is a feeling of fear and provoked reactions in the state. By implication, terrorism encourages a cycle whereby an attack causes a reaction that influences further attacks.[927] Interestingly, one of the ways through which this can happen is by some of the counterterrorism measures causing resentment in society. For instance, the situation in Australia where 16 out of 17 organisations proscribed by the Australian government are in some way associated with Islamic objectives and ideology.[928] Perhaps, the Muslim community might feel that the measure is disproportional and unfair towards them. Hence, out of resentment some individuals in the society are probably less likely to cooperate with the security agents, such as the police and intelligent agencies in the community who seek to thwart future attacks.[929] In consequence, the disproportionality in some counter terrorism measures could make some people vulnerable for recruitment as terrorists by terrorist organisations. Nevertheless, based on the dissection of the definition of 'national security' in this book, and for further analysis into the tenets of national security perceived in this book, a theory will be formulated against the background of counter terrorism, namely, the 'theory of preservative legitimacy'.

---

926 *Saadi v Italy* (2008) ECtHR 37201/06 Grand Chamber

927 G. Williams, 'A decade of Australian anti-terror laws' (2011) vol 35 Melbourne University Law Review 1136

928 ibid

929 T. Tyler, et al., 'Why does the public cooperate with the law enforcement? The influence of the purposes and targets of policing' (2011) vol 7(3) Public Law and Legal Theory Working Papers No. 339

6.4 THEORY OF 'PRESERVATIVE LEGITIMACY'

The promulgation of such theory stemmed from the analysis in Chapter 4 of this book. Such theory is predicated upon the assessment of the depth of violation of the rule of law and human rights in the fight against terrorism. As stated above, post-9/11, nation states embarked on anticipatory and pre-emptive actions geared towards the obstruction of prospective terrorist violence. A variety of contentious preventive measures have been formulated by nation states to thwart future violence, some of which are: indefinite detention of suspected terrorists, control orders, extensions of period of detention without charge, anticipatory strikes against freedom of expression (such as counter radicalisation policies), restrictions over positive acts of expression (for instance, UK adopted the complementary and contentious technique of criminalising the failure to divulge information to the police about suspected terrorist activities). Hence, family members and friends have been forcibly co-opted into matters of risk anticipation.[930] Countries have been attacked, wars have been fought, and people have been arbitrarily moved to other jurisdictions, tortured.[931] All such and more precipitated the "**theory of "preservative legitimacy**" formulated in this book, which:

> "Queries the legality and rationality of the formulation and implementation of some counterterrorism measures or legislations to prevailing circumstances in the fight against terrorism. It evaluates the objectivity of the deployment of certain counterterrorism measures in favour of national security at the expense of human rights against the background of the war on terror. It prescribes compliance with the principles of the rule of law in the fight against terrorism."

The above theory could be illustrated through one of the aspects of national security identified in the third chapter of this book, namely, 'self-defence'. This part of my work will evaluate the security aspect of 'self-defence' through 'military defence'.

930 I. Cram, 'Failing Justice Brennan's quest? Anticipating terrorism risk and the US Supreme Court' (2013) (1) Public Law Journal 30-51

931 M. Sattherwaite, et al., '*Gender, national security and counter-terrorism: Human rights perspective*' (Routledge publishers, Abingdon 2013)

6.4.1 THEORY OF PRESERVATIVE LEGITIMACY AND SELF-DEFENCE IN THE FIGHT AGAINST TERRORISM

Notably, the right to self-defence is a long established custom immanent to a state's sovereignty. It constitutes an exception to prohibition of the use of force. Nation states have been exercising the right to self-defence under customary international law, before it was stipulated in the UN Charter.[932] Thus, Article 51 of the UN Charter states:

> "Nothing in the present Charter shall impair the inherent right of individual or collective self-defence if an armed attack occurs against a Member of the United Nations, until the Security Council has taken measures necessary to maintain international peace and security. Measures taken by Members in the exercise of this right of self-defence shall be immediately reported to the Security Council and shall not in any way affect the authority and responsibility of the Security Council under the present Charter to take at any time such action as it deems necessary to maintain or restore international peace and security".[933]

The UN Charter clearly provides that self-defence of a state is 'inherent' and that nothing in the Charter will vitiate it.[934] Under international law, such right is the right to resist or defeat an unlawful use of force amounting to an armed attack. The UN Charter recognises the right to self-defence as a pre-existing right of states under customary international law. Such right is integrated into the UN Charter of collective security for the provision of an explicit basis of collective self defence.[935]

932 S. Lee, 'Inherent right of self-defense through the lens of 2010 Cheonan attack' (2013) vol 216 Military Law Review 212

933 UN Charter 1945

934 S. Lee, op.cit

935 T. Gill, et al., 'Anticipatory self-defense in the cyber context' (2013) vol 89(1) International Law Studies 6

The right of self-defence is purposed to preserve legal order by allowing every person the right to repel unlawful attacks.[936] Hence, Article 2(4) UN Charter provides:

> "All members shall refrain in their international relations from the threat or use of force against the territorial integrity or political independence of any state, or in any other manner inconsistent with the purposes of the United Nations."[937]

Such right could be viewed through the purview of anticipatory and pre-emptive self-defence, as pointed out in the second chapter of this book. Professor Sean Murphy clearly states that anticipatory self-defence is disparate from pre-emptive self-defence. He maintains that anticipatory self-defence "refers to the use of armed coercion by a state to halt an imminent act of armed coercion by another state or (non-state actor operating from that other state)"[938]; while "pre-emptive self-defence is used to refer to the use of armed coercion by a state to prevent another state (or non-state actor) from pursuing a particular course of action which is not yet directly threatening, but which, if permitted to continue could result at some future point in an act of armed coercion against the first state."[939] Anticipatory self-defence is not expressly authorised by the UN Charter, hence, it allows for a unilateral action; while pre-emptive self-defence requires the authority of the UN Security Council.[940]

Modern terrorism has become one of the greatest challenges for the security and stability of nation states in the world.[941] Terrorists intentionally target innocent civilians in total disregard of legality and morality. Such attacks by non-state actors have been characterised by both random and intentional attacks against innocent civilians. This has sparked conflicts between state and non-state

936 D. Moore, 'Reasonable provocation: Distinguishing the vigilant from the vigilante in self-defense law' (2013) vol 78(4) Brooklyn Law Review 1659

937 UN Charter 1945

938 S. Murphy, 'The doctrine of preemptive self-defense' (2005) vol 50(3) Villanova Law Review 699

939 ibid

940 ibid

941 A. Amet, 'Terrorism and international law: Cure the underlying problem not just the symptom' (2013) vol 19 (1) International and comparative Law 17

actors, especially in the bid to counter such attacks. Nation states have adopted and implemented operational counterterrorism measures for enhancement of national security.[942] In line with a nation's obligation to protect its citizenry, territorial sovereignty and natural resources, force is applied. This ignites the question regarding the 'degree' and 'nature' of force to be applied, especially in a situation where self-defence is invoked by state actors.

The right to self-defence is as old as history. Thus, it is:

> "a law... not written but born with us...which we have taken from nature herself...that if our life be in danger from...open violence, or from the weapons of robbers or enemies every means of securing our safety is honourable".[943]

Essentially, the right of self-defence is hinged on natural law. This deeply informs the right of individuals and nation states to plunge into action in the event of any threat. In view of national security, states have responded to terrorism either through law enforcement measures or through military action. However, in relation to the theory of 'preservative legitimacy' propounded in this book, this part of my work will look into the legality, rationality and objectivity of the US attack on Afghanistan post-9/11 against the background of the "war against terror".

Accordingly, national and global security in the 21st century have been exceedingly affected by 9/11, the "war on terror" (counterterrorism), the war of the United States and its allies against Afghanistan and Iraq respectively, and the subsequent installation of new governments in such nations.[944] Perhaps, it could be argued that peace and security of the world today is unstable. Hence, the security of most nation states is characterised by challenges, questions and

942 A. Guiora, 'Targeted killing: When proportionality gets all out of proportion' (2012) vol 45(1) Case Western Reserve Journal of International Law 235

943 Y. Dinstein, *War, aggression and self-defense* (4th edn, Cambridge University Press, New York 2005), 175

944 M. Krajewski, *Humanitarian intervention and other use of force? Preventive use of force and military actions against non-state actors: Revisiting the right of self-defense in insecure times* (2nd edn, Martinus Nijh of Publishers, Netherlands 2005)

confusion.[945] In the bid to take care of such challenges, answer the questions and bring clarity to some of the security concerns, sovereign states apply force. However, Article 2(4) UN Charter expressly prohibits 'threat' or 'use of force' in international relations of members of the UN. The question arises, as to what extent is it legal to apply force in self-defence to enhance national security? Against the backdrop of national security, could it be said that the US attack on Taliban-Afghanistan was legal? Was the method of the attack by the US reasonable? Is the objective of the attack in consonance with the principle of the rule of law?

Legally speaking, the spirit of Article 51 of the UN Charter protects and recognises not only an individual's intrinsic right to self-defence, but also the inherent collective right to self-defence. By implication, the right to self-defence is also available to nation states, groups or organisations. Such right, according to international law, can only be invoked in the event of an illegal attack measuring up to an armed attack. It becomes a puzzle whether such right of self-defence is available to nation states in their fight against terrorism. It also arouses some level of curiosity regarding whether terrorist attacks amount to armed attack. Basically, many resolutions have been passed by the UN Security Council (S.C.) declaring terrorist acts as acts against international peace and security.[946] The S.C. has condemned acts of terrorism and has encouraged states to desist from rendering any form of support like financial, prevent and curb terrorist activities, and dynamically cooperate amongst themselves to prevent terrorist acts originating within their borders.[947] Nonetheless, no S.C. Resolution has declared the right to 'use of force' on grounds of terrorism,[948] even when Al-Qaeda accepted responsibility for the Kenya terrorist attack in 2002.[949] For instance, the S.C. Resolution 1368 adopted subsequent to 9/11 emphasised that the right of self-defence and terrorism, both amount to "a threat to international peace and

945 D. Aaron, *In their own words: Voices of jihad-compilation and commentary* (RAND Corporation, California 2008), 1

946 C. Gary, *International law and the use of force* (3rd edn, Oxford University Press, USA 2008), 227

947 United Nations Security Council Resolution 53/1189., United Nations Security Council Resolution 54/1259

948 C. Gary, op cit

949 United Nations Security Council Resolution 57/1450

security" without specific reference to chapter VII.[950] S.C. Resolution 1373, passed on the 28th of September 2001, reiterated the above fact. It follows that none such resolutions settled whether the 9/11 attack qualifies as "an armed attack" and, as such, the 'use of force' is not authorised in the fight against terrorism.[951] More so, subsequent S.C. resolutions have also concentrated on dealing with international terrorism through peaceful means.[952] Similarly, the General Assembly has also adopted a peaceful approach in curbing terrorism.[953] It has passed many resolutions,[954] declarations, conventions before, after, and subsequent to 9/11. The General Assembly has condemned the use of force on other states in the fight against terrorism and has declared reprisals illegal.[955] Hence, the implementation of counterterrorism measures, to a large extent, necessitates self-imposed caution to avert violations of domestic and international laws.

Nevertheless, on grounds of self-defence, some states (like US and Israel) have employed force in attacking other states in a bid to counter terrorism.[956] Unmanned aerial vehicles or drones were developed or acquired by nation states in the "war against terror".[957] For instance, since 2001, the US adopted the lethal hellfire missile; armed, predator drones to attack Afghanistan. Subsequently, they have been deployed in Iraq and other parts of the world.[958] The US has drone bases around the world and their deployment is usually controlled from its Creech air force base in American Nevada desert.[959] Hence, at the click of a computer mouse on American soil, drones are employed for clandestine

950 United Nations Security Council Resolution 56/1373, UN DOC S/Res (Sept 28, 2001)

951 Y. Dinstein, *War, aggression and self-defense* (4th edn Cambridge University Press, London 2005), 207

952 C. Gray, op.cit

953 United Nations General Assembly Resolution 2625 (XXV), United Nations General Assembly Resolution 49/60

954 General Assembly Resolution 62/71, UN Doc A RES 62/71 (Jan. 8, 2008)

955 United Nations General Assembly Resolution 2625 (XXV)

956 A. Cassese, *International Law* (2nd edn Oxford University Press, London 2005), 472

957 A. Ogunfolu, et al., 'I have a drone: The implications of American drone policy for Africa and international humanitarian law' (2015) vol 23(1) African Journal of international and comparative law106

958 N. Sharkey, 'Saying no to lethal autonomous targeting' (2010) vol 9(4) Journal of Military Ethics 369

959 ibid

operations to kill Al-Qaeda suspected operatives in non-armed conflict areas.[960] Such drones are robots that lack the proficiency of human decision making. As a result, innocent civilians who find themselves within the vicinity where drones are deployed may be accidentally murdered.[961] Drones are unable to comply with the principles of distinction and proportionality, which regulate the deployment of lethal force in armed conflicts.[962] While declaring it was exercising its intrinsic right to self-defence, the US applied excessive force on Afghanistan that has no place either in the UN Charter or rules of customary international law.

Arguably, to a great extent, the assessment of the legality of the amount of force needed in self-defence by a sovereign state could be dependent on international law requirements of 'necessity' and 'proportionality'. For instance, the US set out to do three things in Afghanistan, namely: (a) the destruction of terrorist training camps and infrastructure within Afghanistan (b) the capturing of Al-Qaeda and Taliban leaders and (c) the cessation of terrorist activities in Afghanistan.[963] Critically, such goals seem reasonable. Again, because the US was attacked (9/11) and there was a clear and compelling evidence of Afghanistan's responsibility for both past and planned attacks, there was a global consensus that ab initio US attack on Afghanistan was 'necessary' and 'proportional'.[964] Perhaps at such point, it could be argued that the US attack on Afghanistan was legal.

However, by December 2001, the Taliban government was extinguished and to a considerable extent Al-Qaeda was expunged from Afghanistan.[965] However, the US persisted in bombing and killing many Afghan civilians.[966] In 2009, the

960 R. Arkin, 'The case for ethical autonomy in unmanned systems' (2010) vol 9(4) Journal of Military Ethics 339

961 ibid

962 P. Singer, 'The ethics of killer applications: Why is it so hard to talk about morality when it comes to new military technology' (2010) vol 9(4) Journal of Military Ethics 299

963 R. Williams, 'Dangerous precedent: America's illegal war in Afghanistan' (2011) vol 33(2) University of Pennsylvania Journal of International Law 582

964 K. Royal, et al., 'Burning the barn to roast the pig? Proportionality concerns in the war on terror and the Damadola incident' (2006) Vol 14 Willamette Journal of International Law and Dispute Resolution 55

965 R. Williams, 582

966 ibid, 583

US deployed additional 30,000 troops in Afghanistan.[967] In 2010, the US doubled its number of troops in Afghanistan to eradicate the Taliban completely.[968] One begins to wonder whether the continued war against Taliban is 'necessary' under international law, when Al-Qaeda was the group that attacked the US many years ago. There is also a contention concerning the proportionality of the continuous US attacks in Afghanistan.[969] Clearly, international law does not see proportionality in terms of the original aggression.[970] Rather, it perceives proportionality in terms of what is required to counteract and deter future aggression; it contemplates responses parallel in intensity to an initial aggression, which is purposed to discourage future attacks.[971]It could be safely said that the US' continued military attack on Afghanistan is in violation of the spirit of Article 2(4) of the U.N. as the US-Afghan attack left the Afghanistan population dispirited and ignited the resurgence of the Taliban movement.[972] Notably, sovereign states are precluded from taking actions inimical to the maintenance of international peace and security.[973]

On the other hand, one might ask whether it is necessary for the US to militarily defeat the Taliban for the US to be secure. Obviously, there are no claims in the international community that the Taliban was responsible for 9/11. Perhaps, the Taliban administration could be guilty of providing 'state support' to Al-Qaeda and its activities, but, as was delineated in Nicaragua's case, it never exerted 'effective control' or 'overall control' as seen in the Tadic judgment[974] on America (9/11). The Taliban had no state sponsorship of Al-Qaeda and its

967 ibid, 576

968 ibid, 584

969 M. O'Connel, 'Lawful self-defense to terrorism' (2002) vol 63(889) University of Pittsburg Law Review 908

970 E. Cannizzaro, 'The role of proportionality in the law of international countermeasures' (2001) vol 12(5) European Journal of International Law 889

971 K. Royal, et al., pages 59-60

972 A. Rashid, '*Descent into chaos: The United States and the failure of nation building in Pakistan, Afghanistan and Central Asia*' (1st edn, Viking Penguin Group, New York 2008), 135

973 ibid

974 S. Shah, 'War on terrorism: Self-defense, operation enduring freedom, and the legality of US drone attacks in Pakistan' (2010) vol 9(1) Washington University Global Studies Law Review 77

activities on US soil. Al-Qaeda was completely responsible for 9/11.[975] Although some international law scholars recognise the Taliban's non-involvement in the 9/11 attack, they still argue that the Taliban was an accomplice to 9/11 by not taking measures against Al-Qaeda and Bin Laden.[976] They contend that by continued harbouring of Al-Qaeda within the Taliban territory, Afghanistan validated the attack against US, and that the Taliban-led government accepted responsibility of the terrorist act. This, according to them, constitutes enough reason for the US to invoke their right of self-defence against Afghanistan.[977] They maintained that it is reasonable for the US to carry out an armed attack against Taliban-Afghanistan either preceding or after 9/11 for providing a safe haven to Al-Qaeda.[978]

Critically, could it be said that US relied upon the Preamble to the UNSC Resolution 1368, which reaffirmed its determination to combat terrorism 'by all means' in recognition of the inherent right to individual or collective self-defence?[979] Alternatively, could the US attack on Afghanistan be justified on grounds of Article 3 of UNSC Resolution 1368, which asserts that those responsible for aiding, supporting or harbouring the perpetrators, organisers and sponsors of terrorist attacks will be held accountable?[980] Arguably, in accord with Article 51 of the UN Charter, harbouring of terrorists and endorsement of a terrorist attack on US soil does not qualify the Taliban as a perpetrator of the 9/11 attack. Under international law, state involvement is an essential element for the occurrence of an armed attack. It follows that a state cannot be responsible for an armed attack after the fact or through imputation.[981] Also, an armed attack can only be committed by a state, its organs or agents.[982] Critically, the 9/11 attack lacks some basic ingredients of an armed attack as seen above. As such, the US lacks the locus standi to engage in what could be described as a 'punitive

975 J. Mueller, 'How dangerous are the Taliban?' (2015) <*http://www.foreignaffairs.com/articles/64932/john-mueller/how-dangerous-are-the-taliban?page=show*> (accessed 3rd December 2016)

976 Y. Dinstein, op cit., 236

977 ibid

978 S. Shah, op cit

979 United Nations Security Council Resolution 1368 (12 September 2001) U.N. Doc. S/RES/1368

980 ibid

981 S. Shah, op.cit

982 *Nicaragua v US.*, op.cit para 103

reprisal attack' on Taliban-Afghanistan. However, assuming the 9/11 attack was an armed attack; the reactionary attack by the US on the Taliban ought to have been on the same day of 9/11. In which case, the requirements of 'immediacy', 'necessity' and 'proportionality', which were popularly delineated in the famous Caroline case, and which are contingent to the right to self-defence will spring into action.[983] According to Daniel Webster, a state is allowed to respond in legitimate self-defence[984] only when the danger posed to it is "instant, overwhelming, leaving no choice of means, and no moments of deliberation..."[985]. Obviously, the element of 'immediacy' seems to have been lost in the US-Afghan attack, which appeared more like a 'punitive reprisal attack' that is largely illegal under international law. Accordingly, the customary law requirements of 'immediacy' and 'necessity' are inevitably connected.[986] Again, the principle of "necessity" can only be met when other peaceful means of settlements have been sought and exhausted.[987]

Additionally, the US must comply with procedural requirements of law. For instance, pursuant to Article 51 of the UN Charter, a member state is compelled to report, without delay, to the Security Council any action taken in the exercise of their right to self-defence and in response to an armed attack. It must not at any time inhibit an attempt by the UNSC to take any steps, which are channelled towards the maintenance of international peace and security. Impliedly, even though US has an inherent right to self-defence, she does not have the exclusive right to act in such a way that the authority and responsibility of the Security Council towards the maintenance of international peace and security can be impeded. Arguably, for the sake of security, the fact that a sovereign state suffered an armed attack is not a guarantee for it to retaliate with an armed attack, unless such use of armed attack is necessary for the maintenance of international peace and security.

983 E. Schwartz, 'US security strategy: Empowering Jim Jong-il?' (2008) vol 30(1) Loyola of Los Angeles International and Comparative Law Review 1

984 N. White, et al., 'The twin towers attack: An unlimited right to self-defense' (2002) vol 7(1) Journal of Conflict and Security Law 5-17

985 S. Shah, op.cit

986 ibid; N. White, *Democracy Goes to War: British Military Deployments under International Law* (Oxford University Press, Oxford 2009), 171

987 ibid; M. Evans, *Just War Theory: A Reappraisal* (Palgrave Macmillan, New York 2006), 55-56

Furthermore, on grounds of rationality (reasonableness of the US method of attack on Afghanistan), the US employed high-handed weapons, which led to innumerable civilian casualties, more dilapidation of public infrastructure, immense suffering [988] and unprecedented damage that might be deemed highly unnecessary.[989] Afghanistan also experienced massive collateral damage.[990] In addition, non-deployment of armed US ground forces in Afghanistan created the opportunity for Osama bin Laden and top Taliban leaders to abscond and an appreciable number of Taliban prisoners were exterminated by the Northern Alliance forces.[991] This, to a considerable extent, defeated the main objective of the US-Afghan attack, namely, countervailing Al-Qaeda leadership. Arguably, on the premise of the theory of 'preservative legitimacy' propounded in this book, the depth of attack on Afghanistan could be described as 'irrational'. The US failed to seriously pursue and exhaust all peaceful means of resolution, and the armament employed was controversial, i.e. carpet and cluster bombs. For instance, the US discharged 1,228 bombs, which released a quarter of a million bomb-lets that continued to kill or maim civilians' years later.[992] The weaponry utilised was not precision-guided. The war was undermining, the tactics and modus operandi of the war ignited and invigorated global terrorism.[993]

To some extent, the question of rationality is connected to proportionality. On one hand, the US aerial bombing proved effective in reducing military casualties but, on the other, it led to extensive loss of civilian life and associated suffering. Hospitals, mosques, homes, as well as, structures belonging to international aid agencies were bombed, resulting in millions of Afghan citizens becoming refugees.[994] The method of attack on Afghanistan could be considered 'unreasonable', as the element of proportionality was ignored. The US administration deployed inadequate US ground troops. The US funded, supported and depended on barbarous and fraudulent local warlords, whose brutal rule instigated the initial inception of the Taliban from the proletariat to overcome Al-Qaeda and the

---

988 ibid, 28-32

989 S. Shah, op.cit

990 ibid

991 A. Rashid, op.cit

992 ibid

993 S. Shah, op.cit

994 ibid

Taliban.[995] Critically, if put on a scale, the weaponry employed by US is hardly proportional to the small arms and launch of small group guerrilla tactics the Taliban employed.[996]

Ultimately, one might be tempted to ask whether the counterterrorism measure adopted by the US in the Afghan attack is 'for' or 'against' national security. Today, the entire world has been plunged into a dilemma that is precipitated by present day terrorism, and the insatiable quest for international peace and security. Ordinarily, one might be tempted to think that the US attack on Afghanistan is justified considering the damage and the loss the US suffered from the 9/11 attack. Some see the "war against terror" as justification for states to invade and violate the territorial sovereignty of other states, where terrorist networks seem to thrive. They act in anticipatory and pre-emptive self-defence even in circumstances where elements of 'immediacy' and 'necessity' are absent.[997] However, with respect to the US-Afghan attack, a critical review of the rules of international law reveals that there has been both substantive and procedural violation of the rules under the UN law of the Charter. This provides for two exceptions to the use of force, namely: the use of force authorised by the Security Council and the use of force in the exercise of an individual or a collective right to self-defence against an armed attack.[998]

6.4.2 THE THEORY OF PRESERVATIVE LEGITIMACY AND ARTICLE 3 OF THE ECHR IN THE FIGHT AGAINST TERRORISM

The theory of 'preservative legitimacy' propounded in this book can also be illustrated by evaluating the violation of Article 3 of the ECHR in the fight against terrorism. Looking at the case of ***Al Nashiri v Poland***[999]***,*** the applicant was captured in Dubai in October 2002. In November 2002, he was transferred

995 A. Rashid, op.cit

996 M. Bhatia, et al., *Afghanistan, arms an conflict: Armed groups, disarmament and security in a post war society* (1st edn, Routledge, Abingdon 2008)

997 A. Cassese, op.cit., 476

998 M. Krajewski, *Humanitarian intervention and other use of force? Preventive use of force and military actions against non-state actors: Revisiting the right of self-defense in insecure times* (2nd edn, Martinus Nijhof, Netherlands 2005)

999 *Al-Nashiri v Poland* (2014) 28761/11 Strasbourg

to the custody of the CIA.[1000] Later, US agents took him to a secret CIA detention facility in Afghanistan called the 'salt pit'.[1001] After a brief stay in the salt pit, he was taken to another CIA prison in Bangkok, Thailand (code named Catseye).[1002] From Catseye, the applicant was moved to another secret CIA facility. In all such secret detentions, the applicant was subjected to EITs (enhanced interrogation techniques), such as water boarding.[1003] He alleged among other things a violation of procedural and substantive aspects of his right under Article 3 of the ECHR.[1004]

In analysing the element of 'legality' in the theory of 'preservative legitimacy' propounded in this book, the present case will be used as a case study. I will consider the three elements of the theory in relation to torture in the "war against terror": (a) the 'legality' of torture in the fight against terrorism; (b) the 'rationality' of torture in the fight against terrorism and (c) the 'objectivity' of torture in the fight against terrorism.

6.4.2.1 THE LEGALITY OF TORTURE IN THE FIGHT AGAINST TERRORISM

The status of the unlawfulness of torture is reinforced by Article 3 of the ECHR. The provision of Article 3 of the ECHR is in consonance with Article 5 of the Universal Declaration of Human Rights (UDHR), adopted by the General Assembly of the UN on 10th December 1948.[1005] This article set a prototype of a large collection of contemporary Constitutions, Conventions and Declarations. For instance, Article XXV of the American Declaration of the Rights and Duties of Man states that "every individual who has been deprived of his liberty has the right to humane treatment during the time he is in custody".[1006] Article 7 of the International Covenant on Civil and Political Rights[1007] and Article 5(2) of

1000 ibid, para 83

1001 ibid, para 84

1002 ibid, para 85

1003 ibid, para 87

1004 ibid, para 460

1005 Resolution 217A (111) (Cmd) 7662

1006 Adopted by the Ninth International Conference of American States on 2nd May 1948

1007 Adopted by a Resolution of the General Assembly of the United Nations on 16th Dec 1966

the American Convention on Human Rights,[1008] both state that "no one shall be subjected to torture or to cruel, inhuman or degrading treatment or punishment." By virtue of Article 12(1) (d) of the Bill of Rights in the Constitution of South Africa 1996, "everyone has the right to freedom and security of the person, which includes the right not to be tortured in any way."[1009] Interestingly, some nation states did not expressly prohibit torture in their body of law. However, many of them still formulated expressions, which could be inferred as implying a prohibition of torture. For instance, the 1982 Canadian Charter of Rights and Freedom did not explicitly mention torture. Nevertheless, its prohibition could be inferred from the wordings of two of its sections. For example, Section 11 (c) provides that "any person charged with an offence has the right not to be compelled to be a witness against himself in proceedings in respect of that offence", and Section 12 provides that "everyone has the right not to be subjected to cruel and unusual punishment."[1010]

It is a settled principle of international law that detainees are entitled to their right not to be tortured. A host of international treaties and domestic laws expressly prohibit the offence of torture or cruel, inhuman or degrading treatment or punishment.[1011] No derogation from it is permissible under Article 15(2) of the ECHR. As pointed out in the previous chapter, the right not to be tortured is an "absolute right". It cannot be derogated from under any circumstance, such as national security or national emergency. Thus, Article 2(2) of the UNCAT states, "No exceptional circumstances whatsoever, whether a state of war or a threat of war, internal political instability or any other public emergency, may be invoked as a justification of torture." By virtue of this Article, states are required to take effective legislative, administrative, judicial or other measures to prevent acts of torture in any territory under their jurisdiction. Article 4 of the UNCAT also requires each State Party to ensure that all acts of torture are offences under its criminal law. However, Article 16 of the UNCAT provides:

> "Each State Party shall undertake to prevent in any territory under its jurisdiction other acts of cruel, inhuman or degrading treatment or

1008 Signed at San Jose, Costa Rica on 22nd Nov 1969

1009 D. Hope, 'Torture' (2004) vol53 International and Comparative Law 807

1010 Constitution Act 1982., Part 1

1011 European Convention on Human Rights

> punishment which do not amount to torture as defined in Article I, when such acts are committed by or at the instigation of or with the consent or acquiescence of a public official or other person acting in an official capacity..."[1012]

A critical look at the provisions of Article 16 of the UNCAT might raise questions regarding whether the said Article sets out to encourage the prohibition of cruel, inhuman and degrading treatment as opposed to torture. Importantly, the interpretation of this Article ought to be in alignment with the provisions of Article 2 (1) (2) of the UNCAT. Article 16 could be interpreted as either an extension of or a continuation of Article 2 of the UNCAT. Hence, the words "other acts" in Article 16 should not be taken to imply that torture is condoned to the exclusion of other acts of cruel, inhuman or degrading treatment/punishment as torture could be considered as an 'aggravated' form of cruel, inhuman or degrading treatment/punishment.

Also, it could be argued that the wording of Article 16 of the UNCAT implies that not every ill, inhuman or degrading treatment or punishment amounts to torture. For an act to be described as torture, it must attain a minimum level of severity. To determine torture, peculiar circumstances of a case must be considered, such as the duration of the treatment or punishment, the impact of the treatment, the sex, age, health condition of the victim, and the reason behind the torture.[1013] However, in August 2002, the US Department of Justice provided a report with 10 'authorised' enhanced interrogation techniques (EITs) stating that the application of such EITs will not violate Article 3 of the ECHR. According to the report, the EITs "... are designed to psychologically 'dislocate' the detainee, maximise his feeling of vulnerability and helplessness, and reduce or eliminate his will to resist ... efforts to obtain critical intelligence."[1014] This report raises some questions. Will such EITs cease from amounting to torture because they are considered as 'legal opinion' from the Department of Justice or will the threshold still be dependent on the elements espoused under law, such as in Article 1 of the UNCAT?

1012 United Nations Convention Against Torture 1984

1013 *Ireland v United Kingdom* (1978) 5310/71 Strasbourg., para 162-163

1014 *Al-Nashiri v Poland* (2014) 28761/11 Strasbourg., Para 55

The question of 'legality' in the theory of 'preservative legitimacy' goes to the 'lawfulness' of an act/s. It addresses the issue of compliance with the principles and dictates of law in a particular case. Impliedly, the issue of legality of the violation of Article 3 of the ECHR in ***Al-Nashiri v Poland*** goes to the issue of lawfulness of subjecting terrorist suspects to torture or to cruel, inhuman or degrading treatment or punishment. The applicant in ***Al-Nashiri v Poland*** was subjected to a series of EITs, while in detention. For example, among other things, the interrogators subjected him to prolonged stress standing positions, during which his wrists were shackled to a bar or hook in the ceiling above the head for at least two days.[1015] During wall standing, the detainee must stand about 4 to 5 feet from a wall with his feet spread approximately to his shoulder width. His arms are stretched out in front of him and his fingers rest on the wall to support all his body weight. The detainee was not allowed to reposition his hands or feet.[1016] The applicant was placed in a confinement box with harmless insects inside. He had two water board sessions in 2002. The water board technique involves binding the detainee to a bench with his feet elevated above his head. The detainee's head is immobilised, and an interrogator places a cloth over the detainee's mouth and nose, while pouring water onto the cloth in a controlled manner. Airflow is restricted for 20 to 40 seconds and the technique produces the sensation of drowning and suffocation.[1017]

In determining the legality of the act or treatment suffered by the applicant in the present case, it is pertinent to ascertain whether such acts fall under the category of treatments or punishments considered as 'torture' as defined under Article 1 of the UN Convention. Importantly, the task of determining whether a treatment or punishment falls within the ambit of 'torture' is a question of facts and degree. It is a matter of assessment, which excludes law and legal principles, but includes an evaluation of the entire circumstance of the interrogation.[1018] The 2004 CIA report reveals that the applicant was interrogated using EITs continuously for 2 weeks in 2002. Subsequently, a senior operations officer debriefed and assessed him as withholding information. The report also reveals that between 28th December 2002 and 1st January 2003, specific unauthorised and

1015 ibid, para 84

1016 ibid, para 54

1017 ibid, para 86

1018 D. Hope, 'Torture' (2004) vol 53 (4) International and Comparative Law quarterly 807

undocumented techniques were administered to the applicant.[1019] The disclosed CIA material evidently demonstrated that the applicant was intentionally subjected to a combination and systematic mode of EITs for a prolonged length of time for obtaining information from him. Clearly, the applicant must have experienced severe pain and suffering. Analytically, considering the type of treatment or punishment the applicant was subjected to, such as water boarding, the shortness of the time within which the water boarding was administered to the applicant becomes immaterial considering the severity of such interrogation technique. Such ill treatments or punishments inflict psychological and physical suffering on an interrogated person.[1020] Such EITs were administered to the applicant by US CIA officials. Legally speaking, it is immaterial that the treatments were not administered on US soil. As long as the US agents acted in an official capacity, the treatment fell within the threshold of Article 3 of the ECHR. Thus, it can be safely said that the treatment received by the applicant in the CIA detention facility in Poland, amounted to 'torture'.

Torture has been applied as an interrogation tool from time immemorial, particularly with respect to crimes against the state, sexual offences, heresy and witchcraft.[1021] Nonetheless, the international prohibition of torture is a fundamental and undeniable aspect of international human rights law, as observed by the US Court of Appeal Second Circuit in ***Filartiga v Pena-Irala.***[1022] The prohibition is evidently conventional and at the same time customary. As pointed out in the previous chapter, it is a norm of jus cogens.[1023] In other words, torture is unacceptable in every circumstance and its prohibition and the right not to be tortured is absolute. In ***Chahal v The United Kingdom***[1024], the Court established that despite difficult circumstances, such as the fight against terrorism and organised crime, the ECHR prohibits, in absolute terms, torture and inhuman or degrading treatment or punishment irrespective of the person's conduct. The qualification that applies to other Convention rights such as the right to

1019 *Al-Nashiri v Poland.*, para 99

1020 Ibid., para 502

1021 Maio, 'The historical evolution of the arguments against torture and the history of human rights' (2000) vol 46 World Medical Journal 75

1022 *Filartiga v Pena-Irala* (2nd cir 1980) 630 F 2d 876 at 890

1023 G. Ert, 'Torture and the Supreme Court of Canada' (2014) University of New Brunswick Law Journal

1024 *Chahal v The United Kingdom.*, op.cit

freedom of expression for the sake of national security or public interest is not applicable to Article 3 of the ECHR. Paradoxically, torture is extensively applied with its method refined to a great extent, especially post-9/11. Thus, Nowak, former UN Special Rapporteur on torture states: "Torture is practiced in more than 90 percent of all countries and constitutes a wide-spread practice in more than 50 percent of all the countries."[1025] Torture is very much practised today in prisons and detention centres. However, the fact that torture is widely practiced does not make it 'legal'.

Hence, in ***Gafgen v Germany***[1026] the applicant lured J an 11year old boy into his flat by pretending his sister's jacket was in the flat and killed him through suffocation[1027] For a ransom of one million euros. The applicant drove for approximately one hour and dropped the corpse of the child in a property close to a pond.[1028] After picking the ransom, the applicant was arrested by the police. He was informed by the police that he was suspected of kidnapping J. The applicant was questioned by the police with the intention to find J. The applicant indicated that J was kidnapped by two people who had hidden him in a hut in a lake. Meanwhile, the police, having searched the applicant's flat, found half of the ransom money and a note concerning the planning of the crime.[1029] In order to find out J's whereabout, the police threatened the applicant with considerable pain. The officer further threatened to lock the applicant in a cell with two huge black men who would sexually abuse him. The officer hit him severally on his chest and on one occasion, his head hit the wall. For fear of being exposed to the measures he was threatened with, the applicant disclosed J's whereabouts.[1030] The applicant alleged that his Article 3 right under the ECHR was violated by the police officers during interrogation. The government contested the applicant's allegation. The ECtHR held that the applicant's Article 3 right was violated.

1025 S. Greer, 'Is the prohibition against torture, Cruel, Inhuman and Degrading treatment really absolute in International Human Rights law' (2015) vol 15(1) Human Rights Law Review 1

1026 Gafgen v Germany (2010) ECHR 22978/05 Grand Chamber

1027 ibid., para 11

1028 ibid., para12

1029 ibid., para 14

1030 ibid., paras 15, 16

Arguably, considering the legal element of the theory of 'preservative legitimacy' propounded in this book, the question is whether the detective officers in this case, complied with the dictates of the law while interrogating the applicant. Accordingly, by virtue of Article 104 (1) of the Basic Law, the applicant should not be subjected to any mental or physical ill treatment. Also, Article 1(1) of the Basic law provides that, it is the duty of all state authorities to respect and protect human dignity which is inviolable under this law. Pursuant to Article 3 ECHR, no one should be subjected to torture, inhuman or degrading treatment/punishment.

Legally, for an act to fall within the ambit of Article 3 ECHR, such an act will be assessed to ascertain if it attained the minimum level of severity that will categories it as 'torture' or as other treatments mentioned under Article 3 ECHR. To determine the severity, the length of time the treatment/punishment lasted will be considered, the effects of the treatment on the detainee (such as the mental and physical effects), the purpose, intent and the context within which the treatment/punishment is inflicted.[1031] In the present case, the applicant was threatened and subjected to considerable pain for an estimated duration of ten minutes. Perhaps, the severity of the pain will be of such intensity that will help in achieving the intended goal. Hence, after the threat and the pain inflicted on him, the applicant confessed as to where he hid J's dead body. It could be alleged that the applicant suffered 'substantial fear' and 'mental suffering'. On account of physical effects of the ill treatment, the facts reveal that the applicant had injuries on his arm, legs, knees and blisters on his feet. Also, the ill treatment was not impromptu. It was premeditated. Thus, the threat and the pain inflicted on the applicant was intended to induce him to disclose J's whereabout.[1032] The officers who threatened and inflicted pain on the applicant were acting in an official capacity with the clear intention to inflict 'considerable pain'. A holistic consideration of the treatment given to the applicant by the officers in the course of interrogation depicts non-compliance with legal principles. Hence, the applicant's Article 3 right was violated. The absolute and non-derogable nature of Article 3 renders the intention of the officers immaterial.

1031 ibid., para 88

1032 ibid., paras 15, 16

Pursuant to Article 26 of the Vienna Convention on the Law of Treaty, parties to treaties are bound by the treaties and must perform treaty obligations in good faith.[1033] Again, Article 17 of the ECHR could be interpreted as being formulated as a deterrent on sovereign states or groups from the performance of any act or activity, which is geared towards the destruction or limitation of any right provided for under the ECHR. These reinforce the illegality of torture. Legally speaking, the defence of 'necessity' as in the case of 'national emergency' or 'public order', as many sovereign states will allege as justification, does not make the offence of torture 'legal'. It remains an aberration to mainstream understanding of the implications of the rule of law (respect for fundamental human rights). At the same time, the fact that international treaties and domestic laws have, in express terms, declared freedom from torture as an absolute right has also not deterred sovereign states, who are signatories to such treaties and whose legislators have promulgated laws, which reinforced the prohibition of torture from violating the right not to be tortured. What then do we do? Also, where do we go from here?

6.4.2.2 THE RATIONALITY OF TORTURE, INHUMAN OR DEGRADING TREATMENT/PUNISHMENT IN THE FIGHT AGAINST TERRORISM

The question of rationality in the theory of 'preservative legitimacy' looks at the entire circumstance in a case to ascertain whether the counterterrorism measure was 'rational' against the background of 'necessity' and 'proportionality'. It goes to the issue of what is legally, morally, psychologically and mentally 'necessary' and 'proportional' in a particular case. As it relates to torture, it goes to the issue of what is legally, morally, psychologically and mentally 'necessary' and 'proportional' in a specific circumstance. The case of torture is a controversial one, especially against the background of counterterrorism. Some scholars affirm that absolute ban on torture ought to be applied irrespective of exceptional circumstances. They argue that torture defiles the physical and mental integrity of the person tortured, negates their liberty and humanity and robs them of human dignity.[1034] They contend that it diminishes them to an ordinary object, a body from which information is obtained, while at the same time coercing them to act

1033 Vienna Convention on the Law of Treaty

1034 E. Scarry, *The body in pain* (1st edn, Oxford University Press, Inc., New York 1985)

in a manner that might be adverse to their most significant beliefs, values and interests.[1035] They see the acceptance of torture in any circumstance as a miscalculation emanating from distorted concentration on isolated cases, while overlooking the long-lasting and systematic effects of specific courses of action.[1036]

On the contrary, some scholars uphold the 'conditional ban' approach arguing that there does not seem to be a comprehensive, absolute, *a priori* prohibition on the use of torture. They argue that their subscription for torture is predicated upon the magnitude of the threat to society (which might be averted or reduced by applying torture). In such case, the threat must be on a huge scale. There is a strong presupposition against the use of torture under such approach. However, such presupposition is refutable. According to such approach, the risk/threat level on national security must be highly exceptional for such rebuttal to hold its ground.[1037]

Importantly, the categorisation of a treatment/punishment as 'torture', according to the ECHR jurisprudence, hovers around the premise of the 'severity of suffering' test. Pursuant to such test, a distinction could be drawn between different forms of ill treatment (degrading treatment, inhuman treatment or torture), as well as treatment that does not cross into the threshold of suffering.[1038] Arguably, governments have taken refuge under the cloak of 'severe suffering' test where their agents are accused of 'torture'. They argue in favour of the offence of torture even in situations where the acts of government agents have been rough and coercive.[1039] They argue that such acts did not cause so much suffering as to constitute 'torture'. Essentially, governments adopt such test to mitigate against the veracity of the absolute prohibition of torture. On the contrary, the theory of 'preservative legitimacy' in this book looks at the entire circumstance of a case to ascertain whether the treatments/punishment were 'rational' against the background of 'necessity' and 'proportionality' for the maintenance

1035 ibid

1036 O. Gross, *The prohibition on torture and the limits of the law* (Oxford University Press, Inc., Sanford Levinson 2004)

1037 ibid

1038 Y. Arai-Yokoi, 'Grading scale of degradation: Identifying the threshold of degrading treatment or Punishment under article 3 ECHR.' (2003) vol 21(3) Netherlands Quarterly Human Rights 387

1039 *El-masri v The former Yugoslav Republic of Macedonia.*, op.cit., para 173

of national security. By implication torture can be applied but to the extent that is necessary in a case.

To a great extent, 'necessity' and 'proportionality' are interrelated. Hence, the effectiveness of a counterterrorism measure indicates whether such a measure can counter a perceived threat. By implication, if the measure adopted against the perpetrators of a terrorist attack escalates the threat of terrorism, it points to the fact that the measure has fallen short of its intention.[1040] To such degree, issues concerning the effect of the use of force as a counterterrorism measure and the tendency of enhancing or obstructing future acts of terrorism are issues of potential relevance to the rationality of the use of force. Thus, proportionality requires that the force used be no more than necessary to repel the threat presented.[1041] Hence, some relevant treaties such as The Hague Conventions of 1899 and 1907, the Geneva Conventions of 1949 and their Additional Protocols of 1977 clearly delineate limits on states concerning the 'use of force'. They are all hinged on the principle of discernment and proportionality. For instance, Article 33 of the Geneva Convention of 1949 expressly states:

> "No protected person may be punished for an offence he or she has not personally committed. Collective penalties and likewise all measures of intimidation or of terrorism are prohibited. Pillage is prohibited. Reprisals against protected persons and their property are prohibited."[1042]

In other words, states must desist from causing suffering amongst the civilian population. Proportionality connotes that there ought to be a reasonable relationship between measures adopted and destruction orchestrated by the enemy, as well as between such same measures and expected results.[1043]

1040 H. Duffy, *The 'war on terror' and the framework of International Law* (2nd edition United Kingdom: Cambridge University Press., 2015), 267

1041 ibid; C. Michelson, op cit; Human Rights Act 1998 (Designated Derogation) Order 2001, No.3644; Lawless v Ireland, (No.3) (1961) 1 EHRR 15; Ireland v United Kingdom., op cit., para 207; J. Oraa, *Human rights in states of emergency in International law* (Clarendon Press, Oxford 1992), 178

1042 Geneva Convention 1949

1043 S. Cohen, *Democracies at war against terrorism: Comparative Perspective* (2nd edn, Palgrave Macmillan Publishers Limited, United Kingdom 2009), 3

For instance, in ***Aksoy v Turkey,*** the applicant stated that while in detention, he was stripped naked and blindfolded. His hands were tied behind his back and he was strung up by his arms in a form of torture referred to as 'Palestinian hanging'. While he was hanging, the police connected electrodes to his genitals and threw water over him as they electrocuted him. Such torture lasted for at least thirty-five minutes. Two days later, he was allegedly beaten continuously without cessation. The applicant claimed that he lost the movement of his arms and hands because of the torture.[1044] He also claimed that his interrogators declined his request to see a doctor.[1045] He contended that he was subjected to treatment contrary to Article 3 of the ECHR. Nevertheless, he was eventually shot and killed.[1046]

On the other hand, the government argued that there were significant doubts regarding whether the applicant had been tortured in detention.[1047] They considered the applicant's allegations of ill treatment to be unfounded.[1048] The Commission observed as a matter of fact that although the government denied that the applicant suffered torture while in detention, it failed to disclose an alternative explanation for the applicant's injuries.[1049] Nevertheless, the Commission found that the applicant's Article 3 right was violated. Subsequently, the court upheld the decision of the Commission.[1050] However, this book attempts to briefly assess the proportionality of the torture suffered by the applicant in relation to the national security situation of the Turkish region.

In ***Aksoy's case,*** there were serious disturbances in the South East of Turkey between the security forces and members of the PKK (Workers' Party of Kudistan). According to the government, such disturbances had claimed the lives of 4,036 civilians and 3,884 members of the security forces.[1051] Hence, the level of threat the national security in South East Anatolia was facing at that

1044 Akosy v Turkey (1996) 100/1995/606/694 European Court of Human Rights., para 14

1045 ibid, para 15

1046 ibid, para 7

1047 ibid., para 17

1048 ibid., para 58

1049 ibid., para 23(f)

1050 ibid., para 64

1051 ibid., para 8

time was of such intensity that it amounted to a threat to the life of a nation within the meaning of Article 15 of the ECHR.[1052] Nevertheless, the question that quickly comes to mind is whether the intensity of the torture the applicant was subjected to is proportionate to the security condition of the Turkish region.

Agreeably, the national security situation in the South-East Anatolia region of Turkey was seriously threatened, but could it justify the gravity of the inhuman treatment given to the applicant? Contentions that the gravity of force applied in self-defence must be about the same magnitude defended against are detached from the proportionality calculus. In effect, proportionality is not to be assessed against potential harm, but rather against what is strictly required to thwart the threat.[1053] In Aksoy's case, necessity could be demonstrated by the level of insecurity (shoot outs between PKK and security agents) within the region. However, in line with the theory of 'preservative legitimacy' propounded in this book, all the circumstances of the case must be assessed in determining the rationality of the torture in question, which is in consonance with the element of proportionality. Any means or methods of treatment/punishment that do not intend to discourage further violations of human rights and aggravation of human suffering are contrary to the spirit of national security advocated in this book.[1054]

Looking at the circumstances of Aksoy's death and the degree of torture he was subjected to, could it be said that the state was complying with its positive duty to protect other individuals from harm, as enshrined under Article 2(1) UNCAT? Legally, Articles 243 and 245 of the Turkish Criminal Code respectfully make it an offence for a government employee to subject someone to torture or ill-treatment. Also, morally speaking, the act of the police connecting electrodes to the applicant's genitals could be considered as a disregard to his human dignity.[1055] More so, a critical examination of Article 33 of the Geneva Convention of 1949 illustrates that no one should be punished for an offence he or she did not commit. The same Article also prohibits reprisals.

1052 ibid., para 31

1053 F. Kirgis., 'Some proportionality issues raised by Israel's use of armed force in Lebanon' (2006) vol 10(20) American Society of International Law

1054 M. Weller, *The Oxford Handbook of the Use of Force in International Law* (1st edn, Oxford University Press, UK 2015), 1206

1055 *Aksoy v Turkey.*, para 14

Basically, the inhuman treatment/punishment the applicant was subjected to by the Turkish security officers was predicated upon a mere 'suspicion' that he belonged to a terrorist organisation. However, even if he was a member of the PKK, Article 3 of the ECHR expressly prohibits the nature and intensity of inhuman and degrading treatment/punishment he was subjected to in the name of national security. Obviously, in the fight against terrorism, there seems to be a clear danger that security imperatives always undermine human right concerns in the bid to enhance national security. Clearly, the 'severity' of the pain and suffering, which the applicant was subjected to, especially through 'Palestinian hanging', coupled with the means through which he was killed could be considered 'unreasonable' and 'disproportionate' in manner and extent. The facts of the case did not reveal the perpetrators of the applicant's death. However, assuming they were the government agents, would such an act be considered reasonable?

Article 2(2) of the ECHR allows intentional deprivation of life. Nevertheless, such deprivation of life would have to result from the use of force, which is 'absolutely necessary' in defence of any person from unlawful violence..." Impliedly, Article 2(2) of the ECHR prohibits deliberate killing by the state, unless the force used is strictly proportionate to a legitimate aim, such as preventing unlawful violence.[1056] Cumulatively, the assessment of the treatment given to the applicant against the background of proportionality could be that the treatment/punishment suffered by the applicant was disproportionate to the exigencies of the situation in Turkey at that time. Thus, proportionality entails a thorough assessment of the appropriateness and effectiveness of the counterterrorism measure in place and its obvious side effects on particular groups or people in the society.[1057] The rule of law maintains that state actions that limits rights be justified in judicial review proceedings.[1058] The court could be seen as an ideal agent for the assessment of proportionality cases, because relegating it to the executive or legislators might mean giving them the opportunity to reaffirm the perpetrated act/s in violation of human rights.

1056 I. Turner, 'Human rights and anti-terrorism: A positive legal duty to infringe freedom from torture' (2012) vol 35(11) Studies in Conflict and terrorism 760

1057 D. Moeckli, *Human rights and non-discrimination in the war against terror* (Oxford University Press, New York 2008), 10

1058 A. Barak, *Proportionality and Pretense* (Cambridge University Press Ltd., New York 2012), 229

It follows that Article 3 of the ECHR enshrines one of the most substantive values of a democratic society. However, in the fight against terrorism, people are also hand-picked indiscriminately and subjected to 'extreme physical force' in the bid to obtain intelligence concerning terrorism or terrorism-related activities. Innocent people are abducted and taken to areas outside judicial jurisdictions, where they cannot seek legal assistance. Using ***El-masri v The Former Yugoslav Republic of Macedonia*** as a case study, the applicant was subjected to an uninterrupted watch by the agents of the respondent's security forces. He was interrogated in an alien language in which he was not conversant, endangered at gun point and was constantly denied access to the outside world, except his interrogators. Such treatments precipitated the applicant's ten-day hunger strike.[1059] The applicant was transferred from the hotel, handcuffed and blindfolded, to the airport. He was severely beaten, stripped and sodomised with an object, placed in an adult nappy, hooded and subjected to complete sensory deprivation. He was forcefully marched to CIA aircraft where he was thrown to the floor, chained down and forcefully tranquilised.[1060]

Critically, a look at the definition of torture in Article 1 of the UNCAT reveals that mental suffering or pain can equate to torture if it gets to a certain level of severity. In other words, torture need not necessarily be 'physical'. It is agreed that the applicant was not subjected to any 'physical force' while detained in the hotel but, no doubt, such type of lonely detention in a hotel (an unusual place for incarceration) could generate a condition of 'anguish' and 'stress' in the applicant. Also, the fact that the applicant was subjected to emotional and psychological torment while in such incommunicado detention for twenty-three days cannot be erased. He experienced an enduring state of anxiety as a result of the uncertainty, which characterised such form of detention and interrogation. His extended internment in the hotel paved the way to his vulnerability to torture, inhuman, or degrading treatment.[1061]

Obviously, an assessment of the level and type of treatment/punishment terrorist suspects are subjected to in the fight against terrorism ignites a critical question about the rationality behind torture, inhuman, or degrading treatment.

1059 *El-masri v The former Yugoslav Republic of Macedonia.*, op.cit., para 18

1060 ibid., para 205

1061 ibid., para 202,203

The applicant was subjected to many offensive interrogative methods referred to as 'enhanced interrogation techniques'. The threat he was subjected to in Skopje hotel and the cruelty used to transfer him to the CIA plane was 'unreasonable', especially regarding the fact that he was a mere 'suspect'. Such cruelty was imposed on him to debase him or to break his spirit.[1062] Such treatments are impermissible under the principles of the rule of law.[1063] Arguably, a reliance on physical force, which was not predicated by an applicant's personal conduct has the proficiency of deflating the applicant's human dignity and legally amounts to a violation of the applicant's right not to be tortured. Evidently, from the facts of the case, the applicant's transfer from the hotel to the custody of the CIA was 'intentional' and 'irrational', as the applicant did not pose any "risk to national security" or a threat to his interrogators.

An assessment of the applicant's treatment/punishment in the custody of the respondent's agents and the CIA, based on the element of 'rationality' would perhaps be that the applicant's right not to be tortured was violated flagrantly. Sequentially, the respondents had no convincing reason for the treatments they subjected the applicant to. For instance, the suppository was not medically prescribed.[1064] The respondent did not present arguments or adduce justifications for the use of physical restraint either. Analytically, the treatments/punishments made no logical sense. It was not revealed in the facts of the case that the applicant had an 'anti-security' history. Even if he did, international human rights law demands that his fundamental rights should have been observed and respected. The principle of the rule of law (criminal law) in a democratic society stipulates that he should be considered innocent, until the contrary is proven. Arguably, in the war against terror, sovereign states are influenced by tunnel vision, fear and stereotypes.[1065]

Critically, the assessment of the rationality of torture, ill, inhuman, or degrading treatment in the fight against terrorism might not be dependent on the acts of torture alone. The element of rationality might perhaps question the grounds of

1062 *El-masri v The former Yugoslav Republic of Macedonia.*, op.cit., para 170

1063 ibid., paras 18,20,21

1064 *El-masri v The Former Yugoslav Republic of Macedonia.*, op.cit., para 21

1065 G. Trotter, et al., 'Miscarriages of justice in the war against terror' (2005) vol. 109(4) Penn state law review 967

an applicant's detention and subsequent torture. It might also question a security agent's conviction in his use of excessive force on a terrorist suspect. For example, it queries whether the security agent's conviction is predicated on the terrorist suspect's outward appearance, religious affiliation, or racial profiling. Accordingly, in the present case, El-masri was questioned by the respondent's border officials, who were suspicious of the authenticity of El-masri's recently issued German passport.[1066] On security grounds, it could be argued that such initial questioning was rational, whereas the act of putting the applicant through an incommunicado detention in an unusual place of detention for twenty-three days to ascertain his affiliation with Al-Qaeda or any other terrorist group could be considered 'unreasonable'.[1067]

The facts of the case never revealed that the applicant had any incriminating material in his possession. Neither did any evidence tag him with Al-Qaeda or any other terrorist group. The element of rationality in such circumstance might not reconcile the conflicting acts of torture with the legitimate interest of national security and, to a large extent, international human rights law. Such element evaluates an acceptable standard of treatment, which terrorist suspects ought to receive. The basic axiom of my theory of 'preservative legitimacy' with respect to rationality is for the evaluation of counterterrorism measures adopted in every circumstance to satisfy respect for the principles of rule of law. Essentially, the assessment of acts of torture in the fight against terrorism in this book could be an additional perception and values that could complement the position of law on the rights of a terrorist suspect not to be tortured.

By way of contrast, in ***Gafgen v Germany*** the treatment given to the applicant by the detective officers during interrogation did not reach the level of severity that qualifies it as torture, but it fell within the purview of Article 3 ECHR. The 'rationality' element of the theory of 'preservative legitimacy' propounded in this book queries the 'reasonability' of the detective officer's treatment on the applicant during his interrogation. It evaluates the act of the officers against the background of 'necessity' and 'proportionality' in the prevailing circumstance. It seeks to determine whether the treatment/punishment given to the applicant is necessary and proportional when compared with the security need at the

1066 *El-masri v The Former Yugoslav Republic of Macedonia.*, op.cit., para 17

1067 ibid., paras 18 and 19

time. To ascertain this, the entire circumstance of the case will be evaluated. Thus, in this present case, J's security was in jeopardy. The applicant killed J an 11year old boy through suffocation for a ransom. In the course of determining the boy's whereabout, the interrogating officers subjected the applicant to ill treatment. The court held that the applicant's Article 3 right was violated by the interrogating officers.

Analytically, through some tangible evidence (among other things, the applicant picked up the ransom, had half of the ransom in his flat, a note concerning the planning of the crime was found in his flat) it was clear the applicant was involved in the crime (J's death). Perhaps, when it seemed like the applicant was not forth coming with any useful information on J's whereabout, the detective officer resorted to ill treatment. Legally, torture, ill or degrading treatment/punishment is outrightly prohibited irrespective of the conduct of the accused. Nevertheless, it was explicitly stated that the applicant was subjected to considerable pain solely for the purpose of disclosing J's whereabout. The officer pointed out expressly that he was concerned with saving the child's life as opposed to furthering a criminal proceeding for kidnapping. The facts of the case also showed that the officers in that department previously opposed to the infliction of ill or degrading treatment on detainees.[1068] Perhaps, it was not the norm in that office to subject detainees to torture, ill or degrading treatment.

It could be argued that, on the grounds of necessity the treatment given to the applicant in that circumstance was appropriate since it was geared towards saving the life of the child. Contentiously, it is in consonance with the state's positive obligation to protect J's convention right from an imminent danger. The police officer ordered that the applicant be threatened and subjected to considerable pain on the assumption that the boy was still alive. The officer also asserted that, he believed the child was in great danger as a result of lack of food and the temperature outside.[1069] Assuming the child was still alive, and it is certain the applicant has information of the child's whereabout but refuses to divulge it, would it be rational in that circumstance to take necessary measures such as torture to compel the applicant to release the relevant information needed to save the child's life? If the answer is still in the negative perhaps because of the

1068 ibid., para 15

1069 ibid., para 20

absolute nature of Article 3 ECHR; then, this work continues to question the rationale behind the trade-off of the right to life with the right not to be tortured or subjected to ill or degrading treatment/punishment of detainees.

Furthermore, the applicant asserted that he disclosed J's whereabout because he was afraid that the officers will carry out the threats on him. What if the applicant was not threatened or subjected to ill treatment and as a result no one could trace J's dead body? Would it had been legally and morally justifiable for the applicant to escape justice and the family of the innocent dead child languish in perpetual 'emotional torture', 'pain' and 'suffering' which could also lead to the death of at least one family member such as J's parent? In applying the rationality principle of the 'theory of preservative legitimacy', moral reasoning could be exercised in favour of torture where torturing one person will lead to the preservation of another person's life.

Again, on grounds of proportionality it could be contended that the treatment the applicant was subjected to is not 'excessive' when compared with the intention behind the treatment (namely, to save the life of an innocent kidnapped child). A careful assessment of the treatment inflicted on the applicant has shown that it did not attain the minimum level of severity that will categorise it as 'torture'. Clearly, this book does not advocate for torture but points towards that direction if that will be the last resort to save life. However, it maintains that only what is reasonably necessary for the exigencies of the situation is allowed. The applicant's Article 3 right was not only at stake, J's right to life was much more implicated. The right to life could be described as a platform for Article 3 right. Realistically, the absolute nature of Article 3 ECHR constitutes a legal and moral dilemma in certain circumstances such as the Gafgen case. A holistic consideration of the entire circumstance of the case, ignites a question as to the moral justification of the absolute nature of Article 3 ECHR when an applicant is reasonably seen to have intentionally deprived another person his right.

On the other hand, it could be argued that the applicant had an original intention to kill the child and not necessarily for ransom. Based on the facts of the case, the applicant killed the child even before he sent out the note for ransom[1070]. By implication, the money he took was not a 'ransom' because there was nothing

1070 ibid., paras 11, 12

to redeem (the boy was already dead). He extorted the money from the deceased child's parents through threat. Clearly, Article 17 ECHR prohibits the applicant from taking away the life of the child through any activity or act that is aimed at the destruction of the child's convention right (in this case, his right to life). The child died through suffocation. The child's suffering must have exceeded the minimum level of severity that is required for an act to be classified as 'torture'. Accordingly, the child was subjected to mental, physical, psychological, emotional pain and suffering and he eventually died. The applicant was not tortured but was subjected to ill treatment in the course of the determination of J's whereabout, but J was tortured and through torture he lost his life. On moral grounds the treatment given to the applicant by the officer for the singular reason of saving the life of a vulnerable child and in compliance with the spirit of Article 2 ECHR (positive duty to prevent foreseeable loss of life) could be declared 'rational'. Ultimately, considering the entire circumstance of this case, the 'theory of preservative legitimacy' formulated in this book, will point towards the direction of taking 'necessary' measures that are 'proportional' to save the life of the child.

Undoubtedly, terrorism generates fear and anxiety that fuels sovereign states into caustic measures to catch and punish terrorists or suspects.[1071] Thus, the horrors of terrorism render security agents vulnerable to mete out torture and other ill, inhuman, and degrading treatment/punishment. They fail to respect the legitimate interests and rights of terrorist suspects, whose intense suffering and pain could be inimical; because of its potency to give rise to false confessions conjured as a mechanism for escaping distress. However, my rationality argument advocates for a consideration of the costs and benefits of acts of torture, ill, inhuman, and degrading treatments towards terrorist suspects and national security in the fight against terrorism. The fact that acts of torture, towards innocent suspects particularly, have the potential to yield anti-security results in the long run must be considered. Accordingly, counterterrorism measures must comply with the principles of proportionality and non-discrimination.[1072] Obviously, terrorism constitutes an undeniable threat to human rights. The courts deem it legal

1071 B. Ackerman, 'The emergency constitution' (2004) vol. 113 Yale Law Journal 1029

1072 I. Sampson, 'Between Boko Haram and the Joint Task Force: Assessing the dilemma of counterterrorism and human right in Northern Nigeria' (2015) vol 59(1) Journal of African Law 25

for sovereign states to adopt a firm stand against perpetrators of terrorist acts.[1073] However, such stand ought to be 'rational' and 'proportionate'.[1074] If torture is legally wrong, why do states embark on such torture?

6.4.2.3 THE OBJECTIVITY OF TORTURE IN THE FIGHT AGAINST TERRORISM

> "There have been, and are now, certain foreign nations. . . which convict individuals with testimony obtained by police organisations possessed of unrestrained power to seize persons . . . hold them in secret custody and wring from them confessions by physical or mental torture. So long as the Constitution remains the basic law of this Republic, America will not have that kind of government."[1075]

Nevertheless, the events of 9/11 altered many things and lives around the world. For instance, it is not startling that the events of 9/11 could change some nation's ideas of criminal procedure. It has become a notorious fact that the criminal law position of voluntary confession has been seriously influenced by the occurrence of 9/11. At the same time, the discourse on 'interrogation' and 'torture' has also been influenced.[1076] Hence, Alan Dershowitz noted, "The events of September 11th require us to imagine the unimaginable and to think the unthinkable".[1077] He maintained that 9/11 ought to arouse a different trend of thoughts towards our most fundamental beliefs about law. Clearly, the 9/11 tragedy navigated the minds of many to issues, which they had never contemplated, especially in a democratic society. For instance, some scholars advocated some imprudent measures such as 'truth scrum' and even 'torture'.[1078]

1073 *Othoman Abu Qatada v United Kingdom.*, op cit., para 183

1074 D. Whittaker, *Counterterrorism and human rights* (Routledge Taylor and Francis Group, New York 2013)

1075 *Ashcroft v Tennessee* (1944) 322 U.S. 143, 155

1076 A. Dershowitz, 'The torture warrant: A response to Professor Strauss' (2003) vol 48 New York Law School Law Review

1077 ibid; J. Samaha, *Criminal Procedure* (Cengage Learning, Boston 2015), 615

1078 ibid; W. Biddle, *Immigrants' Rights after 9/11*(Chelsea House, New York 2008), 67

However, the objectivity of torture in my theory of 'preservative legitimacy' relates to 'why' use torture in the fight against terrorism. It permeates into the goal or purpose of torture in countering terrorism. Thus, interrogating agents were increasingly frustrated by the silence of detained terrorist suspects allied with Al-Qaeda and the resistance they put up against traditional interrogation techniques. The agents observed that such terrorist suspects are trained to resist conventional interrogation methods. As a result, in order to extract intelligence about 9/11, and to thwart possible future terrorists attacks, the FBI and CIA agents began to make calls for innovative interrogation techniques.[1079] The clamour for such techniques arose more with the arrest of the so called 'shoe bomber', who had attempted to blow up an American Airlines jet from Paris to Miami.[1080] Similar calls for additional questioning techniques were also made when Abu Zabaydah, a prominent Osama bin Laden loyalist, was apprehended.[1081] Ultimately, the detention of a likely co-conspirator of the New York attack and the detention of possible suspects, who were tongue-tied in the course of their interrogation, re-established torture and other unconventional methods of interrogation. Accordingly, an authoritative US government document specified that the "goal of interrogation [was] to create a state of learned helplessness and dependence conducive to the collection of intelligence in a predictable, reliable, and sustainable manner", and that interrogation procedures were used "to persuade High-Value Detainees to provide threat information and terrorist intelligence in a timely manner".[1082]

Again, pursuant to a UN General Assembly resolution, an incommunicado detention or detention in a secret place has the potential to facilitate the infliction of torture and other cruel, inhuman, or degrading treatment/punishment and, at the same time, constitute 'torture' in itself.[1083] This is not referring to acts of torture, but is suggesting that incommunicado detention can in itself constitute torture and is employed by nation states to obtain information about

1079 W. Pincus, 'Silence of 4 terror probe suspects poses dilemma for FBI' (2001) <*http://www.infowars.com/police_state/torture.htm*> accessed 3rd September 2016

1080 ibid; J. Wolfendale, *Torture and the Military Profession* (Palgrave Macmillan, New York 2007), 105

1081 ibid; R. Leo, *Police Interrogation and American Justice* (Harvard University Press, Massachusetts 2008), 6-7

1082 *Al-Nashiri v Poland.*, op cit., para 502

1083 United Nations General Assembly Resolution 60/148 on torture and other cruel, inhuman and degrading treatment or punishment adopted on 16 December 2005

terrorist attacks and in fact terrorism in general. Essentially, terrorist suspects are subjected to prolonged incarceration, which is intended to render them helpless to the point of vulnerability for the release of intelligence.

Terrorism and torture are controversial issues. Torture is a defined set of practices that are unambiguously prohibited and criminalised by a catalogue of international treaties and principles of international customary law.[1084] Clearly, the fear of more terrorist attacks against civilians has rolled back some human right protections, both de jure and de facto.[1085] Hence, states have neglected the pre-emptory norms, which prohibit torture, cruel, inhuman, and degrading treatment/punishment.[1086]

After the debate on torture post-9/11, the focus of investigators has shifted from the procurement of viable evidence for prosecution to the procurement of information for the determent of potential terrorist attacks. Many experts have opined that 'coercive' interrogation tactics which, ordinarily, should not be used on suspects should be employed in the "war against terror".[1087] Torture is on the menu of potential responses to suspicious behaviour. This is a paradigm shift in international human rights law and criminal law, respectively. Many sovereign states, such as the US, recognise international law standards on torture and cruel, inhuman, and degrading treatment. Nevertheless, they have circumvented their application and, in some circumstances, have intentionally watered it down. The picture is foggy.

Accordingly, the imposition of torture or ill, inhuman, or degrading treatment disregards national law and international legal obligations. Thus, in ***Ramdan v Rumsfeld,***[1088] the Supreme Court pointed out that Conventions can be a source of law, but it remains uncertain whether they are self-executing and whether

---

1084 K. Bennoune, 'Terror/Torture' (2008) vol 26(1) Berkeley Journal of International Law 3

1085 Amnesty International., 'USA: five years on 'the dark side': A look back on 'war against terror' detentions' (2006) <*http://web.amnesty.org/library/index/ENGAMR511952006?open&of=ENG-USA*> accessed 4th June 2016

1086 M. O'Connell, 'Affirming the ban on harsh interrogation' (2005) vol 66(6) Ohio State Journal 1231

1087 ibid

1088 *Ramdan v Rumsfeld* (2006) 548 U.S. 557

they would be interpreted to confer personal rights in US Courts.[1089] Hence, one might be tempted to question the compatibility of torture with the principles of such international Conventions, when administered for the sole purpose of obtaining information for the prevention of future terrorist attack. Is it antithetical to national security, which the supposed interrogating agents set out to protect? Or does it enhance national security? Where is the force of such international Conventions, which nations are signatories to in an ongoing terrorist world?

6.5 SUMMARY

In summary, the weakness and fragility of democracies and civil liberties against sudden, chaotic and barbarous attacks from terrorist organisations were revealed by the 9/11 attack and were further revealed by the painful aftershocks in Bali, Madrid, Casablanca, London and Mumbai.[1090] In essence, the dynamism of modern terrorism has such capacity to make governments of nation states react excessively. As a result, sovereign states engage in the formulation of counterterrorism measures and policies to wage war against terror. However, most counterterrorism measures, such as the ones seen above, violate some of the basic principles of the rule of law, as well as fundamental human rights as enshrined under international treaties or international human rights law. Accordingly, some such measures create an enabling environment for violence in the society. For instance, the implementation of some counterterrorism measures stir up feelings of alienation within particular groups of people who feel that they have been specifically singled out from society for some reason, such as their religion. Such sense of alienation undermines social cohesion and support for national security imperatives.[1091]

Arguably, if the degree of terrorist threat is further reinforced with persistence, frequency, access to domestic soil, to weapons of mass destruction, and to

1089 D. Sloss, et al., 'Is the president bound by Geneva Conventions?' (2004) vol 90(1) Cornell Law Review124

1090 A. Ozturk, 'The war on terror or the war on civil liberties: the state, the society and the civil liberties since 2001' (2010) vol 6(22) Review of International Law and Politics 105

1091 K. Roach, 'Must we trade rights for security? The choice between smart, Harsh or proportionate security strategies in Canada and Britain' (2006) vol 27(5) Cardozo Law Review 2151

suicide bombers, the cost to the target population for protecting fundamental liberties can, presumably, be raised sufficiently to generate potentially significant concessions.[1092] Critically, the practical effectiveness of the implementation of anti-terror measures could be predicated upon maintaining a feasible balance between the three most-contending interests in the fight against terrorism (national security, rule of law, and human rights). Events have proven over the years that much of the harsh anti-terror laws and measures such as the ones highlighted above were counterproductive. For instance, some of the detainees who were released from the black sites reportedly returned to hostilities,[1093] and the application of extreme interrogation techniques has sometimes generated inaccurate intelligence and contaminated the use of statements in criminal prosecutions.[1094] Hence, the question regarding whether it is necessary to sacrifice fundamental rights for security becomes an integral puzzle in this whole dilemma. It is paradoxical for counterterrorism measures to undermine fundamental liberties; which terrorism seeks to take away.[1095]

Axiomatically, states are obliged to protect their citizens against every sovereign and individual existential threat, such as terrorism. Undoubtedly, the security of the individual in society is a fundamental human right and the protection of individuals is an essential responsibility of the government. In fulfilling such obligation, the definition of national security in this book propagates for rule of law-compliant strategies in the fight against terrorism. Ultimately, it would be illogical for counterterrorism measures to instil the same sense of psychological fear, anxiety and insecurity that terrorism produces.[1096] Hence, precautionary steps need to be taken in the formulation and implementation of counterterrorism measures and policies so that such measures will not end up stirring up the type of terror, which they set out to prevent.[1097]

1092 G. Spann, 'Terror and race' (2005) vol 45 Washburn Law Journal 89-112

1093 K. Roach, et al., 'Miscarriages of Justice in the war against terrorism' (2005) vol 109(4) Penn State Law Review 967

1094 D. Cole, *Enemy aliens: Double standards and constitutional freedoms in the war against terrorism* (1st edn, The New Press, New York 2003)

1095 G. Spann, 'Terror and race' (2005) vol 45 Washburn Law Journal 89-112

1096 ibid

1097 J. Mccullock, 'War at home: National security arrangements post 11 September 2011' (2002) vol 27(2) Alternative Law Journal 87-91

6.6 CONCLUSION

This chapter set out to address one of the challenges in countering terrorism. It set out to develop a revised definition of national security based on the findings from the third chapter of this book. The aim is to supplement the existing academic literature with a more comprehensive definition of national security that will be resolving difficulties within it. Ultimately, it was found that one major impediment to the efforts made towards countering terrorism is the failure of both the judiciary and international law to formulate a comprehensive definition of national security. Hence, most nation states have traded their democratic nature in the bid to counter terrorism as most counterterrorism measures have deviated from the principles of the rule of law as seen above.

No doubt, the terrorist attack of 2001 and the ongoing fight against terrorism reignited public and academic discussions on torture tolerance.[1098] Clearly, the unprecedented attacks on the US World Trade Centre and the Pentagon, coupled with some counterterrorism measures like such discussed above, have plunged the world into a new historical epoch.[1099] Despite the fact that nation states rallied around the US in support of national and global security at the time of the 9/11 attack, they also chorused their concern about the morality and legality of the assault of the military on terrorist suspects. They expressed their concern on the myopic and antipodal way terrorism is defined and in which security is prioritised over the principles of rule of law. As a result, the prudence and effectiveness of most counterterrorism strategies has also been questioned.[1100] Hence, human rights, the rule of law and national security are portrayed as unaffordable luxuries in view of the security challenges posed by terrorism.

Categorically, counterterrorism measures play significant roles in the fight against terrorism. Realistically, the formulation of such measures has the potential of incurring some costs or concessions on human rights. Therefore, there is a need to create and maintain a viable balance between national security, the rule of law and human rights. Undeniably, the issue of creating a balance

---

1098 Gross O., op.cit

1099 J. McCullock, 'War at home: National security arrangements post 11 September 2011' (2002) vol 27(2) Alternative Law Journal 87-112

1100 ibid

between such three competing interests has constituted a continued challenge for democracies of the world seeking to guard themselves against issues of future insecurity. However, it is important that security interests of sovereign states must be pursued in an accountable way, which will balance out the government's responsibility to protect its territorial sovereignty, the personal interest of its citizens, and the principles of rule of law. Essentially, such balance, if achieved, must be maintained and, of necessity, must constitute a conscious aspect of the national security policy development. Nevertheless, a pertinent question remains. Considering the challenges posed by terrorism, should issues relating to human rights, rule of law and national security remain issues that are considered as unaffordable luxuries, in pursuit of national security and to a large extent global security? Where are we with terrorism and comprehensively where is the place of national security? There is an urgent need to rethink the politics of national security of sovereign states.

CHAPTER 7
CONCLUSION AND RECOMMENDATIONS

7.1 INTRODUCTION

This book set out to critically review and ultimately revise existing legal/judicial conceptions of 'national security'. The aim was to embark on an exhaustive search for the formulation of a comprehensive definition of national security against the background of counterterrorism. The adoption of the black letter approach in combination with the immanent critique and social-legal studies of law in action in this book was believed to offer an original approach to the existing academic scholarship. The adoption of such methodologies has resulted in many findings and recommendations for improving national security in an ongoing world of terrorism.

The preceding chapters of this book has shown that national security issues, perceptions and ideologies are multifaceted. Hence, one might be tempted to ask why this work chooses to view national security from a legal perspective. This book highlights the disagreements in the existing scholarship to the extent to which the definition of national security has been expanded. However, the acute shift in security concerns post 9/11 makes an evaluation and interpretation of national security measures by the courts crucial in an evolving terrorist environment. Hence, it becomes necessary for human rights violations emanating from national security concerns to be determined by the courts in a way that makes it clear that justice is being done.

7.2 MAJOR FINDINGS

7.2.1 THE NARROW PERSPECTIVE OF NATIONAL SECURITY

The first finding is relating to the definition of national security. This book found that existing scholarship has largely viewed national security from a narrow perspective (see Chapter 1 and 2). Regrettably, scholars have examined the issue of national security from one aspect at a time (for instance, defining national security specifically from the perspective of 'military security' or other singular aspects only). Also, they often lack conceptual underpinnings. However, this work has gone a step further from the existing scholarship to define national security conceptually, and at the same time, it has holistically applied the black-letter doctrinal approach. The national security definition formulated in this book is shown to be contextually appropriate to anti-terrorism measures in the fight against terrorism. It adopts a suitable interpretation of national security. It thereby bridges the gap between the existing scholarship on the definition of national security as prompted by reference to violations of human rights and controversial anti-terror laws. Subsequent definition of national security stretches across divergent elements of national security. For instance, anti-terrorism, and people's security, immigration, self-defence, regional security and intelligence sharing. Hence, national security is widely analysed from different contexts, which are either directly or indirectly connected to each other.

7.2.2 THE ABSENCE OF JUDICIAL DEFINITION OF NATIONAL SECURITY

This book found that national security has not been explicitly defined by judges; rather inferences could be drawn from the context which a judge perceives as threatening national security in a particular circumstance. It has been found that, national security could be perceived either from a narrow or wide perspective. Thus, chapter 6 has suggested an alternative account of a comprehensive definition of 'national security' and its implications for reforming the general understanding of national security. This will promote the maintenance of a viable balance between the competing interests (human rights, rule of law and national security) in the fight against terrorism. Existing published researches show that there is still no clearly expounded or definitive definition of 'national security' that answers some critical questions ("what" "when", "why" and "how" of national security) about this topic based on the black letter approach. Hence, this work is significant as a comprehensive definition of national security aligning with the liberal communitarian school of thought was explicitly formulated in the chapter 6 of this book.

The definition of national security formulated in this book was achieved by evaluating relevant cases in the third chapter of this book where only some basic elements of national security were revealed. Based upon the findings from those cases, national security was expressly explicated through the lens of each of these national security elements identified. These composite definitions of national security via its elements were then crafted into a comprehensive whole to formulate this work's more integrated and comprehensive definition of national security. It was also found that some of those aspects of national security constitute in themselves counterterrorism measures adopted in the fight against terrorism. For instance, intelligence sharing was shown to be an integral aspect of the prevailing ideas of national security. At the same time, such sharing constitutes one of the counterterrorism measures adopted by sovereign states in the fight against terrorism. It helps sovereign states with timely imminent and remote 'intelligence' on terrorist attacks or threats against national security.

7.2.3 THE CONCEPT OF NATIONAL SECURITY IS MULTIDIMENSIONAL IN NATURE

Chapter 6 of this book recognised the multidimensional nature of the concept of 'national security' and subcategorised the concept into its 'security' and 'national' dimensions. It also uncovered the unavoidable intersection between the 'national' and the 'security' elements of 'national security'. This intersection unveiled the competing interests in the fight against terrorism namely; rule of law, human rights and national security. Accordingly, this book discovered that there is a need for a viable balance between these inevitable competing interests in the fight against terrorism for the promotion of public order. Some contentious counterterrorism measures (such as unlawful detention) employed by sovereign states were highlighted too. These measures are perpetrated by states who are signatories of international conventions that declare such acts impermissible in a democratic society, creating a tension between legal commitments in theory and legally relevant activities in practice. Hence, the practicability of the strict adherence to some of the rules of international law enshrined in some conventions such as the ECHR is questioned.

This work discovered that in the bid to fight terrorism some rights (such as right to life) have suffered flagrant violation by sovereign states. Significantly, the definition of national security developed in this book recognises 'human security' as an integral aspect of it. It might be safe to say that there is no national security without human security (people's security). As a result, in line with Article 17 of the ECHR, this book questions reliance mostly in deportation cases on Article 3 ECHR by terrorist/suspects whose activities are 'manifestly' seen as threat/s to the life of others and the nation. Such reliance encourages the precedent in ECHR case law, which has led to the trade-off of the rights of innocent civilians in the contracting country.

7.2.4 SOME COUNTERTERRORISM MEASURES ARE ANTI-SECURITY

Thus, it has been found that anti-terrorism measures which violate the principles of the rule of law may ignite the spirit of radicalisation amongst people. As claimed in Chapter 4, some of the counterterrorism measures adopted in the fight against terrorism could be said to be 'anti-security'. For instance, arbitrary detentions practiced in the fight against terrorism constitute violations of treaty obligations (such as Article 5 ECHR) of sovereign states. Pre-charge detention has the unwanted danger of radicalising potentially innocent detainees (Chapter 4). Also, extraordinary detention programmes are more likely to plunge the world into a state of uncertainty and insecurity than curing the ails of terrorism. Terrorism has become one of the major challenges in the world today. It could be deeply rooted and unpredictable. In recent times, the threat and existence of terrorism have grown increasingly, and it is very challenging for the sovereign nations to counter terrorism. Through research, this work shows that human rights constitute an integral component of national security. However, one of the greatest challenges is how to effectively enhance security without unduly infringing the fundamental rights of individuals. At the same time, this book also found that national security and human rights reinforce each other since a threat to human rights, to some extent, is a threat to national security. It was deduced in this book that counterterrorism policies can only be sustainable if they will support the very subjects they intend to protect. Hence, it was found that national security is incomplete without the maintenance of high level of human security. Essentially, people's security must be prioritised in national security policies. Notably, human rights and national security are not only interconnected but are equally reinforcing.

Hence, the alienation of democratic freedom as a mechanism for the enhancement of national security will only cripple security further. In essence, by radicalising and isolating particular populations this might have some negative ripple effects on national security.[1101] Critically, excessive political radicalisation breeds violence. The big fight notion of 'total-action-defeats-total-terror' has a beguiling simplicity and an unproductive dividend[1102]. It becomes paramount that the task of countering terrorism be carried out with due regard for the preservation of human rights. Thus, Benjamin Franklin famously, and scathingly, said: 'Those who would give up essential liberty to purchase a little temporary safety deserve neither liberty nor safety'.[1103]

7.2.5 THE UNAVOIDABLE VIOLATION OF HUMAN RIGHTS IN COUNTERING TERRORISM

Realistically, this book found that human rights must be violated in the bid to counter terrorism because of the type of terrorism in recent times (such as the 9/11). However, pursuant to Article 15 ECHR, states could derogate from their obligations under the ECHR. Permissible derogations under Article 15 ECHR must meet three substantive conditions (discussed in detail below). Accordingly, the element of proportionality is indispensable in any action/measure purported to be adopted by sovereign states to enhance national security.[1104] Arguably, individuals (terrorists included) have a negative obligation towards engaging in activities that will destabilise national security or interrupt public order. Emphatically, people's security is an integral aspect of national security. Hence, the reciprocity in obligations between individuals and the government is fundamental for the enhancement of national security.

1101 A. Megan, et al., op cit

1102 D. Whittaker, op cit

1103 ibid, 3

1104 C..Michelson, op cit; Human Rights Act 1998, op cit; Lawless v Ireland, op cit; Ireland v United Kingdom, op cit, para 207; Oral J, op cit

7.2.6 UNCONTROLLED IMMIGRATION IS A CONDUIT FOR TERRORISM

Again, this book identifies immigration as a crucial element of national security. It was found that 'uncontrolled immigration' is one of the conduits for terrorism. Illustratively, an apprehended terrorist state:

> '... several Al-Qaeda leaders believe operatives can pay their way through Mexico and believe that illegal entry is more advantageous than legal entry for operational security reasons...'[1105]

Consequently, states have adopted immigration laws or policies as counterterrorism measures. Thus Spain's foreign minister contends: 'The fight against illegal immigration is a reinforcement of the fight against terrorism'.[1106]At the same time, a terrorist might not necessarily migrate to a 'targeted' country for a terrorist attack to take place.[1107] Radicalisation, extremism and terrorist networks could be maintained and sustained via information technology.[1108]Hence, through information technology terrorist/s suspect could network with each other without physical contact.[1109]Nevertheless, an effective border and immigration control may not be ignored in the enhancement of national security.

How successful have sovereign states been in the implementation of immigration policies as counterterrorism measures? Have they been able to operate in their capacity as 'sovereign' states in cases of deportation where it has been found that an immigrant poses a security risk to the society? This book illustrates the difficulties encountered by sovereign states in removing individuals who are deemed security risk to the society. Terrorist suspects often invoke Article 3 of the ECHR[1110] as a defence to obstruct deportation knowing it is an absolute right and is non-derogable.[1111] States have also attempted to circumvent

1105 J. Hayworth, et al., op cit

1106 J. Kirshner, op cit

1107 M. Todd, op cit

1108 ibid; M. Conway, ibid; K. McGuire, et al., op cit

1109 B. Kyrgyzstan, op cit

1110 J. Kirshner, op cit

1111 European Convention on Human Rights 1950

the defence of Article 3 of the ECHR by relying on MOU's or diplomatic assurances. Unfortunately, MOU's and related assurances are not regarded as binding by the courts. They are seen as legally unenforceable agreements.[1112]International experts criticise assurances as wrong in principle and ineffective in practice.[1113]

Many of the existing scholarships uphold the absolute nature of Article 3 of the ECHR even in the face of potential violation of Article 2 rights of innocent individuals through terrorist activities.[1114] However, this book contends with the trade-off of the right to life of innocent civilians as opposed to the Article 3 – right of a terrorist/suspect. Obviously, this work does not advocate torture, rather it advocates for the adoption of the principle of 'necessity' and 'proportionality' whenever issues that might involve human rights violation arise in the fight against terrorism. Importantly, governments should ensure that the right to life of individuals secures their lives as reasonably as possible. One of the implications of the definition of national security in this book is the attainment of a 'viable balance' in conflicts between issues of national security, human rights and the rule of law

7.2.7 REGIONAL SECURITY IS INTEGRAL TO NATIONAL SECURITY

Furthermore, this book acknowledges regional security as a key player of national security. Hence, it admits that the propagation of non-traditional security concerns, such as uncontrolled immigration, international terrorism and drug trafficking, as opposed to traditional military security, are extremely challenging to national security. It follows that the transnational nature of these security concerns may attract the cooperative security support or assistance of other nation states or organisations such as NATO, AU, or Arab League.[1115] In view of this, is it possible to boast of sovereignty in modern times? Pragmatically, absolute and exclusive sovereignty may not be seen in recent times.[1116] Realistically, the complexities of modern international terrorism are such that interdependence of

1112 A. Scheonholtz, et al., op cit

1113 Othman (Abu Qatada) v United Kingdom, op cit, para 175

1114 Saadi v Italy, op cit, para 125; Soering v United Kingdom, op cit, para 90–91

1115 T. Paul, et al., op cit

1116 W. Sidhu, et al., op cit

states is crucial for the enhancement of national security. Practically speaking, security issues may transcend territorial boundaries. As a result, national unilateral security measures may not be enough to quell modern day domestic security threats. Nevertheless, some scholars posit that sovereignty always works against regional organisations, particularly in issues of security.[1117] Accordingly, while recognising and respecting the sovereign position of a nation state, regional intervention could be carried out within clearly delineated lines during negotiation. It follows that, where intervention is predicated upon invitation, the form and validity conditions of the consent should be open to dialogue. For instance, the 2015 Arab League's military intervention in Yemen.[1118]

Basically, regional support cannot happen without a compelling intelligence arrangement. In effect, it might be safe to say that there cannot be an effective enhancement of national security without efficient mechanisms for intelligence sharing within and among nation states. Surprisingly, some scholars regard intelligence with contempt. For example, Carl Von Clausewitz states: 'Many intelligence reports in war are contradictory; even more are false, and most are uncertain... In short most intelligence is false'.[1119]

7.2.8 INTELLIGENCE SHARING IS CRUCIAL TO NATIONAL SECURITY

Against all odds, this work concedes that intelligence sharing is indispensable in national security issues. This work also illustrates that intelligence sharing is one of the elements through which national security is defined and at the same time constitutes an integral element for the implementation of national security. It demonstrates that the actuality of limitations in intelligence sharing does not nullify its necessity and practicality in the enhancement of national security. Some of the legal and human rights challenges that emanate from intelligence sharing arrangements/agreements in the fight against terrorism were exposed in this book. For instance, the level of secrecy involved in intelligence sharing cooperation among states implicates Article 6 of the ECHR (the right to fair

1117 ibid

1118 N. Aloupi, 'The right to non-intervention and non-interference' (2015) vol4(3) Cambridge Journal of Comparative and International Law 566

1119 R. Kline, et al., *Intelligence and the national security strategist: Enduring issues and challenges* (Rowman and Littlefield Publishers Inc, Maryland 2006), 11

hearing). Often, applicants do not have complete knowledge of the evidence against them.[1120] Intelligence sharing may have provided concerted collaborative means to address potential terrorist attacks. Sadly, the fear of unearthing classified information during the prosecution of suspects has given rise to closed material procedures. This precludes the accused from understanding the full nature of the charges against them. Implicitly, in the bid to protect some of the evidence and the source of intelligence, national security is implicated too. Perhaps, there is an impasse between the conditions of intelligence sharing in the fight against terrorism (such as the duty of non-disclosure) and human rights.

Paradoxically, pursuant to the principle of the rule of law (stated in chapter 6) democratic states have a legal and moral duty to adopt appropriate measures for the protection of individuals within their jurisdiction.[1121] By implication, this may include adoption of measures, which violate human rights. However, the extent of derogation might give rise to some legal and moral concerns. Hence, there is a need for a viable balance between national security directives and human rights imperatives. Essentially, national security cannot be ignored under the pretext of human rights protection and vice versa. Nevertheless, how easy is it to strike this balance?

This book exposes the difficulty involved in the great task of attempting to create a viable balance between the competing interests. Accordingly, the ratification of some international treaties (such as ECHR) by nation states has placed some legal constraints on them in implementing some counterterrorism measures.

To create a balance between national security and human rights in times of emergency, nation states have derogated from their treaty obligation. As a result, counterterrorism measures can be considered controversial. It might be argued that it is not the purport of democratic governments to adopt measures that will undermine democracy. Nevertheless, they may be guilty of welcoming the thought of an inevitable trade-off between national security and human rights. Hence, short sighted measures may be adopted because of fear of inability to prevent a terrorist attack that could cause loss of many innocent lives.[1122]

1120 A and Others v United Kingdom, op cit, para 111

1121 E. Gross, ibid

1122 M. Crenshaw, op cit

Accordingly, this book distinctively propounded the 'theory of preservative legitimacy'. Its conception more adequately encompasses existing, largely implicit, judicial and legislative interpretations of the meaning, scope and purpose of national security as contained within existing legal and constitutional scholarship. Thus, it expressly supplements the existing academic literature in ways that will be resolving difficulties within it. This theory is applied to understand whether self-defence reasonably enhances national security. It questions whether 1) legally, 2) rationally, and 3) objectively, the adoption of some counterterrorism measures in the fight against terrorism is favourable to national security.

However, when examined under the rationality element, it becomes a question of 'necessity' or 'proportion'. Arguably, at this level of examination, while self-defence is a right, detainees are entitled not to be tortured. However, if we are to employ the 'preservative legitimacy' paradigm propounded in this book, it becomes clear that, in some circumstances, torture may be found acceptable. For instance, where a person's activities threaten national security to the point that lives may be lost in a contracting state, perhaps, it might not be 'reasonable' for the terrorist to invoke his Article 3 rights on the grounds of a likelihood of torture in the case of deportation. Hence, Article 17 of the ECHR precludes a suspect from enjoying his Article 3 right at the expense of Article 2 rights of others. Finally, when moving to the objective element of the theory, the final question becomes 'why' use torture in the fight against terrorism? Categorically, under international law the issue of torture is settled. A detainee has the right not to be tortured. Nonetheless, in the right set of circumstances involving an attack devastating enough, where a nation state feels the need for self-defence, the 'preservative legitimacy' theory may point in the direction of torture.

Clearly, the dynamism of modern terrorism constitutes a challenge. In fact, this book found that the fight against terrorism seems endless with the increase in the off shoot of terrorists. As a matter of fact, terrorist organisations constantly recruit fresh members, adopt new practices and redefine their goals.[1123] It becomes pertinent that responses be considered in the light of contemporary circumstances. No doubt, terrorist acts create fear and the impending threats of terrorism instigate states to re-evaluate their security strategy. An atmosphere

1123 D. Aaron, op cit, 1

of fear in perilous times can cause people to amplify the sense of threat and a readiness to forego liberties as a trade-off for security. In view of this, governments need to conscientiously assess their targets before implementing any counterterrorism measure. Also, states' perception of threat must be 'rational' and 'realistic'. In the spirit of national security, counterterrorism measures that are not compatible with human rights and the principles of the rule of law have proven, overtime, to be counterproductive to national security.

Obviously, the game of countering terrorism took a different turn after the 9/11 incident.[1124] Post-9/11, a challenge of the question as to whether, and to what extent, it was and is necessary to curtail human rights in the fight against terrorism has gripped sovereign states in their attempt to counter terrorism. As a result, sovereign states are challenged with uncertainties and contradictions which have given rise to the issue of attempts to create a viable balance between the various norms. These norms (the norms of national security and human rights) are some of the basic elements of a democratic society.[1125]

Interestingly, one might think that creating a viable balance between national security and human rights protection will go a long way to cushion the pain of violations of human rights and, perhaps, reduce the threat of terrorism. But, for some reason it has become notoriously difficult to establish the required balance. Obviously, challenges arise in the society where the government categorically tilts towards one of the norms. Sometimes, some basic rights are derogated from in the fight against terrorism under 'temporary' measure. However, it becomes saddening to see such temporary measures lasting for a long time. In the quest for a viable balance between national security and human rights, one begins to ask the question: how 'temporary' is 'temporary'? How long can sovereign states interrupt human rights while security measures remain in operation?

Arguably, new laws ought to be enacted or existing ones to be reviewed and amended in response to the growing threat of this modern form of terrorism. This precludes vague and unclear provisions of the law. Those might attract ambiguous interpretations that could plunge the nation into a dilemma of radicalisation of some individuals. Additionally, discriminatory and stigmatising

1124 ibid

1125 M. Feinberg, op cit

provisions could also affect the society. (such as Part 4 allowed for the Home Secretary to certify any non-British citizen whom he suspected to be a terrorist and detain them indefinitely, pending deportation, even when such a deportation would be prohibited).This may result in further marginalisation and probably radicalisation of some of the vulnerable members of the society. Hence, careful drafting of counterterrorism legislation becomes pertinent as conditions favourable to the spread of terrorism could emanate from discrimination and disenfranchisement. Realistically, some counterterrorism legislation/measures might contain provisions, which implicate some fundamental human rights. Ultimately, it might be safe to say that violation of these rights should not be to the extent that is more than necessary in a specific circumstance.

7.3 RESEARCH CONTRIBUTION

This book set out to accomplish one major objective. As pointed out earlier, the existing constitutional scholarship contains various definitions of national security, but it has shown that there is no comprehensive and viable definition of national security. Most of these definitions are 'conceptually' deficient. Again, some of the existing definitions of national security have not successfully articulated most of the crucial aspects; rather, they contain fragments of national security. Also, this book found that there is still no clearly expounded judicial definition of national security. As a result, this book has defined national security comprehensively (chapter 6) adopting the black letter standard. This definition has expressly answered some crucial national security questions in chapter 3 of this book. It was achieved through evaluation of some cases. It analysed judicial interpretation of these cases from which it identified some essential and indispensable aspects of national security against the background of 'terrorism' and 'counterterrorism'. It examined each of these identified elements of national security through the lens of case law. It formulated separate definitions of national security based on each of these elements and, ultimately, integrated these definitions into a comprehensive whole to define 'national security' broadly. To further add to the body of knowledge as well as illustrate the practicality of this definition in the fight against terrorism, the 'theory of preservative legitimacy' was propounded in this book. This theory explored the 'legality', 'rationality' and 'objectivity' of the formulation and implementation of some of the counterterrorism measures adopted by sovereign states in the fight against terrorism.

7.4 RESEARCH IMPLICATIONS

7.4.1 POLICY IMPLICATION OF THE DEFINITION OF NATIONAL SECURITY FORMULATED IN THIS BOOK

The assignment of countering terrorism necessitates policy articulation and enforcement through legislation. However, the issue of vague and incomprehensive definitions of some terms such as 'national security' pose significant challenges in countering terrorism. Perhaps a comprehensive and generally acceptable definition of such term as 'national security' would go a long way in bringing consistency to measures formulated and adopted for countering terrorism by sovereign states. This leads us to the overall purpose of this work. It set out to analyse national security related cases, to devise a comprehensive definition based on a close 'hermeneutic reading' of express, but also implicit, understandings and interpretations contained within a range of judicial and legislative documents. This analysis includes inferences drawn from the way the courts interpret and apply this idea in practice. In addition to the attempt to resolve the acute conflict between national security and human rights protection in the 'fight against terrorism', this comprehensive definition of national security could, perhaps, serve as a normative category (evaluative standard: a criteria/model). More practically speaking, policy makers need to clearly understand the 'core' of the policy under formulation. The absence of a clear and expansive definition of national security will result in misdirected and costly counterterrorism policies. To a reasonable extent, in countering terrorism, policy makers need to delve into, and understand, the question: What is national security? Also, the proper evaluation of the elements of national security crafted into the national security definition in this book, will further illustrate the answer to this question.

Policy makers might employ the definition of national security in this book as a framework for the formulation of effective counterterrorism measures. It might assist them as a useful tool in the analysis of national security imperatives. Hence, it could reorient the way they perceive and regard national security as its various aspects have been integrated into the definition as 'essential elements' and 'indispensable' in security considerations. Accordingly, these elements will be considered holistically and not in isolation when counterterrorism policies are being formulated. Perhaps this consideration might assist in resolving issues of imbalance among the competing norms. Obviously, a comprehensive definition of national security is not a conclusive mechanism for countering terrorism, but it is a vital starting point.

7.4.2 SOCIAL IMPLICATION OF THE DEFINITION OF NATIONAL SECURITY FORMULATED IN THIS BOOK

This definition of 'national security' has some social implications. To counter terrorism, sovereign states have a corresponding obligation to respect the rights of individuals within their territory. Unfortunately, the fight against terrorism has been characterised with flagrant violations of human rights, such as arbitrary detentions, indiscriminate loss of lives and property. These violations are publicised by the media and human rights activists. Loss of confidence on the government by the masses on the protection of their human rights could lead to a violent reaction against the authorities. Notably, it is immaterial if the reaction is from a single individual. In recent times, individuals have detonated bombs in public places. Consequently, a grave feeling of insecurity of lives and property in the society could be a conduit for national insecurity. Some of the human rights cases espoused in this book reveal the laxity (lack of care) with which some government agents handle terrorist suspects.[1126] Some of these suspects may have been killed before it was found that they had nothing to do with terrorism, some have been arrested for terrorism followed by releases without explanations. All this might aggravate the feeling of social discrimination and social alienation; And perhaps, heighten radicalisation.

Hence, the important policy question remains; how far has the existing counterterrorism models gone in combating terrorism? Accordingly, the definition of national security formulated in this book fosters the recognition of 'people's security'. Its application as a model in the formulation of counterterrorism policies brings the 'interest' and 'welfare' of people into focus in any national security considerations. Perhaps it might assist in reducing the social impact (such

1126 El-masri v Former Republic of Macedonia, op cit, para 51

as radicalism) of some counterterrorism measures, which infringe on the principles of human rights law. Where the situation demands a withdrawal of certain human rights for the enhancement of national security then, the extent of the right to be withdrawn will not be more than the exigencies of the situation.[1127] This is in line with the element of 'rationality' elucidated in the 'theory of preservative legitimacy' formulated in this book and Article 15 ECHR respectively.

7.4.3 ACADEMIC IMPLICATIONS OF THE DEFINITION OF NATIONAL SECURITY FORMULATED IN THIS BOOK

The definition developed in this book will serve as a good reference for academics and researchers in their evaluation of national security issues. It provides a broad landscape for understanding the concept and crucial elements of national security, irrespective of jurisdiction, and the effect/s of these elements on it. Researchers might use it as a platform for critical analysis of the competing interests in national security matters especially in democratic societies. For instance, in issues relating to the evaluation of the effectiveness of the rule of law in countering terrorism in a democratic society. Ultimately, it provides a background for further research in considerations of national security and human rights law and policy. Its application can be extended to other academic areas such as sociology and political science.

7.5 POLICY IMPLICATION OF THE 'THEORY OF PRESERVATIVE LEGITIMACY' PROPOUNDED IN THIS BOOK

This theory is anchored on three principal questions: what is the 'legality', 'rationality' and 'objectivity' of a counter terrorism measure or legislation? Hence, the contemplation of these questions in policy making might assist a policy maker in the formulation of counterterrorism policies, which reflect respect for the rule of law. Perhaps the question of legality will be a guide for the formulation of 'lawful' counterterrorism policies; it seeks policies, which are in consonance with treaty obligations of the sovereign state in question. It prescribes, for

1127 European Convention on Human Rights

compliant policies, with the principles and dictates of the law in ways that will resolve conflicts within the competing interests of national security.

The element of 'rationality' puts the policy maker on a pedestal of 'reasonableness'. This element provides a policy maker with a holistic assessment of the policy to be formulated. In other words, it contemplates the legal, moral, psychological and mental acceptance of the proposed counterterrorism policy. In effect, this element might assist a policy maker in the examination of whether the proposed policy has a human face (people's security). Nevertheless, the prevailing circumstance in the sovereign state is considered too. It puts the policy maker on 'check' as to whether the proposed policy is 'proportional' to the ill to be curbed. Perhaps, the proper assessment of this element in policy making may assist in attempting to strike a viable balance between the competing interests in the fight against terrorism.

The 'objectivity' element begs the question: 'why'. It ignites the policy makers' consciousness towards the purpose or goal of the policy to be formulated as it is pertinent that he understands the underlying aim of the proposed policy. As a result, it cuts deep into the pros and cons of the policy. At this point, the policy maker analyses the implication/s of the proposed policy on national security. Where the definition of national security formulated in this book is adopted side by side with this element, the policy maker manifests a broad understanding of the idea and concept of national security. Conceivably, he will be able to properly articulate the counterterrorism measures that are not anti-security in the bid to enhance national security. This work calls for more activism in promoting the principles of the rule of law in formulating and implementing counterterrorism measures in the fight against terror. Realistically, if democracies are to counter terrorism effectively, is it possible that human rights will not be sacrificed?

7.6 RECOMMENDATIONS

Terrorism poses a unique challenge to democracy.[1128] It is characterised by political, security and emotional implications. As a result, the evaluation of some counterterrorism measures of some sovereign states in this book reveal repeated

1128 D. Cole, et al., op cit

violations of human rights in the fight against terrorism which is antithetical to the spirit of democracy. Obviously, there is tension between national security, human rights and the rule of law. Hence, there is a question as to the capability of sovereign states to 'effectively' enhance their national security (according to this book peoples' security inclusive).

The UK was well ahead of the game by passing an Act (Terrorism Act 2000) before the 9/11 that dealt with the very acts that occurred on US soil. However, when the 'war on terror' began, it was not clear whether all nations were discussing the same thing. John Amos and Russel Stolfi state

> 'each discipline, even each writer, tends to treat terrorism, local or international, from given, narrow perspective shaped by the parameters of the discipline or the author's orientation'.[1129]

Terrorism as a concept inevitably appears within the framework of national security and human rights policy. Terrorist acts often culminate in loss of life, destruction of property, and disruption of public peace and order. Unfortunately, there are instances where some perpetrators of these acts undertake the act of terrorism as suicide bombers. It therefore becomes immaterial whether they are intercepted by law enforcement and subsequently prosecuted. For example, the act committed on 9/11 is a clear case in point. The sophistication that characterised the tactics used reveals that the act of 9/11 was premeditated. Thus, to forestall similar or greater acts of terrorism, sovereign states adopt relevant counterterrorism measures for the enhancement of their national security and human rights policies. This book has delved into and evaluated some of these counterterrorism measures against the background of national security and the protection of human rights. Axiomatically, it discovers a critical need to create a viable balance between national security interests and human rights concerns in the fight against terrorism, especially in a free and democratic society. At the same time, it questions the attitude of the courts towards the trade-off of the Article 2 of the ECHR rights of many innocent civilians against the Article 3 right of someone whose activities poses a threat to the life of others or the nation.

1129 A. John, et al., 'Controlling international terrorism: Alternatives palatable and unpalatable' (1982) vol 463 The Annals of American Academy 70–71

In addition, one of the significant elements of terrorism is a claimed political motive and, on the grounds of that motive, there is a perceived need for sovereign states to pass specific legislation/s adequate to the specific challenges. Hence, on the grounds of this political motive, a claimed resistance to law enforcement and the synthesis of a crime has led to the lack of a generally accepted definition and consequently, to enforcement challenges.[1130] The concept of 'terrorism' could be deemed ambiguous just like the concept of 'national security'. It means different things to different people, groups, and organisations. It might be safe to say that the complexity surrounding the absence of a generally acceptable definition of terrorism is predicated on the varying political motives of different terrorist organisations and their complicated models of operation. The major terrorist organisations such as Al-Qaeda might have a main political motive. However, there are other known or unknown terrorist movements/organisations with different political motives. The diverse or varying political motives of these terrorist groups constitute a challenge to national security and its imperatives in the fight against terrorism. The issue of 'insecurity' via terrorism, especially post-9/11, prompted this work into the task of attempting to identify and elucidate the various aspects of national security and to further synthesise these aspects into a comprehensive whole.

The political motive of Al-Qaeda and their mission to destroy all that is Western became the beacon call for many terrorists who now targeted American-allied, or Western nations. Now, in a post-9/11 society, a balancing exercise has become crucial. It has long been posited that governments cannot maximise both security and human rights at the same time.[1131] Realistically, this trade-off perhaps could be because of the interference of rights and liberties with governments' ability to pursue effective counterterrorism campaigns.[1132]

Clearly, for many sovereign states, the trade-off is a complicated issue because it does not constitute a simple issue of abstract weighing mechanisms, especially in democratic nations. Sovereign states find themselves weighing up those options in tandem with treaty and Convention obligations to ideally afford all people their human rights regardless of their status as an enemy or suspected

1130 ibid

1131 G. Stoudmann, op cit, 283

1132 J. Piazza, et al., op cit, 125

terrorist. Thus, despite the real and present danger facing many nations, the question remains, when determining appropriate actions by democratic member states in a post-9/11 environment, what weight should be given to:

1) The public's perception/s of the nation states applied terrorism fighting policies
2) Extinguishment of known terrorist cells or
3) Blind adherence to some of the rules of transnational law such as the ECHR.

One might be tempted to ask what could happen if current terrorist campaigns escalate and intensify. Several European nation states may find themselves addressing those questions given the current state of the Convention rights. Therefore, this chapter suggests how some of the convention rights under the ECHR might be amended so that nation states may address the need for security while maintaining priority rights of suspected terrorists.

The discussion will begin with Article 3 of the ECHR, and any such implications on member states' ability to address the threat of suspected terrorists. It will turn to some safeguards which Article 5 ECHR may provide, either currently or as amended, where Article 3 no longer constitutes an absolute right. It will also discuss the safeguard provided by Article 15 ECHR in derogation cases while countering terrorism. There will be a succinct discussion on Article 2 and its possible use in balancing a potential re-imagining of Article 3. Then, it will delve into some post deportation safeguards, a review of the UN delisting procedure in terrorist funding. Finally, this paper will conclude with a brief discussion on the adoption of a socio-legal approach in countering terrorism and areas for further research.

Proposed Amendments

7.6.1 THIS BOOK PROPOSES A POTENTIAL RE-IMAGINING OF ARTICLE 3 OF THE ECHR IN AN ONGOING TERRORIST WORLD WHERE ARTICLE 3 OF THE ECHR BECOMES A DEROGABLE RIGHT.

A review of the absolute nature of Article 3 of the ECHR is needed, especially in relation to terrorist suspects/applicants whose actions 'manifestly endanger' the lives of other people, or has the potential to do so, or, who evidently constitute a threat to national security. Impliedly, it advocates for exceptions to be enshrined in Article 3 of the ECHR. Often, nation states attempt to eliminate potential 'threats' to their nation through the deportation of terrorist suspects. However, the precedent in ***A and Others v United Kingdom*** makes it clear that member states could be limited in such situations.

The right under Article 3 of the ECHR is absolute. This right may not be applied differently when an individual is suspected of terrorist activity.[1133] Thus, the ECHR in ***Saadi v Italy*** stated that 'the danger an individual may pose to the community cannot be taken into account when assessing the risk to the individual upon transfer to another nation state'.[1134] However, the yardstick for assessing the legality of a potential deportation emerged in the ***Chahal*** case. In which case, the contracting country must consider whether serious proof has been shown for presuming that there is a real risk of being subjected to treatment contrary to Article 3 if removed to another State. If such grounds are probable, it becomes incumbent on the contracting state to put safe measures in place to protect the deportee (terrorist suspect) against such treatment in the event of deportation. More so, in determining such grounds, the activities of such individual/s become immaterial. In other words, the actions of the deportee in the contracting state might not stand to deprive him of his Article 3 right in the receiving state. Basically, the court will investigate the human rights situation in the receiving state. It will also examine the information held or ought to have been held by the contracting state at the time of deportation concerning the human rights condition in the receiving state.

1133 F. De Londras, op cit, 616–622.

1134 Ibid, 616

In ***Saadi v Italy,*** the third party interveners (UK) opined that the ECHR's standard for evaluating a terrorist suspect's transfer risk, delineated in ***Chahal's*** case, be amended and recast against the background of individuals who pose a specific danger to the society as a whole.[1135]This would be particularly significant considering the serious nature of potential harm posed by certain individuals in the post-9/11 terrorist setting.[1136]Again, since states adopt immigration measures in protecting themselves against extrinsic terrorist threats, they ought to be entitled to ask that dangerous individuals demonstrate a higher risk before a potential deportation will invoke the protection enshrined in Article 3 of the ECHR.[1137]

This view echoes the UK's post-9/11 position that the threat posed by international terrorism is fundamentally distinct from that which existed before.[1138] As a result, reconsideration or rebalancing of legal standards in international human rights law is pertinent to deal with the current security issues. In specific terms, the UK emphasised that the right to deport alien nationals taking part in terrorist acts pursuant to MOUs with, or diplomatic assurances by, the receiving state should be a more acknowledged practice.[1139] Currently, this practice has attracted criticism as human rights advocates contend that they are not binding, unenforceable, and provide insufficient protection for preserving Article 3 rights. By implication, the potential harm on suspected terrorists caused by their mistreatment abroad is prioritised over the more likely harm to citizens of the holding nation state.[1140] This difficult 'trade-off' of interests presents tension between affording terrorist suspects the full absolute extent of their human rights, while quietly denying innocent citizens their Article 2 right to life. Arguably, the latter should be an absolute right, except maybe in cases of murder. The potential Article 3 violation of a suspected terrorist should be amendable, within clearly articulated lines.

1135 Ibid, 617, Soering v United Kingdom, op cit, para 89, Articles 32 and 33 of the UN 1951 Convention on the Status of Refugees

1136 F. De Londras, 618

1137 ibid

1138 ibid, 620

1139 ibid

1140 ibid

The European Convention on Human Rights was primarily enacted to protect personal freedoms. The spirit of Article 3 of the ECHR simply posits that treatment must reach an intense level of severity for a challenge under this provision to succeed.[1141] It is settled that international law and the several Conventions on human rights prohibit the principle of Non-Refoulment (prohibits nation states from sending asylum seekers to where they will be tortured), especially under Article 3 of the ECHR in relation to terrorist suspects.[1142] However, it is important to note that Article 3 was primarily related to asylum seekers. Following the 9/11 attacks, a variety of attempts have been made to modify the interpretation of Article 3 of the ECHR as providing absolute protection against refoulment and expanding the individuals involved to include terrorists. The issues are two pronged. (a)Is the right to life of victims being unfairly traded off against the right of the terrorist/terrorist suspect to be transferred and (b) should contracting states be concerned with what happens to terrorist suspects when transferred/deported to their countries of origin or recipient states?

Notably, Article 2 of the ECHR not only urges sovereign states to desist from deliberate and illegal taking of life, but also to take proper steps to safeguard the lives of those within its jurisdiction. The state's obligation in this regard stretches beyond its basic duty to safeguard the right to life by putting in place necessary criminal law provisions. These provisions set out to obstruct the infringement of the Article 2 right in addition to law enforcement machinery for the prevention, suppression and sanctioning of violation of such provisions.[1143] There is also an implied positive obligation on sovereign states to adopt preventive operational measures to safeguard individuals whose lives are at risk from the criminal acts of others.[1144] In effect, states are legally obliged to protect their citizens and persons within their jurisdiction from acts of violence through terrorism or other means. Extradition is one of the ways through which states have exercised this positive duty in the fight against terrorism.[1145]

1141 European Convention on Human Rights as amended by Protocols Nos. 11 and 14 supplemented by Protocols Nos 1, 4, 6, 7, 12 and 13, op cit, para 54

1142 Chahal v United Kingdom, op cit

1143 D. Ehlers, et al., op cit,

1144 ibid

1145 R (Wellington) v Secretary of State for Home Department, op cit; RB(Algeria) and another v Secretary of State for the Home Department, ibid; Ben Khemais v Italy, op cit

Critically, in pursuing its positive obligation of protecting the lives of individuals within their jurisdiction, Article 3 of the ECHR perhaps operates as a restraint on sovereign states in deportation cases. As previously, stated, terrorist suspects often evoke Article 3 of the ECHR whenever there is an intention to deport them to a receiving country.[1146] Analytically, terrorist acts are intentional and therefore preconceived. Thus, in consonance with the spirit of Article 2(1) of the ECHR, no one (terrorists inclusive) should deliberately take away the life of another. Terrorist attacks, most times, culminate in loss of innocent lives. The right to life attracts significant attention in international law. Obviously, the absence of this right renders the other rights purposeless. Hence, the UN Human Rights Committee also recognises the right to life as the 'supreme right' of human beings.[1147] Accordingly, the law controls and restricts any condition or situation through which the lives of individuals could be endangered. However, it might be safe to say that where obligations are concerned, Conventions ought to be interpreted in the light of current developments. The wording of Article 3 of the ECHR mainly comprises prohibitions; the assertion of such duty is judge-made. Essentially, laws are made for the people.

Importantly, the state's positive duty to protect the right to life of the citizens and individuals within its jurisdiction does not justify the adoption of unreasonable measures that may infringe on other rights. This includes the rights of terrorist suspects. However, in line with the 'theory of preservative legitimacy' propounded in this book, the duty to protect life implies that every measure adopted to protect life must be 'absolutely necessary'. The deportation of terrorist/terrorist suspects could be considered 'reasonable' and 'necessary' considering the exigencies of the situation in the contracting country. In extradition cases, perhaps the court could carry out a balancing exercise between the Article 3 right of a terrorist suspect and the Article 2 right of innocent individuals in the contracting nation. On these grounds, which way do we go? Terrorism or deportation?

Based on ***Saadi*** and ***Othman***, a framework arose for member states to deport terrorist suspects. However, the concern remained that the court had categorically rejected any form of balancing between the interests of the member state

1146 Chahal v United Kingdom, op cit, para 26

1147 Human Rights Committee, op cit

to protect their citizens from harm, and the potential for Article 3 violations. This rejection gives rise to the 'trade-off' mentioned earlier between the member states citizens' Article 2 rights (right to life) and the terrorist suspect's Article 3 rights. In the absence of some form of amendment, the ECHR has established an unfortunate precedent that prioritises freedom from torture and inhuman treatment or punishment over the right to life. The right to life could be taken as the 'anchor' or foundation stone for every other right. In this case, a comparatively 'secondary right', which is derivative, is being prioritised over an axiomatic 'primary right' from which it derives in ways that are contradictory. There is a case for either treating both rights on par or for prioritising Article 2 as axiomatic but not for prioritising Article 3 over Article 2.

A singular amendment to the criteria presented in the Saadi and Othman cases may be proposed. The court may allow a nation state to derogate from its convention obligations where there is strong evidence of near-likely harm, or attack, against the nation and its citizenry if the suspected individual is not deported. In this case, the suspected individual's evidence of potential torture and or inhuman treatment is not prioritised over the rights of innocent civilians. Such balancing could be submitted before the judicial branch of the nation and would be appealable to the Convention Court. Where the member state's evidence is more credible and imminent than evidence of torture, then the suspect should be deported subject to additional safeguards outlined later in this chapter. These safeguards illustrate the fact that the terrorist suspects Article 3 right is not neglected.

Morally speaking, is it logical for a terrorist to allege a violation of his human rights when he is guilty of an infringement of human rights? Or for a terrorist suspect to allege a violation of his human rights when it is evidently seen that he is connected to terrorism? Pursuant to Article 17 of the ECHR, a terrorist suspect cannot enjoy his Article 3 right at the expense of the Article 2 right of thousands of people in the contracting country. Therefore, in the event of deportation terrorists/terrorist suspects should not hide under the cloak of some human rights provision (such as Article 3 ECHR) especially where their activities are evidently seen to threaten national security, which includes people's security as defined in this book. Analytically, as a citizen of a sovereign state, perhaps it is rational for a terrorist/terrorist suspect to desist from any act which has the potential to destabilise the security of the nation or acts which violate the rights of others in the nation. In an attempt to strike a viable balance, perhaps national security should gain priority over the rights of a single individual who is 'reasonably' suspected as a terrorist.

7.6.2 THIS BOOK RECOMMENDS THE MAINTENANCE AND STRICT COMPLIANCE TO THE CONDITIONS OF ARTICLE 15 OF THE ECHR AS A VIABLE SAFEGUARD AGAINST VIOLATIONS OF HUMAN RIGHTS IN CASES OF DEROGATION WHILE COUNTERING TERRORISM.

The fight against terrorism is liable to erode essential fundamental human rights.[1148] For most member nations, accusations of rights infringement may begin with an infringement of Article 5 of the ECHR (the right to liberty and security of persons). Such accusations take place where a nation's detention of a suspected person drifts from the articulated ECHR requirements. To ascertain if there has been abuse, the court will first examine whether the applicants were legally detained in accordance with Article 5(1) (f) of the ECHR. If there has been an illegal detention, then the court must determine whether the member state validly derogated from its obligations under Article 5(1) of the ECHR.

In ***A and others v United Kingdom*** the courts investigated the first element of the test by specifying the requirements of Article 5 of the ECHR. The provisions of Article 5(outlined earlier in the 3rd chapter of this book) reveal clearly that the guarantees under the ECHR relates to 'everyone'.[1149] Sub-sections (a) to (f) of Article 5(1) of the ECHR consist of a comprehensive list of permissible grounds upon which the liberty of individuals may be deprived. In other words, no deprivation of liberty will be legal unless it falls within one of the sub-sections of Article 5 of the ECHR. For instance, Article 5(1) (f), allows the state to control the liberty of non-nationals in an immigration context. The United Kingdom contended that the applicants' detention was permissible because they were legally detained as persons 'against whom action is being taken with a view to deportation or extradition'.[1150]There is no reasonably necessary standard attached to Article 5(1) of the ECHR where the member state hopes to prevent fleeing or

1148 S. Sottiaux, op cit

1149 ibid, 162

1150 ibid, 163

further offence.[1151]Hence, in this case, the court found that the applicant was not awaiting imminent immigration processes and therefore was not being detained legally. As a result, the second element of the test was applied.

Accordingly, Article 15 of the ECHR allows contracting states to derogate from certain rights guaranteed by the Convention in time of 'war or other public emergency threatening the life of the nation'. However, permissible derogations under Article 15 must meet three substantive conditions. Nonetheless, two will be discussed with respect to this present case:

1. There must be a public emergency threatening the life of the nation;
2. Any measures taken in response must be 'strictly required by the exigencies of the situation', and
3. The measures taken in response to it must be in compliance with a state's other obligations under international law.[1152]

It follows that derogation from the obligation of the convention is permissible by the contracting state where it holds that the life of the nation is under threat or that the nation is confronted with public emergency. Notably, the court may not ascertain what constitutes a public emergency, but it is incumbent on the court to establish whether the state undertook only those actions which are expedient considering the exigencies of public emergency or threat[1153], for instance, deportation. Although member states have the right to manage and detain potential terrorists, contracting parties do not enjoy an unlimited discretion. The court must still determine whether, amongst other things, the states have gone beyond the 'extent strictly required by the exigencies' of the situation. In carrying out this task, the court must give proper weight to such pertinent factors like the nature of the rights affected by the derogation, the conditions leading to, and the duration of the emergency situation.[1154] In ascertaining the lawfulness of the member state action, the court will inquire as to: (1) whether there was a 'public emergency threatening the life of the nation', and (2) whether the measures

1151 A and others v United Kingdom, op cit, para 164

1152 European Convention on Human Rights 1950

1153 A and Others v United Kingdom, op cit, para 173

1154 ibid

were strictly required by the exigencies of the situation.[1155] Sequel to the results of each inquiry, the court will establish whether the member state acted within the obligated confines of their right to derogate.

a) Whether there was a 'Public Emergency Threatening the Life of The Nation'?

Based on three reasons, the applicants in ***A and Others v United Kingdom*** contended that there had been no public emergency threatening the life of the British nation. They pointed out, firstly, that the emergency was neither actual nor imminent; secondly, that it was not of a temporary nature; and, thirdly, that no state had derogated from the ECHR. This, coupled with the informed views of other national and international bodies, suggested that the existence of a public emergency had not been established.[1156] In addition, the court stated that the requirement of 'imminence' cannot be so narrowly interpreted as to expect a state to wait for a disaster to strike before taking measures to handle it.[1157] Hence, on this first question, the court agreed with the government that there was indeed a 'public emergency threatening the life of the nation'.[1158]

However, does this imply that an application for derogation will always be granted whenever there is a clear evidence of danger threatening the life of a nation? Essentially, the element of 'imminence' might not always stand the test of ascertaining the existence of 'public emergency' in a nation state. Thus, once there are proven signs of 'danger' threatening the life of a nation, derogation could be valid. The danger need not be probable. Again, does the validity of derogation in a public emergency threatening the life of a nation authorise the government of that nation to adopt 'any' measure, which they deem fit for the maintenance of their national security?

1155 Article 15(1) (2) European Convention on Human Rights 1950; A and others v United Kingdom, op cit

1156 A and others v United Kingdom, op cit, para 175

1157 ibid, para 177

1158 ibid, para 181; Ireland v United Kingdom (1978) application no 5310/71 Strasbourg para 205, 212; Denmark, Norway, Sweden and Netherlands v Greece (1969) application no 3321/67, 3322/67, 3323/67, 3344/67, Yearbook 12, para 113, page 70

b) Whether the measures were strictly required by the exigencies of the situation?

With respect to the second question, the court considered Article 15, which provides that the State may take measures derogating from its obligations under the Convention only 'to the extent strictly required by the exigencies of the situation'.[1159] In other words, contracting states do not enjoy unlimited power in adopting measures to avert the emergency. Thus, the measure adopted must be 'proportional' to the emergency to be averted. In the case of ***A and Others v United Kingdom***, the House of Lords opposed to the government's contention when it observed that the measures adopted were disproportionate to the exigencies of the situation as they discriminated unjustifiably between nationals and non-nationals. Hence, the court established that there has been a violation of Article 5(1) of the ECHR.[1160] In the present case, the court found a violation of Article 5 of the ECHR because the unlawful detention was not justified by a valid derogation.[1161] Notably, the ECHR pointed out that the issue of the determination of 'public emergency' should be within the discretion of the national authorities. It also allowed the national authorities a wide margin of appreciation in issues relating to the measures to be adopted to forestall an emergency. Accordingly, the determination of the kind of measures to be adopted has been considered 'political' as opposed to 'judicial'.[1162] However, it becomes incumbent upon the courts to determine whether the measures are 'strictly required by the exigencies of the situation'.

This procedure remains a safeguard against member state decisions to deport suspect individuals where an MOU may exist but is in effect, not enforceable in nature. In that sense, the Article 5 right to liberty and security is maintained. This safeguard reflects a major ingredient of national security as defined in this book ('legal certainty' (predictability), which is one of the basic requirements for the rule of law). However, like the disconnect between Articles 3 and 2, here the court allows that, even where a member state determines there is held to be 'an emergency threatening the life of its nation', deportation will be forestalled

1159 A and Others v United Kingdom, op cit, para 182

1160 ibid, para 190

1161 ibid

1162 ibid, para 183, 184

by the ECtHR if the member state exceeded the scope of actions necessary to avoid the emergency. Ultimately, this could be determined on the grounds of proportionality.

7.6.3 SUGGESTED POST-DEPORTATION SAFEGUARDS

(a) This Proposal is an additional safeguard to the present ECHR Protocol of 'Visitation' and 'Reporting' in cases of Detention of Deportees.

It may be proposed that the ECHR work with another organisation. This is to ensure that, the receiving nation accepts additional review and examination of post-deportation detention conditions. The rationale is to make certain, the suspect individual's rights under the Convention are not violated. In the event an individual is deported for acts of terror, or suspected acts of terror, a protocol must be created to ensure safe delivery, installation, and continued dignity upon arrival in the home nation or a third country. To facilitate such a protocol, a neutral party from a non-sender or receiver state may accompany the individual during the deportation. This individual would ensure that no harassment would occur in the process of transporting the suspect individual to their home country or a third country.

Upon arriving at the home country or a third country, the neutral party would deliver the individual to a pre-selected receiver who is charged with ensuring the safety of the individual. Then, the designated receiver would escort the individual to any legal proceedings, and ultimately visit the individual in incarceration on a regular basis. This individual will deliver reports of incarceration condition, inmate treatment, and facility compliance with agreed upon holding standards. At agreed upon intervals, a neutral non-receiving or sending party would be given access to the individual, periodically drafted reports on his/her holding and condition for follow up interviews. This neutral party may investigate all violations under the ECHR or deportation agreement. Where a violation occurs, the violation is reported to the ECHR.

The benefits to a closed system with very careful safety protocols that requires a non-participating neutral party is that there are some guarantees that the suspected or convicted individual will arrive to his home country unmolested.

Then, the pre-selected receiving individual will be screened and introduced to the deportee prior to deportation to ensure the deportee develops a relationship with the receiving individual. With that relationship, the deportee will be willing to communicate when violations occur, and the receiving party, due to the pre-screening, will report it.

The disadvantages deal mainly with 'national sovereignty'. The involvement and role non-citizens play in the transportation, and receipt of the suspected terrorist may not be a welcome intrusion for either the sending or receiving nation states. It may be seen as an imposition to include human chaperones in addition to the drafted and approved transporting agreement which was required by the court to justify deportation to begin with. Additionally, even if the nation states cooperate, there is no guarantee that the deportee will be treated better because safeguards are in place. In some nations, the simple fact that more safeguards are placed to protect the deportee may make them a target, not only for those working in the government, or the holding facility, but the inmates whom they share space within the facility.

It is likely that any program that requires extensive monitoring and chaperoning will need careful manoeuvring and modification depending on the nation states involved in the deportation. It is possible that different protocols will be needed in different cases. The only aspect of the protocol that may remain the same is the visitation and reporting that is a component of ECHR protocols presently. This proposal would simply allow for additional safeguards which can be modified if the situation warrants it. For example, the transportation of a globally wanted and convicted terrorist who has killed both abroad and in his home country. Such an individual may require additional safety protocols for deportation, as well as holding, given the likelihood that many individuals would not be restrained in torture or ultimately killing the deportee.

(b) Access to Counsel of their Choice:

It may also seem that the clearest amendment for suspected individuals be that they have access to counsel of their choice. Article 14 (3) (b) of the ICCPR states; 'everyone charged with a criminal offence is to be entitled to have adequate time and facilities for the preparation of his defence and to communicate with counsel of his own choosing'. The Human Rights Committee, in its General Comment

20 (1992) on Article 14, stated that the protection of the detainee requires that prompt and regular access to lawyers be given to him. Failure to provide access to a lawyer for five days was found to violate Article 14 in ***Gridin v Russian Federation.*** [1163] Furthermore, in its General Comment No. 2 the Committee Against Torture reiterated that the right of arrested persons to notify someone of their detention, to have prompt access to a lawyer... as fundamental safeguards against torture, especially in the first hours and days of detention when the risk of torture is greatest.[1164]

Evidently, the right of a detainee to consult a counsel of his choice while in detention is not enshrined under the ECHR. Thus, to avoid some of the violations of Convention rights in the fight against terrorism, detainees should have access to communication with privileged people outside the detention facility especially counsel of their choice. This suggests that, it might be pertinent to enshrine 'the right to have counsel of your own choice while in detention' into the ECHR body of laws as a possible safeguard to Article 5 of the ECHR. This right is conspicuously absent in the ECHR. Notably, this access is different from having access to appear before a judge. This access is such that will help a detainee understand fully the case against him and acquaints him with the legal options available to him as the case may be.

An access to appear before a judge only allows that the detained may have an audience before a legal decision maker who can determine their guilt or innocence, then pass a sentence. The legal system in most countries is not one that is easily navigated by laypersons. Often, an individual represents themselves in the court of law by necessity and not by choice. It is conceivable that a layperson, unschooled in matters of the law would not be aware of all possible defences, or methods of argument to bolster their claim in court.

Simply providing legal counsel does not cure the inherent power imbalance when a detainee represents themselves. Simple access to legal counsel of their choice does not forestall attempts to provide legal counsel whose loyalties are to parties other than the detained. Therefore, access to counsel of the detainee's choice allows comprehensive and competent representation of the detainee

1163 Othman (Abu Qatada) v United Kingdom, op cit, para 156

1164 ibid

and ensures that the legal counsel's loyalties are appropriately aligned with the detainee.

This book concludes that it is time to look to an existing organisation within the ECHR and perhaps increase its responsibilities and resources with which it must perform any expanded obligations. The ECHR supranational organisation Convention for Prevention of Torture and Inhuman or Degrading Treatment of (or) Punishment (CPT), is a committee that evaluates the conditions of deported individuals in receiving countries to guarantee compliance of MOUs.[1165] The Council of Europe's Committee of Ministers embraced the CPT collectively in 1987. The CPT was allowed almost unrestricted access to all places of detention, including the right to interview detainees without witnesses. The purpose was to create a compelling extra-judicial mechanism to prohibit torture and ill-treatment via exposure of high-risk situations. Then, through reports and proposals to national authorities, the CPT can help in the reinforcement of human rights protections.[1166]

The CPT's main method of work depends on the collaboration of different nation states and the confidentiality of its operation. The CPT operates through on-site visitations by a member delegation of 2-5 members each visit, in conjunction with professionals and, usually, interpreters. After the visits, the CPT formulates and sends confidential reports to the governments involved. These include observations, recommendations and requests for more information, and do not contain the names of prisoners concerned. Once the report is received, the government then sends a reply to the CPT. Contingent to the response provided by the government, the CPT may request further information.[1167]Currently, occasional visits are made to every nation that ratified the Convention. Such visits can last from one to two weeks and cover different places of detention designated by the CPT, based on advice received from non-governmental organisations and other sources. Impromptu visits are made to definite institutions or regions from which information indicates a particularly high risk of torture or ill treatment.[1168]

1165 D. Bertrand, et al., op cit

1166 ibid, 234–242

1167 ibid

1168 ibid

Given the present role of the CPT, this book goes a step further by proposing that the ECHR develops a follow-up program by mandating a receiving state to include a mandatory clause into every MOU, affirming that once a detention facility is found to be in violation of the MOU, they are automatically investigated by a body independent from the CPT and constituted by the European Commission. If the investigation determines that the facility's violation is a result of an extensive flagrant violation of human rights, the detention facility will be immediately placed on 'a no-deportation list' (this might affect their foreign relations with other countries depending on what the interest is). Further, any presently held deportees would be transferred to a compliant facility. Also, in the case where a detention facility is a repeat violator of MOUs, then that facility could be placed on a no-deportation list either for a period (i.e. several years subject to re-evaluation), or permanently, if the violation was egregious enough. This could perhaps serve as an additional procedural safeguard for those transfers that do occur in locations with borderline acceptable MOUs. In essence, where it is evidently seen that effective monitoring mechanisms have been put in place by the contracting sovereign state, perhaps there could be a strong presumption in favour of deportation. Ultimately, the positive duty imposed on states to prevent acts of torture would be much less effective if a corresponding obligation to investigate allegations of torture, ill or degrading treatment did not exist.

7.6.4 THIS BOOK RECOMMENDS THE POSSIBILITY OF ARTICLE 2 RE-IMAGINED WITH ENFORCEABLE 'TEETH'.

Much of what has been discussed thus far involves the 'absolute' nature of Article 3 of the ECHR in contrast to the non-absolute nature of Article 2 of the ECHR. This work has considered the safeguards put in place through Article 5 ECHR. It has also examined potential amendments to increase the CPT's jurisdiction as a further safeguard in deportation cases against the background of the fight against terrorism. Further, this book advocates consideration of the power or force of Article 2 of the ECHR (right to life). It looks at how that Article, or an amendment to it, could strike a balance where the court feel that their primary obligation is to ascertain the protection of Article 3 rights of the deportee in the receiving country as opposed to the effect of the deportees' presence/conduct on national security in the contracting nation state.

On the other hand, member states may feel that they must exchange the rights of 'one' for the rights of many. In the spirit of national security, considering the after effects of terrorist acts such as, loss of innocent life, this paper recommends that 'right to life' takes priority, in the face of any balancing with Article 3 of the ECHR, particularly where it is evident that the terrorist/terrorist suspect constitutes a 'danger' to the life of others and the nation at large. Where Article 3 of the ECHR is implicated in the Court's determination it must be adjusted to an amended position to always preserve the life of many. Finally, where the life of one or few terrorist/terrorists suspect is likely to be at risk in cases of deportation (because of torture, ill or degrading treatment) in a receiving country as opposed to the life of many in a contracting country, ultimately, the right to be prioritised in that circumstance remains an Article 2 right. Hence, if the right to life of many is in sharp contrast with the rights of few suspected terrorists, the court must examine whether the expulsion of the suspected terrorists to their original nation state or a third country will remove the risk to life. If so, then the court must examine what the consequence of such an expulsion could be. If such an expulsion would likely result in loss of life of a deportee, then expulsion may only be completed upon the drafting of an MOU with a mandatory CPT review clause.

However, where the risk to the suspected terrorist is a possible Article 3 violation, then an MOU would still be required. Nonetheless, the suspected terrorists should be required to present evidence that it is more likely than not that they will suffer an Article 3 violation at the hands of their receiving nation. Upon such a demonstration, the Contracting State may extend additional post-expulsion support. For instance, CPT review, an attorney to represent the suspect's interests in the receiving nation state, as well as financial support to appeal any unfavourable determinations in the contracting state to an international body. By providing such a framework, the ECHR would display a clear priority for life, while maintaining that Article 3 violations, while not absolute, are significant. Perhaps by distinguishing the two, member states may better construct internal policies within their law enforcement and immigration departments to address such situations. Once such policies are in place, they will leave the government free to pursue counterterrorism programs, which will protect the nation's citizens and national security at large. In conclusion, in pursuing the interest of many, it is pertinent that the government adopts measures, which are not more than required in the circumstance.

There are several considerations for the ECHR in the configuration, or the prioritisation of its given rights, but also for nation states, in terms of the interests they must weigh up in securing a viable and legitimate balance. For the ECHR, there are areas in need of clarification or perhaps amendments that can give member states guidance as to how to conceptualise and incorporate a rights system that places their citizens' rights lower than those of individuals who are 'reasonably' suspected of terrorism. For nation states, it is important to determine what the priority is. Hence, whether in the end the goal is to promote the security of its citizens, balance the interest of the nation against the greater calling to ensure human rights for all individuals, or to prioritise the tenets of the Convention at all costs. With each interest, comes an equally challenging trade-off.

When stepping from the legal or pseudo-legal framework of the ECHR Court system, and the companion international tribunals, there are a few final recommendations that can be made to member states battling this constant dilemma. First, a nation state may withdraw from the agreement with the Convention and decide to focus only on the safety of its citizens. Such an option would follow if the member state holds no interest in participating in international human rights initiatives. Secondly, where the member states care somewhat for the international human rights initiative, then the nation state can be mindful of the information disseminated amongst the public about its counterterrorism initiatives. Returning to the concept of nations increasing terrorism by engaging in killings and disappearances, it is possible for a nation to balance citizens' rights with suspected individual's rights if the information about detention is managed.

Finally, a nation that does not wish to manipulate the media or its citizens may consider managing the expectations of its public, by providing meaningful, and useful educational information about the processes involved in counterterrorism (transparency) and the ways in which they impact everyday citizens. Perhaps a greater understanding for the decisions that are to be made, and the trade-offs that are involved, will garner greater public awareness and acceptance for the often-complicated counterterrorism programs that exist. Where none of the above-mentioned recommendations are deemed possible or effective, then it would be in the member state's interest to encourage the ECHR to consider amendments to Articles 3, 5, and 2. By so doing, a more realistic, manageable and human counterterrorism program can emerge in the various nations that require it. Without such amendment, the ECHR runs the risk that future terrorists will utilise the very same human rights to plan attacks and escape serious punishment, thereby turning ECHR member states into targets weakened by their international agreements.

7.7 ADOPTION OF SOCIO-LEGAL MEASURES IN COUNTERING TERRORISM

Finally, one of the major concerns while countering terrorism is the challenge of human rights violation. The flagrant violation of human rights in the fight against terror has created a grave imbalance in the attempt to protect national security. This challenge might not be strictly legal. It could be social too. As a result, addressing the issues of human rights violations in the fight against terrorism might not wholly depend upon the dictates of the law.[1169] Striking the required balance between national security and human rights violations might demand other disciplines such as sociology, political science. Thus, the sole adoption of a doctrinal approach in enhancing national security might not proffer all the solutions to the challenges of terrorism as that approach looks at an instant solution to the problems totally from legal perspective with no connection outside the ambit of the law.[1170]

On the other hand, socio-legal measures adopt a bigger picture of the issue at hand. They put law back and apply it within the social context. They critically examine the moral, political and religious justifications of terrorism. Perhaps, they might bring out possible reason/s why people get radicalised and get involved in terrorism. It examines the cultural, geographical and religious implications of terrorism as well. On that account, sovereign states could adopt, consultation, negotiation, mediation where necessary in the resolution of issues relating to national security namely terrorism. In this event, this work advocates for policy recommendations outside the purview of the law. Hence, it highlights the need for terrorism to be dealt with from its root. For instance, it recommends the need for nation states to dialogue with non-state actors to ascertain what

1169 S. Queshi, op cit

1170 ibid

the agitations are, if any, and consequently negotiate for settlements where necessary. Perhaps this will help create the desired balance to enhance national security.

7.8 FURTHER RESEARCH

The conclusions reached, and recommendations made in this book are earnestly expected to attract the attention of policy makers. They should be considered as modest contributions toward the urgent need for reform in relation to the acute imbalance fostered by the absolute nature of Article 3 of the ECHR against the background of national security and some counterterrorism measures that are antithetical to national security and the rule of law in a democratic society. The concern this work has expressed in relation to the trade-off of rights in the fight against terrorism is intended to ignite policy considerations and possible legislative reviews for the enhancement of national security.

Again, the difficulty inherent in striking a viable balance between the competing interests in a post-9/11 world is a potential roadmap for researchers to build upon this work and carry out further research in the future. For instance, in areas such as law, sociology and political science where research or discussions on the topic: 'Is ethnicity and religion a national security issue'? or 'Is human rights a challenge to national security: Article 9 ECHR (Freedom of thought, conscience and religion) a case in view? 'could be explored as a guide, such further research could take the definition of national security formulated in this book into consideration.

Again, since the challenge of terrorism is an issue of national security, the definition of 'national security' propounded in this book could provide a background for further research into the research topic: 'Why terrorism?'. The incidence of terrorism seems to be on an increase post 9/11.Such research may investigate the root cause of modern type of terrorism adopting the black-letter and socio-legal approach. An exposure into the reasons for terrorism perhaps might be a pointer in the right direction towards the enhancement of 'national security'. This book has made an innovative and pioneering move of formulating an expansive definition of 'national security' against the background of terrorism and counterterrorism and the theory of preservative legitimacy. Addressing issues of terrorism and counterterrorism is tantamount to addressing issues, which obstruct the enhancement of national security. It has also attempted to proffer solutions to the acute conflicts between security and human rights in countering terrorism. Ultimately, the existence of terrorism and the dilemma of how to react to its challenges 'legally' and 'pragmatically' demand a radical approach. Hence, the question; what should be done next?[1171]

1171

Bibliography

BOOKS

Aaron D, *In their own words: Voices of jihad-compilation and commentary* (RAND Corporation, California 2008)

Abubakar I., *Anti-Money Laundering and Counterterrorism Financing: Law and Practice in Nigeria* (Malthouse Press Limited, Nigeria 2015)

Akpeninor J., *Modern concepts of security* (AuthorHouse Publishers USA, Indiana 2012)

Akrivopoulou C., et al., *Digital Democracy and the Impact of Technology on Governance and Politics: New Globalised Practices* (IGI Global, Pennsylvania 2013)

Alexander Y, *Counterterrorism strategies: Successes and failures of six nations* (Potomac Books Inc, Washington DC 2006)

Allawi A., *The Occupation of Iraq: Winning the War, Losing the Battle* (Yale University Press Publication, Finey 2008)

Allhoff F, *Terrorism, Ticking Time-Bombs and Torture: A Philosophical Analysis* (The University of Chicago Press, Chicago 2012)

Amiri A., *Freedom of Information and National Security: A study Of Judicial Review Under US Law* (Herbert UtzVerlag GmbH, EU 2014)

Amnesty International, *The Circle of injustice: Security operations and human rights violations in Ingushetia* (Amnesty International limited, London 2012)

Amos A., et al., *American National Security* (6th edn, The John Hopkins University Press, Maryland 2009)

Amos M., *Human Rights Law* (Hart Publishing, Portland 2014)

Art R., et al., *Militant democracy and counterterrorism: Lessons from the past* (United States Institute of Peace, Washington 2007)

Atkins S., *The 9/11 Encyclopedia* (2[nd]edn ABC-CLIO, California 2011)

Aubrey S., *The new dimension of international terrorism:(Strategie und konflikt-forschung*, VdfHochschulverlag 2004)

Auerswald D., et al., *NATO in Afghanistan: Fighting Together, Fighting Alone* (Princeton University Press, New Jersey 2014)

Bailliet M., et al., *Promoting Peace Through International Law* (Oxford University Press, United Kingdom 2015)

Bandarage A, *The Separatist Conflict in Sri Lanka: Terrorism, Ethnicity, Political Economy* (Routledge Taylor & Francis Group, New York 2009)

Barak A, *Proportionality and Pretense* (Cambridge University Press Ltd., New York 2012)

Barros V, et al., *Climate Change 2014: Impacts, Adaptation and Vulnerability* (Cambridge University Press, New York 2014)

Bartrop P., et al., *Modern Genocide: The Definitive Resource and Document Collection* (ABC-CLIO LLC, California 2015)

Basoglu M, *Torture and its Consequences: Current Treatment Approaches* (Cambridge University Press, Cambridge 1992)

Baylis J., et al., *The globalization of world politics: An introduction to international relations* (5th edn Oxford University Press United States, New York 2011)

Beckman J., *Comparative Legal Approaches to Homeland Security and Anti-Terrorism* (Routledge Taylor & Francis Group, New York 2016)

Belluck D., *Environmental security, critical infrastructure and risk management: Definitions and current trend* (Springer Publisher Ltd, Netherlands 2006)

Benjamin D., *The Next Attack: The Failure of The War on Terror and A Strategy for Getting It Right* (Henry Holt and Company LLC, New York 2006)

Betts R., *Enemies of Intelligence: Knowledge and Power in American National Security* (Columbia University Press, New York 2007)

Bhatia M, et al., *Afghanistan, arms and conflict: Armed groups, disarmament and security in a post war society* (1st edn, Routledge, Abingdon 2008)

Biddle W, *Immigrants' Rights after 9/11* (Chelsea House, New York 2008)

Bilgin P., et al., *Global security and international political economy* (vol 111 EOLSS Publication Co Ltd United Kingdom, Oxford 2010)

Biswaro J, *The Quest for Regional Integration in the Twenty First Century* (Mkuki Na Nyota Publishers, Salaam 2012)

Bjola C, et al., *Secret Diplomacy, Concepts, Contexts* (Taylor and Francis, London 2016)

Bloss W, *Under a Watchful Eye: Privacy Rights and Criminal Justice* (ABC-CLIO-LLC Press, California 2009)

Bollinger L, *The tolerant society: freedom of speech and extremist speech in America* (Oxford University Press, New York 1986)

Bonner D., *Executive measures, terrorism and national security: Have the rules of the game changed?* (Ashgate Publishing Limited, England 2007)

Borjas G, *Immigration Economics* (Harvard University Press, Cambridge 2014)

Born H., et al, *Democratic Control of Intelligence Services: Containing Rogue Elephants* (Ashgate Publishing Company, England 2016)

Boschiero N., et al., *International Courts and the Development of International Law* (T.M.C. Asser Press, Netherlands 2013)

Bourantonis D, et al, *The United Nations in the New World Order: The World Organisation at Fifty* (Macmillan Press Limited, London 2016)

Bove M, et al., *Pre-trial detention in 20th and 21st century common law and civil law systems* (1st edn, Cambridge Scholars Publishing, London 2014)

Brecher R, *Is the use of coercive interrogation or torture permissible and effective as a counterterrorism model: Contemporary debates on terrorism* (Routledge, Oxon 2012)

Budania R, *India's National Security Dilemma: The Pakistan Factor and India's Policy Response* (Indus Publishing Company, New Delhi 2001)

Bunck J, et al., *Law, power and the sovereign state: The evolution of and the application of the concept of sovereignty* (University of Pennsylvania State University Press, Pennsylvania 2010)

Burgers J, et al., *The United Nations Convention against torture: A handbook on the Convention against torture and other cruel, inhuman and degrading treatment or punishment* (MartinusNijhoff Publishers, Dordrecht 1988)

Bush G, *The national security strategy of the United States of America* (Morgan James Publishing, New York 2009)

Byers M., *War Law: Understanding International Law and Armed Conflict* (Atlantic Books, London 2007)

Caine T, *Stamping out Rights: The Impact of Anti-Terrorism Laws on Policing* (CHRI 2007 REPORT)

Carlsnaes W., et al., *Handbook of International Relations* (1st edn Sage Publication Ltd United Kingdom, London 2002)

Caselia J, et al., *Hell is a very small place: Voices from solitary confinement* (New Press, London 2016)

Cassese A, *International Law* (2nd edn Oxford University Press, London 2005)

Castles S, et al., *The Age of Migration: International Population Movements in the Modern World* (5th edn The Palgrave Macmillan, England 2014)

Chandler D, *Critical perspective on human security: Rethinking emancipation and power in international relations* (Routledge publishing limited, New York 2011)

Chatterji M, et al., *Conflict and Peace in South Asia* (Emerald Group Publishing Limited 2008)

Chen T, et al., *Cyber terrorism: Understanding, assessment and response* (Springer Publishing Company, New York 2014)

Chivas C., et al., *Libya after Qaddafi: Lessons and Implications for the Future* (Rand Corporation, Boston 2014)

Christiano T., *The Constitution of Equality: Democratic Authority and its Limits* (Oxford University Press, Oxford 2008)

Cizre U., *Democratic Oversight and Reform of The Security Sector in Turkey* (Deutsche Nationalbibliothek, Germany 2005)

Clapham A., et al., *The Oxford Handbook of International Law in Armed Conflict* (Oxford University Press: Oxford 2014)

Clarke A, *Rendition to Torture* (Rutgers university Press, Newbrunswick New Jersey 2012)

Cohen J., *How many people can the earth support* (W.W. Norton & Company, Inc United Kingdom, New York 1995)

Cohen S, *Democracies at war against terrorism: Comparative Perspective* (2nd edn, Palgrave Macmillan Publishers Limited, United Kingdom 2009)

Cole D., et al., *Terrorism and The Constitution: Sacrificing Civil Liberties in The Name of National Security* (3rd edn, The New Press Company Inc, New York 2006)

Colvin M, *Developing Key Privacy Rights* (Hart Publishing, Portland 2002)

Conca K., et al., *Green Planet Blues: Critical Perspective on Global Environmental Politics* (5thedn, Westview Press, Colorado 2015)

Constant A, et al., *International Handbook on the Economics of Migration* (Edward Elgar Publishing Limited, Cheltenham 2013)

Cooper S., et al., Psychology serving humanity: Proceedings of the 30th international congress of psychology (Psychology Press, New York 2014)

Cornelisse G, *Immigration Detention and Human Rights: Rethinking Territorial Sovereignty* (Marinus Nijhoff Publishers, Leiden 2010)

Costigliola F., et al, *Explaining the history of American Foreign relations* (3rd edn Cambridge University Press United States, New York 2016)

Cottey A., *Security in 21st century Europe* (2nd edn Palgrave Macmillan United Kingdom, London 2013)

Council of Europe, *"Apologie Du Terrorisme" and "Incitement to Terrorism"* (Council of Europe Publishing, Strasbourg 2006)

Couvreur P., *The International Court of Justice and the effectiveness of International Law* (Koninklijke Brill nv Incorporates, Netherlands 2016)

Cremer H, *Human Rights and the Protection of Privacy in Tort Law* (Routledge-Cavendish, New York 2010)

Crenshaw M, *The consequences of counterterrorism* (Russell Sage Foundation, New York 2012)

Criminal Justice Handbook Series, *Handbook on Criminal Justice Responses to Terrorism* (United Nations Publication, New York 2009)

Cronin A, et al., *Attacking Terrorism: Elements of a Grand Strategy* (Georgetown University Press, Washington, D.C 2004)

D. Cole, *Enemy aliens: Double standards and constitutional freedoms in the war against terrorism* (1st edn, The New Press, New York 2003)

Dadwal S, et al., *Non-traditional Security Challenges in Asia: Approaches and Responses* (New Delhi: Routledge Taylor & Francis Group 2015)

Danner M, *Spiral: Trapped in the Forever War* (Simon & Schuster Paperbacks, New York 2017)

David C, et al., *"Jousting at windmills": the laws of armed conflict in an age of terror-state actors and nonstate elements* (Columbia University Press, New York 2011)

Davis J, et al., *International handbook of war, torture and terrorism: Perspectives of torture in Great Britain, Northern Ireland, United States, Canada and Australia* (Springer New York, New York 2013)

Dinstein Y, *War, aggression and self-defense* (4th edn Cambridge University Press, London 2005)

Dudziak M, *Wartime: An idea, its history, its consequences* (Oxford University Press, New York 2012)

E. Balabanova, *The Media and Human Rights: The Cosmopolitan Promise* (Routledge Publishers, London 2014)

Eckersley R., *The Green State: Rethinking Democracy and Sovereignty* (The MIT Press, Massachusetts 2004)

Ehlers D, et al., *European fundamental rights and freedoms* (Hubert & Co Gottingen, Germany 2007)

Ehlers D., *European Fundamental Rights and Freedoms* (De Gruyter Recht, Berlin 2007)

Eisenman J., et al., *China and the Developing World: Beijing's Strategy for the Twenty-first Century* (M. E Sharpe Inc, New York 2007)

Emmerson B., et al, *Human Rights and Criminal Justice* (3rd edn Sweet and Maxwell, London 2012)

Etzioni A., et al., *Privacy in A Cyber Age: Policy and Practice* (1st edn, Palgrave Macmillan, New York 2015)

Evans D, *Not an Ordinary Life* (Coogee Creations LLC, Florida 2014)

Evans M, *Just War Theory: A Reappraisal* (Palgrave Macmillan, New York 2006)

F. Burton, et al., *Under Fire: The Untold Story of the Attack in Benghazi* (1st edn St Martin's Press, New York 2013)

Feinberg M., *Sovereignty in the Age of Global Terrorism: The Role of International Organizations* (Brill Nijhoff, Boston 2016)

Fenwick H, *Civil Liberties and Human Rights* (Cavendish Publishing Limited, London 2002)

Fernando H., et al., *National Security and Human Health Implications of Climate Change* (Springer Publishing Company, Netherlands 2011)

Floyd R, et al., *Environmental Security: Approaches and Issues* (1st edn Routledge Publishers, New York 2013)

Floyd R., et al., *Environmental Security: Approaches and Issues* (Routledge: London 2013)

Flynn M, *Screening torture: Media representations of the state of torture and political domination* (Columbia University Press, New York 2012)

Fuller G, *The Telegraph History of The World: An Anthology of The Telegraphs Finest Reporting* (Aurum Press, London 2015)

Gaan N., *Climate Change and International Politics* (Kalpaz Publications, New Delhi 2008)

Gandhi N., *National security: Emerging dimensions and threats* (Pentagon Security International India, New Delhi 2010)

Ganor B, et al., *Hypermedia Seduction of Terrorist Recruiting: NATO Science for Peace and Security Series* (IOS Press, Amsterdam 2007)

Gary C, *International law and the use of force* (3rd edn, Oxford University Press, USA 2008)

Ghosh P, *Migrants Refugees and the stateless in South Asia* (Sage Publications India Pvt Ltd, New Delhi 2016)

Ghosh P, *Migrants, Refugees and the Stateless in South Asia* (Sage Publications, California 2016)

Gibbs L, et al., *Addressing the health impacts of 9-11: Reports and Recommendations to Mayor Michael R. Bloomberg* (Diane Publishing Company, Pennsylvania 2007)

Goodhart M, et al., *Human Rights in the 21st Century: Continuity and Change Since 9/11* (Palgrave Macmillan, New York 2011)

Graber M, *A New Introduction to American Constitutionalism* (Oxford University Press, New York 2015)

Gross E, *The struggle of democracy against terrorism: Lessons from United States, United Kingdom and Israel* (University of Virginia Press, Charlottesville 2006)

Gross O, *The prohibition on torture and the limits of the law* (Oxford University Press, Inc., Sanford Levinson 2004)

Grozdanova M, *What Motivates Suicide Terrorism?* (Grin Publishing, Germany 2016)

Guan A., *Singapore, Asean and Cambodia Conflict 1978-1999* (National University of Singapore Press, Singapore 2013)

Guiora A., *Top ten global justice law review articles* (Oxford University Press, New York 2008)

Harris F., *Global Environmental issues* (2nd edn Wiley Blackwell Publishers, New Jersey 2012)

Harrison B, *Power and Society: An Introduction to The Social Sciences* (12th edn, Cengage Learning, Wadsworth 2010)

Haynes J., et al, *The world politics: International relations and globalization in the 21st century* (Routledge Publishers USA, New York 2013)

Hayworth J., et al., *Whatever it takes: Illegal Immigration, Border Security and The War on Terror* (Regnery Publishing Inc., Washington DC 2006)

Herik L., *Counter-Terrorism Strategies in a Fragmented International Legal Order* (Cambridge University Press, Cambridge 2013)

Heywood A., *Global Politics* (2nd edn Palgrave Macmillan, England 2014)

Hobbes Thomas., *Leviathan or the matter, form and power of a common-wealth ecclesiastical and civil* (Andrew Crooke, London 1961)

Holtzman E, et al., *Cheating Justice: How Bush and Cheney Attacked the Rule of Law, Plotted to Avoid Prosecution and What We Can Do About It* (Beacon Press, Boston 2012)

Hough P, *Understanding global security* (3rd edn, Routledge Publishers, Abingdon 2013)

Howorth J., *Security and Defence Policy in the European Union* (2nd edn Palgrave Macmillan, New York 2014)

Hughes C, et al., *Security studies: A reader* (1st edn, Routledge publisher USA, New York 2011)

Hughes C., et al., *Security studies: A reader* (1st edn, Routledge publisher USA, New York 2011)

Hunt M., *Using Human Rights Law in English Courts* (Hart Publishing, Oxford 1997)

IBP Inc, *Global National Security and Intelligence Agencies Handbook* (1st vol International Business Publications, Washington D.C 2015)

Ignateiff M, *The lesser evil: Political ethics in an age of error* (4th edn, Princeton University Press, New Jersey 2004)

Inc I., *Global national security and intelligence agency handbook: Strategic information and contacts* (International Business Publications United States of America, Washington 2015)

International encyclopedia of the social sciences

International Monetary Fund, *Maldives: Detailed Assessment Report on Anti-Money Laundering and Combating the Financing of Terrorism* (International Monetary Fund Publication Services, Washington D.C 2012)

International Organization for Migration, *'World Migration 2005: Costs and benefits of international migration'* (Academic Foundation press, India 2006)

Jacobs D., World Book Focus on Terrorism (World Book Inc. Chicago 2003)

Jaishanka K., et al., *Global Criminology: Crime and Victimization in a Globalised Era* (Taylor and Francis Group, London)

Jarvis L, et al., Anti-terrorism, Citizenship and Security (Manchester University Press, Manchester 2015)

Jarvis S., *Adorno: A Critical Introduction* (Polity Press and Blackwell Publishers Ltd, New York1998)

Johnson K, et al., *Immigration law and the US-Mexico border: Si se puede?* (University of Arizona Press, Arizona 2011)

Johnson R, et al., *Battles and Leaders of The Civil War: The Tide Shifts* (Castle Books, Tullamarine 1985)

Johnson T, *Power National Security, and Transformational Global Events* (CRC Press, New York 2012)

Jordan A., et al., American *National Security* (6th edn The John Hopkins University Press, Baltimore 2011)

Kan P, *Drug Trafficking and International Security* (Rowman & Littlefield, Lanham 2016)

Kavanagh A, Arguing *about the law* (Routledge Publishers, Abingdon 2009)

Kendall D, *Sociology in Our Time* (11th edn Cengage Learning, Boston 2016)

Khatchadourian H, *The Morality of Terrorism* (Wipf and Stock Publishers, Oregon 2011)

Kim S, et al., *North Korea And Nuclear Weapons: Entering the New Era of Deterrence* (Georgetown University Press, Washington D.C 2017)

Kirshner J, *Globalization and national security* (Routledge Taylor and Francis Group, New York 2013)

Kline R, et al., *Intelligence and the national security strategist: Enduring issues and challenges* (Rowman and Littlefield Publishers Inc, Maryland 2006)

Kline R., et al., *Intelligence and The National Security Strategist: Enduring Issues and Challenges* (Rowan and Littlefield Publishers Inc, Maryland 2006)

Koh J., *Suppressing Terrorist Financing and Money Laundering* (Springer, Germany 2006)

Krajewski M., *Humanitarian intervention and other use of force? Preventive use of force and military actions against non-state actors: Revisiting the right of self-defense in insecure times* (2nd edn, Martinus Nijh of Publishers, Netherlands 2005)

Krieger H., *The Kosovo Conflict and International Law: An Analytical* (Cambridge University Press, Cambridge 2001)

Kyi A., Empowerment for a culture of peace and development: Freedom from fear and other writings (New edn, Penguin Book Publishers, London 2010)

Kyrgyzstan B, *Capacity building in the fight against terrorism* (Netherlands IOS Press BV, Amsterdam 2013)

Langford M., et al, Global Justice, State Duties: *The Extraterritorial Scope of Economic, Social and Cultural Rights in International Law* (Cambridge University Press, New York 2013)

Larsen K, *The Human Rights Treaty Obligation of Peacekeepers* (Cambridge University Press, Cambridge 2012)

Larsen K, *The Human Rights Treaty Obligations of Peacekeepers* (Cambridge University Press, New York 2012)

Legrain P, *Immigrants: Your Country Needs Them* (Princeton University Press, Princeton 2014)

Leo R, et al., *The Miranda Debate: Law, Justice, and Policing* (North-eastern University Press, Boston 1998)

Leo R, *Police Interrogation and American Justice* (Harvard University Press, Massachusetts 2008)

Letsas G., et al., *Current Legal Problems* (Oxford University Press, New York 2010)

Levinson S, *Torture: A collection* (Oxford University Press, New York 2004)

Lewis C, et al., *Counter-Terrorism and the Post-Democratic State* (Edward Elgar Publishing Limited, Cheltenham 2007)

Lokanneta J, *Transnational torture: Law, violence and state power in the United States and India* (New York University Press, New York 2011)

Lombardi M, et al., *Countering Radicalisation And Violent Extremism Among Youths to Prevent Terrorism* (IOS Press Inc, Netherlands 2014)

Londras F, *Detention in the 'war against terror': Can human rights fight back?* (Cambridge University Press, New York 2011)

Lowenthal *M, Intelligence from Secrets to Policy* (7th edn Congressional Quarterly Inc, 2016)

Lucarelli S, et al., *The EU and multilateral security governance* (1st edn, Routledge Publishers, New York 2013)

Ludsin H, *Preventive detention and the democratic state* (Cambridge University Press, India 2016)

Lugar R, et al., *Russia, its Neighbours and an Enlarging NATO: Report of an Independent Task* (Council on Foreign Relations Inc, New York 1997)

Macken C., *Counter-Terrorism and The Detention of Suspected Terrorist* (Routledge Taylor & Francis Group, New York 2013)

Macovei M., *Freedom of Expression: A guide to the implementation of article 10 of the European Convention on Human Rights* (2nd edn, Human Rights Handbooks, Germany 2004)

Macovei M., *The Right to Liberty and the Security of the Person: A Guide to the implementation of Article 5 of the European Convention on Human Rights* (Council of Europe, Germany 2004)

Magsig B., *International Water Law and the Quest for Common Security* (Routledge, New York 2015)

Maniscalco P, et al., *Homeland Security: Principles and Practice of Terrorism Response* (1st edn Jones and Bartlett Publishers LLC, Maryland 2011)

Manwaring M., *Strategic Studies Institute Monograph: The Strategic Logic of the Contemporary Security Dilemma* (Strategic Study Institute, US Army War College 2011)

Mbote P., *Gender, Conflict and Regional Security* (Heinrich Boll Foundation, Nairobi 2004)

McMahon R., et al, *Guide to U.S. Foreign policy: A diplomatic history* (vol 1 SAGE Publications Inc. United States, Los Angeles 2012)

Meese M., et al., *American national security* (7th edn, John Hopkins University Press USA, Maryland 2018)

Metzler H., *County Reports on Terrorism 2007* (Nova Science Publishers, Incorporated, Hauppauge 2010)

Miklaucic M., et al., *Convergence: Illicit Networks and National Security in The Age of Globalization* (National Defense University Press, Washington D.C 2013)

Mill J, *On Liberty* (Broadview press, Canada 1999)

Minnerop P., et al., *World Court Digest 2001-2005* (Springer, New York 2005)

Moeckli D, *Human rights and non-discrimination in the war against terror* (Oxford University Press, New York 2008)

Moran G., *Silencing scientists and scholars in other fields: Power, paradigm controls, peer review and scholarly communication* (Ablex Publishing Corporation, England 1998)

Morgan P., *Security in international politics: Traditional approaches [in] contemporary security studies* (Oxford University Press United States, New York 2007)

Morkuniene J., *Social Philosophy: Paradigm of Contemporary Thinking* (1st edn, The Council for Research in Values and Philosophy, Washington D.C 2004)

Morris C., et al., *Getting A PHD In Law* (Hart Publishing Ltd, Oxford 2011)

Morrison K, et al., *International Handbook of War, Torture, and Terrorism* (Springer, New York 2012)

Moucheboeuf A., *Minority Rights Jurisprudence Digest* (Council of Europe Publishing, Strasbourg Cedex 2006)

Mroz J, *Beyond security: Private perceptions among Arabs and Israelis* (International Peace Academy, New York 1980)

Mroz J., *Beyond security: Private perceptions among Arabs and Israelis* (International Peace Academy, New York 1980)

Mueller K., *Precision and Purpose: Airpower in the Libyan Civil War* (Rand Corporation: Santa Monica 2015)

Murdock E, *Obama Won but Romney Was President: How the Democrats Targeted Electoral College Votes to Win the 2012 President Election* (H.O.T Press, 2012)

Murphy C., *EU Counter-terrorism Law: Pre-Emption and the Rule of Law* (Hart Publishing Ltd, Oxford 2012)

N. Al-Rodhan N., *Neo statecraft and meta-geopolitics: Reconciliation of power, interests and justice in the 21st Century* (LIT VERLAG GmbH & Co. KG. Wien Germany, Zurich 2009)

Nacos B., *Terrorism and Counterterrorism* (5th edn, Taylor and Francis Group, Abingdon 2016)

Neack L., *Elusive Security: States First, People Last* (Rowman & Littlefield Publishers Inc, Maryland 2007)

Neal A, *Security in a Small Nation: Scotland, Democracy, Politics* (Open Book Publishers, Cambridge 2017)

Neocleous M., *Critique of security* (Edinburgh University Press Ltd United Kingdom, Edinburgh 2008)

Neufeld, M. *The Restructuring of International Relations Theory* (Cambridge University Press, Cambridge 1995)

Nnoli O., *National security in Africa: A radical new perspective* (Pan African Centre for Research on Peace and Conflict Resolution (PACREP) Nigeria, Enugu 2006)

Nowak M., *U.N. Covenant on Civil and Political Rights: CCPR Commentary'* (2nd edn, Kehl am Rhein, Engel 2005)

O'Connor Vivienne, et al., *Model Codes for Post-Conflict Criminal Justice Volume 1* (United States Institute of Peace Press, Washington D.C 2007)

Oberleitner G., *Human Rights in Armed Conflict: Law, Practice,* Policy (Cambridge University Press, Cambridge 2015)

Oraa J, *Human rights in states of emergency in International law* (Clarendon Press, Oxford 1992)

Orakhelashvili A., *Collective Security* (Oxford University Press, New York 2011)

Ostreng W, *National and International Environmental Cooperation in the Arctic-the Case of the Northern Sea Route* (Springer Science and Business Media, 2012)

Ostreng W., *National security and international environmental cooperation in the Arctic: The Case of the Northern sea route* (Kluwer Academic Publishers, Netherlands 1999)

P. Paleri, *National security: Imperatives and challenges* (Tata McGraw-Hill Publishing Company Limited India, New Delhi 2008)

P. Thunberg, 'National economic security: Interdependence and vulnerability' in Frans A.M. Alting von Geuseu and Jacques Pelkman (Tilburg: John. F. Kennedy Institute 1982)

Paleri P., *National Security: Imperatives and Challenges* (Tata McGraw-Hill Publishing Company Limited, New Delhi 2008)

Paul T, et al., *Globalization and National Security State* (Oxford University Press, New York 2010)

Pavliuk O, et al., *The Black Sea Region: Cooperation and Security Building* (Routledge, New York 2016)

Payan T, *The Three US-Mexico Border Walls: Drugs, Immigration and Border Security* (2nd edn Praeger Security International, California 2016)

Peer S., et al., *The EU Charter of Fundamental Rights: A Commentary* (Hart Publishing, Oxford 2014)

Peters D., *Constrained balancing: The EU's security policy* (Palgrave Macmillan United States, New York 2010)

Pongsawat P., *Border Partial Citizenship, Border Towns, and Thai-Myanmar Cross Border Development: Case Studies at the Thai Border Towns* (University of California Berkeley Press, Berkeley 2007)

Quille G, *The Nordic countries and the European Security and Defence Policy: The impact of EU capability targets and operational demands on defence concepts and planning* (1st edn Oxford University Press, New York 2006)

R. Budania, *India's national security dilemma: The Pakistan factor and India's policy Response* (Indus Publishing Company India, New Delhi 2001)

R. Fawn R., *Globalising the regional, Regionalising the global* (Cambridge University Press United Kingdom, Cambridge 2009)

Ramage S, *Privacy-Law of Civil Liberties* (iUniverse Inc. Lincoln 2007)

Ramraj V., et al., *Global Anti-Terrorism Law and Policy* (Cambridge University Press, Cambridge 2012)

Rashid A, '*Descent into chaos: The United States and the failure of nation building in Pakistan, Afghanistan and Central Asia* (Penguin Group, New York 1988)

Reed E., *Civil Liberties, National Security and Prospects for Consensus: Legal, Philosophical and Religious Perspectives* (Cambridge University Press, New York 2012)

Richelson J, *The US intelligence community* (4th edn, Westview Press, Colorado 1999)

Ripsman N., et al., *Globalisation and The National Security State* (Oxford University Press, New York 2010)

Roach K., The *9/11 effect: Comparative Counter-terrorism* (Cambridge University Press, New York 2011)

Robb J., *Brave New War: The Next Stage of Terrorism and The End of Globalisation* (John Wiley & Sons Inc, New Jersey 2007)

Rodley N, *The definitions of torture in International Law* (Oxford University Press, London 2002)

Ronis S., *Economic Security Neglected Dimension of National Security* (National Defense University Press, Washington DC 2011)

Ronis S., *Economic Security: Neglected Dimension of National Security?* (National Defense University Press, Washington D.C 2011)

Room J., *Defining national security: the non-military aspect* (Council on Foreign Relations Press USA, New York 1993)

Rose D, *Guantanamo: The War on Human Rights* (New Press, New York 2006)

Roy D., *The new security agenda in the Asia-Pacific region* (Macmillan Press Ltd United Kingdom, London 1997)

Rudolph C., *National Security and Immigration: Policy Development in The United States and Western Europe Since 1945* (Stanford University Press, California 2006)

Ryder N., *The Financial War on Terrorism: A Review of Counter-Terrorists Financing Strategies Since 2001* (Routledge, New York 2015)

Sageman M, *Leaderless jihad: Terror networks in the twenty-first century* (University of Pennsylvania, Philadelphia 2008)

Sajo A, Militant *democracy* (Eleven International Publishing, Netherlands 2004)

Samaha J, *Criminal Procedure* (10th edn Cengage Learning, Boston 2016)

Samaha J, *Criminal Procedure* (Cengage Learning, Boston 2015)

Sattherwaite M, et al., '*Gender, national security and counter-terrorism: Human rights perspective*' (Routledge publishers, Abingdon 2013)

Saulnier F., et al., *The Practical Guide to Humanitarian Law* (Rowman & Littlefield Publishers, New York 2008)

Scarry E, *The body in pain* (1st edn, Oxford University Press, Inc., New York 1985)

Scharia D., *Judicial Review of National Security* (Oxford University Press, New York 2015)

Schellnhuber H., *Climate Change as a Security Risk* (Earthscan, London 2010)

Schilder K., et al., *Civilian Perspective or Security Strategy? European Development Policy Confronting New Challenges in Foreign and Security Policy* (Friedrich-Ebert-Stiftung, Germany 2005)

Schmitt M., et al., Yearbook of International Humanitarian Law (Cambridge University Press, London 2011)

Schmitt M., et al., *Yearbook of International Humanitarian Law 2011*(Cambridge University Press, Cambridge 2012)

Sharma R., *Afghanistan and Central Asia'* (1st edn, Viking Penguin Group, New York 2008)

Shaw M., Transnational Organised Crime in Africa: An Overview from Six Governments (Sage Publishers, Los Angeles 2013)

Shen S., *Multidimensional Diplomacy of Contemporary China* (Rowman and Littlefield Publishers Inc, Maryland 2010)

Shepard W., *Islam: The E-book* (Journal of Buddhist Ethics Online Books Ltd, Utah 2009)

Shetty S, et al., *The Baltic States, NATO and Non-strategic nuclear weapons in Europe* (Stephen Austin and Sons Ltd., United Kingdom 2012)

Sidhu W., et al., *The United Nations and Regional security: Europe and Beyond* (Lynne Rienner Publishers Inc, London 2003)

Singh J, *National Security: An Outline of Our Concerns* (Lancer Publishers and Distributors, India 1996)

Singh L., *National security problem in India: A case study of the insurgency problem in Nagaland and Manipur* (A.P.H Publishing Corporation India, New Delhi 2000)

Skerker M, *An Ethics of Interrogation* (University of Chicago Press, London 2010)

Slapper G., et al., *The English Legal System* (Routledge Taylor & Francis, New York 2017)

Smith D, *The Baltic States and Their Regional: New Europe or Old?* (Rodopi, Amsterdam 2005)

Smith P., *Terrorism and Violence in Southeast Asia: Transnational Challenges to States* (Taylor and Francis Group, London 2015)

Smith S., et al., *Foreign Policy: Theories. Actors. Cases* (1st edn, Oxford University Press USA, New York 2008)

Snow D, *National Security* (Routledge Taylor & Francis Group 2017)

Solis G, *The Law of Armed Conflict: International Humanitarian Law in War* (Cambridge University Press, New York 2016)

Sottiaux S., *Terrorism and the limitation of rights: The ECHR and the US Constitution* (Hart Publishing USA, Portland 2008)

Spalek B., *Ethnicity and Crime: A Reader* (Open University Press, England 2008)

Staniforth A, *Routledge Companion to UK Counter-Terrorism* (Routledge Taylor& Francis Group, London 2013)

Stec S., et al, *Energy and Environmental Challenges to Security* (Springer Publishers, Netherlands 2009)

Stephen, D. et al, *Counterterrorism Law* (Aspen Publishers, New York 2007)

Stone J, *Interrogation: World War II, Vietnam, and Iraq* (NDIC Press, Washington, D.C 2010)

Stritzke W, et al., *Terrorism and Torture: An interdisciplinary perspective* (Cambridge University Press, London 2013)

Takahashi Y, *The margin of appreciation doctrine and the principle of proportionality in the jurisprudence of the ECHR* (Oxford University Printing Press, New York 2002)

Tang S, et al., *Asia-Pacific Security Cooperation: National Interest and Regional Order* (ME Sharpe, 2004)

Thakur R., et al., *International Commissions and The Power of Ideas* (United Nations University Press, New York 2006)

Thiel M, *Militant democracy principle in modern democracy* (Ashgate Publishing Limited, Surrey 2009)

Thillaye B., *Politico-Strategic Forecasting* (MA thesis, Royal Military College of Canada 1972)

Tobin K., et al., *Doing Educational Research: A Handbook* (Sense Publishers, Rotterdam 2006)

Torres T, 'How National Security Limits Speech in Four Anglophone States' (Seton Hall Law eRepository 2013)

Tripathy P, *Contemporary Social Problems and the Law* (A.P.H Publishing Corporation, New Delhi 2000)

Tucker S., *US Conflicts in the 21st Century: Afghanistan War, Iraq War and the War on Terror* (Praeger Publishers, California 2015)

Veldhuis T, *Prisoner Radicalization and Terrorism Detention Policy: Institutionalized fear or evidenced-based policy making?* (Routledge, New York 2016)

Ventre D, *Information Warfare* (Iste Ltd.& John Wiley and Sons Inc, New York 2016)

Viljoen F, *International Human Rights Law in Africa* (Oxford University Press, Oxford 2012)

Waldron J, *Torture, terror and trade-offs: Philosophy of the White House* (Oxford University Press, New York 2010)

Walker C., *Terrorism and The Law* (Oxford University Press, New York 2011)

Watson C., *US National Security: A Reference Handbook* (ABC-CLIO Inc, Santa Barbara 2002)

Watson R, *White House Studies Compendium, Volume 4* (Nova Science Publishers Inc, New York 2007)

Webber D., *Preventive Detention of Terror Suspects: A New Legal Framework* (Routledge Taylor & Francis, New York 2016)

Webley L, et al., *Complete Public Law: Texts, Cases, and Materials* (Oxford University Press, Oxford 2015)

Weiner J., *Referral of Iranian President Ahmadinejad on the Charge of Incitement to Commit Genocide* (The Jerusalem Centre for Public Affairs, Jerusalem 2007)

Weisband E, et al., *Political Culture and The Making of Modern Nation-States* (Paradigm Publishers, Colorado 2015)

Weller M, *The Oxford Handbook of the Use of Force in International Law* (1st edn, Oxford University Press, UK 2015)

West D., et al., *Reality check: The unreported good news about America* (Regnery Publishing Inc, Washington DC 2008)

White N, *Democracy Goes to War: British Military Deployments under International Law* (Oxford University Press, Oxford 2009)

Whittaker D, *Counterterrorism and human rights* (Routledge Taylor and Francis Group, New York 2013)

Wiener J., et al, *International relations* (EOLSS Publishers Co Ltd United Kingdom, Oxford 2009)

Wiktorowicz Q., *Radical Islam rising: Muslin extremism in the West* (Rowman & Littlefield Publishers Inc., Lanham 2005)

Wilkinson P, *Terrorism and the liberal state* (New York University Press, New York 1986)

Wilkinson P, *Terrorism versus Democracy: The liberal state response* (Frank Cass Publishers, London 2001)

Wilkinson P, *Terrorism Versus Democracy: The Liberal State Response* (3rd edn Routledge, Abingdon Oxon 2011)

Winkler T., et al., *Combating Terrorism and Its Implication for The Security Sector* (DCAF & The Swedish National Defence College, Stockholm 2005)

Wisner B., et al., *At Risk: Natural Hazards Peoples' Vulnerability and Disasters* (2nd edn Routledge, London 2004)

Wolfendale J, *Torture and the Military Profession* (Palgrave Macmillan, New York 2007)

Wolfson M., *The Political Economy of War and Peace* (Springer Publishers, New York 2012)

Womack B., *China and Vietnam: The Politics of Asymmetry* (Cambridge University Press, Cambridge 2006)

Youde J, *Global Health Governance* (Polity Press, Cambridge 2013)

Youngs R., Climate Change and European Security (Taylor and Francis Group, London 2015)

Zartner D, Courts, *Codes, and Custom: Legal Tradition and State Policy toward International Human Rights and Environmental Law* (Oxford University Press, Oxford 2014)

Zhou M, *Contemporary Chinese America: Immigration, Ethnicity and Community Transformation* (Temple University Press, Philadelphia 2009)

JOURNAL

Ackerman B., 'The emergency constitution' (2004) vol. 113 Yale Law Journal

Adamson F., 'Crossing borders: International Migration and National Security' (2006) vol 31(1) International security

Akhtar Z., 'Malicious communications, media platforms and legal sanctions' (2014) 20(6) Computer and Telecommunications Law Review

Alarid M., Recruitment and Radicalisation: The Role of Social Media and New Technology (2016) Centre for Complex Operations

Aloupi N., 'The Right to Non-Intervention and Non-Interference' (2015) vol 4(3) Cambridge Journal of Comparative and International Law

Amet A., 'Terrorism and international law: Cure the underlying problem not just the symptom' (2013) vol 19 (1) International and comparative Law

Anderson D., 'Control Orders in 2011: Final Report of the Independent Reviewer on the Prevention of Terrorism Act 2005' (2005) The Stationery Office

Anderson S., et al., 'Climate change as a national security threat' (2012) The Centre for Climate and Security

Arai-Yokoi Y., 'Grading scale of degradation: Identifying the threshold of degrading treatment or Punishment under article 3 ECHR.' (2003) vol 21(3) Netherlands Quarterly Human Rights

Arbour L., 'In our name and on our behalf' (2006) vol 55(3) International and Comparative Law Quarterly

Arkin R., 'The case for ethical autonomy in unmanned systems' (2010) vol 9(4) Journal of Military Ethics

Asif N., 'United we stand, divided we all: Terrorism as an international crime versus terrorism as a transnational crime' (2016) vol1(1) Birmingham Student Law Review

Axworthy L., 'Human security: Safety for people in a changing world' (2007) Centre for Peace and Development Studies

Bailes A., et al., 'Regional Security Cooperation in The Early 21st Century' (1992) In Conference on Interaction

Bailin A., 'Criminalising free speech' (2011) vol 9 Criminal Law Review

Baldwin D., "The Concept of Security" (1997) vol 23 Review of International Studies

Balkin J., 'Digital speech and Democratic culture: A theory of freedom of expression for the information society' (2004) vol 79(1) New York University Law Review

Banisar D., 'Speaking of terror' (2008) Media and Information Society Division, Council of Europe

Barnett M., 'Extraordinary rendition: International law and the prohibition of torture' (2008) Law and Government Division Parliament of Canada

Bassiouni M., 'Challenges facing a rule of law-oriented world order' (2010) vol 8(1) Santa Clara Journal of International Law

Bellany I., "Towards a theory of national security" (1981) vol 29 (1) Political Studies

Bem K., et al., 'A Price Too High: The Cost of Australia's Approach to Asylum Seekers' (2007) Oxfam Australia

Benhabib S., 'Borders, boundaries and citizenship' (2005) vol 38(4) Political Science and Politics

Benjamin P., 'Green wars making environmental degradation a national security issue puts peace and security at risk' (2000) No. 369 Policy Analysis

Bennoune K., 'Terror/Torture' (2008) vol 26(1) Berkeley Journal of International Law

Bernstein S., 'The Responsibility to Protect After Libya: Humanitarian Prevention as Customary International Law' (2012) vol 38(1) Brooklyn Journal of International Law

Bertrand D., et al., 'Preventing human rights violations in places of detention: A European initiative' (1995) vol1(3) Health and Human Rights

Bhoumik A., 'Democratic responses to terrorism: A comparative study of the United States, Israel and India' (2004) Paper 287 Bepress Legal Serie

Bigo D., et al., 'The EU counterterrorism policy Responses to the attacks in Paris towards an EU security and liberty agenda' (2015) No 81 CEPS Paper in liberty and security in Europe

Biswas N, 'Is the environment a security threat? Environment Security beyond securitization' (2011) vol XX (1) International Affairs Review

Blank L., 'A square peg in a round hole: Stretching law of war detention too far' (2011) vol 64(1) Rutgers Law Review

Boin A., 'Managing Transboundary Crisis: What Role for the European Union' (2008) vol 10(1) International Studies Review

Bollingtoft D., et al., 'Under the guise of national security: Surveillance, Snowden and the challenges to democracy' (2014) Roskilde University: Department of Society and Globalization

Brandon B., 'Terrorism, Human Rights and the Rule of Law: 120 years of the UK legal response to terrorism' (2004) Criminal Law Review

Brooks B., 'Law enforcement's role in US counterterrorism strategy' (2010) vol 83(2) The Police Journal

Bruderlein C., 'People's Security as a new measure of Global Stability' (2001) vol 83 (842) International Review of the Red Cross

Bucci S., et al., 'After Hurricane Sandy: Time to Learn and Implement the Lessons in Preparedness, Response and Resilience' (2013) Special Report No.144 The Heritage Foundation

Buyse A., 'Dangerous expressions: ECHR, violence and free speech' (2014) vol 63(2) International and Comparative Law Reform

Cannizzaro E., 'The role of proportionality in the law of international countermeasures' (2001) vol 12(5) European Journal of International Law

Cassel D., 'Pretrial and preventive detention of suspected terrorists: Options and constraints under international law' (2008) vol 98(3) The Journal of Criminal Law and Criminology

Chau A., 'Security Community and Southeast Asia: Australia, the US and ASEAN's Counter-Terror Strategy' (2008) vol 48(4) Asian Survey

Chesterman S., 'The spy who came in from the cold war: Intelligence and international law' (2007) vol. 27(4) Michigan Journal of International Law

Cohen-Jonathan G., 'Television without frontiers and Human Rights in Europe' (1992) International Business Law Journal

Cole D., 'Where liberty lies: Civil society and individual lies after 9/11' (2012) vol 57 Wayne Law Review

Conway M., 'Terrorism and the internet: New Media-New threat'? (2006) vol 59(2) Parliamentary Affairs

Conway M., 'Terrorists "use" of the internet and fighting back' (2006) vol19 Information and Security

Coupland R., 'Security, insecurity and health' (2007) 85 Bulletin of the World Health Organisation

Cram I, 'Failing Justice Brennan quest? Anticipating terrorism risks and the US Supreme Court' (2013) (1) Public Law

Cram I., 'Beyond Lockean Majoritarianism? Emergency, Institutional Failure and the UK Constitution' (2010) vol 10 (3) Human Rights Law Review

Cram I., 'Failing Justice Brennan's quest? Anticipating terrorism risk and the US Supreme Court' (2013) (1) Public Law Journal

Cuyckens H., Revisiting the Law of Occupation (Koninklijke Brill NV Incorporates, The Netherlands 2017)

Daalder I., et al., 'NATO's Victory in Libya: The Right Way to Run an Intervention' (2012) vol 91(2) Foreign Affairs

Danziger Y., 'Changes in methods of freezing funds of terrorist organizations since 9/11: A comparative analysis' (2012) vol 15(2) Journal of Money Laundering Control

Davis M., 'The moral justifiability of torture and other cruel, inhuman and degrading treatment' (2005) vol19 (2) International Journal of Applied Philosophy

Day M., 'Frankfurt airport shooter shouted 'Allahu Akhbar' before opening fire' (2011) The Telegraph

De Vos C., 'Mind the gap: Purpose, pain, and the difference between torture and inhuman treatment' (2007) vol 14(2) Human Rights Brief

Denbeaux M., et al., 'National security deserves better: "odd" recidivism numbers undermine the Guantanamo policy debate' (2013) vol 43 Seton Hall Law Review

Dershowitz A., 'The torture warrant: A response to Professor Strauss' (2003) vol 48 New York Law School Law Review

Deudney D., 'The Case Against Linking Environmental Degradation and National Security' (1990) vol 19(3) Journal of International Studies

Dominik-Bachmann S., et al., 'Control orders post 9/11 and human rights in the United Kingdom, Australia and Canada: A Kafkaesque dilemma' (2010) vol 15(2) Deakin Law Review

Downs D., et al., 'Predicting the importance of the freedom of speech and the perceived harm of hate speech' (2012) vol 42(2) Journal of Applied Social Psychology

Draper A., et al., 'Media in the UK' (2013) Hong Kong University, Faculty of Social Sciences

Duffy H., The 'war on terror' and the framework of International Law (2nd edition United Kingdom: Cambridge University Press., 2015)

Dupont A., et al., 'Australia's National Security Priorities: Addressing Strategic Risk in A Globalised World' (2012) vol 66(1) Australian Journal of International Affairs

Eatwell T., 'Selling the pass: Habeas corpus, diplomatic relations and the protection of liberty and security of persons detained abroad' (2013) vol 62(3) International and Comparative Law Quarterly

Ekaratne S., 'Redundant restriction: The UK's offence of glorifying terrorism' (2010) vol 23 Harvard Human Rights Journal

Eppinger M., 'Reality check: Detention in the war on terror' (2013) vol 62(2) Catholic University Law Review

Etzioni A., 'A Liberal Communitarian Approach to Security Limitations on The Freedom of The Press' (2014) vol 22(4) William &Mary Bill of Rights Journal

Etzioni A., 'A liberal communitarian conception of privacy' (2012) vol 29 (3) Journal of Computer and Information Law

Etzioni A., 'The standing of the public interest' (2014) vol (20) Barry Law Review

EU Focus, Stronger EU action to tackle violent radicalization leading to terrorism (2016) vol 345 EU Focus

Facchini G., et al., 'From individual attitudes towards migrants to migration policy outcomes: Theory and evidence' (2008) vol 23(56) Economic Policy

Farah D., 'The League of Arab States and regional security: Towards an Arab security Community?' (2012) vol 39(2) British Journal of Middle East Studies

Fenwick H., 'The Human Rights Act or a British Bill of Rights: Creating a downgrading recalibration of rights against the counter-terror backdrop' (2012) Public Law

Field A., 'New Terrorism: Revolution or Evolution?' (2009) vol 7(2) Political Studies Review

Fillippo M., 'Terrorist Crimes and International Co-operation: Critical Remarks on The Definition and Inclusion of Terrorism in The Category of International Crimes' (2008) vol 19(3) The European Journal of International Law

Fiona A., 'Crossing borders: "International migration and national security"' (2006) vol 31(1) International security

Flynn E., 'Counterterrorism and Human Rights: The View from The United Nations' (2005) vol 1 European Human Rights Law Review

Foot R., 'The United Nations, Counter Terrorism and Human Rights: Institutional Adaptation and Embedded Ideas' (2007) vol 29 (2) Human Rights Quarterly

Foster S., 'Are we becoming afraid of free speech' (2013) vol 18(1) Coventry Law Journal

Gathii J., 'Torture, Extra-Territoriality, Terrorism and International Law' (2004) vol 67 Albany Law Review

Gentili G., 'An absolute ban on deportation of foreign citizens to countries where torture or ill treatment is a genuine risk' (2010) vol 8(2) International Journal of constitutional Law

George E., 'Whose line in the sand: Can environmental protection and national security coexist, and can the government be held liable for not attaining this goal?' (2003) vol 27(3) William & Mary Environmental Law and Policy Review

Geyer F., 'Fruit of the poisonous tree: Member states' indirect use of extraordinary rendition and the EU counterterrorism strategy' (2007) Centre for European Policy Studies Working Document

Gheciu A., 'Security institutions as agents of socialization? NATO and "The New Europe"' (2005) vol 59(4) International Organization

Gibbs C, 'Securing the nation: Radicalism and security in 1970s Britain' (2013) Research Paper, University of York

Gill T., et al., 'Anticipatory self-defense in the cyber context' (2013) vol 89(1) International Law Studies

Goderis B., et al., 'Human rights violation after 9/11 and the role of constitutional constraint' (2012) vol 40(1) The Journal of Legal Studies

Gordon E., 'Freedom of expression and its limits in blogs as means of contemporary communication' (2013) vol 37(4) Teme: CasopiszaDrustveneNauke

Great Britain Parliament, House of Lords, Journals of the House of Lords Volume 240 (HM Stationery Office, London 2006)

Great Britain Parliament: House of Lords, House of Commons, Joint Committee on Human Rights., Allegations of UK complicity in torture (2008-09) Twenty-third report of session

Greer S., 'Human Rights and The Struggle Against Terrorism in The United Kingdom' (2008) vol 2 European Human Rights Law Review

Gross O., 'Are torture warrants warranted? Pragmatic absolutism and official disobedience' (2004) vol 88 Minnesota Law Review

Guiora A., 'Targeted killing: When proportionality gets all out of proportion' (2012) vol 45(1) Case Western Reserve Journal of International Law

Guzman A., 'Climate is a security issue' (2012) Legal Planet, The Environmental Law and Policy

H. Lovell, et al., 'Converging agenda's? Energy and climate change policies in the UK' (2009) vol 27 (1) Environment and Planning C: Government and Policy

Hafetz J., 'Detention without end? Re-examining the indefinite confinement of terrorism suspects through the lens of criminal sentencing' (2014) vol 61 University of California Los Angeles Law Review

Hafetz J., 'Redefining state power and individual rights in the war on terrorism' (2012) vol 46(3) Valparaiso University Law Review

Hafetz J., 'Torture, judicial review and the regulation of custodial interrogations' (2007) vol 62(3) NYU Annual Survey of American Law

Hague Yearbook of International Law-Annuaire De La Haye De Driot International (Koninklijke Brill NV Incorpora44tes, The Netherlands 2012)

Hammond K., National defense authorization Act and the unbound authority to detain: A call to congress (2013) vol 22 Southern California Interdisciplinary Law Journal

Haren F., 'The global environmental challenge: Is the developed world up to it?' (2003) vol 5(1) Environmental Law Review

Haris D., 'Immigration and National Security: the illusion of safety through local law enforcement action' (2011) vol 28(2) Arizona Journal of International and Comparative Law

Hathaway O., et al., 'Tortured reasoning: The intent to torture under international and domestic law' (2012) vol 52 Virginia Journal of International Law

Henning V., 'Anti-terrorism Crime and Security Act 2001: Has the United Kingdom made a valid derogation from the European Convention on Human Rights' (2002) vol 17(6) American University International Law Review

Herz J., 'Idealist internationalism and the security dilemma' (1950) vol 2(2) World Politics

Hinnen T., The cyber front in the war against terrorism: Curbing terrorist use of the internet (2004) vol 5(5) The Columbia Science and Technology Law Review

Hoffman B., 'Rethinking Terrorism and Counterterrorism Since 9/11' (2002) vol 25(5) Studies in Conflict and Terrorism

Hope D., 'Torture' (2004) vol 53 (4) International and Comparative Law quarterly

Imoedemhe O., 'Unpacking the tension between the African Union and the international criminal court: A way forward' (2015) vol 23(1) African Journal of International and Comparative Law

Innes M., 'A Destructive Influence? "Prevent-ing" Problems and Countering Violent Extremism Policy in Practice' (2017) vol 51(2) Law and Society Review

ısaac K., 'A regime in need of balance: The UN counterterrorism regimes of security and human rights' (2013) vol 4 University of Miami National Security and Armed Conflict Law Review

Jack S., 'One World, Rival Theories' (2004) vol 1(145) Foreign Policy

Jacobsen J., et al., 'East Africa: Regional Security organizations and dynamics' (2012) Danish Institute for International Studies

Jadhav J., et al., 'Views of medical students on torture in Ahmadabad city' (2013) vol 5 (7) International Journal of Current Research and Review

Jividen D., 'It Takes a Region: A Proposal for An Alternative Regional Approach to UN Collective Force Humanitarian Intervention' (1999) 10 United States Air Force Academic Journal of Legal Studies

Jody R., Cyber war v Cyber stability (2009) Paper for the 42nd Session World Federation of Scientists International Seminars on Planetary Emergencies

John A., et al., 'Controlling international terrorism: Alternatives palatable and unpalatable' (1982) vol 463 The Annals of American Academy

Jopling L., 'Chemical, biological, radiological or nuclear (CBRN) detection: A technological overview' (2005) Special Report to NATO Parliamentary Assembly

Keller H., et al., 'State Security v Freedom of Expression: Legitimate Fight against Terrorism or Suppression of Political Opposition?' (2010) vol 10(1) Human Rights Law Review

Kerwin D., 'The use and misuse of 'National Security' rationale in crafting US refugee and immigration policies' (2005) vol 17(4) International Refugee Law

King H., 'Extraterritorial human rights obligations of state' (2009) vol 9(4) Human Rights Law Review Elliot M., 'United Kingdom: The "war on terror" UK style-the detention and deportation of terrorist suspects' (2010) vol 8(1) International Journal of Constitutional Law

Kirgis F., 'Some proportionality issues raised by Israel's use of armed force in Lebanon' (2006) vol 10(20) American Society of International Law

Kochenov D., et al., 'Monitoring and enforcement of the rule of law in the EU: Rhetoric and reality' (2015) vol11(3) European Constitutional Law Review

Kohlmann E., 'Homegrown terrorists: Theory and cases in the war on terror's newest front' (2008) vol 618(1) The ANNALS of the American Academy of Political and Social Science

Krickovic A., 'All Politics Is Regional": Emerging Powers and The Regionalisation of Global Governance' (2015) vol 21(4) Regional Governance

Kwasi T., et al., 'African union's new security agenda: Is Africa closer to a pax-pan Africana' (2005) vol 60(4) International Journal

Lanteigne M., 'In Medias Res: The development of the Shanghai Co-operation Organization as a security community' (2006/2007) vol79(4) Pacific Affairs, University of British Columbia

Lee S., 'Inherent right of self-defense through the lens of 2010 Cheonan attack' (2013) vol 216 Military Law Review

Leffler M., "National Security" (1990) vol 77 (1) The Journal of America History

Levy M., 'Is the environment a national security issue?' (1995) vol 20(2) International Security

Liff A., et al., "Racing toward tragedy? China's rise, military competition in the Asia Pacific and the security dilemma" (2014) vol 39 (2) International Security

Londras F, 'International decision: Saadi v Italy' (2008) vol 102(3) The American Journal of International Law

Longhi S., et al., 'A meta-analytic assessment of the effect of immigration on wages' (2005) vol19(3) Journal of Economic Surveys

Loyka S., et al., 'Protecting your community from terrorism: The strategies for local law enforcement series' (2005) vol. 4 Police Executive Research Forum, US Department of Justice office of community oriented policing services

Luciani G., 'The economic content of security' (1989) vol 8(2) Journal of Public Policy

Luciani G., 'The economic content of security' (1989) vol 8(2) Journal of Public Policy

Lumina C., 'Counterterrorism legislation and the protection of human rights: A survey of selected international law practice' (2007) vol 7(1) African Human Rights Law Journal

Lumina C., 'Counterterrorism legislation and the protection of human rights: A survey of selected international law practice' (2007) vol 7(1) African Human Rights Law Journal

Macovei M., 'The Right to liberty and the security of the person: A guide to the implementation of Article 5 of the European Convention on Human Rights' (2002) Human Rights Handbook

Maher J., 'The Europa World Yearbook 2008' (Taylor and Francis Group, New York 2008)

Mahmud H., 'Human security or national security: The problems and prospects of the norm of human security' (2008) vol1(4) Journal of Politics and Law

Maio, 'The historical evolution of the arguments against torture and the history of human rights' (2000) vol 46 World Medical Journal

Makinda S., 'Sovereignty and global security' (1998) vol 29(3) Sage Journals

Marino C., 'Freedom of expression and the internet' (2013) Inter American Commission on Human Rights

Marong C., 'Protecting the public? Challenging the indefinite preventive detention of non-citizens' (2014) vol 3(1) Journal of Law and Jurisprudence

Martin L., 'Can there be national security in an insecure age?' (1983) Vol 60(3) Encounter

Martin L., 'Can there be national security in an insecure age?' (1983) vol 60(3) Encounter

Mathieu R., 'Defence against terrorism: What kind of co-operation between NATO and the EU?' (2006) vol X11(23) Agenda Internacional

McCulloch J., 'Pre-Crime and Counter-Terrorism: Imagining Future Crime on the 'War on Terror'' (2009) British vol 49(5) Journal of Criminology

Mccullock J., 'War at home: National Security Arrangements Post 11 September 2011' (2002) vol 27(2) Alternative Law Journal

McFarlane J., 'Regional and international cooperation in tackling transnational crime, terrorism, and the problems of disrupted states' (2005) vol 12(4) Journal of Financial Crime

McGuire K., et al., 'State of the union report: A road map addressing reform possibilities based upon a comparative analysis of the legal regulation of hate speech and hate crime' (2013) Central Lancashire online Knowledge

Mckeever D., 'The Human Rights Act and Anti-Terrorism in the UK: One Great Leap Forward by the Parliament, but are the Court able to slow the steady Retreat that has followed?' (2010) vol 110 Public Law Journal

McNeal G., 'The Status Bias and Counterterrorism Detention' (2011) vol 101(3) Journal of Criminal Law and Criminology

McNeal G., 'The status quo bias and counterterrorism detention' (2011) vol 101 (3) The Journal of Criminal Law and Criminology

Megret F., "War'? Legal semantics and the move to violence' (2002) vol13(2) European Journal of International Law

Meyerrose A., 'Possible cause for the increased susceptibility of radicalization among British and American Muslims' (2012) Department of International Studies Rhodes College Memphis Tennessee

Michaelsen C., 'Derogating from International Human Rights Obligations in the War Against Terrorism'? A British/Australian perspective' (2005) vol17 (1-2) Terrorism and Political Violence

Michaelson C., 'Derogating from international human rights obligations in the 'War Against Terrorism'? A British/Australian perspective' (2005) vol 17(1-2) Terrorism and Political Violence

Michaelson C., 'The renaissance of non-refoulement? The Othman (Abu Qatada) decision of European Court of Human rights' (2012) vol 61(3) International and comparative Law Quarterly

Middleton B., 'Rebalancing, Reviewing or Rebranding the treatment of terrorists' suspects: The counterterrorism review 2011' (2011) vol 75(3) Journal of Criminal Law

Middleton B., 'Terrorism prevention and investigation measures: Constitutional evolution not revolution?' (2013) vol 77(6) The Journal of Criminal Law

Mikhaylova A., 'Region in The National Security System of Russia' (2015) vol 1(1) Social and Economic Geography

Miller P., 'Torture approval in comparative perspective' (2011) vol 12(4) Human Rights Review

Mohammed Nia M., 'From Old to New Terrorism: The Changing Nature of International Security' (2010) vol 1 (18) Globality Studies Journal

Moller B., 'The African union as security actor: African solutions to African problems?' (2009) Working paper no.59 Regional and Global Axes of Conflict., Danish Institute of International Studies

Moore C., 'The world spins madly on: How the P5 caused a paradigm shift in norm diffusion' (2013) Social Science Research Network

Moore D., 'Reasonable provocation: Distinguishing the vigilant from the vigilante in self-defense law' (2013) vol 78(4) Brooklyn Law Review

Murithi T., 'The African Union's Evolving Role in Peace Operations: The African Union Mission in Burundi, The African Union Mission in Sudan, The African Union Mission in Somalia' (2008) vol 17(1) African Security Review

Murphy S., 'The doctrine of preemptive self-defense' (2005) vol 50(3) Villanova Law Review 699

Murray C., 'Out of the shadows: The courts and the United Kingdom's malfunctioning International counter-terrorism partnership' (2013) vol 18(2) Journal of conflict and security law

Mylonaki E., et al., 'An Assessment of UK anti-terrorism strategy and the human rights implications associated with its implementation' (2011) Journal on terrorism and security analysis

Nick G., 'Enforcing the London 2012 airspace restrictions: Lessons arising from the "lethal force option' (2014) vol 2 European Human Rights Law Review

Nielson C., 'Preventing disorder and protecting private and family life: Case Comment' (2011) vol 70 (1) Cambridge Law Journal

O'Boyle M., 'Emergency government and derogation under the ECHR' (2016) Law Society of England and Wales

O'Connel M., 'Lawful self-defense to terrorism' (2002) vol 63(889) University of Pittsburg Law Review

O'Connell M., 'Affirming the ban on harsh interrogation' (2005) vol 66(6) Ohio State Journal

Ogunfolu A., et al., 'I have a drone: The implications of American drone policy for Africa and international humanitarian law' (2015) vol 23(1) African Journal of international and comparative law

Owen E, 'State security vs. human rights: Finding a proportionate balance', (2010) E-International Relations

Ozturk A., 'The war on terror or the war on civil liberties: the state, the society and the civil liberties since 2001' (2010) vol 6(22) Review of International Law and Politics

Papademetriou D., et al., 'Migration and economic downturn: What to expect in the European Union' (2009) Transatlantic Council on immigration, Migration Policy Institute

Parker E., 'Implementation of the UK Terrorism Act 2006-The relationship between counterterrorism law, free speech and the Muslim community in the United Kingdom versus the United States' (2007)

Peterson R., et al., 'Exploring the implications of the internet for consumer marketing' (1997) vol 25(4)

Piazza J., et al., 'Transnational terror and human rights' (2009) vol 53(1) International Studies Quarterly

Plache B., 'Soldiers for democracy: Karl Lowenstein, John H Herz, militant democracy and the defense of democratic states' (Virginia Commonwealth University Theses and Dissertations Paper 2995, 2013)

Podesta J., et al., 'The security implication of climate change' (2007) vol 31(1) The Washington Quarterly

Poling K, 'Protecting freedom of expression in times of terrorism: A comparison of United States, Germany and South Korea' (2014) Law School Student Scholarship Paper

Prieto D., 'War About Terror: Civil Liberties and National Security After 9/11' (2009) Council on Foreign Relations

Prieto D., 'War about terror: Civil liberties and national security after 9/11' (2009) Council On Foreign Relations

Raikka J., 'The argument from truth as a basis for legislation concerning freedom of speech' (2003) vol 7(4) Trames

Raleigh C., et al., 'Climate change, environmental degradation and armed conflict' (2007) vol 26(6) Political Geography

Ramraj V., 'Global Anti-Terrorism Law and Policy' (Cambridge University Press, Cambridge 2012)

Rice S., 'The new national security strategy: Focus on failed states' (2003) The Brookings Institution Policy Briefs Policy Brief

Ridley N., et al., 'Combating terrorists financing in the first decade of the twenty first century' (2012) vol 15(1) Journal of Money Laundering Control

Roach K., 'Must we trade rights for security? The choice between smart, Harsh or proportionate security strategies in Canada and Britain' (2006) vol 27(5) Cardozo Law Review

Roach K., et al., 'Miscarriages of Justice in the war against terrorism' (2005) vol 109(4) Penn State Law Review

Ronen Y., 'Incitement to terrorist acts and international law' (2010) vol 23(3) Leiden Journal of International Law

Ronen Y., 'The ties that bind: Family and private life as bars to the deportation of immigrants (2012) vol 8(2) International Journal of Law

Royal K., et al., 'Burning the barn to roast the pig? Proportionality concerns in the war on terror and the Damadola incident' (2006) Vol 14 Willamette Journal of International Law and Dispute Resolution 55

Ruhle M., 'NATO after Prague: Learning the lesson of 9/11' (2003) vol 32(2) Parameters

Sah N., et al., 'Cyber-attack armed attack? The implications and challenges' (2013) vol 19(8) Computer and Telecommunications Law Review

Salem H., 'Issues in chemical and biological terrorism' (2003) vol 22(6) International journal of toxicology

Sampson I., 'Between Boko Haram and the Joint Task Force: Assessing the dilemma of counterterrorism and human right in Northern Nigeria' (2015) vol 59(1) Journal of African Law

Scheonholtz A., et al., 'The immigration control of terrorism and the prevention of terror' (2009) Institute for the study of International Migration, Walsh school of Foreign Service Georgetown University

Schepple K., 'Global Security Law and the Challenge to Constitutionalism after 9/11' (2011) vol 2 Public Law

Schwartz E., 'US security strategy: Empowering Jim Jong-il?' (2008) vol 30(1) Loyola of Los Angeles International and Comparative Law Review

Sciolino E., et al., 'For decade, London thrived as a busy crossroads of terror' New York Times (2005) New York Times

Shah N., 'Self Defence, Anticipatory Self-Defence and Pre-emption: International Law's Response to Terrorism' (2007) vol 12(1) Journal of Conflict and Security Law

Shah S., 'War on terrorism: Self-defense, operation enduring freedom, and the legality of US drone attacks in Pakistan' (2010) vol 9(1) Washington University Global Studies Law Review 77

Sharkey N., 'Saying no to lethal autonomous targeting' (2010) vol 9(4) Journal of Military Ethics

Sharma M., 'How not to fight terrorism' (2009) vol 44(5) Economic and Political Weekly

Shetret L., et al., 'Promoting organizational change to ensure respect for human rights while countering terrorism' (2012) Center on Global Counterterrorism cooperation; Policy Brief

Singer P., 'The ethics of killer applications: Why is it so hard to talk about morality when it comes to new military technology' (2010) vol 9(4) Journal of Military Ethics

Sloss D., et al., 'Is the president bound by Geneva Conventions?' (2004) vol 90(1) Cornell Law Review

Spann G., 'Terror and race' (2005) vol 45 Washburn Law Journal

Sperotto F., 'The use of force against terrorists: a reply to Christian J. Tams (2009) vol 20(4) European Journal of International Law

Stancic D., et al., 'Study on the assessment of regional security threats and challenges in the Western Balkans' (2007) Geneva Centre for the Democratic control of armed forces

Tamanaha B., 'The history and elements of the rule of law' (2012) Singapore Journal of Legal Studies 232

Thunberg P., 'National economic security: Interdependence and vulnerability' in Frans A.M. Alting von Geuseu and Jacques Pelkman (Tilburg: John. F. Kennedy Institute 1982)

Thym D., 'Respect for private and family life under article 8 of ECHR in immigration cases: A human right to regularize illegal stay?' (2008) 57 (1) International and Comparative Law Quarterly

Trotter G., et al., 'Miscarriages of justice in the war against terror' (2005) vol. 109(4) Penn state law review

Trujillo B., et al., 'Immigration reform, national security after September 11 and the future of North (2007) vol 28 Immigration and Nationality Law Review

Tuba T., 'War on terror in the US and the UK: An evaluation with regard to civil liberties' (2006) vol2(7) Review of International Politics

Tucker K., 'Abduction, torture, interrogation: An argument against extraordinary rendition' (2014) vol 10(2) Brazilian Journal of International Law

Turner I, 'A Communitarian Justification for Measures to Prevent Terrorism in the UK' (2016) vol 10(5) Perspective on Terrorism

Turner I., 'Freedom from torture in the war on terror: Is it absolute?' (2011) vol 23(3) Terrorism and Political Violence

Turner I., 'Human rights and anti-terrorism: A positive legal duty to infringe freedom from torture' (2012) vol 35(11) Studies in Conflict and terrorism

Tushnet M., et al., 'Handbook of Constitutional Law' (Routledge Publishing, London 2013)

Tyler T., et al., 'Why does the public cooperate with the law enforcement? The influence of the purposes and targets of policing' (2011) vol 7(3) Public Law and Legal Theory Working Papers

Ullman R., 'Redefining Security' (1983) vol 8(1) International Security

Vella A., 'From national security to environmental security: A historical overview' (2012) Thesis submitted to the Graduate faculty of George Mason University, Malta

Ville G., 'Climate Change: Bad News for Environmental Security' (2008) vol 10(3) Environmental Law Review

Walker C., 'The reshaping of control orders in the United Kingdom: Time for a fairer go, Australia!' (2013) vol 37(1) Melbourne University Law Review

Walsh J., 'Intelligence Sharing in the European Union: Institutions are not enough' (2006) vol 44 (3) University of North Carolina

Walt S., 'The renaissance of security studies' (1991) vol 35(2) International Quarterly Studies

Warren T., 'ISAF and Afghanistan: The impact of failure on NATO's future' (2010) Research Project, USAWC

Waxman M., 'Administrative detention of terrorists: Why detain, and detain whom?' (2009) vol 3(1) Journal of National Security Law and Policy

Waxman M., 'Police and national security: American local law enforcement and counterterrorism after 9/11' (2009) (3) Journal of National Security Law & Policy

Wellman D., 'Terrorism and counterterrorism: A moral assessment' (2013) vol 9 Springer Briefs in Law

White N., et al., 'The twin towers attack: An unlimited right to self-defense' (2002) vol 7(1) Journal of Conflict and Security Law

William G., et al., 'Balancing national security and human rights: Assessing the legal response of common law nations to the threat of terrorism' (2006) vol 8(1) Journal of Comparative Political Analysis

Williams A., et al., 'The psychological impact of torture' (2013) vol 7(2) British Journal of Pain

Williams G., 'A decade of Australian anti-terror laws' (2011) vol 35 Melbourne University Law Review

Williams R., 'Dangerous precedent: America's illegal war in Afghanistan' (2011) vol 33(2) University of Pennsylvania Journal of International Law

Wolfendale J., 'Terrorism, security and the threat of counterterrorism' (2007) vol 30(1) Studies in Conflict and Terrorism

WordNet 3.0., Farlex clipart collection (2003/2012) Princeton University Farlex Inc

WEBSITES, REPORTS AND NEWSPAPER PUBLICATIONS

'US-European cooperation on counterterrorism: Congressional hearing' (2004) <*http://0-Congressional.proquest.com.library.ggu.edu/congressional/docview/t29.d30.hrg-2004-hir-0109*?accountid=25283> accessed 29 December 2015

Aaronson S., 'Internet governance or internet control: How to safeguard internet freedom' (2013) <www.cicerofoundation.org> accessed 29 April 2014

Article 19 global campaign for free expression., 'The impact of UK anti-terror laws on freedom of expression' (2006) <www.article 19.org/pdf/.../terrorism-submission-to-icj-panel.pd...> accessed 23 April 2014)

Bailey R., et al., 'Latin America and the debate over environmental protection and national security' (2008) <www.redorbit.com/news/science/1257019/latin-america-and...-> accessed 26 November 2012

BBC News., 'Three guilty of airline bomb plot' (2009) <*http://news.bbc.co.uk/1/hi/UK/8242238.stm*> accessed 19 July 2016

BBC News., 'What is a fascist?' (2009) <news.bbc.co.uk/2/hi/UK_news/magazine/8316271.stm> accessed 14 January 2017

Beckett M., 'Beckett admits Guantanamo camp should be shut down', (2006) <*http://news.independent.co.uk/uk/politics/article/1868066.ece.*> accessed 17 February 2014

Bowers D., 'The world dilemma: National security vs environmental protection' (2009) <webspace.ship.edu/ajdieterichward/Exhibits/.../Bowers-Exhibit.pdf> accessed 30 November 2012

Buerk M., 'What are the limits of freedom of expression?' (2014) <www.bbc.co.uk/podcast/series/moralmaze> accessed 3rd July 2014

Carabin D., 'An Intelligence sharing continuum: Next generation requirements for U.S counterterrorism efforts' (2011) <oai.dtic.mil/oai/oai?verb=getRecord&metadataPrefix=html...> accessed 5 September 2012

Carabin D., 'An Intelligence sharing continuum: Next generation requirements for U.S counterterrorism efforts' (2011) <oai.dtic.mil/oai/oai?verb=getRecord&metadataPrefix=html...> accessed 5 September 2012

Chalecki E., 'Environmental security: a case study of climate change' (2008) *Pacific Institute of Studies in Development, environment and Securities* <pacinst.org/report/environment and security/env...> accessed 18 November 2012

Counterterrorism' (2009) <*www.ohchr.org/Documents/Publications/Factsheet32EN*> accessed 14 April 2014

Dresen J., 'Economic growth and environmental security in Russia' (2011) <www.wilsoncentre.org> accessed 1st December 2017

European Convention on Human Rights as amended by Protocols No.11 and 14., Supplemented by protocols 1, 4, 6, 7, 12 and 13, <www.echr.int/.../Convention-ENG.pd...> accessed 7 February 2014

European Convention on Human Rights as amended by Protocols Nos. 11 and 14 supplemented by Protocols Nos. 1, 4, 6, 7, 12 and 13. *"Article 3—Prohibition of Torture. Anti-torture and inhumane treatment."* <*https://ukhumanrightsblog.*

com/incorporated-rights/articles-index/article-3-of-the-echr.> accessed 1st August 2016.

European Convention on Human Rights as amended by Protocols Nos. 11 and 14 supplemented by Protocols Nos. 1, 4, 6, 7, 12 and 13. *"Article 3—Prohibition of Torture. Anti-torture and inhumane treatment."* *<https://ukhumanrights-blog.com/incorporated-rights/articles-index/article-3-of-the-echr.>* accessed 1st August 2016.

Forcese C., 'The collateral casualties of collaboration: The consequence for civil and human rights of transnational intelligence sharing' (2008) *<www.http://ssm.com/abstract=1354022>* accessed 27 August 2012

Gibbs L., et al., *Addressing the health impacts of 9-11: Reports and Recommendations to Mayor Michael R Bloomberg* <www.nyc.gov/html/om/pdf/9/11_health_impacts_reports.pdf> accessed 4th June 2016

Gordes J., 'Environmental security part 1: The basics' (2010) <www.nesea.org/uncategorised/environment-security-part> accessed 25 November 2012

Hampshire J., et al., 'Migration, Integration and Security in the UK since July' (2006) <www.migrationinformatiom.org/USFocus/display.cfm?ID=383> accessed 21 August 2012

Hampshire J., et al., 'Migration, Integration and Security in the UK since July' (2006) <www.migrationinformatiom.org/USFocus/display.cfm?ID=383> accessed 21 August 2012

Hom T., 'Drug smugglers shoot drugs across borders with cannon' (2012) America Broadcasting Company Network abcnews.go.com/blotter/drug-smugglers-shoot-drugs-border-cannon/story? id... accessed 12 December 2012

Hom T., 'Drug smugglers shoot drugs across borders with cannon' (2012) America Broadcasting Company Network abcnews.go.com/blotter/drug-smugglers-shoot-drugs-border-cannon/story? id... accessed 12 December 2012

Hosenball M., 'US intelligence agencies didn't issue high alert about Mideast unrest threat' *American Broadcasting Corporation News Network* (2012) Copyright Thompson Reuters <URL> accessed 14 September 2012

Hosenball M., 'US intelligence agencies didn't issue high alert about Mideast unrest threat' *American Broadcasting Corporation News Network* (2012) Copyright Thompson Reuters <URL> accessed 14 September 2012

Human Rights Watch, 'In the name of security: Counterterrorism laws worldwide since September 11' (2012) <*https://www.hrw.org/.../name-security/counterterrorism-laws-worldwide-*> (accessed 3 January 2017)

Human Rights Watch, 'Not the way forward: The UK's dangerous reliance on diplomatic assurance' (2008) <*http://www.hrw.org/sites/default/files/reports/uk1008web.pdf&gt*> accessed 27 April 2015

International encyclopedia of the social sciences, 'National security' (2008) *https://www.encyclopedia.com/social-sciences/applied-and-social-sciences-magazines/national-security-0* accessed 15 November 2018

Kelling G., et al., 'Policing terrorism: Civic bulletin' (2006) <*http://www.manhattan-institute.org/html/cb43.htm*> accessed 7 May 2015

Mataconis D., 'Final Costs of hurricane sandy could exceed $60 billion' (2012) <www.outsidethebeltway.com/final-costs-of-hurricane-sandy> accessed 1st December 2012

McCain J., 'Bin Laden's death and the debate against torture' (2011) *http://www.washingtonpost.com/opinions/bin-ladens-death-and-the-debate-over* torture/2011/05/AFdimdsG_story.html, accessed 2nd December 2017

Megan A., et al., 'National security and Human rights' (2006) Woodrow Wilson International Center for Scholars <www.wisoncenter.org/kennan> accessed 19 July 2012)

Mueller J., 'How dangerous are the Taliban?' (2015) <*http://www.foreignaffairs.com/articles/64932/john-mueller/how-dangerous-are-the-taliban?page=show*> (accessed 3rd December 2016)

Muller-Willie B., 'For our eyes only? Shaping an intelligence community within the EU' (2004) vol 50 European Union Institute for Security Studies <*http://www.iss.europa.eu/upload/media/occ50.pdf*> accessed 27 February 2015

Myers N., et al, 'Environmental security: What's New and Different?' (2002) www.envirosecurity.org/conference/working/newanddifferent.pdf., accessed 13 December 2017

Nicklaus D., 'Immigrant entrepreneurs could help jump start the economy' (2012) www.stltoday.com/...nicklaus/immigrant-enterpreneurs-could-help-start-the-eco... accessed 20 August 2012

Obama B., 'Strategy to combat transnational organized crime' (2011) <www.whitehouse.gov/.../eop/nsc/transnational-crime/threat> accessed 5th December 2012

Obama B., 'Transnational organized crime: A growing threat to national and international security' (2011) National Security Council, <www.whitehouse.org/.../eop/nsc/transnational-crime/threat> accessed 20 December 2012

Obama B., 'Transnational organized crime: A growing threat to national and international security' (2011) National Security Council, <www.whitehouse.org/.../eop/nsc/transnational-crime/threat> accessed 20 December 2012

Owen E., 'State security vs. human rights: Finding a proportionate balance', (2010) <www.e-ir.info/2010/08/28/state-security-v-human-rights> accessed 2nd January 2013

Patel F., et al., 'What went wrong with the Fisa Court—Brennan Court for Justice' (2015) <*https://wwwbrennancentre.org/.../what_went_%20wrong* _with_The_FISA. Court.p....> accessed 13 December 2017

Picchi A., 'How would deporting undocumented workers affect the US economy?' (2016) *CBS News* <URL https//:www.cbsnews.com>moneywatch>work accessed 19 May 2017

Pincus W., 'Silence of 4 terror probe suspects poses dilemma for FBI' (2001) <http://www.infowars.com/police_state/torture.htm> accessed 3rd September 2016

Prieto D., 'War about terror: Civil liberties and national security after 9/11' (2009) <www.cfr.org/content/publications/.../Civil_Liberties_WorkingPaper> accessed 1st December 2017)

Qureshi A., 'Fabricating terrorism 111: British complicity in renditions and torture' (2011) <www.therenditionproject.org.uk/documents/eur-comlicity.html> accessed 10 March 2014

Singh M., 'Tehran, a threat to security' (2012) The Voice of Bahrain: Gulf Daily News <URL> www.gdnonline.com/Deatails/269068/Iran-a-threat-to-the-security-of-Gulf-countries> accessed 9 December 2012

Sukma R., Indonesia and regional security: The quest for cooperation security (2002) Institute of Defence and Strategic Studies Singapore (IDSS) www.

propatria.or.id/loaddown/paper%20Diskusi/Indonesia..., accessed 3rd march 2016

The New York Times., 9/11 Congressional Report Faults F.B.I-C.I.A Lapses (2003) www.nytimes.com/2003/07/24/.../9-11-congressional-report-faults-fbi-cia-lapses.html, accessed

The New York Times., Storm Gains Strength as It Nears Florida (2017) https://www.nytimes.com/2017/09/09/us/hurricane-irma-florida.html?mcubz=3, assessed 15 September 2017

The Washington Post, Hurricane Maria Churns Through Caribbean As Ravaged Puerto Rico Takes Stock of An Island Destroyed (2017) https;//www.washingtonpost.com/.../post-nation/21/hurricane-maria-churns-through-c... Assessed 1/10/2017

UN Committee on Economic, Social and Cultural Rights (CESCR)., General Comment No. 14., 'The Right to the Highest Attainable Standard of Health (Art. 12 of the Covenant)' (2000) E/C.12/2000/4 <http://www.unhcr.org/refworld/docid/4538838d0.html> accessed 13 December 2017, para 12(b)

UN General Assembly Report of the Special Rapporteur of the Commission on Human Rights on the question of Torture and other Cruel, inhuman or degrading treatment or punishment 2002 (A/57/173)

CASES

A and Others v United Kingdom (2009) 3455/05 Strasbourg

A.K. and A.R. v Uzbekistan (2009) CCPR/C/95/D/1233/2003; 16 IHRR 719

Agiza v Sweden (2005) Communication no 233/2003, UN Doc CAT/C/34/D/233/2003

Akosy v Turkey (1996) 100/1995/606/694 European Court of Human Rights

Akosy v Turkey (1996) 23 EHRR 553 European Court of Human Rights

Al Hanchi v Bosnia and Herzegovina (2011) ECHR 48205/09 Grand Chamber

Al Nashiri v Poland (2014) 28761/11 Strasbourg

Al-Jedda v The United Kingdom (2011) ECHR 27021/08 Grand Chamber

Al-Skeini and Others v The United Kingdom (2011) ECHR 55721/07 Strasbourg

Alzery v Sweden (2006) Human Rights Committee Communication No 1416/2005, CCPR/C/88/D/1416/2005

Alzery v Sweden (2006) UN Doc CCPR/C/88/D/1416/2005

Amministrazione delle Finanze dello Stato v Salumi (1981) ECR 2735

Ashcroft v Tennessee (1944) 322 U.S. 143, 155

Auad v Bulgaria (2011) 46390/10 Strasbourg

B.H., M.W., H.P. and G.K. v Austria (1989) European Commission 12774/87

Ben Khemais v Italy (2009) ECtHR application no. 246/07 Grand Chamber

Binyam Mohammed v Secretary of state for Foreign and Commonwealth Affairs (2008) EWCH 2048

Boujlifa v France (1997) 122/1996/741/940

Chahal v United Kingdom (1996) 22414/93 Strasbourg

CIA v Sims (1985) 471 U.S. 159, 17

Denmark, Norway, Sweden and Netherlands v Greece (1969) application no 3321/67, 3322/67, 3323/67, 3344/67, Yearbook 12

DPP v Morgan (1976) AC 182 at 216-217, 1975 WL 44975

El-Masri v The Former Yugoslav Republic of Macedonia (2012) 39630/09 Strasbourg

Esmukhambetov and Others v. Russia (2011) ECHR 23445/03 Strasbourg

Filartiga v Pena-Irala (2nd cir 1980) 630 F 2d 876 at 890

Gerger v Turkey (1999) ECHR 24919/94 Grand Chamber

Gafgen v Germany (2010) ECHR 22978/05 Grand Chamber

Guerra & Others v Italy (1998) ECHR 116/1996/735/932 Strasbourg

Gul and Others v Turkey (2010) Strasbourg 4870/02

Guzzardi v Italy (1980) A/39 ECHR 7367/76 ECtHR

Hoechst v Commission (1989) ECR 02859

Huseyn and Others v Azerbaijan (2011) ECHR 35485/05, 45553/05, 35680/05 and 36085/05 Grand Chamber

Ireland v UK (1978) 2 EHRR 25

Ireland v United Kingdom (1978) 5310/71 Strasbourg

Ireland v United Kingdom (1978) application no 5310/71 Strasbourg

Isayeva v Russia (2005) ECHR 57950/00 Strasbourg

Keenan v United Kingdom (2001) ECtHR 27229/95

Kolyadenko and Others v Russia (2012) ECHR 17423/05, 20534/05, 20678/05, 23263/05, 24283/05 and 35673/05 Strasbourg

Lawless v Ireland (No.3) (1961) 1 EHRR

Liberty v The United Kingdom (2008) ECHR 58243/00 Strasbourg

Mangouras v Spain (2010) ECHR 12050/04 Strasbourg

McCann and Others v United Kingdom (1995) ECHR 18984/91 Strasbourg

Mckerr v The United Kingdom (2001) ECHR 28883/95 Strasbourg

Nada v Switzerland (2012) ECHR 10593/08 Strasbourg

Osman v United Kingdom (2000) 29 EHRR 245

R (Adam, Limbuela and Tesema) v Home Secretary (2005) UKHL 66

R(Wellington) v Secretary of State for Home Department (2008) UKHL 72 (2009) 1 A.C 335

RB(Algeria) and another v Secretary of State for the Home Department (2009) UKHL 10

R.A.V v City of St. Paul (1992) 505 US 377

Ramdan v Rumsfeld (2006) 548 U.S. 557

Ramzy v Netherlands (2010) 25424/05 Strasbourg

Rotaru v Romania (2000) ECHR 28341/95 Strasbourg

Saadi v Italy (2008) 37201/06 Strasbourg

Saadi v Italy (2008) ECtHR 37201/06 Grand Chamber

Saygili and Falakaoglu v Turkey (2008/09) Strasbourg 39457/03

Secretary of State for Home Department v AP (2010) UKSC 24

Secretary of State for Home Department v JJ (2008) 1 AC 385

Secretary of state of home department v E & S (2007) EWCA 459

Soering v The United Kingdom (1989) 14038/88 Strasbourg

Sufi and Elmi v United Kingdom (2011) 8319/07, 11449/07 Strasbourg

Suresh v Canada (Minister of Citizenship and immigration) (2002) 1 SCR 3

Umarovy v Russia (2012) ECHR 2546/08 Strasbourg

Uner v Netherlands (2006) 54 ECHR 46410/99 Strasbourg

Uzunget & Others v Turkey (2009) ECHR 21831/03 Strasbourg

STATUTES

Antiterrorism, Crime and Security Act 2001

Antiterrorism, Crime and Security Act 2001

Constitution Act 1982

Criminal Law Act (Northern Ireland) 1967

Criminal Procedure Act of 1997 (*Закон за кривичната постапка*)

Department of Public Information (1995) United Nations

Duties and Powers of the Police, Law No. 2559

European Convention on Human Rights 1950

General Assembly Resolution 62/71, UN Doc A RES 62/71 (Jan. 8, 2008) United Nations General Assembly Resolution 2625 (XXV)

Geneva Convention 1949

Human Rights Act 1998 (Designated Derogation) Order 2001, No.3644

Human Rights Committee., 'General Comment No. 6 Article 6 (the right to life) (1982)

International Convention for The Protection of All Persons from Enforced Disappearance (CED) 2010

International Covenant on Civil and Political Rights 1966

International Covenant on Civil and Political Rights 1976

Meetings and Demonstration Marches Act, Law No. 2911

Presidential Decree No. 175, 1988

The Prevention of Terrorism Act (Law No 3713 12 April 1991)

Regulation of Investigatory Powers Act 2003

Terrorism Prevention Investigation Measures 2011

Terrorist Act 2005 (The Stationery Office, London 2012)

The Press Act (Law No 5680 15 July 1950)

The Protection of Personal Data in Bosnia and Herzegovina Law No.49/06

Turkish Constitution

United Nations Charter of 1945

United Nations Convention Against Torture 1984

United Nations Convention against Torture and other Cruel, inhuman or degrading Treatment or Punishment 1985

United Nations General Assembly Resolution 2625 (XXV)

United Nations General Assembly Resolution 49/60

United Nations General Assembly Resolution 60/148 on Torture and other Cruel, Inhuman and Degrading Treatment or Punishment Adopted in 2006

United Nations Security Council Resolution 1368 (12 September 2001) U.N. Doc. S/RES/1368

United Nations Security Council Resolution 53/1189.,

United Nations Security Council Resolution 54/1259

United Nations Security Council Resolution 56/1373, UN DOC S/Res (Sept 28, 2001)

United Nations Security Council Resolution 57/1450

Vienna Convention on the Law of Treaty

www.ingramcontent.com/pod-product-compliance
Lightning Source LLC
LaVergne TN
LVHW052224200926
848481LV00001B/202